BABEL OF THE ATLANTIC

THE MAX KADE RESEARCH INSTITUTE SERIES:
GERMANS BEYOND EUROPE

Series Editors
A. Gregg Roeber and Daniel Purdy

The Max Kade Research Institute Series is an outlet for scholarship that examines the history and culture of German-speaking communities in America and across the globe, from the early modern period to the start of the First World War. Books in this series examine the movements of the German-speaking diaspora as influenced by forces such as migration, colonization, war, research, religious missions, or trade. This series explores the historical and cultural depictions of the international networks that connect these communities, as well as linguistic relations between German and other languages within European global networks.

This series is a project of the Max Kade German-American Research Institute located on Penn State's campus. This Institute, co-directed by A. Gregg Roeber and Daniel Purdy, was founded in 1993 thanks to a grant from the Max Kade Foundation, New York.

Babel of the Atlantic

EDITED BY BETHANY WIGGIN

The Pennsylvania State University Press
University Park, Pennsylvania

Library of Congress Cataloging-in-Publication Data

Names: Wiggin, Bethany, 1972– editor.
Title: Babel of the Atlantic / edited by Bethany Wiggin.
Description: University Park, Pennsylvania : The Pennsylvania State
    University Press, [2019] | Series: The Max Kade Research Institute
    series: Germans beyond Europe | Includes bibliographical references
    and index.
Summary: "A collection of essays examining colonial Philadelphia and
    its surroundings as a zone of cultural and linguistic interchange.
    Documents everyday multilingualism and intercultural negotiations
    with special attention to themes of religion, education, race and the
    abolitionist movement, and material culture and architecture"—
    Provided by publisher.
Identifiers: LCCN 2019001033 | ISBN 9780271083230 (cloth : alk. paper)
Subjects: LCSH: Multilingualism—Pennsylvania—History—18th
    century. | Multilingualism—Pennsylvania—Philadelphia—
    History—18th century. | Multilingualism—Middle Atlantic
    States—History—18th century. | Pennsylvania—Religion—
    History—18th century. |
    Antislavery movements—Pennsylvania—History—18th century.
Classification: LCC F152.B165 2019 | DDC 306.44/60974811—dc23
LC record available at https://lccn.loc.gov/2019001033

Copyright © 2019 The Pennsylvania State University
All rights reserved
Printed in the United States of America
Published by The Pennsylvania State University Press,
University Park, PA 16802–1003

The Pennsylvania State University Press is a member
of the Association of University Presses.

It is the policy of The Pennsylvania State University Press to use
acid-free paper. Publications on uncoated stock satisfy the minimum
requirements of American National Standard for Information
Sciences—Permanence of Paper for Printed Library Material,
ANSI Z39.48–1992.

CONTENTS

List of Illustrations (vii)

Acknowledgments (xi)

Introduction: Multilingual Soundings in the Colonial Mid-Atlantic; "Differences of Manners, Languages and Extraction, Was Now No More"? (1)
Bethany Wiggin

PART 1 NEW WORLD, NEW RELIGIONS

1   "Wie ein Nimrod / Like a Nimrod": Babel, Confusion, and Coercive Bilingualism in the Eighteenth-Century Mid-Atlantic (41)
Patrick M. Erben

2   The Moravian Threat to the Old World Establishment (75)
Craig Atwood

3   Women, Migration, and Moravian Mission: Negotiating Pennsylvania's Colonial Landscapes (101)
Katherine Faull

PART 2 THE LANGUAGES OF EDUCATION AND ESTABLISHED RELIGIONS

4   Benjamin Franklin, the Philadelphia Academy, Halle, and Göttingen (131)
Jürgen Overhoff

5   German or English? Halle's Pastors in Pennsylvania and the Search for the Right Language, 1742–1820 (147)
Wolfgang Flügel

PART 3 THE LANGUAGES OF RACE AND (ANTI-)SLAVERY

6   Writing Against Slavery: Germantown, Quakers, and the Ethnic Origins of Early Antislavery Thought (175)
Katharine Gerbner

7 "Ein schrecklicher Zustand": Race, Slavery, and Gradual
  Emancipation in Pennsylvania *(199)*
  Birte Pfleger

8 How the Quakers Worked with Moravians, Germans,
  the French, the British, and Enslaved and Free Africans:
  All in the Antislavery Cause *(228)*
  Maurice Jackson

PART 4 THE LANGUAGES OF WOOD AND STONE

9 Communicating Through Wood and Stone: Building
  a New World Identity in Pennsylvania *(249)*
  Cynthia G. Falk

10 Germans in Colonial Philadelphia: Ethnicity, Hybridity,
   and the Material World *(275)*
   Lisa Minardi

List of Contributors (299)

Index (302)

ILLUSTRATIONS

I.1A. First page of Franklin's *Plain Truth* (Philadelphia, 1747). Courtesy of the Curtis Collection of Franklin Imprints, Kislak Center for Special Collections, Rare Books and Manuscripts, University of Pennsylvania. *(15)*

I.1B. First page of Franklin's *Plain Truth* (Philadelphia, 1747). Courtesy of the Curtis Collection of Franklin Imprints, Kislak Center for Special Collections, Rare Books and Manuscripts, University of Pennsylvania. *(16)*

I.2. German translation, by J. Crell, of Franklin's *Plain Truth*. *(17)*

1.1. Bilingual title page of *Die Hoch Teutsche und Englische Zeitung / The High Dutch and English Gazette*, January 1, 1752. Photograph © 2019 Museum of Fine Arts, Boston. *(47)*

1.2. Anonymous letter printed in German only. *Die Hoch Teutsche und Englische Zeitung / The High Dutch and English Gazette*, January 1, 1752. Photograph © 2019 Museum of Fine Arts, Boston. *(48)*

1.3. Bilingual title page of William Smith, *Eine Kurtze Nachricht Von der Liebreichen Anstalt / A Brief History of the Charitable Scheme* (1755). The Library Company of Philadelphia. *(62)*

1.4. Bilingual double page in William Smith, *Eine Kurtze Nachricht Von der Liebreichen Anstalt / A Brief History of the Charitable Scheme* (1755). The Library Company of Philadelphia. *(67)*

3.1. "Reise Charte durch Pennsylvanie und anderer angränzenden Provinzen," travel map of Pennsylvania, northern Maryland, and New Jersey, ca. 1750. DP f.037.6, Moravian Archives, Bethlehem, Pa. *(103)*

3.2. Taylor's map of traders at the confluence with annotations. *(111)*

3.3. Detail of travel map (fig. 3.1) annotated with dates of Moravian women missionaries' service. DP f.037.6, Moravian Archives, Bethlehem, Pa. *(112)*

3.4. Visualization of strength of connections between Moravian women missionaries at the Moravian missions in the mid-Atlantic states, 1747–75. Rendered by author in Gephi. *(122)*

7.1. Journals of Henry Melchior Muhlenberg, PM95A, September 23, 1742. Lutheran Archives Center at Philadelphia. *(200)*

viii ILLUSTRATIONS

7.2. Journals of Henry Melchior Muhlenberg, PM95A, February 1, 1775. Lutheran Archives Center at Philadelphia. *(200)*

7.3. Journals of Henry Melchior Muhlenberg, PM95A, March 8, 1778. Lutheran Archives Center at Philadelphia. *(201)*

9.1. David Deshler house, Germantown, Pa., 1772–74. Photo: Cynthia G. Falk. *(250)*

9.2. John Wister house, now known as Grumblethorpe, Germantown, Pa., 1744. Photo: Cynthia G. Falk. *(253)*

9.3. Augustus Lutheran Church, Trappe, Upper Providence Township, Montgomery County, Pa., 1743. Photo: Cynthia G. Falk. *(000)*

9.4. Interior, August Lutheran Church, Trappe, Upper Providence Township, Montgomery County, Pa., 1743. Photo: Cynthia G. Falk. *(255)*

9.5. Detail from "To the Honourable Thomas Penn and Richard Penn, Esqrs., true & absolute proprietaries & Governours of the Province of Pennsylvania & counties of New-Castle, Kent & Sussex on Delaware this map of the improved part of the Province of Pennsylvania. / Is humbly dedicated by Nicholas Scull. Engraved by Ja. Turner. Printed by John Davis" (Philadelphia: Nicholas Scull, 1759). Library of Congress, Geography and Map Division, G3820 1759.S3. *(255)*

9.6. Isometric projection of first-floor plan, Hans Mirtel Gerick house, Exeter Township, Berks County, Pa., 1741. Drawn by Hope M. LeVan, from field measurements by James Lewars. *(257)*

9.7. Heinrich and Anna Maria Zeller house (Fort Zeller), Newmanstown, Millcreek Township, Lebanon County, Pa., ca. 1745. The interior plan of the house was made manifest by the slightly off-center placement of the chimney along the roof ridge. Photo: Cynthia G. Falk. *(258)*

9.8. Jamb, or five-plate, iron stove, Isaac Zane, Marlboro Furnace, Frederick, Virginia, ca. 1768. Anonymous gift to Winterthur Museum, 1994.111. Stove support, Philip Erpf, Schaefferstown, Pa., 1765. Courtesy Winterthur Museum. *(259)*

9.9. First Single Brothers' house, later converted to Single Sisters' house, Bethlehem, Northampton County, Pa., 1744. Photo: Cynthia G. Falk. *(261)*

9.10. First-floor plan, first Single Brothers' house, from "Entwurf zum Bau des Gemeinhauses in Bethlehem in Pennsylvania mit Angabe der Nutzung der Räume, Grundriss Erdgeschoss" (1751). Courtesy Moravian Archives Herrnhut, TS Mp.216.15. *(261)*

9.11. Johannes Lesher house (Oley Forge mansion), Oley Township, Berks County, Pa., ca. 1750–55. Photo: Cynthia G. Falk. *(262)*

9.12. Isometric projection of first-floor plan, Johannes Lesher house, Oley Township, Berks County, Pa. Drawn by Hope M. LeVan, from field measurements by Kenneth LeVan and Hope M. LeVan. *(262)*

9.13. Isaac and Catherine Meier house, Myerstown, Lebanon County, Pa., ca. 1757. Photo: Cynthia G. Falk. *(263)*

9.14. James Logan house, Stenton, Germantown, Pa., 1723–30. Library of Congress, Prints and Photographs Division, HABS PA, 51-PHILA, 8-2. *(264)*

9.15. Joseph and Mary Pennock house, now known as Primitive Hall, West Marlboro Township, Chester County, Pa., 1738. Wikimedia Commons, photograph by Smallbones. *(265)*

9.16. Center passage as viewed from the front door, Peter and Rosina Margaretha Wentz house, Worcester Township, Montgomery County, Pa., 1758. Photo: James G. Layton with permission of the Peter Wentz Farmstead, a property of Montgomery County, Pennsylvania. *(266)*

9.17. Date stone, Benedict and Anna Eshleman house, Conestoga Township, Lancaster County, Pa. Photo: Cynthia G. Falk. *(268)*

9.18. Johann Peter and Maria Magdalena Troxell house, Egypt, Lehigh County, Pa., 1756. Photo: Cynthia G. Falk. *(269)*

10.1. Spice box, Philadelphia area, ca. 1740. Private collection. Photo: Gavin Ashworth, reproduced by permission of the Chipstone Foundation. *(276)*

10.2. Pair of side chairs made for Henry Muhlenberg, attributed to Leonard Kessler, Philadelphia, 1763. Photo: Gavin Ashworth, reproduced by permission of the Chipstone Foundation. *(276)*

10.3. *The Parrot of Carolina*, in Mark Catesby, *Natural History of Carolina, Florida and the Bahama Islands* (London, 1729–47). Courtesy Winterthur Library, Printed Book and Periodical Collection. Photo: James Schneck. *(280)*

10.4. Schrank, Philadelphia area, 1741. Courtesy Winterthur Museum, promised gift of William K. du Pont. Photo: Gavin Ashworth. *(281)*

10.5. Detail of the lid of a slant-front desk, Philadelphia area, ca. 1750. Private collection. Photo: Gavin Ashworth, reproduced by permission of the Chipstone Foundation. *(281)*

10.6. Detail of the inlaid parrot on a tall clock case, Philadelphia area, ca. 1745. From the collection of the York County History Center, York, Pa. Photo: Gavin Ashworth. *(282)*

10.7. Old Lutheran Church on Fifth Street, Philadelphia. Drawn and engraved by William Russell Birch and Thomas Birch, Philadelphia, 1800, and published in *Birch's Views of Philadelphia* (Philadelphia:

W. Birch, 1800). Courtesy Winterthur Library, Printed Book and Periodical Collection. Photo: James Schneck. *(290)*

10.8. Chest, Philadelphia, ca. 1750. Courtesy Krauth Memorial Library, United Lutheran Seminary. Photo: Gavin Ashworth. *(291)*

10.9. New Lutheran Church on Fourth Street, Philadelphia. Drawn and engraved by William Russell Birch and Thomas Birch, Philadelphia, 1799, and published in *Birch's Views of Philadelphia* (Philadelphia: W. Birch, 1800). Courtesy Winterthur Library, Printed Book and Periodical Collection. Photo: James Schneck. *(291)*

10.10. Photograph of Zion Lutheran Church interior, Philadelphia, 1866. Private collection. *(293)*

10.11. Teapot, southeastern Pennsylvania, 1779. Courtesy Winterthur Museum, 1960.633. *(294)*

10.12. Sugar bowl by Christian Wiltberger, Philadelphia, ca. 1800. Courtesy Winterthur Museum, 1956.98.2. *(294)*

ACKNOWLEDGMENTS

Edited collections, good ones, are inevitably labors of love. *Babel of the Atlantic* is no different. Gathering these chapters by its scholars, laboring across languages and disciplines, has required countless conversations, careful translations, further clarifications, and seemingly endless corrections. So many people and organizations have helped to bring together these voices and languages scattered "abroad upon the face of all the earth" (Gen 11:9). Together we have endeavored to gather not to build a tower, neither to produce a second "babbling Babylon," as eighteenth-century traveler Gottfried Mittelberger described colonial Pennsylvania. Instead, we wanted to make a *book*, and like the best of those, this one too contains many voices. Special thanks to the volume's authors, with whom it has been a sincere pleasure to talk, to write, and to collaborate.

In addition, and in particular, I would like to thank the staff of the Francke Foundations in Halle, Germany. They enabled me, with the award of a Fritz Thyssen Fellowship for Postdoctoral Research, to carry out research in the beautiful library while my young son attended the beautiful Kindertagesstätte August Hermann Francke next door. Their generosity gave me hours of peace and quiet, while my son had hours of play and sleep, under the guidance of two inspiring teachers who played guitar for every nap time, and to whom I am especially grateful, Frau Wittenbecher and Frau Guenther.

In Halle, and in conversation with other researchers, especially Professor Gregg Roeber, came the first ideas for a conference that became, in November 2012, "Envisioning the 'Old World': Heinrich Melchior Mühlenberg and Imperial Projects in Pennsylvania" and to which the Francke Foundations contributed twenty exhibition panels about the life, travels, writings, and teachings of Mühlenberg, or Muhlenberg as he is more commonly known on the western side of the Atlantic. The conference was hosted by the McNeil Center for Early American Studies at the University of Pennsylvania. As ever, the MCEAS staff showed off their prolific organizing and hosting talents, and I am particularly grateful to conference co-organizer, MCEAS's long-time visionary director,

Dr. Daniel Richter. Thanks too to conference intern and German graduate student Nick Theis.

The conference, and in turn this book, could not have happened without major help from the Kislak Center for Special Collections, Rare Books and Manuscripts, also at the University of Pennsylvania. Interim director David McKnight graciously "lent" me Betsy Bates. Little did I know what a gift that would be. Betsy helped at every step of the grant-writing and application process, even suggesting we arrange meetings so I could work at home with a new baby. I am extraordinarily grateful for her words of encouragement and keen insights. Furthermore, Kislak senior curator Lynne Farrington and early Americanist and Kislak curator John Pollack prepared a terrific installation of print and manuscript materials for the conference. Thanks go also to John for writing the conference review that appeared in *Early American Literature*. Speakers and attendees at this sprawling conference on Penn's campus hailed from the many educational and cultural heritage institutions in the mid-Atlantic that bear witness to the living legacy of early Pennsylvania's linguistic and cultural diversity. The conference was my own first foray into the world of public history. With the help of so many local experts, I haven't once regretted it.

Several members of the Germantown Monthly Meeting of the Society of Friends attended the conference at Penn. They, and in particular Thomas and Joanne Sharpless, dreamt up the idea for a follow-up event, focusing on "the father of abolitionism," Anthony Benezet, to be held in Germantown. One year after the Penn conference, we hosted the two-day symposium "'Equally Entitled to Freedom': Benezet Then, Benezet Now." Versions of some of the papers in this volume were commissioned for the lectures, workshops, tours, and roundtables held up and down Germantown Avenue over two days in November 2013. Once again, I am particularly grateful to John Pollack—this time for the wonderful workshop he convened at Historic Germantown's Concord School House. Special thanks go also to the leadership of Historic Germantown, especially to Laura Keim; to the Colonial Dames; to the Germantown Community Development Corporation, especially Harold "Hask" Haskins; to the William Penn Charter School, especially Darryl Ford; and to the Germantown Friends School, who donated the use of their beautiful spaces and buses.

The editorial team at Penn State University Press has been involved in *Babel* from the very beginning. Thanks again to Gregg as well as to Professor Daniel Purdy, coeditors of the Max Kade Research Institute Series Germans Beyond Europe, for their interest in the book. Special thanks at the Press must to Kathryn Yahner, and indeed her whole team, for their expert guidance in getting *Babel*'s many voices into this beautiful book. Copy editor John Morris has deftly whipped its polyphony into shape, patiently offering helpful suggestions and corrections well beyond the call of duty.

Every step in this labor of love has been accompanied by Theodore and Peter Wiggin Helgerson. Thank you especially to them.

Introduction: Multilingual Soundings in the Colonial Mid-Atlantic

"Differences of Manners, Languages and Extraction, Was Now No More"?

BETHANY WIGGIN

Nec ignoro ingrati ac segnis animi existimari posse merito si obiter atque in transcursu ad hunc modum dicatur terra omnium terrarum alumna eadem et parens, numine deum electa quae caelum ipsum clarius faceret, sparsa congregaret imperia ritusque molliret et tot populorum discordes ferasque linguas sermonis commercio contraheret ad colloquia et humanitatem homini daret, breviterque una cunctarum gentium in toto orbe patria fieret. Sed quid agam?

I am well aware that I may with justice be considered ungrateful and lazy if I describe in this casual and cursory manner a land which is at once the nursling and the mother of all other lands, chosen by the providence of the gods to make heaven itself more glorious, to unite scattered empires, to make manners gentle, to draw together in converse by community of language the jarring and uncouth tongues of so many nations, to give mankind civilization, and in a word to become throughout the world the single fatherland of all the races. But what am I to do?
—PLINY THE ELDER (TRANS. H. RACKHAM)

> Differences of manners, languages and extraction, was now no more [in Cincinnatus's Rome].... The rising generation acquired a conformity in all things. No distinction remained but between a virtuous and vicious citizen.
>
> —WILLIAM SMITH

The relationship of mother tongue to fatherland—and of language to empire—has preoccupied writers ancient as well as modern. Scottish-born Anglican cleric and early American schoolman William Smith (1727–1803), first provost of the University of Pennsylvania, worried that "differences of manners, languages and extraction" dotted the *via imperii*. For Smith, and many other modern students of empire, Roman farmer turned general re-turned farmer Cincinnatus provided a favorite model for how to smooth the path to power. Across the eighteenth-century Atlantic world, a classical education furnished lessons in how to achieve that "conformity in all things" accomplished by Cincinnatus and prized by Smith. Roman "civilization," in the words of Pliny the Elder in this chapter's first epigraph, had brought "the jarring and uncouth tongues of so many nations" into concert. And what civilization and Cincinnatus had done for ancient Rome, Smith aimed to do for Whitehall. Acting from his post in mid-eighteenth-century colonial Philadelphia, as the French and Indian War wore on, Smith promised that "no distinction" would remain "but between a virtuous and vicious citizen."

These "jarring and uncouth tongues of so many nations" as they sounded in the colonial mid-Atlantic unite the essays gathered in *Babel of the Atlantic*. The diversity of the "uncouth tongues" heard there countered the "conformity" that men such as Smith desired. More troublingly for Smith, some of these tongues raised their voices in an anti-imperial key. The colony's various languages elicited anxious comparisons to Babel by British imperial projectors, including German speakers, working in offices of the church or the state, in the metropole or on the periphery. Yet its various languages also produced what we might call a Philadelphia sound—one whose diverse speakers together embodied the promise of a community of brothers.

Babel of the Atlantic aims to recall some of those "differences of manners, languages, and extractions" that collectively sounded attempts at a Philadelphian utopia, sometimes less and sometimes more loudly, in the years leading up to the French and Indian War. Drawing on archives of Delaware, Dutch, English, French, German, and Mohican cultural, linguistic, material, and textual artifacts, *Babel* explores how language, or languages, provided critical tools for building the "new worlds for all" that resulted from early modern globalism.[1] Its ten chapters, along with this introduction, document the many and varied negotiations that the alleged babble of the Atlantic produced. *Babel* suggests how language itself was, in Mary Louise Pratt's seminal formulation, a "contact zone," a place where "highly asymmetrical relations of power" come into sharp relief.[2]

To take soundings in this contact zone is to listen for its silences as well as for its babble. As we cross between languages, we traverse "translation zones" everywhere marked and made by relations of power.[3] Any equivalence between languages or cultures does not lie ready-made; translingual and transcultural equivalence cannot be "natural," it can only be made and remade.[4] Translational equivalence is not equality, for translators and their tools can never be neutral (even when they would prefer to remain invisible).[5] As Lydia Liu reminds us, "In thinking about the translatability between historical languages, one cannot but consider the actual power relations that dictate the degree and magnitude of sacrifice that one language must make in order to achieve some level of commensurability with the other."[6] The colonial mid-Atlantic was a place where languages mixed, crossed, attempted to silence or to draw one another into more or less civil dialogue. Building on powerful work on cultural brokers and the cross-cultural use of metaphor by Daniel Richter, Jane Merritt, and others, *Babel of the Atlantic* focuses squarely on the question of language and the tasks of translation, plunging us into the everyday, uneven, and unequal multilingualism with which empires and other transnational structures, including the antislavery and human rights movements, are necessarily built.[7]

Oceanic Atlantic history has done much to move colonial American historiography beyond the confounding frame of an English-speaking American nation. And yet national historiographical traditions, themselves heirs of powerful imperial traditions, die slowly. The colonial Atlantic world imagined by historians today often seems to remain an English-only place. And, when other language communities are considered, they are considered as monolingual, largely undifferentiated wholes. The work of translation between its language communities often remains, with notable exceptions discussed below, invisible.

These essays jointly demonstrate the continued need to hear non-English voices constitutive of other linguistically defined communities. But this volume also documents how, in this Babel of the mid-eighteenth-century Atlantic, individuals as well as groups often moved fluidly across linguistic borders. Such was their multilingual traffic that in many cases it can be hard to identify discrete single-language communities. Everyday life in the colonial mid-Atlantic necessitated functional multilingualism, as well as other forms of interlingual communication such as patois and pidgins, and nonverbal modes of communication. Some degree of pragmatic multilingualism was the norm, not the exception. Indeed, this introduction suggests how the very prosaicness of multilingualism can make its echoes hard to hear in archives structured by monolingual paradigms. The present volume is thus most interested in the quotidian, polyglot landscape produced for reasons both commercially pragmatic and tolerantly high-minded, and so often commented on by observers of colonial Pennsylvania, even as those voices have been quieted in historical scholarship.

Babel's essays are grounded primarily in the geography of the eastern Atlantic seaboard, centered on Philadelphia and nearby Germantown, with forays north to Bethlehem and west into "Indian country," from the late seventeenth century into the late eighteenth and, in one case, some decades beyond. Highlighting this region's multiple languages allows us to glimpse this translation zone as process, one also reminiscent of Richard White's middle ground: a site of continuous negotiations within and across languages that constituted and reconstituted place.[8] *Babel of the Atlantic* shows how attention to the transactions between languages also helps to "reimagine space not as a surface to be crossed and conquered but rather as the product of inter-relations, be they local or global."[9] Attending to the languages of empire and of those who would resist its reach—in the archives of the everyday, that is, in almanacs and newspapers, and including too the vernaculars of the built environment and the material world—allows us to see how spaces were produced "where people came together to coexist as best they could" (24).[10]

ORGANIZING BABEL

To recover the hum and whir of voices speaking in various languages who talked, laughed, argued, and not infrequently tried to silence one another permanently in eighteenth-century Pennsylvania, this volume draws a variety of fields of historical research into conversation. To hear conversations across and between languages—and to be more attendant to those occasions when their voices have been brought into "conformity"—these essays draw from the fields of European, American and Native American, and African histories; from literary and religious histories; from the history of education; of slavery and abolition; and of material culture and the built environment. *Babel of the Atlantic* is organized along four themes.[11] The first, "New Worlds, New Religions," begins with Patrick Erben's expert reconstruction of the rhetorical (and political) use made by European settler colonists of the Tower of Babel. Erben explores a print skirmish in which printer Christoph Saur was alleged by Smith, Franklin, and their occasional ally, German Lutheran and Pietist preacher Henry Melchior Muhlenberg, to be Babel's ruler, Nimrod. In their contributions to this section foregrounding religion, Craig Atwood and Katherine Faull variously explore the multilingual eighteenth-century world of the Moravians. If Pennsylvania's Philadelphia was named as a place for a dialogue among brothers, Moravian Bethlehem sought to extend the conversation into the mission fields, where sisters too played a vital role. If Pennsylvania's polyglot, multiconfessional society as a whole was a *novum*, it was in Moravian Bethlehem and in the mission field in "Susquehanna country," as Faull calls it, where the "holy experiment" was perhaps pushed to be the most inclusive. For the Moravian sisters, as Faull's essay meticulously documents, spoke, worked, and lived on apparently equal terms with sisters who spoke the English, German, French, Mohican, and Delaware languages.

The essays in the volume's second section attend to "The Languages of Education and Established Religions." Drawing respectively on university and Lutheran archives in Pennsylvania and in Germany, Jürgen Overhoff and Wolfgang Flügel document how men of more established churches, Anglican and Lutheran, sought to reshape the colony's officially tolerant landscape. In some cases, as the chapter by Erben also discusses, the educational institutions they supported were designed explicitly to correct the "error" of supposedly "illiterate" Quaker, Moravian, Anabaptist, and separatist "fantasy." Overhoff's chapter takes up the foundation and expansion of the Philadelphia Academy, forerunner to today's University of Pennsylvania, beginning with the concern that the Academy's expanding curriculum was missing, as awakened English evangelist George Whitefield phrased it in a letter to Franklin, "*aliquid Christi* in it." Whitefield thus recommended a "little Dutch book" to Franklin and the Trustees, the German *Kurtzer Bericht* (Brief description) of a school for gentlemen and part of the Francke Foundations in Halle. When Franklin—ever on the lookout for educational models— later toured the leading eighteenth-century German university, in Göttingen, the professors who hosted him voiced the same concern about the absence of a theological faculty in Pennsylvania. The colony's mixed religious landscape, reflected in the curriculum the trustees implemented, was experienced by German Lutheran pastors sent to Pennsylvania from the Pietist educational center in Halle as a "babbling Babel" (babylonisches Sprachgewirr), as Wolfgang Flügel discusses. His survey of their different language choices, German or English, spans the French and Indian War, stretches across the divide of the War of Independence, and reaches into the early decades of the republic. In the pastors' different language choices, we can observe the variety in their philosophy of language. Some saw the medium (language) as the message (belief), while for others, language provided merely a transparent, incidental vehicle.

Babel's third section turns to "The Languages of Race and (Anti-) Slavery." American notions of race—more aptly termed American racism—had been invented by the eighteenth century.[12] While drawing from older ideas about geography, ethnicity, and skin color, early modern racist thought was developed to justify the persistent denial of subjectivity to persons of African descent upon which the legal system of American slavery came to rest. And it rested there increasingly heavily over the course of the eighteenth century, even as the rights of men were asserted from Philadelphia, to Paris, to Port-au-Prince. Katharine Gerbner's chapter surveys late seventeenth-century German, Welsh, and English Quaker communities in the mid-Atlantic and in the Caribbean, locating amidst German Quakers in Germantown an early formulation of a rights-based argument against slavery, whether that enslavement was of

Africans by European settler colonists in the Atlantic or of Europeans by Ottomans in the Mediterranean world. Birte Pfleger's contribution explicitly counters the notion that Germans and German Americans in colonial Pennsylvania were—especially after the middle of the eighteenth century, as the numbers of migrants from established churches increased—any more opposed to the system legalizing the hereditary slavery of people of African descent. Pfleger frames her chapter with a contrast between Lutheran Pietist pastor Henry Melchior Muhlenberg's account of African slavery in the British Atlantic colonies in 1742 and his observations made three decades later, and she shows how the language of race and the "naturalization" of slavery evolved in tandem with the delineation of rights for European indentured servants and redemptioners ever more carefully distinguished from the disenfranchisement of African slaves. The delineation, she writes, retroactively produced a "natural" difference and so a justification for this most unnatural institution. Maurice Jackson's final chapter in this section on race turns to the French-born Pennsylvania Quaker and Atlantic polyglot Anthony Benezet, and it considers the polyphony of people and books from which Benezet drew as he began his lifelong campaign for educational opportunities for and the enfranchisement of African people across the Atlantic world.

The volume's final section, "The Languages of Stone and Wood," reminds us of the mixtures that fed a European cosmopolitan colonial Atlantic culture especially legible in material culture artifacts. Cynthia Falk makes an elegant end-run around scholarship emphasizing European ethnic and linguistic tribalism with the example of a single, architecturally pathbreaking Germantown home. The Deshler house appealed equally to David Deshler and to his wife, Mary, both from Heidelberg, she of French Huguenot parents; to British general William Howe; and, in the 1780s, to American president George Washington. The influence of this fashionable, cosmopolitan culture is also explored in the final chapter, by Lisa Minardi. In her insightful readings of two groups of exquisite furniture produced in Pennsylvania, Minardi poses powerful questions: Why are sophisticated, worldly objects made by Germans in urban Philadelphia not identified as "German"? And conversely, why have historians not attended to these goods' urban cultural production, deeming only quaint rural folk art German and considering it coterminous with

Germans in Pennsylvania? The answers to these questions, she argues, lie in the mistaken assumption that culture is not always plural—no matter how strong the desire that those "differences of manners, languages and extraction" be "no more." There were differences across languages, to be sure; and there were differences within language too. To disregard them is to fall prey to the myth of monolingualism, or the monolingual fallacy.

MYTHS OF BABEL AND MONOLINGUALISM

The remaining pages of this introduction look at how, when we consider language as such, we run, in the midst of history, straight into the work of myth. Like others working on Germans in the wider world, I have profited from the pioneering work of Werner Sollors and his insistence that the *German American Tradition* needed reconsideration.[13] This volume's title, *Babel of the Atlantic,* indicates a debt also to Marc Shell's work, including *American Babel*, which I return to below.[14] It is time, as Patrick Erben also suggests, to reconsider the valence of the Babel story itself. In the multitude of voices heard after the tower's fall, we hear today a different foundational story: not one according to which "differences of manners, languages and extraction" arose and threatened good order, but, instead, a tale that suggests the variety of languages as a *bonum* to be celebrated rather than overcome.

We remain heirs to an epistemology structured by purification, as Bruno Latour influentially wrote.[15] This division of the natural from the social, constitutive of modernity in the West, the division of objective science from subjective humanist pursuits, relies on an instrumental conception of language. For language, as linguistic anthropologists Richard Bauman and Charles Briggs argue, first had to be made "unimportant" for science to work as the realm of pure fact.[16] Stated otherwise, moderns constructed truth as if it had no social life.[17] If some moderns still have a hard time in recognizing the messy, creative work of language, we have perhaps yet more trouble recognizing a "language" as a deeply plural, multilingual formation. To recognize the myth of modernity, we need to learn to hear linguistic variety. The notion that differences, including those of language, must be made "no more" is rooted in a "monolingual fallacy." This mistake rests on the profoundly ahistorical notion that humans, somehow naturally and more authentically, speak only a single language. As a whole, *Babel of the Atlantic* contributes to the ongoing decolonization of Atlantic archives and the scholarship that colonial archives have enabled, so often organized within a serially monolingual paradigm. Working across and between languages, following the lead of eighteenth-century predecessors other than Smith, we might better hear the many differences that imperial projectors sought to quiet in the Atlantic.

In emphasizing the plurality of Atlantic culture in colonial Pennsylvania, and in calling attention to language as such, *Babel of the Atlantic* offers a twofold intervention. First, it intervenes into the field of Atlantic history, where English often, as we have noted, remains the de facto language. Despite the field's transnational contours—as well as its desire to work in spaces before, beyond, and other than the nation[18]—Atlantic history has retained much of its (English) American inheritance. The American nation continues, often in strange and uncanny ways, to shape Atlantic history no less than early American studies.[19] As Shell observed in *American Babel*, even as American literary and cultural studies began to emphasize cultural diversity, scholarship on the whole has tended to deemphasize language difference. This deafness to language as a material witness, following Shell, "arises from the traditional American pretense that culture is not largely linguistic or, rather," he continues, "that culture ought to be English." But in the normativity of English, the work of myth, not history, is at play. As Shell brilliantly observes, "The monoglottal Tereus fears the nightingale's song."[20]

Following Shell's lead, more recent historical work has begun listening more carefully to multilingual voices and the productive passages between and among languages.[21] Nonetheless, now nearly two decades after *American Babel*, English disciplinary models still provide a powerful normative model for early American scholarship. This state of affairs is surely fed by the fact that for many scholars in the American academy, monolingualism remains the reigning norm of the human condition.

Monolingualism has, as Elizabeth Ellis points out, been the unmarked case since the nineteenth century.[22] It became so with the increase in authority accorded to the figure of the "native" speaker of a mother tongue. This figure requires historicization. As Richard Bauman and Charles L.

Briggs write, "If cultures of the printed word are also ideologies of print, so too are cultures of the spoken word ideologies of orality.... Essentialist conceptions of the spoken word and determinist understandings of how it shapes society, culture, or thought are as much in need of critical examination as corresponding conceptions of print."[23] Birgit Jostes has suggested how a "Herderian, deeply Romantic notion of language gave rise in the nineteenth century to the primacy of the native speaker."[24] Jostes draws on the work of linguist Konrad Ehlich, reminding us again, "The conceptualization of the human being as ... fundamentally monolingual is deeply entrenched." She explains, "As a result of the socio-economic and political generalization of national concepts in the nineteenth century, the concept of monolingualism underwent stabilization and became practically unassailable."[25] It remains constitutive, for example, of the modern (national) language departments, including English no less than the "foreign" languages.

The reign of monolingualism—studded by a welter of disciplinary blind spots—coincides roughly with what Paul Giles, via his reading of Emerson reading German Romantics, identifies as the nationalist phase in American literature and culture, from the end of the American Civil War to roughly 1981. Giles convincingly argues that today's "current transnational phase actually has more in common with writing from the periods on either side of the War of Independence, when national boundaries were much more inchoate and unsettled."[26] Those porous boundaries, then as now, implied, too, a degree of flexibility to stretch and encompass a variety of voices and languages, as we shall see.

From our present vantage point, in plain view of the emergence of global English and global Chinese as powerful hybrid, internally polyglot formations, spoken as second or third languages by many of the planet's citizens, we might recognize monolingualism more as a historical aberration than as a norm. The yoke of nation to language, then as now, was far less binding than Herderian acolytes imagined. Jürgen Leonhardt explains in his introduction to the English version of the magisterial *Latin: Study of a World Language*: "Beginning in the sixteenth century and then more intensively since the eighteenth, the primacy of 'natural' [i.e., oral] language was joined by a second notion, namely, that one's individuality and one's inclusion in a national or social community (*Volksgemeinschaft*) can develop only from within the mother tongue and that the mother tongue alone enables individuals to express their deepest thoughts and yearnings."[27]

The monolingualism with which the Atlantic world is often unwittingly described is perhaps particularly pervasive in Anglophone studies.[28] But if the monolingual fallacy is a snare Anglophone scholars fall into, it has also frequently tripped up studies of other European settler colonists. In the colonial mid-Atlantic, German was the second-most widely spoken language after English, as documented by several of the essays in the following pages. Yet colonial German speakers have most often been considered in the historiography as if they spoke only to one another.[29] Questions of a single ethnic identity continue to dominate, even as ethnicity is today more often considered as a discursive formation rather than as innate or essential.[30]

Babel of the Atlantic aims to tell stories that traverse the Atlantic, and, in some cases, the globe, foregrounding how colonial Pennsylvania was not a national but a transnational space, and also profoundly local: coconstituted by people and objects—including the African slaves whose labor was increasingly at the center of the British imperial project—carried by ships plying Atlantic waters.[31] Stories that begin in Germantown, in present-day Philadelphia, for example, proceed across routes that cross the eastern ocean to the British Isles or flow south to the Caribbean or east to Africa and across the Mediterranean to the Ottoman Empire and on to India. They help us to see how the world entered Philadelphia clergymen's homes and shaped how they chose to furnish and inhabit their houses in the cosmopolitan city as well in the countryside, and, conversely, how those same men's concerns at home went out into the world. As Minardi remind us in this volume's final chapter, German Lutheran pastor Muhlenberg was "keenly aware of the need for keeping up appearances." As he noted in his diary, given here as translated into English by Theodore Tappert and John W. Doberstein, Muhlenberg "would not dare" wear homespun clothing made by his wife, "unless I wanted the children on the streets to laugh at me behind my back."[32] While in Philadelphia, worldly concerns shaped the pastor's appearance as he negotiated the urban landscape.

MULTILINGUAL SOUNDINGS, WILLIAM SMITH, AND GERMANS *IM BUSCHE* (IN THE WILD)

In what follows, two historical sketches, or soundings, offer sharp contrasts to one another, although they share a cast of characters, even beyond William Smith, and are both set in the 1750s in Philadelphia and Germantown, amidst the swirling fear and panic reported in the daily press across the Atlantic during the first global war. This was the Seven Years' War (1756–63), known in North America as the French and Indian War, which in fact was breaking out already in 1755 in the Pennsylvania "backcountry." Its theaters extended across Europe to South America, Africa, and the Indian subcontinent. Rather than remaining unwitting inheritors of Smith's resolve to plane the colony's linguistic and religious differences, which he alleged made the British colony ripe for French invasion—the subject of the first sketch—we might take cues from those in the eighteenth century who opposed him—the subject of the second.

The first sketch features Smith in dialogue with Benjamin Franklin, and it shows a rather nastier side of the favorite founding father than we are perhaps accustomed to seeing. The second sketch features Germantown printer Christoph Saur (1695–1758) and his newspaper's account of the printer's court-martial, overseen by British General Forbes in the company of fourteen regimented *Bergschotten* (Highland Scots) in the *Wirtshaus zum Hirsch* (Deer's Inn). The contrasting sketches help us to hear the diversity of voices that sounded, within and between languages, in the mid-1750s—even at the command headquarters of the British imperial military enterprise.

These sketches offer soundings in the translation zone of colonial Pennsylvania from two different locations. Everywhere he went, Smith spoke an English inspired by imperial Roman models, and he sought to force everyone else to do so as well. The second traces Saur's route, described in the popular newspaper he published, down the high street in Germantown to Lancaster Street and the Deer's Inn. Along his route he passed in and out of German, summarized discussions held in English, and referenced others held with Delaware leaders. Only the first man, Smith, is much remembered in colonial Atlantic world scholarship. But the second, Saur, I argue, provides far better evidence toward a history of the diverse, polyglot places scattered across the colonial Atlantic. His relative obscurity in colonial Atlantic scholarship is symptomatic of how that multilingual story has been made barely audible within a disciplinary framework constituted of and by the monolingual fallacy.

William Smith had taken up the problem of language and empire in his influential educational plan, the *General Idea of the College of Mirania*, published in 1753.[33] *Mirania* proved the young Smith an eager reader of Roman history, and he aspired to translate Roman civilization, now dressed in English garb, to a still farther shore. Along the North American continent's eastern coast, he would work tirelessly to extend the patrimony of the civilization he believed had spawned "the single fatherland of all the races." *Mirania* caught the notice of Franklin, who was heading a committee of Philadelphia men working to expand higher education in colonial Philadelphia, as explored in greater detail by Overhoff in this volume; and, like Smith, Franklin would soon become involved in a plan to create charity schools for poor German children, as both Erben and Flügel discuss in their chapters.

It was likely *Mirania*'s advocacy of mixing classical tradition with practical application that first attracted Franklin's notice, rather than Smith's poetic talent. *Mirania*'s preface marches on leaden feet; its heroic couplets drill Smith's imperial design for gentlemen in the British American colonies into readers' heads:

> Lo! The wild INDIAN, soften'd by their Song,
> Emerging from his *Arbors*, bounds along
> The green *Savannah* patient of the *Lore*
> Of Dove-ey'd *Wisdom*—and is *rude* no more. (6)

Smith aimed to provide an imperial curriculum suitable to "draw together... the jarring and uncouth tongues of so many nations." They would be united in their adulation of the humble plowman ever ready to pick up his sword again. Smith promised to educate boys to bear arms, a readiness Franklin found sorely wanting, especially among the Germans in Quaker Pennsylvania.

At the same historical moment, also in 1753, Franklin wrote to his friend in London Peter Collinson that the Germans "come in droves."[34] Furthermore, he complained to Collinson, while earlier German migrants to Pennsylvania had little influence on local politics, they now "carry all before them, except in one or two Counties." Inconveniently for Franklin, the Germans had not supported his pet project of the 1740s: how to solve the conundrum of funding and training an armed militia in a colony founded on pacifist principles. Indeed, Quaker founder William Penn had included in the colony's guarantees of freedoms the right *not* to bear arms; and, as Erben discusses below, it was *Freyheit* from military service that many German migrants both sought and defended, some having left Europe expressly to avoid conscription into Prussia's growing army. Franklin explained in several letters to Collinson in the early 1750s that the Germans seemed beyond the power of his otherwise influential press. They would not become humble plowmen ready to bear arms, never mind produce a latter-day Cincinnatus.

Six years earlier, in 1747, as Collinson would have known, Franklin had published the pamphlet *Plain Truth*. As Franklin later recalled in his autobiography, it "had a sudden and surprizing Effect."[35] In it, a woodcut (fig. I.1) featured a plowman praying to Hercules to help get his cart unstuck from the mud, with a Latin caption from Sallust's *Bellum Catilinae*, "Non Votis, & C."[36] The woodcut had been recycled from a children's book illustrating Aesop's fables, where it illustrated the tale of the wagoner whose cart got stuck, with its lesson "He that won't help himself, shall have Help from no Body."[37] This was the gospel as Franklin's popular *Poor Richard's Almanac* also preached it. "God helps them that helps themselves" had appeared there already in 1736.[38] *Plain Truth* owed its "sudden and surprizing Effect" to broad segments of the English-speaking audience, particularly those modest "tradesmen" to whom it was addressed and who, like Franklin and Poor Richard, distinguished themselves from the wealthy ruling Quaker elite. They participated in the lottery to support a militia, subscribed money, and began training in brigades.

But the plan to arm and train European settlers was less convincing to many of the colony's German speakers. And yet it did not fail for lack of trying. Franklin had collaborated with Philadelphia German printer Gotthard Armbrüster to bring out J. Crell's translation, *Die Lautere Wahrheit* (fig. I.2). Franklin even lent Armbrüster the woodcut from Aesop's fable.[39] Despite this German translation, Franklin insisted that many Germans' resistance to his plan to form militias was rooted in their linguistic and cultural separatism. That Germans in Pennsylvania, like

FIGURE I.1A First page of Franklin's *Plain Truth* (Philadelphia, 1747).

many of their English Quaker neighbors, might genuinely hold pacifist principles was not a fact he bothered to consider publicly.

In a manuscript that Franklin authored in 1751, four years after the publication of *Plain Truth*, then sent to Collinson and eventually allowed to be printed, he lamented,

> Few of their children in the Country learn English; they import many Books from Germany; and of the six printing houses in the Province, two are entirely German, two half German half English, and but two entirely English; They have one German News-paper, and one half German. Advertisements intended to be general are now printed in Dutch and English; the Signs in our Streets have inscriptions in both languages, and in some places only German: They begin of late to make all their Bonds and other legal Writings

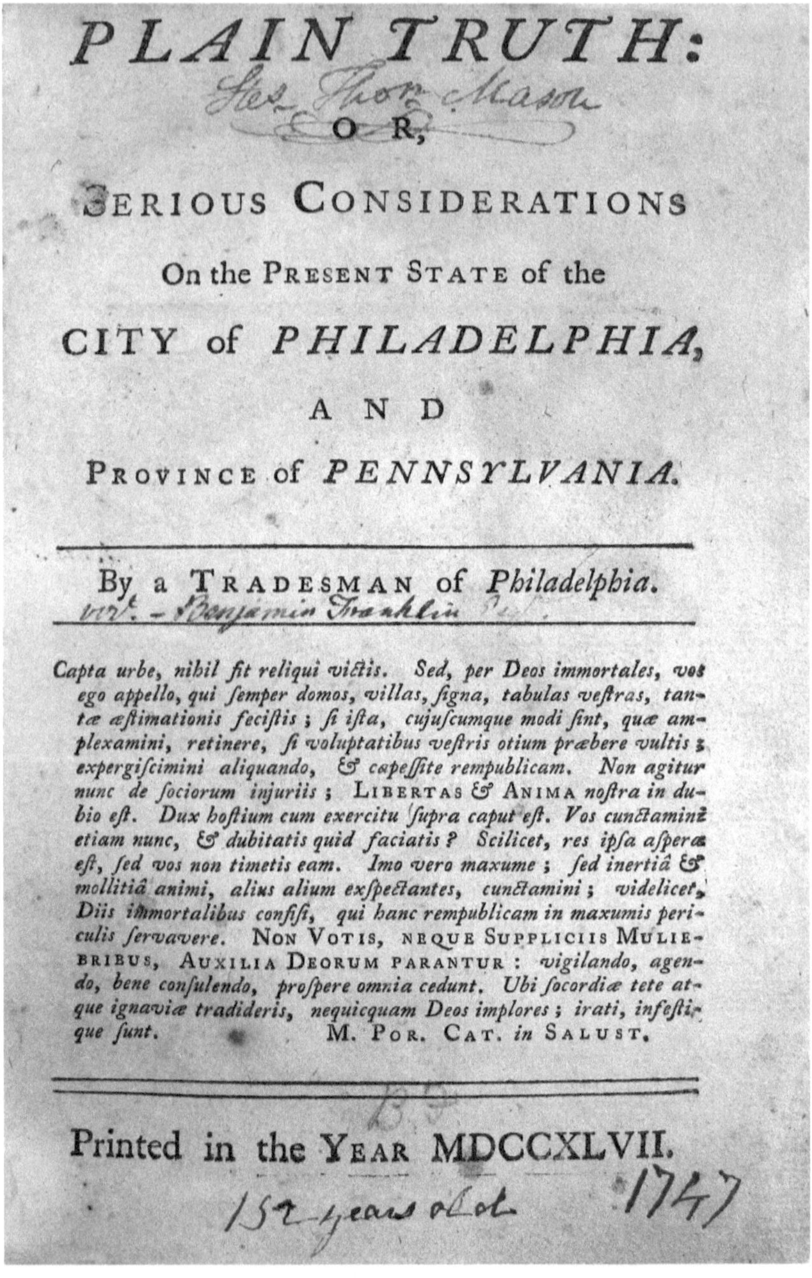

PLAIN TRUTH:

OR,

SERIOUS CONSIDERATIONS

On the PRESENT STATE of the

CITY of PHILADELPHIA,

AND

PROVINCE of PENNSYLVANIA.

By a TRADESMAN of *Philadelphia*.

Capta urbe, nihil fit reliqui victis. Sed, per Deos immortales, vos ego appello, qui semper domos, villas, signa, tabulas vestras, tantæ æstimationis fecistis; si ista, cujuscumque modi sint, quæ amplexamini, retinere, si voluptatibus vestris otium præbere vultis; expergiscimini aliquando, & capessite rempublicam. Non agitur nunc de sociorum injuriis; LIBERTAS & ANIMA *nostra in dubio est. Dux hostium cum exercitu supra caput est. Vos cunctamini etiam nunc, & dubitatis quid faciatis? Scilicet, res ipsa aspera est, sed vos non timetis eam. Imo vero maxume; sed inertia & mollitia animi, alius alium exspectantes, cunctamini; videlicet, Diis immortalibus confisi, qui hanc rempublicam in maximis periculis servavere.* NON VOTIS, NEQUE SUPPLICIIS MULIEBRIBUS, AUXILIA DEORUM PARANTUR : *vigilando, agendo, bene consulendo, prospere omnia cedunt. Ubi socordiæ tete atque ignaviæ tradideris, nequicquam Deos implores; irati, infestique sunt.* M. POR. CAT. *in* SALUST.

Printed in the YEAR MDCCXLVII.

FIGURE I.1B First page of Franklin's *Plain Truth* (Philadelphia, 1747).

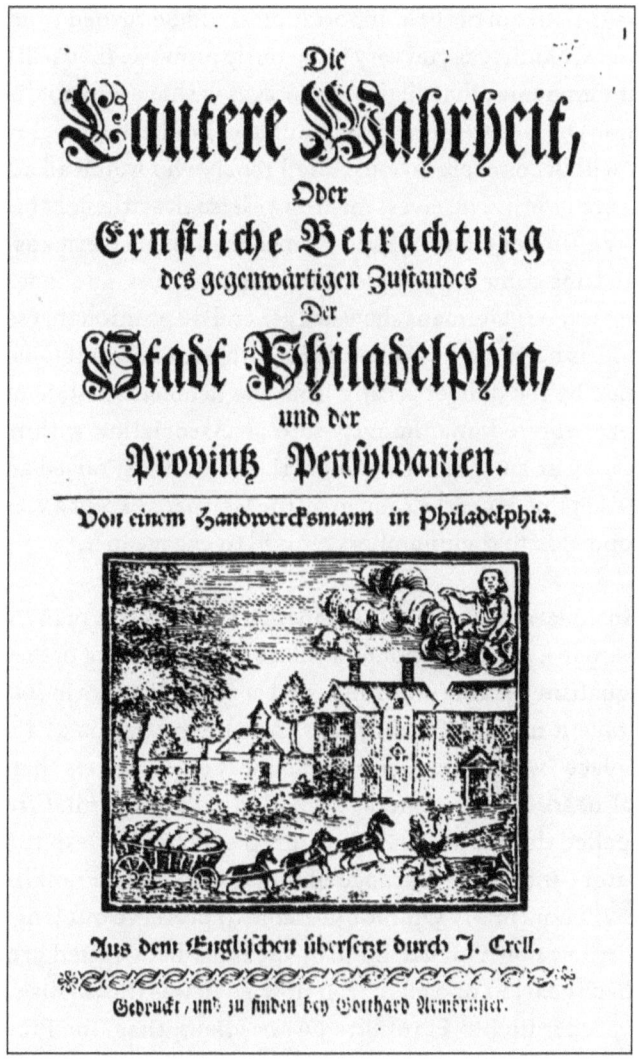

FIGURE I.2 German translation, by J. Crell, of Franklin's *Plain Truth*.

in their own Language, which (though I think it ought not to be) are allowed good in our Courts, where the German Business so encreases that there is continual need of Interpreters; and I suppose in a few years they will be also necessary in the Assembly, to tell one half of our Legislators what the other half say; In short unless the stream of their importation could be turned from this to other Colonies, as you very judiciously propose, they will soon so out number us, that all the advantages we have will not [in My Opinion] be able to preserve our language, and even our Government will become precarious. The French who watch all advantages, are now [themselves] making a German settlement back of us in the Ilinoes Country, and by means of those Germans they may in time come to an understanding with ours, and indeed in the last war our Germans shewed a general disposition that seems to bode us no good; for when the English who were not Quakers, alarmed by the danger arising from the defenceless state of our Country entered unanimously into an Association within this Government and the lower Countries [Counties] raised armed and Disciplined [near] 10,000 men, the Germans except a very few in proportion to their numbers refused to engage in it.[40]

The insinuation of French sympathies infuriated many German Pennsylvanians, pacifist or not. Franklin's disparagement of the colony's multilingualism became notorious, and several chapters in *Babel of the Atlantic* take it up. The *Observations* treat Pennsylvania as a veritable Babel, a place "where the German Business so encreases that there is continual need of Interpreters."[41] For Franklin, this mixture of languages spelled the end of "all the advantages we have." Despite the work of translators and the appearance of bilingual papers, Franklin opines that we "will not [in My Opinion] be able to preserve our language." A decade earlier, non-Quaker English speakers had "raised armed and Disciplined [near] 10,000 men." But now, such was the English colony's precarity, according to Franklin's *Observations*, that "the French who watch all advantages" were ready to pounce. For Franklin, or at least for the Franklin of the late 1740s and '50s, as for Smith, Pennsylvania's linguistic diversity marked the colony's vulnerability; it provided the possible point of entry through which the French and "their" Indians were bound to march. The colony's several mother tongues made "even our Government . . . precarious." Pennsylvania was badly in need of Pliny's "civilization." Non-Quaker Englishmen willing to assemble with guns would be its bearers. And William Smith would be the man to train their leaders.

Smith took up his role at the Academy in May 1754, after first returning to London, where he received ordination as an Anglican cleric. When the Academy was granted a new charter in 1755, making it a degree-granting college, Smith was at the helm.[42] And the college was not the only pedagogical mission Smith embraced. Even before *Mirania*'s publication, Smith had made a *Proposal for Erecting Indian Schools*, prefaced by *Indian Songs of Peace*.[43] Furthermore, as Patrick Erben recounts in extensive detail in the following chapter, while in London in 1753–54, Smith had joined forces with a group of German Lutherans and English Anglicans, and with German and Dutch Reformed allies, on a project, to be funded by donors in North America, Great Britain, and Hanover and Prussia, to educate the colony's German-speaking children. The children's acquisition of English was, as Erben's essay shows, to be cajoled and coerced; Smith would have them learn English, like it or not. For in Smith's view, a monolingual English nation was the rightful inheritor of Rome's imperial power, *translatio imperii*. Thus, just as *Mirania* proclaimed that "the *INDIAN*" must be "*soften'd* by their [English] Song," so too must the German be made "*rude* no more." He must instead be made English—and ready to bear arms.

Throughout the eighteenth and into the nineteenth century, Pennsylvania's multilingual population elicited commentary, delighting some and driving others to despair. Some fifty years after Smith's *Mirania*, the observer of America Hector St. John de Crèvecoeur famously proclaimed that meaningful differences were indeed now no more, subsumed under a "naturalized" American identity: "He is become a freeholder, from perhaps a German boor—he is now an American, a Pennsylvanian, an English subject. He is naturalized. . . . From nothing to start into being; from a servant to the rank of a master; from being the slave of some despotic prince, to become a free man, invested with lands, to which every municipal blessing is annexed! What a change indeed! It is in consequence of that change that he becomes an American" (Letter III).[44] St. John's naturalized American rootstock, "from perhaps a German boor," was hardly incidental; it recalled Franklin's infamous *Observations*, which conclude by racializing Pennsylvania's inhabitants. Germans were judged "swarthy," as Birte Pfleger's chapter in this volume discusses, and they were thus anything but sound stock for future American generations. They were "boors," perhaps a play on the German *Bauern* (farmers), and these colonists, unlike St. John's naturalized, hybrid freeholders in the early republic, would in Franklin's view prove Pennsylvania's undoing. Franklin concluded his *Observations*, "Why should the Palatine Boors be suffered to swarm into our Settlements, and by herding together establish their Language and Manners to the Exclusion of ours? Why should Pennsylvania, founded by the English, become a Colony of *Aliens*, who will shortly be so numerous as to Germanize us instead of our Anglifying them, and will never adopt our Language or Customs, any more than they can acquire our Complexion."[45] Franklin's racist thinking on the eve of the French and Indian War loathed mixtures—whether of peoples or of their languages. His thinking on slavery evolved, as Maurice Jackson's chapter here documents. But, like the Franklin of the *Observations*, William Smith saw multilingualism's messiness as threatening the purity of the civilizing imperial project.

It bears emphasizing that English-speaking imperial projectors were not the only mid-eighteenth-century observers worried about Pennsylvania's hybridizing, plural identities. These identities frightened many German observers too, particularly those employed by the Lutheran or Calvinist Churches. In his well-known *Reise nach Pennsylvanien* (Travels to Pennsylvania), for example, published in 1756, Lutheran Gottlieb Mittelberger (1715–1779) opined that "Pennsylvania's freedom was more harmful than healthy to many a body and soul."[46] According to more educated German observers, while simple farmers and tradespeople might believe they had found heaven on earth, their ignorance led them into error. As Mittelberger reported, "There is a saying: 'Pennsylvania is heaven for farmers, paradise for tradespeople, and hell for government officials and clergy.'"[47]

It was these allegedly uneducated Germans—including those who remained unmoved by Franklin's *Plain Truth*—who were presumably not ready for *die Pennsylvanische Freiheit* (Pennsylvanian freedom). For Franklin and Smith, this freedom must be guarded and defended with military measures; only the Germans' lack of education prevented them from recognizing this necessity. Smith, in league with other men of the cloth, whether speaking German or English, stood ready to school them. Mittelberger returned to Germany, but in Philadelphia Smith found a willing partner in Henry Melchior Muhlenberg.[48] Muhlenberg—as Patrick Erben, Craig Atwood, Wolfgang Flügel, and Birte Pfleger variously discuss below—had been sent in 1742 by Lutheran Pietists from the Francke Foundations in Halle (Saale) specifically to minister to those many Germans alleged to have gone wild *im Busche* (in the wild, or in the wilderness, i.e., "gone native"). These Germans were believed by Lutheran church leaders in Halle to be particularly susceptible to what Atwood, echoing Aaron Fogleman, calls the "Moravian threat."[49] As Mittelberger noted, so many articles of faith and sects ruled over Pennsylvania that they could not all be named, especially since no one confirmed the beliefs they held.[50] Muhlenberg, no less than Smith, aimed to bring these renegades back into conformity. If only they could be educated, they would abandon their troubling pacifism and other "fantasies."

Brought into conformity by educated schoolmen, the Germans *im Busche* might form a united eternal defensive wall against all America's enemies ("ewige Vormauer wider alle ihre Feinde), as Mittelberger's editor expounded (see the quotation below). These men of the cloth, trained in the shared classical curriculum also held up by Smith, would form the bulwark of what Carla Pestana has more recently called the Protestant Empire. Despite the "failure to create a uniformly Anglican Atlantic world under English purview," Pestana argues that the "expansion [out of Europe] established a broadly shared culture that united believers from different Protestant churches (and different ethnic and racial backgrounds) into a common Anglophone spiritual orientation."[51] How far this Protestant culture might move toward the inclusion of Protestant "brothers" speaking languages other than English and of complexions deemed more "swarthy" than their own presented urgent questions, to Smith no less than his various contemporaries. Mittelberger's editor added a long note, from which we have already quoted, amplifying Mittelberger's own concerns that more educated men were needed:

> An English text about the condition of immigrants who have settled in Pennsylvania, Virginia, Maryland, etc, announces the following: The most reliable reports we have from these provinces reveal that the number of immigrants has uncommonly increased in the last years. The greatest part consists of Palatines, Franconians, Swiss. In the colony of Pennsylvania alone there are over one hundred thousand, of which some twenty thousand are Calvinist, and nearly as many are Lutheran, and around seventeen hundred

are devoted to the Roman religion. The rest consist of Baptists, Herrenhuters [Moravians], Brothers of Zion, Rondonfers, and other separatists. Since, among these last, each is his own teacher [Lehrer], so it can be said that they know their articles of faith [Lehrsätze] (if their fantasies can be so called) far better than many of the others who hold similar beliefs. Even though one can meet among them many of no little piety as well as awakened Christians, the vast majority remain in the greatest ignorance, for there are not enough preachers and schoolmasters and the people lack the means to support them. The [English] author of this text thus concludes with the wish that the nation of Great Britain might take into their heart these [poor] brothers in all things spiritual and secular and help them achieve a condition such that America would have in them an eternal outer wall against all her enemies.[52]

For some observers, the mix of voices speaking separatist, often pacifist articles of faith—in German, in English, as well as in other languages—produced a maddening roar. It confirmed Pennsylvania's status as a latter-day Babel, a place brought to a fall and henceforth consigned to disharmony and discord. For some, it bordered on Babylon. For others, however, the colony's various tongues, both religious and linguistic, sounded the freedom that put paid to the Quaker colony's foundational Philadelphian promises of a place in which all were to be recognized as brothers.

MULTILINGUAL SOUNDINGS, CHRISTOPH SAUR, AND THE REGIMENT OF *BERGSCHOTTEN* (HIGHLAND SCOTS)

The July 8, 1758, issue of the *Pensylvanische Berichte* (Pennsylvanian Reports)—a newspaper published twice weekly in Germantown, with a circulation of some four thousand[53]—reported that nine days earlier, on the same day that British general Forbes was to set out on his expedition to Fort Duquesne (soon to be renamed Fort Pitt), fourteen soldiers from the regiment of Highland Scots (*Bergschotten*) had appeared at the paper's offices. They arrived, the article continued, on the High Street in Germantown to escort the paper's founder, printer, and publisher, Christoph

Saur, to an audience with the general before his imminent departure to confront the French and "their Indians."

Saur, the father of a son and printer of the same name, is well known in scholarship on German Americans but sadly less so beyond it.[54] A self-taught printer who also built his own press, the elder Saur is perhaps most famous for publishing the first Bible in North America in a European language, to Muhlenberg's chagrin, as Erben's chapter below discusses. Saur's *Almanac* circulated in print runs of ten thousand annually: the same estimate given for Benjamin Franklin's celebrated *Poor Richard's Almanac*. Franklin's *Almanac* has gone into the canon of American literary history; poor Christoph's has definitely not.[55] Even more linguistically inclusive literary histories of America, including the one edited by Greil Marcus and Werner Sollors, make no mention of him.[56]

Saur's exclusion from the American canon should not be read as a judgment on his wit or originality. He was ridiculed in the eighteenth century by imperial promoters because he was a nonconformist pacifist; he is excluded today because he wrote predominantly in German. But his story is not proper only to German American history; it is a story that points to the need to recover more voices of the multilingual Atlantic. His provides one sounding in a sea of voices that crossed and mixed languages. To hear them, we must bring monolingual, monocultural archives into dialogue; and we must hybridize the disciplinary frameworks of those pedagogical systems constructed as a road to empire. To do so, we might take a hint from Saur himself.

As we have heard above, Saur had opposed Franklin's scheme to militarize the colony since the 1740s. Unsurprisingly, Saur also bore no sympathy for Smith's plans to educate the colony's youth. Until the end of his life in 1758, a few months after his hearing with Forbes, Saur would use his press to restore peace, constantly reminding readers of the colony's pacifist foundation.[57] In 1755, Delaware warriors began to attack European squatters and settlers along the disputed border of Indian country, including Germans, both Lutherans and Moravians. These violent attacks were broadly publicized across the Atlantic world, in newspapers from Philadelphia to Hanover. The reasons why the Lenape had grown so angry with British colonists, switching their support to the French and declaring war, received less spectacular coverage. And yet, English Quakers and German pacifists worked to make their grievances public, forming the Friendly Association and publishing under its auspices histories of Delaware grievances and colonial authorities' broken promises and fraudulent land deals.[58] With Quaker leaders, including the wealthy Israel Pemberton—known derisively in the English-language, prowar press as "King Wampum"—Saur used his press to raise money to gift to dislocated Lenape.[59]

It was, the newspaper article hinted, Saur's refusal to whitewash Penn family dealings and sanctify the new military campaign against the "French and their Indians" that had brought the *Bergschotten* to his door. The article is little known; it deserves a wider audience. Like other examples of Saur's writing, it contains some rhetorical gems. I present it here in a lengthy excerpt as a powerful—if nearly unknown—document of the everyday multilingualism of the colonial mid-Atlantic. Our disciplinary paradigms have made it only barely audible today. It shows, in a matter-of-fact manner, how multilingual voices were heard even at the very headquarters of the British imperial project in North America. And it shows Pennsylvania's babble not as a condition to be overcome, or an index to Babel after the fall. Rather, it documents diverse citizens exercising the freedoms (*Freyheiten*) and privileges (*Privilegien*) enshrined in colonial Pennsylvania's founding charter, freedoms, including the freedom of speech, that they sought to extend—at least to all the colony's males. This was a freedom not to be enforced by a militia, but one designed to tolerate a variety of voices; indeed, this freedom would take its meaning precisely with the multitude of voices who could speak and so instantiate it.

Forbes had been sent to the colonies in the aftermath of the dismal defeat and death of his predecessor, General Braddock. The former—in taking the French Fort Duquesne and rechristening it with the name of the English prime minister who had given him his orders, William Pitt—saved the British Empire in North America. He was celebrated for a time as a second Cincinnatus. William Smith's 1758 panegyric to Forbes on the eve of the troops' departure for Fort Duquesne urged,

> Rise then, my countrymen! as you value the blessings you enjoy, and dread the evils that hang over you, rise and shew yourselves worthy of the name of Britons! rise to secure to your posterity, peace, freedom, and a pure religion! rise to chastize a perfidious

nation for their breach of treaties, their detestable cruelties, and their horrid murders! remember the cries of your captivated brethren, your orphan children, your helpless widows, and thousands of beggar'd families! think of Monongahela, Fort-William Henry, and those scenes of savage death, where the mangled limbs of your fellow citizens lie strewed upon the plain; calling upon you to retrieve the honour of the British name![60]

Forbes, in Smith's unparalleled bombast, was nothing less than a divine instrument:

> This, my dear Countrymen, is happiness indeed! and what still enhances it, is the consideration that we are not only called to enjoy it ourselves, but perhaps to be the instruments of diffusing it over this vast continent, to the nations that sit "in Darkness and the Shadow of Death." ...
>
> ... Or shall a French slave and popish bigot, at this day, do more for the glory of his tyrannical Lord, than a Freeman and Protestant for the best of Kings, and the Father of his people?
>
> This land was given to us for propagating Freedom, establishing useful Arts, and extending the kingdom of Jesus.[61]

For Smith, Forbes was the "instrument" of divine, Anglophone Protestant light. He had been called to propagate "Freedom" in "this land given to us."

For all Smith's and the pacifist Saur's differences, Saur, cannily, also portrayed Forbes as a hero. Despite the general's very raison d'être, Saur styled Forbes as a more loyal son of Pennsylvania's freedoms than were the pastors of the organized churches, whether Anglican or Lutheran. Saur preferred army leaders, "generals in red," to those of the church, "generals in black," quipping, "there is more understanding, intelligence, and moderation among the red generals than among the black." The full news item appeared in the *Pensylvanische Berichte* on July 8, 1758:

> The **Germantown** printer has been accused to General Forbes, probably by adversaries, to be a doer of terrible deeds and to have sinned against the king, the government, and the province. It seems the General wanted to prove his loyalty to the king, the government, and the province. On the day of his departure [for

Fort Duquesne], he sent the printer a written order delivered by fourteen **Highland Scots** that he should appear in front of the General at twelve noon in **Lancaster** Street at the Deer's Inn and answer for a sentence in his recent newspaper. The order, however, was moderated to say that if he would come freely, then the detachment could go on their way. This happened. The **Highland Scots** left one hour before and arrived one hour after him. The general had hardly arrived when he called the printer aside, into a separate room, and read him, in the presence of the Herr Governor, the following sentence [from Saur's newspaper], translated into English, which reads:

> Several days ago the emissaries who had been sent to **Teedyuskung** and the **Delaware** returned to Philadelphia and report that **Teedyuskung** and his people remain in good peace with the **English**, etc.

With this he questioned the printer: Was this not written **against** the king, **against** the governor, and **against** the province? The printer answered: He believed he had been unjustly accused and additionally the translation was not made completely according to his meaning and his words. That in fact the complete opposite was true of him than that of what he had been accused. Indeed, since he had come thirty-four years ago from a bad country into this good country, he had written various letters to **Germany** that had drawn many people to this country: And those who came wrote in their turn and attracted still others; and because he believed that he is the reason why so many people have moved here, he also felt it was his duty to support the welfare of this province via good government by supporting its good government. The general said: **I want to believe you**; but a person can hold a good intention that can nonetheless turn bad. And so he warned the printer with all due seriousness that he should not print anything that might be against the king, against the government, and against the welfare of this province. This the printer willingly promised, indeed he even offered that if there was something in the accusations that proved him wrong, he would correct it in the next newspaper; but the general did not name any points that did not bear out; instead he told the printer to go about his business.

He could have given the printer nothing easier, since he loves the **king** of **England**, he loves a good **government**, and when this **province** fares well, he benefits from it too. And thus within three minutes, the great charges of guilt were heard, explained, and resolved, all at no cost.

After the meal, it is true that another officer gave the printer privately to understand that he hoped the printer would retract and would not write anything inappropriate against this expedition in the newspaper. But as he did not name anything that should be retracted, so [the printer] promised the latter, and himself desires, that he might be able to discover and write nothing but purely appropriate, good, and praiseworthy things about the whole expedition.

The printer claims no cleverness in flattering fancy people; but he can attest in truth to what **Christian Democritus** has written, that there is more understanding, intelligence, and moderation among the red generals than among the black. And if His Excellency General Forbes possesses as much good fortune as he does understanding, seriousness, loyalty, and moderation, the expedition against Fort **Duquesne** will soon be over and we will be able to report on his heroics.

It was desired that the whole episode be passed over in silence, but since so many pernicious, calumnious things have been and may still be spread about the country and people are asking hourly about the course of the thing, we've reported how it is.

On this past Thursday, the sixth of July, **Teedyuskung** and forty **Indians** traveled through **Germantown** to **Philadelphia**. It is reported that some of these Indians had stood in friendship with the English; there are also two other foreign nations which until then had remained independent or had been in peace with the French. They have two wagons full of gifts with them, the best deerskins among them. It is reported that one person is in their midst who had previously captured two children and had wanted to bring them back; but they had not wanted to come. They also have brought a Low Dutch woman with them who was supposed to have stayed in **Bethlehem**, but she had not wanted to leave the Indians' side and so also came to Philadelphia, and it seems she wants to return back with them; maybe she considers such an idle life to be freedom.

A man named **Hochstättler**—who had been a prisoner of the Indians for eight months and escaped—reports that as the French have very little rations, so too are the **Indians** in short supply, and that this might do much to move them to peace with the English.[62]

Saur was an American original. Largely self-taught, he became by the end of his life an adept rhetorician and master of well-placed rhetorical questions. He deftly employs parallel structures and notes with refreshing understatement that some contemporaries, "probably adversaries," have reported him to military authorities. They alleged him "to have sinned against the king, the government, and the province," whereupon he was summoned by the commanding officer, who pressed him on his account of Friendly Association emissaries to the Delaware, lately "returned to Philadelphia." The emissaries, and Saur's newspaper, had reported "that Teedyuskung and his people remain in good peace with the English, etc." Together, they begged the question why Forbes was on a war footing. And Forbes, echoing Saur's accusers, demanded, "Was this not written against the king, against the governor and against the province?" But then the article cleverly overturns the parallel formulation, insisting that in fact the "red generals" were much more understanding than those who wore black.

In the following chapter, Patrick Erben shows how Saur delighted in vilifying paid clergy. He often did so with understatement and humor; he is relatively free of the bombast of churchmen such as William Smith. We would be wrong to conflate Saur's separatist religious beliefs with quietism. It was not the case, as Gregg Roeber has suggested, that Christoph Saur "assaulted closer English-German union in religious or political affairs in Pennsylvania." Saur assaulted a union that would have curtailed religious and personal freedoms to nonchurch members. He did not have, as Roeber argues, "one simple lesson" that he simple-mindedly "hammered home": "Support the Quakers and avoid courts, lawyers, politics, and unnecessary involvement with English-speakers that might endanger our language, our families and customs, and our faith."[63] On the contrary, Saur's position entailed no withdrawal from the public sphere: he used his press to expand the space for civil discourse, and to make it, no less than Pennsylvania itself, a place where pacifist voices, some speaking German, might continue to be heard even amidst a war.⁶⁴

His press, as this report also shows, was influential. Governors and generals had to reckon with it. They did so across languages. The article shows Forbes and Saur arguing the finer points of translation. Saur told the general, "He believed he had been unjustly accused." Indeed, the English translation of the originally German article reporting on the emissaries, Teedyuskung, and the continued peace they enjoyed "was not made completely according to his meaning and his words." The English translation, the German account hints, had been made according to remarkably un-Philadelphian principles. It was religiously partisan, the work of the "generals in black," and Saur received far fairer treatment from Forbes, a man distinguished by his "understanding, seriousness, loyalty, and moderation." American history has given Saur a less fair hearing.

This introduction has set Christoph Saur in contrast to William Smith. It has done so in part to contextualize Saur's suspicions of the colony's educational institutions, including the leading establishment, run by Provost Smith. Saur's resistance to Smith's various educational schemes does not signal the printer's ignorance—or that he was capable of only "one simple lesson." Rather, it shows Saur as a witness to and participant in contests to give shape to British imperialism, contests that still bear on American legacies. The contrast between Smith and Saur also helps bring into view the other "possible pasts" obscured by the monolingual fallacy, reminding us how things might have gone otherwise.⁶⁵

Saur's print shop provides us with a microcosm of the colony's multilingualism. It is rather unremarkable, in many ways; it was the business of everyday colonial Pennsylvania. But it is also here, in the multilingual commerce of Saur's shop, where we find outstanding historical figures such as Anthony Benezet, as Maurice Jackson discusses in his contribution to the volume. Both men were active in the Friendly Association; Saur, as we have seen, printed for the Association. And Saur's son would go on to print, also in English, Benezet's pioneering work against slavery. In the print shop, we can again hear the mixed babble of life and languages in the colonial mid-Atlantic, a discourse carried out in several languages all at once, a place unspectacular and yet also productive of a powerful tradition of human rights advocacy.

In Saur's work with the Friendly Association, we recognize Saur as a cultural broker, to use Daniel Richter's now classic formulation. In a multilingual history, Saur can no longer be read as an icon of an insular German American historical tradition. Cultural brokers, often translators, remind us, in Richter's words, how "the fate of both the imperial powers of the modern world-system and the native peoples that system sought to absorb" lay at key moments in local hands.[66] But, as the following chapters richly illustrate, cultural and linguistic negotiations were not the exclusive purview of official translators. Instead, transactions and exchanges across and between languages made up the mid-Atlantic, the public sphere no less than the physical world that print culture sought to represent. Language itself, as we have seen, was under debate. Across languages, various meanings of freedom were at stake.

In a globalized world, myths of the monoglot nation have lost their magic. As sociologist Ulrich Beck and historian Martin Mulsow together write, questions of perception, cultural translations, and negotiations among different cultural codes take center stage.[67] These are the translations and negotiations that also provide the focus of *Babel of the Atlantic*. Perhaps, we want to suggest, it is time to reconsider the meaning of Babel. It is past time to return to this rich trope, the *locus classicus* of all the "differences of manners, languages and extraction" that William Smith would have made "no more."

Notes

1. Colin Calloway, *New Worlds for All: Indians, Europeans, and the Remaking of Early America* (Baltimore: Johns Hopkins University Press, 1997).

2. Mary Louise Pratt, "Arts of the Contact Zone," *Profession* (1991): 34.

3. Emily Apter, *The Translation Zone: A New Comparative Literature* (Princeton: Princeton University Press, 2005).

4. See also Rey Chow, "Translator, Traitor; Translator, Mourner (or, Dreaming of Intercultural Equivalence)," in *Not Like a Native Speaker: On Languaging as a Postcolonial Experience* (New York: Columbia University Press, 2014), 61–77.

5. Lawrence Venuti, *The Translator's Invisibility: A History of Translation* (New York: Routledge, 1995).

6. Lydia Liu, quoted in Chow, "Translator, Traitor," 68.

7. Daniel K. Richter, "Cultural Brokers and Intercultural Politics: New York–Iroquois Relations, 1664–1701," *Journal of American History* 75, no. 1 (1988): 40–67; Jane T. Merritt, *At the Crossroads: Indians and Empires on a Mid-Atlantic Frontier*,

1700–1763 (Chapel Hill: University of North Carolina Press, 2003).

8. Richard White, *The Middle Ground: Indians, Empires, and Republics in the Great Lakes Region, 1680–1815* (New York: Cambridge University Press, 1991).

9. Juliana Barr and Edward Countryman, eds., *The Contested Spaces of Early America* (Philadelphia: University of Pennsylvania Press, 2014), 24.

10. James Taylor Carson, "Ethnogeography and the Native American Past," *Ethnohistory* 49, no. 4 (2002): 775.

11. Some chapters originated in a conference held in December 2012 at the McNeil Center for Early American Studies at the University of Pennsylvania called "Envisioning the 'Old World.'" John Pollack offers a conference review, "Lumping or Splitting: Fresh Perspectives on the 'German-Speaking Peoples' of Early Pennsylvania," *Early American Literature* 48, no. 3 (2013): 801–9. The "Old World" conference, in turn, inspired a public history workshop in November 2013, "'Equally Entitled to Freedom': Benezet Now, Benezet Then," convened by Historic Germantown with cosponsorship from the Germantown Monthly Meeting, the Germantown Friends School, the William Penn Charter School Germantown United CDC, and the National Society of the Colonial Dames of America in the Commonwealth of Pennsylvania. The program is available online: see "'Equally Entitled to Freedom': Benezet Now, Benezet Then," accessed November 18, 2017, http://www.freedomsbackyard.com/programs-events/anthony-benezet-symposium/.

12. Ta-Nehisi Coates, "How Racism Invented Race in America: The Case for Reparations; A Narrative Bibliography," *Atlantic*, accessed July 28, 2016, http://www.theatlantic.com/politics/archive/2014/06/the-case-for-reparations-a-narrative-bibliography/372000/. Coates's essay provides a wealth of further materials on the history of American racism. Also drawing on decades of work on the black Atlantic and slavery, Susan Buck-Morss situates racism at the very center of European idealism, rather than at the margins. She insists, correctly, that we reimagine what has been rendered invisible by the long "construction of disciplinary discourses through which knowledge of the past has been inherited." That which has been rendered invisible includes the racism at the heart of universalism. It is, as she writes, the limits of disciplines that long made pairing such as Hegel and Haiti hard to conceive, rather than inconceivable. Susan Buck-Morss, *Hegel, Haiti, and Universal History* (Pittsburgh: University of Pittsburgh Press, 2009), 50.

13. Werner Sollors, "The German American Tradition Reconsidered," in *German? American? Literature? New Directions in German-American Studies*, ed. Winfried Fluck and Werner Sollors (New York: Peter Lang, 2002), 3–5.

14. Marc Shell, ed., *American Babel: Literatures of the United States from Abnaki to Zuni* (Cambridge, Mass.: Harvard University Press, 2002).

15. Bruno Latour, *We Have Never Been Modern*, trans. Catharine Porter (Cambridge, Mass.: Harvard University Press, 1993).

16. "While purification and hybridization render society and science visible and seemingly omnipotent, these processes measured their success in constructing language and managing discursive practices by the degree to which they could render language unimportant—only worthy of attention by linguists and grammar teachers. Locke only thought to worry about language, he tells us, when it got in the way." Richard Bauman and Charles L. Briggs, "Introduction," in *Voices of Modernity: Language Ideologies and the Politics of Inequality* (New York: Cambridge University Press, 2003), 8.

17. Steven Shapin, *A Social History of Truth: Science and Civility in Seventeenth-Century England* (Chicago: University of Chicago Press, 1994).

18. A survey of approaches and paradigms adopted, often explicitly, to counteract the narrative pull of the nation is provided by Eric Hinderaker and Rebecca Horn, "Territorial Crossings: Histories and Historiographies of the Early Americas," *William and Mary Quarterly*, 3rd ser., 67, no. 3 (2010): 395–432. They include oceanic studies (Atlantic world) as well as continental and hemispheric approaches.

19. Consider, for example, Stievermann's description of the American Atlantic perspective. He describes how it "involves attention to the myriad ways in which events and developments in the territory of the (future) United States were connected to and influenced by happenings and changes across the Atlantic world, and vice versa." The specter of the nation haunts its prehistory. Jan Stievermann, "Introduction," in *A Peculiar Mixture: German-Language Cultures and Identities in Eighteenth-Century North America*, ed. Jan Stievermann and Oliver Scheiding (University Park: Penn State University Press, 2013), 7.

20. Marc Shell, "Babel in America," in *American Babel*, ed. Marc Shell (Cambridge, Mass.: Harvard University Press, 2002), 14.

21. Exemplary in this regard in American scholarship is Wai-Chee Dimock, *Through Other Continents: American Literature Across Deep Time* (Princeton, N.J.: Princeton University Press, 2006); Paul Giles, *Global Remapping of American Literature* (Princeton: Princeton University Press, 2011); and Patrick M. Erben, also a contributor to the present volume, *A Harmony of the Spirits: Translation and the Language of Community in Early Pennsylvania* (Chapel Hill: University of North Carolina Press for the Omohundro Institute of Early American History and Culture, 2012). Emily Apter, in dialogue with the work of a multilingual team led by Barbara Cassin, has published widely on the instrumental concept of language that Apter locates too at the heart of a concept of world literature that fails to account adequately for the work of translation. See, most recently, Emily Apter, *Against World Literature: On the Politics of Untranslatablity* (New York: Verso, 2014). And for an account, drawing on both Apter and Cassin, of how scholarship on German literature has often remained deaf to "Wörter aus der Fremde" (words from abroad), to use Theodor Adorno's wonderful title, see also Bethany Wiggin, Catriona MacLeod, Daniel DiMassa, and Nicholas Theis, "Un/Translatables: An Introduction," in *Un/Translatables: New Maps for Germanic Literatures*, ed. Bethany Wiggin and Catriona MacLeod (Evanston, Ill.: Northwestern University Press, 2016), 1–25.

22. Elizabeth Ellis, "Monolingualism: The Unmarked Case," *Estudios de sociolingüística: Linguas, sociedades e culturas* 7, no. 2 (2006): 173–96.

23. Bauman and Briggs, "Introduction," 14.

24. Brigitte Jostes, "Monolingualism: An Outline of an Unpopular Research Programme," *Language and History* 53, no. 1 (2010): 27–47.

25. Ehlich, quoted in Jostes, "Monolingualism," 29.

26. Giles, *Global Remapping*, 21.

27. Jürgen Leonhardt, *Latin: Study of a World Language* (Cambridge, Mass.: Harvard University Press, 2012), 7.

28. Consider, to take one representative example, how rapidly Eve Tavor Bannet and Susan Manning align transatlantic and Anglophone. In the introduction to their essay collection, they first assert that encounters with others surely matter: "On land and at sea in this multinational Atlantic world, Britons and Americans repeatedly encountered others who resisted incorporation, even as they were themselves unwillingly incorporated through captivity in the societies of others. British and American treatment of others and by others was a key part of transatlantic experiences, and increasingly, of violent differences and debates." Then, however, they declare that they will consider only texts in English. Finally, they assert, "Before about 1830, however, Anglophone lines of transatlantic circulation and exchange dominated in both Britain and America." Given that they only consider texts in English, can they be so sure? How might those lines become considerably more complex, even tangled, were their intersections with non-Anglophone lines ever accounted for? Eve Tavor Bannet and Susan Manning, "Introduction: British and American Genres," in *Translatlantic Literary Studies, 1660–1830*, ed. Eve Tavor Bannet and Susan Manning (New York: Cambridge University Press, 2012), 2–3.

29. Pennsylvania historians' persistent assumption of separate, insular communities is a topic I consider at greater length in Bethany Wiggin, "'Birds of Different Feathers': Recent Publications from the Max Kade Series," *Early American Literature* 50, no. 1

(2015): 153–66. As that essay discusses in greater detail, Bannet and Manning's circuitous English-only logic, as discussed in the previous note, is mirrored by Hermann Wellenreuther's German-only examples in *Citizens in a Strange Land*. As Wellenreuther notes, "We have intentionally limited ourselves to [German printers in America] and excluded any discussion of English printers, who made no contribution to Pennsylvania German broadsides and who have already received lavish scholarly attention." Hermann Wellenreuther, *Citizens in a Strange Land: A Study of German-American Broadsides and Their Meaning for Germans in North America, 1730–1830* (University Park: Penn State University Press, 2013), 9.

30. On colonial historians' adoption of a discursive model of German ethnicity, see Stievermann, "Introduction."

31. An excellent review of American and Atlantic historians' gradual recognition of the importance of enslaved labor to the British Empire and the early American republic is presented by Sven Beckert, *Empire of Cotton: A Global History* (New York: Knopf, 2014). Nineteenth-century white American abolitionists' entanglement in the slave economy is the subject of Bethany Wiggin, "The German Calico Quilt," in *Future Remains: A Cabinet of Curiosities for the Anthropocene*, ed. Gregg Mitman, Marco Armiero, and Robert Emmett (Chicago: University of Chicago Press, 2018), 149–58.

32. English-speaking scholarship on Muhlenberg sometimes fails to consider that he actually wrote his journals in German and quotes uncritically from the far more readily available translated edition by Theodore G. Tappert and John W. Doberstein. Birte Pfleger has compared some of the original German journal entries with the English translation and notes how consulting the fragile, unpublished original German caused her to "rethink some of my interpretations [based solely on the English translation]: for example, while Tappert and Doberstein had used the term 'huge Negro,' Muhlenberg actually wrote 'fremder [foreign] Neger'" (e-mail communication to the author, August 16, 2015).

33. William Smith, *A General Idea of the College of Mirania* (New York: J. Parker and W. Weyman, 1753).

34. Benjamin Franklin, letter to Peter Collinson, May 9, 1753, http://founders.archives .gov/documents/Franklin/01-04-02-0173 #BNFN-01-04-02-0173-fn-0015-ptr.

35. The Library Company of Philadelphia has an informative online exhibit of Franklin and other sympathizers' print efforts to fund what was to be a voluntary militia, including the lottery tickets sold to fund its training. James N. Green and Peter Stallybrass, *Benjamin Franklin: Writer and Printer*, section 1, "Plain Truth," accessed March 12, 2016, http://www.librarycompany.org/BFWriter /plain.htm.

36. Lemay explains that Franklin gave the whole quotation in full capitals: "NON VOTIS, NEQUE SUPLICIIS MULIEBRIBUS, AUXILIA DEORUM PARANTUR." Franklin provided the English translation two days later in the *Gazette*: "Divine Assistance and Protection are not to be obtained by timorous Prayers and womanish Supplications." J. A. Leo Lemay, *The Life of Benjamin Franklin*, vol. 3, *Soldier, Scientist, and Politician, 1748–1757* (Philadelphia: University of Pennsylvania Press, 2009), 5.

37. Green and Stallybrass, *Benjamin Franklin*, section 1, "Plain Truth."

38. Lemay, *Life of Benjamin Franklin*, 5.

39. Franklin lent Armbrüster the title-page woodcut of Hercules and the farmer. See Green and Stallybrass, *Benjamin Franklin*, section 1, "Plain Truth," fig. 5.3, http://www .librarycompany.org/BFWriter/images /large/5.3.jpg.

40. "Observations Concerning the Increase of Mankind, 1751," Founders Online, National Archives, http://founders.archives.gov /documents/Franklin/01-04-02-0080. Source: Leonard W. Labaree et al., eds., *The Papers of Benjamin Franklin*, 41 vols. to date (New Haven: Yale University Press, 1961–), 4:225–34.

41. The publication history of the essay is sketched by Leonard Labaree in the notes introducing the essay as printed in the Franklin Papers, and now available at Founders Online, National Archives, accessed June 8,

2015, http://founders.archives.gov/documents/Franklin/01-04-02-0080. While Franklin came to regret the anti-German remarks and sought to have the language about "Palatine boors" in the final sections of the essay omitted from subsequent print editions after 1755, he had only modest success in repressing it. And in any case, his language was adumbrated upon by William Smith. In 1764, in the run-up to the Pennsylvania election, Franklin's "Observations" were reprinted with the offending final two paragraphs. Franklin lost, and he attributed it to his failure to attract German voters, who were no doubt swayed by being reminded that he had called them "boors."

42. The University of Pennsylvania recognizes William Smith as its first provost. http://www.archives.upenn.edu/faids/upt/upt50/smith_w.html#ref3.

43. William Smith, *Indian Songs of Peace with a Proposal, in a prefatory Epistle, for Erecting Indian Schools. And a Postscript by the Editor, introducing Yariza, an Indian Maid's Letter, to the Principal Ladies of the Province and City of New-York* (New York: J. Parker and W. Wayman, 1752).

44. Quoted from the e-edition: Hector St. John de Crèvecoeur, *Letters from an American Farmer*, accessed June 6, 2015, http://xroads.virginia.edu/~hyper/CREV/letter03.html.

45. "Observations Concerning the Increase of Mankind, 1751," Founders Online; in Labaree et al., *Papers of Benjamin Franklin*, 4:234.

46. "Die Pennsylvanische Freyheit [ist] einem manchen Menschen an Seel und Leib mehr schädlich als nutzlich." Gottlieb Mittelberger, *Reise nach Pennsylvanien im Jahr 1750 und Rückreise nach Teutschland im Jahr 1754* (Frankfurt, 1756), 51.

47. "Sonst ist ein Sprichwort darinnen: Pennsylvania ist der Bauren ihr Himmel, der Handwerksleute ihr Paradis, der Beamten und Prediger ihre Hölle." Ibid.

48. Mittelberger's travel narrative provided an account of higher education in Philadelphia on the eve of William Smith's guidance. The *Gymnasium*, as Mittelberger calls it, was designed to educate students in a variety of languages so that they might better train the colony's diverse population: "Es ist in dieser Stadt auch schon ein *Gymnasium* erbauet, worinnen mancherley Sprachen tractiret werden, dann es sind in dieser Stadt und in diesem Land Leute aus allen Theilen der ganzen Welt zu sehen, sonderheitlich Europäer und könnte man derer mehr dann ein hundert Tausend zehlen. Die grösste Anzahl der Inwohner von Pennsylvanien sind die Teutschen. Es studiren auch in gedachtem *Gymnasio* viele von denen Teutschen in unterschiedlichen Sprachen." Ibid., 39.

49. Aaron Spencer Fogleman, *Jesus Is Female: Moravians and Radical Religion in Early America* (Philadelphia: University of Pennsylvania Press, 2007).

50. "In Pennsylvanien herrschen so vielerley Glaubens-Lehren und Secten, die nicht alle können nahmhaft gemacht werden, weilen mancher es niemanden bekennet, was er vor einen Glauben habe." Mittelberger, *Reise nach Pennsylvanien*, 20.

51. Carla Gardina Pestana, *Protestant Empire: Religion and the Making of the British Atlantic World* (Philadelphia: University of Pennsylvania Press, 2009), 6.

52. Mittelberger, *Reise nach Pennsylvanien*, 50–51n.

In einer Englischen Schrift, welche von dem Zustande der Emigranten handelt, die sich in Pennsylvanien, Virginien, Maryland u. niedergelassen haben, wird unter andern folgendes gemeldet: Aus den glaubwürdigsten Berichten, die man von diesen Provinzen hat, erhellet, daß die Anzahl der Emigranten sich daselbst seit den letzern Jahren ganz ungemein vermehret habe. Der gröste Theil derselben bestehet aus Pfälzern, Franken, Schweizern. In der einzigen Colonie von Pennsylvanien befinden sich über 100000. davon sind ungefehr 20000. der Reformirten, fast eben so viel der Lutherischen und ungefehr 1700. der Römischen Religion zugethan. Der Rest bestehet aus Wiedertäufern, Herrnhütern, Zionsbrüdern, Rondonfern und andern Separatisten. Da von diesen leztern [sic] fast ein jeder sein eigener Lehrer ist; so kan man von ihnen sagen, daß sie ihre Lehrsätze (wenn man anders die Geisttreibereyen dieser

Menschen so nennen kan) besser inne haben, als viele der andern Glaubens-Verwandten, denn obgleich unter denselben nicht wenig Fromme und erleuchtete Christen angetroffen werden, so steckt doch der gröste Haufe in der tieffsten Unwissenheit, woran der Mangel an gnugsamen Predigern und Schulmeistern schuld ist, zu deren Unterhaltung den Einwohnern die Mittel fehlen. Der Verfasser dieser Schrift endiget dieselbe, mit dem Wunsche, die Großbrittanische Nation den Zustand dieser ihrer Brüder sowohl im geistlichen als weltlichen bestens beherzigen und sie in den Stand setzen möge, um an ihnen in Amerika eine ewige Vormauer wider alle ihre Feinde zu haben.

53. Saur was also publisher of an even more widely read annual *Almanac*, whose print runs are estimated at ten thousand per year. The estimate of four thousand readers for the biweekly newspaper comes from the February 1, 1752, edition of the paper itself, as Erben discusses at greater length in the following chapter.

54. His name, for reasons I cannot understand, is often spelled Sauer; and, more understandably, in English, as Sower. His press's many imprints consistently spell the name Saur, and I, like Erben, use this spelling.

55. See also Bethany Wiggin, "Poor Christoph's Almanac: Popular Media and Imperial Education in Colonial Pennsylvania," in *New Perspectives on German-American Educational History: Topics, Trends, Fields of Research*, ed. Anne Overbeck and Jürgen Overhoff (Bad Heilbrunn: Klinkhardt Verlag, 2017), 1–22.

56. Greil Marcus and Werner Sollors, eds., *A New Literary History of America* (Cambridge, Mass.: Harvard University Press, 2009).

57. On the Saur press's steady stream of newspaper articles and almanac essays to try to keep the peace, see Bethany Wiggin, "'For Each and Every House to Wish for Peace': Christoph Saur's *High German Almanac* on the Eve of the French and Indian War," in *Empires of God: Religious Encounters in the Early Modern Atlantic*, ed. Linda K. Gregerson and Susan Juster (Philadelphia: University of Pennsylvania Press, 2010), 154–71, 295–302.

58. See, for example, To William Denny, Esquire lieutenant governor and commander in cheif [sic] of the province of Pennsylvania, &c. The address of the trustees and treasurer of the Friendly Association for Regaining and Preserving Peace with the Indians by Pacific Measures (Philadelphia, 1757). The Papers of the Friendly Association, held by Haverford College, document how Friendly Association activists—including Pemberton, Anthony Benezet, and others—worked across languages and added their voices to Delaware leader Teedyuskung, who sought clarification of promises made by Governor William Denny at the controversial council meeting in Easton of 1756, and then another in Philadelphia in July of 1758. James Merrell has meticulously demonstrated how contentious the minutes of these meetings were, as various parties vied for how they would be recorded, with pacifist activists working with Teedyuskung to provide their own council meeting minutes. James Merrill, "'I desire all that I have said . . . may be taken down aright': Revisiting Teedyuscung's 1756 Treaty Council Speeches," William and Mary Quarterly, 3rd ser., 73, no. 4 (2006): 777–826.

A new multilingual history of the Friendly Association is overdue. Useful in this regard will be the Moravian archival reports, now increasingly available in digital editions by Kate Carte Engel, Katherine Faull, and others. Faull provides bibliographic references in her chapter in this volume. The Moravian Indian Diaries, published via the Bethelehem Digital History Project, also have records of the refuge built on Province Island: accessed August 20, 2016, http://bdhp.moravian.edu/community_records/christianindians/indiandiaryintro.html. A revised history of the Friendly Association would also draw on the lives of the German Moravian Christian Frederick Post as well as the Scots Charles Thomson. The latter, Teedyuskung's secretary at the Treaties in Easton, is also the author of the excellent *An Enquiry into the Causes of the Alienation of the Delaware and Shawenese Indians from the British Interest* (London: J. Wilkie, 1759). See too Merritt, *At the Crossroads*, 228.

59. As Peter Silver also notes, the work of the so-called Friendly Association needs

retelling. Peter Silver, *Our Savage Neighbors: How Indian War Transformed Early America* (New York: W. W. Norton, 2008), 100.

60. William Smith, "An Earnest Address to the Colonies, Particularly Those of the Southern District; on the Opening of the Campaign, 1758: Written and Published at the Desire of Brigadier-General Forbes, when Levying Forces for the Expedition Against Fort Du Quesne, Which Was Afterward Taken by Him," appendix I, no. 2 in William Smith, *Discourses on Public Occasions in America*, 2nd ed. (London: A. Millar, D. Wilson, T. Becket, P. A. De Hondt, and G. Keith, 1762), 30–31.

61. Ibid., 27–28.

62. Bold in original.

Der Drucker zu **Germanton** ist vermuthlich von Wiedrig-Gesinneten beym Genral hefftig verklagt worden / als ein groser Uebelthäter der sich versündigt habe an dem König, am Governement und an dieser Prozintz. Wie es scheinet so hat der Genral seine Treue gegen den König / gegen das Governement, und gegen diese Provintz beweisen wollen. Er sandte dan am Tag seiner Abreise einen schriftlichen Befehl an den Drucker mit 14 **Bergschotten**, daß er um 12 Uhr bey ihm seyn soll, an der **Lancäster** Straß im Wirthshauß zum Hirsch, und antworten auf einen Satz in seiner letzten Zeitung; jedoch mit solcher Moderation daß wan er willig sey allein zu kommen, so möge das Detaschement ihres wegs gehen. Das geschah. Die **Bergschotten** gingen eine Stunde vorher, und kamen auch eine Stunde nach ihm dahin. Kaum war der Genral daselbst angelanget, so rief er den Drucker beyseit, in ein apartes Zimmer, las ihm in Gegenwart unsers Herrn Governörs den folgenden Satz vor, in Englisch übersetzt: da es heißt

> Vor etlichen Tagen sind die Bottschaffter welche zu **Tiediuskung** und den **Dellawar** Indianer gesandt worden, wieder nach Philadelphia gekommen, welche berichten, daß **Tiediuskung** mit den Seinigen noch in gutem Frieden mit den **Englischen** stehen u. u.

Hierbey stellete Er den Drucker vor: Ob dieses nicht **gegen** den König, **gegen** das Governement, und **gegen** die Provintz geschrieben sey? Der Drucker antwortete: Er glaube, Er sey unrecht beschuldiget, auch sey die Uebersetzung nicht völlig nach seinem Sinn und Worten: Ja es sey bey ihm gantz das Gegentheil dessen, was Er beschuldiget worden. Dann weil Er vor 34 Jahren aus einem schlechten Land in diß gute Land gekommen, so habe Er verschiedene Briefe nach **Teutschland** geschreiben, welche sehr viele Leute in diß Land herein gereitzet: Und die gekommen sind, haben wieder so geschrieben, und noch mehr gelocket; und weil Er geglaubet, daß Er Ursach daran ist, daß viele Menschen herein gezogen, so habe Er es seine Schuldigkeit erachtet, das Wohlseyn in dieser Provintz zu unterstützen durch ein gutes Governement und das gute Governement so viel möglich zu unterhalten. Der Genral sagte: **Ich will euch glauben**; aber man kann doch eine gute Meynung haben und kan doch übel ablauffen. Dabey warnete Er den Drucker mit allem Ernst, das er ins künfftige nichts drucken soll, das gegen den König, gegen das Governement, und gegen die Wohlfahrt dieser Provintz seyn möge. Das versprach der Drucker gar willig, ja er erboth sich auch, daß wan etwas in den Klag-Puncten ware, das nicht so ist, so wolle ers verbessern in der nechsten Zeitung; es hat aber der Genral keinen Puncten benahmet, der sich nicht so verhalten; sondern sagte dem Drucker: Er soll seinen Geschäfften nachgehen.

Nichts leichters hätte der Genral dem Drucker auferlegen könne, dan Er liebet den **König** von **Engelland**, er liebet ein gutes **Governement**, und wan es der **Provintz** wohlgeht, so geneißt ers mit. Also war die große Beschuldigung in 3 Minuten verhört, erklärt, und geschlichtet, ohne Kosten.

Es hat zwar nach der Mahlzeit ein anderer Officier dem Drucker in privat zu verstehen gegeben, wie er hoffe der Drucker werde wiederrufen, und werde nicht ungeziemendes gegen diese Expedition in die Zeitung schreiben. Weil er aber nichts benahmet, was wiederrufen werden soll, so versprach er das Letzte, und verlanget selber, das er nichts als lauter Geziemendes, Gutes, und Löbliches von der gantzen Expedition erfahren und schreiben könne.

Der Drucker verlanget keine Geschicklichkeit vornehmen Leuten zu schmeicheln; aber er kan doch mit Warheit bezeugen, was **Christian Democritus** schreibt, daß er mehr Verstand, Klugheit und Moderation bey den rothen Genralen gefunden, als bey den schwartzen Genralen. Und wan Sr. Exellentz General Forbes in der gegenwärtigen Expedition so viel Glück haben wird, als er Verstand, Ernst, Treue und Moderation besitzt, so wird die Expedition gegen Fort **du Quesne** in kurtzer Zeit zu Ende seyn, und wir werden etwas Heldenmäsiges von ihm berichten können.

Man hatte die Sache gantzlich wollen mit Stillschweigen übergehen; aber weil so viele verkehrte und lügenhafftige Reden im Land außgebreitet sind, und noch außgebreitet werden möchten, und man täglich und stündlich im den Verlauff der Sache gefraget worden, so hat man es dargelegt wie es ist.

Am verwichenen Donnerstag den 6 July ist **Tidiuskung** und 40 **Indianer** durch **Germanton** nach **Philadelphia** gereißt. Wie man höret, so sind es solche Indianer, welche zum theil mit den Englischen in Freundschafft stunden; es seyen aber auch von 2 fremden Nationen, welche biß daher entweder allein oder mit den Frantzosen friedlich waren. Sie haben 2 Pferde-Last mit Geschenken bey sich, von den besten Hirschfellen. Wie man höret so ist einer unter ihnen, der ehemahls 2 Kinder gefangen weggeführet, und wolte sie wieder mitbringen; sie hätten aber nicht mit gewolt: Auch haben sie eine niederteutsche Weibs=person mit sich gebracht, die hat sollen zu **Bethlehem** bleiben; sie aber wolte nicht von den Indianern weichen, und ist auch mit nach **Philadelphia**, und wie es scheinet, so will sie wieder mit ihnen zurück; vielleicht halt sie so ein müssiges Leben für eine Freyhiet [sic].

Ein Mann Names **Hochstättler**, der bey 8 Monat ein Gefangener unter den Indianern war u. eschappiert ist, meldet daß weil die Frantzosen sehr wenig Proviant haben, so mangle es den **Indianern** auch, und das mögt noch mehr bewegen Frieden zu machen mit den Englischen.

63. A. Gregg Roeber, "'The Origin of Whatever Is Not English Among Us': The Dutch-Speaking and the German-Speaking Peoples of Colonial British America," in *Strangers Within the Realm: Cultural Margins of the First British Empire*, ed. Bernard Bailyn and Philip D. Morgan (Chapel Hill: University of North Carolina Press for the Omohundro Institute of Early American History and Culture, 1991), 252.

64. Some of the peace churches, including the Church of the Brethren, shared a common background with the separatist older Saur. Saur hailed from Laasphe, near Berleburg, home to "Christian Democritus," whom Saur evokes in the account of his hearing with Forbes. The name was an occasional pseudonym for Johann Konrad Dippel, a Pietist and alchemist active in and around Berleburg, sometimes said to be Mary Shelley's model for Frankenstein. Berleburg is well known as a home for radical Pietist and Philadelphian thought, including the famed Berleburg Bible.

65. Robert Blair St. George, ed., *Possible Pasts: Becoming Colonial in Early America* (Ithaca: Cornell University Press, 2000).

66. Richter, "Cultural Brokers."

67. "Wahrnehmungsfragen, kulturelle Übersetzungen, Aushandlungen zwischen Typen mit unterschiedlichen kulturellen Kodierungen treten in den Mittelpunkt des Interesses." Ulrich Beck and Martin Mulsow, "Einleitung: Soziologie und Geschichtswissenschaft," in *Vergangenheit und Zukunft der Moderne*, ed. Ulrich Beck and Martin Mulsow (Berlin: Suhrkamp, 2014), 16–17.

PART 1

New World, New Religions

CHAPTER 1

"Wie ein Nimrod / Like a Nimrod"
Babel, Confusion, and Coercive Bilingualism in the Eighteenth-Century Mid-Atlantic

PATRICK M. ERBEN

On January 1, 1752, Benjamin Franklin's struggling bilingual English-German newspaper, *Die Hoch-Teutsche und Englische Zeitung / High Dutch and English Gazette*, printed a gossip column about Christoph Saur, the most influential German-language printer in British North America. The column ridiculed him for supposedly running around Ephrata "like a Nimrod" with a rifle, trying to shoot his wife, Marie Christine, who had left her family and joined the celibate Seventh-Day Baptist community.[1] While playing with the familiar association of Nimrod as a "mighty hunter" (the notion of "a stupid or contemptible person" appeared in American English later), Franklin's lampoon reverberated with several pejorative political, social, cultural, and religious connotations.[2] What meanings and values did the term hold in eighteenth-century Pennsylvania, specifically among the German settlers whom Franklin's paper tried to lead away from Saur?

Historically, interpretations of Genesis 10 described King Nimrod not only as a mighty hunter but also as the tyrannical ruler of Babel who rebelled against God in building the infamous Tower—considered in the early modern age to be the beginning of linguistic and spiritual confusion.[3] In the rabbinical literature, Nimrod was identified as the first to wage war, in a battle between his kinsmen, the Hamites, against the Japhetites. Victorious, Nimrod made himself king over all humans and ordered the construction of the Tower in defiance of God's authority.[4] The result of Nimrod's hubris and rebellion was the confusion of a hitherto unified language, wrought by God as punishment. The tradition identifying Nimrod as the instigator exculpated the rest of humanity as led astray by a cunning, powerful manipulator of words and minds.[5]

Early church fathers such as Augustine referred to Nimrod as the first tyrant but believed that the Christian Church would unite the languages and peoples dispersed by the events at Babel.[6] Martin Luther, in the sixteenth century, began to equate the Catholic Church and intolerant potentates with Nimrod the tyrant, while identifying the orthodox churches, temporal governments, and academic institutions as Babel.[7] Importantly for the development of radical Protestantism, the German mystic Jacob Boehme interpreted the Tower of Babel as a figure of fallen men—the children of Nimrod—who no longer saw God and were sinking into perpetual darkness. The "natural language" spoken until Babel, therefore, was confused by humans' desire for self-determination and corrupted by their idolatrous groveling before Nimrod and his Tower.[8] August Hermann Francke, the founder of the Halle orphanages and mentor to the influential founder of the American Lutheran Church, Heinrich Melchior Mühlenberg (or Muhlenberg), urged Pietists not merely to search for Babel in other denominations and former times, but to oust Nimrods confusing the faith within their own church.[9] The Nimrod epithet thus reverberated in the early modern age with accusations of tyrannical power, enslavement of the people, rebellion against authority, confusion of language, and the resulting breach in the divine harmony pervading human society.

In colonial Pennsylvania, Benjamin Franklin and his German printing partners, orthodox German ministers such as Mühlenberg, and imperialist schemers such as Anglican minister William Smith leveled similar charges at Saur: as a publisher, he allegedly ruled his readers' minds like a tyrant; as an advocate for German linguistic and cultural independence, he confused the civic unity of the province; as a self-educated printer, he corrupted the German language with his numerous errors; as a supporter of the colony's Quaker Party and defender of William Penn's legacy of religious freedom, he challenged political elites in the province; and, as a sectarian critic of the orthodox Lutheran and Reformed Churches and their clergy, he rebelled against divine authority and undermined the religious harmony of his community. In short, he was a true Nimrod.

The conflict between emerging discourses of empire and its friction with the proliferation of ideas, people, denominations, and languages in Pennsylvania has been well studied.[10] This essay attends to the often-neglected issue of language unity, difference, multiplicity, and confusion at the center of the debate, symbolized by the figure of the confounder, tyrant, and rebel: King Nimrod. After examining in detail the various invectives against Saur, I turn the table on his accusers—Franklin, Mühlenberg, and Smith—to probe the political and cultural motivations behind their attempts to police the German printer and their larger agenda of controlling and assimilating the German immigrant population. In evaluating each figure's use of and response to language, especially their negotiation of linguistic difference, I thus consider who (or what institution) in colonial Pennsylvania deserved the title of Nimrod. While Mühlenberg, Franklin, and Smith professed to unite Pennsylvania under a single religious and linguistic umbrella to achieve internal harmony and security from external enemies, they established—especially through the controversial "Charity School" movement—an oppressive, imperialist regime governed by Anglophone and orthodox religious ideals. For this purpose, the *High Dutch and English Gazette* (hereafter *HDEG*) and other publications promoting the Charity Schools (or "Charitable Scheme") deployed translation and bilingualism as tools of power and coercion.

In fact, the imperialist promoters of language unity and monolingualism targeted Saur as Nimrod—ostensibly confusing and enslaving his German readers—as a convenient distraction from their agendas. When imperial warfare against France, Spain, and their Native American proxies threatened Pennsylvania in the 1740s and '50s, Franklin and Smith searched for scapegoats for the supposed weakness and defenselessness of the province. They found a large group of non-English-speaking aliens, the Pennsylvania Germans, and their irascible printer Saur, who refused to succumb to English cultural and linguistic as well as orthodox religious rule. In examining the cultural and imperial politics of language use in early Pennsylvania, we need to disentangle the association of language difference with rebellion or confusion. Whereas Saur's insistence on German-language rights and cultural distinctiveness was allegedly a form of rebellion against the British Empire, Franklin and Smith's imperial schemes deployed English and German bilingualism in their newspapers and pamphlets to delegitimize equality between both languages and language groups. Their bilingualism had one main goal: to disparage German as an inferior language and German immigrants as inferior members of the British Empire, whose loyalty and citizenship could only be ensured through a comprehensive assimilation policy and the suppression of linguistic, political, cultural multivocality. Therefore, I award the title of King Nimrod to Franklin and Smith, with Mühlenberg as their accomplice.

I have previously studied the role that translation and bilingualism played in promoting intercultural exchange in early Pennsylvania, establishing greater harmony among disparate ethnicities, religions, political factions, and languages.[11] The radical Protestant groups who conceived Pennsylvania as a holy experiment carried with them the desire to overcome factionalism and religious strife by cultivating a common spiritual language.[12] The use imperial boosters like Franklin and Smith made of translation and bilingualism radically departed from this earlier model of translation.[13] Granted, Enlightenment language theory was already leaving behind the earlier, neo-Platonist concept of diverse languages being somehow—perhaps mystically—related to a single original language and to each other, replacing it with a more conventionalist, Aristotelian approach that regarded languages as arbitrary signifiers constructed by specific and changing human cultures.[14]

In addition to philosophical and epistemological changes, the proponents of fitting Pennsylvania into the structures and discourses of the British Empire tapped into another long-standing tradition—the use of translation as a tool of imperial conquest. As Stephen Greenblatt and Eric Cheyfitz have argued, the enterprise of settlement and conquest relied upon translation to dispossess indigenous people not only of their land but of their language and knowledge systems.[15] Cheyfitz sees the "European process of translation" displacing Native Americans to the "territory of the figurative," making "the relation between *property* and *identity* . . . inviolable, and thus dispossessing them of both.[16] Franklin tried a similar strategy in his pamphlet *Plain Truth*, hoping to recruit German immigrants into his "Voluntary Association" for the defense of Pennsylvania. Here, Franklin created the fiction of *pacifist* Pietist and Anabaptist immigrants transformed into members of a *"Warlike Nation . . . the brave and steady* GERMANS." Their *"newly acquired and most precious Liberty and Property,"* Franklin averred, had to be deserved and earned by joining the English majority "in Defence."[17] Notably, Franklin had *Plain Truth* translated into German as *Lautere Wahrheit* and distributed free of charge among Pennsylvania Germans. Christoph Saur's defiance of such coercion in several pamphlets opposing the "Association" accomplished what Anna Brickhouse has recently defined as the unsettling function of translation in early America.[18] Saur exposed Franklin's discourse of common sense and self-interest into an imperialist seduction reducing German residents to mindless henchmen. Translation and bilingualism in mid-eighteenth-century Pennsylvania, therefore, served as a means of imperial coercion and dispossession as well a form of "unsettlement" through misdirection.

Saur successfully rebutted Franklin's call to arms by lambasting the author of *Plain Truth* as anti-Christian and his arguments as a violation of the liberties—particularly freedom of conscience and thus the right *not* to bear arms—that William Penn had inscribed in his 1701 Charter of Privileges, translated and published by Saur in 1743.[19] Most Pennsylvania Germans, as Bethany Wiggin's introduction to this volume also discusses, boycotted the Association; and Franklin later expressed his grudge in a letter to his English correspondent Peter Collinson, claiming that "in the last war our Germans shewed a general disposition that seems to bode us no good."[20] Franklin also sponsored several German printing partners, including Anthon and Gotthard Armbrüster, to break the Saur family's monopoly on the German print market in the mid-Atlantic—with varying success.[21]

Underlying Franklin's initiatives to enter German-language printing was a broader fear that German immigrants would undermine the dominance that Anglo-Pennsylvanian political elites and the city of Philadelphia exerted over the colony. Channeled primarily through Philadelphia, German-speaking immigration to the British colonies in North America doubled from 16,000 in the 1740s to over 29,000 in the 1750s.[22] As early as 1691, the incorporation of Germantown, located only a few miles from

Philadelphia, "alarmed" the members of the Provincial Council, who feared "that German settlers had such independent and influential correspondence with Penn" that they would be able to garner their own charter and thus gain broad powers of self-government.[23] The midcentury demographic shifts further ramped up German immigrant involvement in Philadelphia and Pennsylvania politics. In 1742, provincial secretary Richard Peters "claimed that the Proprietary Party lost [the election to the Quaker Party] because" of the meddling of "some of the German leadership, including the pacifist printer Christopher Saur."[24] Yet colonial Pennsylvania did not present a simple binary between an English urban center and German hinterland; rather, Philadelphia itself became a multiethnic city, with Germans as the strongest non-English contingent.[25] As historian Marie Basile McDaniel has shown, almost one half of the German population in Philadelphia married outside of their ethnic group; "in Philadelphia, German speakers associated with people from a variety of linguistic and religious backgrounds, which was made possible by the diversity of the city."[26] Franklin and other Anglophone Philadelphians confronted the complex task of influencing the political behaviors of German-speaking residents, who had become an integral part of the political, social, and religious fabric of both town and country. Their first goal was to disenchant them with Christoph Saur.

In the winter of 1751/52, Franklin's bilingual newspaper, *Die Hoch Teutsche und Englische Zeitung / High Dutch and English Gazette*, retaliated against Saur's thwarting of Franklin's Association and Saur's perceived stranglehold on the political opinions and behaviors of Pennsylvania Germans. The January 1 issue included a letter by an anonymous German reader chastising Saur for the supposedly aggressive style of his publications, as well as an editorial written by an "Evangelical preacher" scrutinizing Saur's frequent commentary on religious issues. Both contributions underscored Saur's supposed unfitness to serve as the mouthpiece of the rapidly growing German immigrant population in Pennsylvania. Accusing Saur of partisanship, libel, and other offenses against Christian and journalistic ethics, Franklin's paper itself pursued a strategy of verbal mudslinging. The otherwise bilingual *HDEG* printed these ungraceful transactions only in German, thus presenting them as a strictly German affair (figs. 1.1 and 1.2). Franklin himself may have adopted the personae of two different "German" writers, as he had done

FIGURE 1.1 Bilingual title page of *Die Hoch Teutsche und Englische Zeitung / The High Dutch and English Gazette*, January 1, 1752. Photograph © 2019 Museum of Fine Arts, Boston.

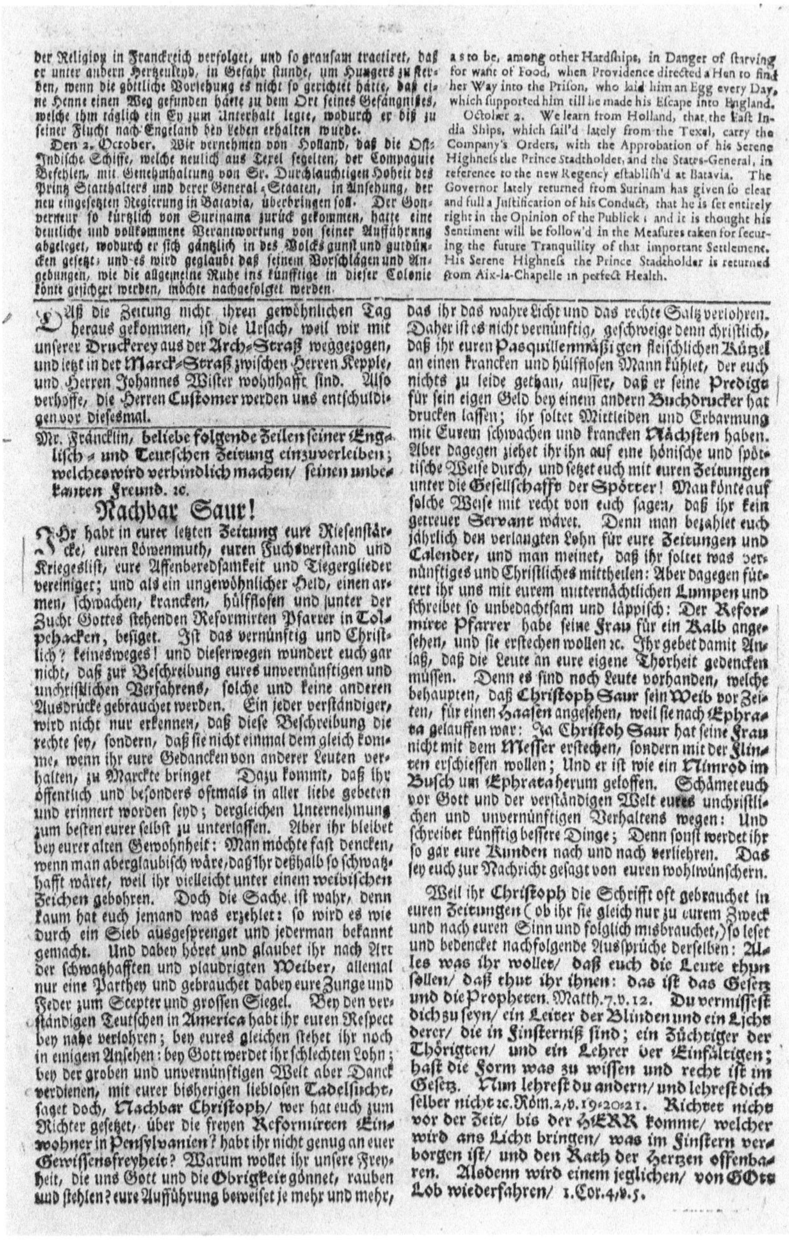

der Religion in Franckreich verfolget, und so grausam tractiret, daß er unter andern Hertzeleyd, in Gefahr stunde, um Hungers zu sterben, wenn die göttliche Vorsehung es nicht so gerichtet hätte, daß eine Henne einen Weg gefunden hätte zu dem Ort seines Gefängnißes, welche ihm täglich ein Ey zum Unterhalt legte, wodurch er biß zu seiner Flucht nach Engeland ben Leben erhalten wurde.

Den 2. October. Wir vernehmen von Holland, daß die Ost-Indische Schiffe, welche neulich aus Texel segelten, der Compagnie Befehlen, mit Genehmhaltung von Sr. Durchlauchtigen Hoheit des Printz Statthalters und derer General-Staaten, in Ansehung, der neu eingesetzten Regierung in Batavia, überbringen soll. Der Gouverneur so kürtzlich von Surinama zurück gekommen, hatte eine deutliche und vollkommene Verantwortung von seiner Aufführung abgeleget, wodurch er sich gäntzlich in des Volcks gunst und gutdüncken gesetzt; und es wird geglaubt daß seinem Vorschlägen und Angebungen, wie die allgemeine Ruhe ins künfftige in dieser Colonie könte gesichert werden, möchte nachgefolget werden.

as to be, among other Hardships, in Danger of starving for want of Food, when Providence directed a Hen to find her Way into the Prison, who laid him an Egg every Day, which supported him till he made his Escape into England.

October 2. We learn from Holland, that the East India Ships, which sail'd lately from the Texel, carry the Company's Orders, with the Approbation of his Serene Highness the Prince Stadtholder, and the States-General, in reference to the new Regency establish'd at Batavia. The Governor lately returned from Surinam has given so clear and full a Justification of his Conduct, that he is set entirely right in the Opinion of the Publick; and it is thought his Sentiment will be follow'd in the Measures taken for securing the future Tranquility of that important Settlement. His Serene Highness the Prince Stadtholder is returned from Aix-la-Chapelle in perfect Health.

Daß die Zeitung nicht ihren gewöhnlichen Tag heraus gekommen, ist die Ursach, weil wir mit unserer Druckerey aus der Arch-Straß weggezogen, und letzt in der Marck-Straß zwischen Herren Kepple, und Herren Johannes Wister wohnhafft sind. Also verhoffe, die Herren Customer werden uns entschuldigen vor diesesmal.

Mr. Francklin, beliebe folgende Zeilen seiner Englisch- und Teutschen Zeitung einzuverleiben; welches wird verbindlich machen/ seinen unbekanten Freund. &c.

Nachbar Saur!

Ihr habt in eurer letzten Zeitung eure Riesenstärcke, euren Löwenmuth, euren Fuchsverstand und Kriegeslist, eure Affenberedsamkeit und Tiegerglieder vereiniget; und als ein ungewöhnlicher Held, einen armen, schwachen, krancken, hülfflosen und unter der Zucht Gottes stehenden Reformirten Pfarrer in Tolpehacken, besiget. Ist das vernünftig und Christlich? keinesweges! und dieserwegen wundert euch gar nicht, daß zur Beschreibung eures unvernünftigen und unchristlichen Verfahrens, solche und keine anderen Ausdrücke gebrauchet werden. Ein jeder verständiger, wird nicht nur erkennen, daß diese Beschreibung die rechte sey, sondern, daß sie nicht einmal dem gleich komme, wenn ihr eure Gedancken von anderer Leuten verhalten, zu Marckte bringet. Dazu kommt, daß ihr öffentlich und besonders oftmals in aller liebe gebeten und erinnert worden seyd; dergleichen Unternehmung zum besten eurer selbst zu unterlassen. Aber ihr bleibet bey eurer alten Gewohnheit: Man möchte fast dencken, wenn man abergläubisch wäre, daß ihr deßhalb so schwatzhafft wäret, weil ihr vielleicht unter einem weibischen Zeichen gebohren. Doch die Sache ist wahr, denn kaum hat euch jemand was erzehlet: so wird es wie durch ein Sieb ausgesprenget und jederman bekannt gemacht. Und dabey höret und glaubet ihr nach Art der schwatzhafften und plaudrigten Weiber, allemal nur eine Parthey und gebrauchet dabey eure Zunge und Feder zum Scepter und grossen Siegel. Bey den verständigen Teutschen in America habt ihr euren Respect bey nahe verlohren; bey eures gleichen stehet ihr noch in einigem Ansehen: bey Gott werdet ihr schlechten Lohn; bey der groben und unvernünftigen Welt aber Danck verdienen, mit eurer bisherigen lieblosen Tadelsucht, saget doch, Nachbar Christoph/ wer hat euch zum Richter gesetzet, über die freyen Reformirten Einwohner in Pensylvanien? habt ihr nicht genug an euer Gewissensfreyheit? Warum wollet ihr unsere Freyheit, die uns Gott und die Obrigkeit gönnet, rauben und stehlen? eure Aufführung beweiset je mehr und mehr, das ihr das wahre Licht und das rechte Saltz verlohren. Daher ist es nicht vernünftig, geschweige denn christlich, daß ihr euren Pasquillenmäßigen fleischlichen Kützel an einen krancken und hülfflosen Mann kühlet, der euch nichts zu leide gethan, ausser, daß er seine Predigt für sein eigen Geld bey einem andern Buchdrucker hat drucken lassen; ihr soltet Mittleiden und Erbarmung mit Eurem schwachen und krancken Nächsten haben. Aber dagegen ziehet ihr ihn auf eine hönische und spöttische Weise durch, und setzet euch mit euren Zeitungen unter die Gesellschafft der Spötter! Man könte auf solche Weise mit recht von euch sagen, daß ihr kein getreuer Servant wäret. Denn man bezahlet euch jährlich den verlangten Lohn für eure Zeitungen und Calender, und man meinet, daß ihr soltet was vernünftiges und Christliches mittheilen: Aber dagegen füttert ihr uns mit eurem nutternächtlichen Lumpen und schreibet so unbedachtsam und läppisch: Der Reformirte Pfarrer habe seine Frau für ein Kalb angesehen, und sie erstechen wollen &c. Ihr gebet damit Anlaß, daß die Leute an eure eigene Thorheit gedencken müssen. Denn es sind noch Leute vorhanden, welche behaupten, daß Christoph Saur sein Weib vor Zeiten, für einen Haasen angesehen, weil sie nach Ephrata gelauffen war: Ja Christoh Saur hat seine Frau nicht mit dem Messer erstechen, sondern mit der Flinten erschiessen wollen; Und er ist wie ein Nimrod im Busch um Ephrata herum geloffen. Schämet euch vor Gott und der verständigen Welt eures unchristlichen und unvernünftigen Verhaltens wegen: Und schreibet künfftig bessere Dinge; Denn sonst werdet ihr so gar eure Kunden nach und nach verliehren. Das sey euch zur Nachricht gesagt von euren wohlwünschern.

Weil ihr Christoph die Schrifft oft gebrauchet in euren Zeitungen (ob ihr sie gleich nur zu eurem Zweck und nach euren Sinn und folglich misbrauchet,) so leset und bedencket nachfolgende Aussprüche derselben: Alles was ihr wollet/ daß euch die Leute thun sollen/ daß thut ihr ihnen: das ist das Gesetz und die Propheten. Matth. 7. v. 12. Du vermissest dich zu seyn/ ein Leiter der Blinden und ein Licht derer/ die in Finsterniß sind; ein Züchtiger der Thörigten/ und ein Lehrer der Einfältigen; hast die Form was zu wissen und recht ist im Gesetz. Nun lehrest du andern/ und lehrest dich selber nicht &c. Röm. 2, v. 19-20-21. Richtet nicht vor der Zeit/ bis der HERR kommt/ welcher wird ans Licht bringen/ was im Finstern verborgen ist/ und den Rath der Hertzen offenbaren. Alsdenn wird einem jeglichen/ von GOtt Lob wiederfahren/ 1. Cor. 4, v. 5.

FIGURE 1.2 Anonymous letter printed in German only. *Die Hoch Teutsche und Englische Zeitung / The High Dutch and English Gazette*, January 1, 1752. Photograph © 2019 Museum of Fine Arts, Boston.

with many English-speaking pseudonyms, allowing him to debunk his competitor through a seemingly authentic German voice.[27] In that case, the German translation of Franklin's own words dissembled as contributions *originally* written by German readers, making the process of translation disingenuous and coercive. If German-speaking writers were actually behind these anonymous articles, their contributions nevertheless reflected a spirit of contention. Either way, the *HDEG* satirized the German writers and readers as irrational quarrelers and discredited German immigrants as unreliable citizens of a putatively Anglophone, British imperial society.

The letter responds to a story Saur had published in the November 1, 1751, issue of his newspaper, the *Pensylvanische Berichte*, concerning the Reformed pastor Bartholemä[us]. The pastor had supposedly lost his mind and attempted to stab his wife after mistaking her for a calf. In turn, the letter in the *HDEG* satirizes the German printer as a predatory animal by assigning him mock attributes of great strength and courage: "Neighbor Saur! In your last newspaper, you joined the strength of a giant, the courage of a lion, the slyness and stratagem of a fox, the eloquence of a monkey, and the roar of a tiger; and, as an extraordinary hero, you vanquished a poor, weak, sick, and helpless Reformed preacher in Tolpehacken, who is suffering under God's affliction. Is this reasonable and Christian? Not in the least!"[28] Saur was cast as an uncanny multispecies creature whose many qualities were as threatening as his multivocality. This hybrid nature undermined his trustworthiness, while highlighting his allegedly tyrannical behavior. The rumor of Saur hunting for his wife thus lampooned the inconsistency between his avowed pacifism and his tendency toward violence: "There are still people around who claim that Christoph Saur had some time ago mistaken his wife for a rabbit, because she had run away to Ephrata: Yes, indeed, rather than stabbing her with a knife, he wanted to shoot her with a rifle, and he ran through the woods around Ephrata *like a Nimrod*" (emphasis added).[29] Saur had been transformed from a pacifist sectarian into a mighty hunter and tyrannical oppressor.

Virtually attacking the celibate brothers and sisters at Ephrata, Saur apparently tried to assert dominance over his wife as well as the religious community founded by Conrad Beissel. Although Saur and Beissel had known each other before emigrating from Germany and were neighbors in the Conestoga area, their animosity began in 1728, when Saur criticized Beissel for his decision to reject the baptism Beissel had received from the Dunker community in Germantown and allow one of his followers to rebaptize him.[30] Saur's wife, Marie Christine, joined Beissel's community in 1730 as Sister Marcella, where she remained until her son Christoph Jr. entreated her to return to her family. In 1739, Saur attacked one of Beissel's hymn compositions for its allegedly self-aggrandizing content, which resulted in a heated correspondence between the men.[31] The relationship between Saur and Ephrata, in other words, already stood out through its profusion of words and confusion of opinions. Styling Saur as Nimrod, the *HDEG* further evoked the German printer's association with Babel and the confusion of languages. The anonymous letter casts Saur as deliberately abusing language by "cooling [his] carnal lust by lampooning a sick and helpless man."[32] Saur's "pen and tongue"—symbols of written and spoken language as well as patriarchal power—were transformed into the "scepter and great seal" of the mighty Nimrod.[33] Saur, the letter accuses, always used this kind of extreme partisanship to victimize helpless individuals, especially the orthodox ministers of Pennsylvania's Lutheran and Reformed congregations.

The author of the lengthy editorial appended to the *HDEG* of January 1, 1752, identified himself as an "Evangelical preacher"—possibly a screen for Heinrich Melchior Mühlenberg, the "patriarch" of Lutheranism in colonial America. Indeed, Saur had repeatedly criticized the two orthodox Protestant denominations among the Pennsylvania Germans (Lutheran and Reformed) and their clergy.[34] The writer argues that Saur must be disqualified as a "judge" of church matters because his reporting violated the freedom of conscience of the orthodox clergymen and their followers. Ironically, the author calls into question his own judgment by heaping insults on Saur: "You have for many years, without calling or commission[,] . . . spread your coarse, uncharitable, unsalted [raw], and libelous slaver over the world of religion, thus imitating Satan, who confuses everything and throws out the baby with the bathwater! . . . We don't like to reprimand you, however, because you are (even though a freak of nature) one of our own German nation and blood."[35] The anonymous contributor to the *HDEG* outs the sectarian Saur as arch-heretic and seducer, both product and producer of religious error and confusion. Though the identification with "German nation and blood" seems to preserve a shred of solidarity between Saur and the writer, Saur's alleged freakishness disrupts any allegiance and tarnishes the reputation of the Pennsylvania Germans. The writer continues by calling the German printer an embarrassment to his nation, because he "is not even able to spell correctly in his mother tongue." The printer's alleged linguistic confusion thus served the *HDEG* (and its English-speaking publisher) by casting not just Saur but also his German-speaking readers as semiliterate people, in need of guidance and (re)education.

Franklin's paper, in other words, presented the bickering between Saur and his anonymous nemeses as endemic to Pennsylvania Germans. The anonymous "Evangelical preacher" admonishes Saur to "see how peaceful and without injury our English fellow citizens live and enjoy their liberty! They also have printers, but they are more judicious and wise than our pert Saur."[36] While praising the English printers and citizens as peaceable and wise, the title page of the *HDEG* visually held up the English language in a separate column, with the German on the left-hand and the English on the right-hand side. These bilingual portions of the newspaper covered the news and other presumably useful and objective information (fig. 1.1). The sections exclusively printed in German, however, vented vituperative language and thus displayed irrational behavior (fig. 1.2). English language and English manners, therefore, modeled good behavior to the German readers and their aberrant printer.

The opinion piece by the "Evangelical preacher" attacks Saur's language as confused, vitriolic, loveless, and thus thoroughly Babylonian. Though Saur was skilled at printing, the writer alleges that his spiritual powers were "still too weak, unclear, and confused," and even his sentences were "unclear and confused."[37] Playing up his own credentials and authority as a presumably university-trained minister, the "Evangelical preacher" disqualified Saur from discussing theological matters, for "he cannot understand the Holy Scriptures in their original languages according to the sense of the Holy Spirit, yea he cannot even comprehend the Protestant denominations in their languages, and thus cannot judge in how far each agrees with or deviates from the word of God."[38] This gibe at Saur's lack of formal theological and linguistic training rehearsed the warnings that orthodox preachers in Pennsylvania had issued against Saur's 1743 Bible-printing project—the first printed in North America in a European language. The Lutheran and Reformed clergy had incited their parishioners against Saur's Bible because he had affixed apocryphal sections from the radical Protestant Berleburg Bible, calling it the "usual appendix." Saur was deemed liable for infusing a sectarian bias into the Holy Scriptures and thus confusing or corrupting the Word of God.[39] Finally, the "Evangelical preacher" threatened to report Saur's "rebellious and vulgar writing style" to the "high Christian authorities."[40] Saur's linguistic performances and theological opinions were judged devious, rebellious, and confused, thus threatening religious and political authorities. The preacher's threat, however, was empty: considering the freedom of conscience granted by Pennsylvania's Charter and the still tentative reach of the Lutheran Church in the province, Saur was free to say and print whatever he wanted.

Allegedly offensive words provoked no official sanction but rather a flood of words attempting to unveil the truth and discredit the perpetrator. What had Saur said that so infuriated the anonymous letter writer and the so-called "Evangelical preacher"? In the November 1, 1751, issue of his newspaper *Pensylvanische Berichte, Oder: Sammlung Wichtiger Nachrichten aus dem Natur- und Kirchen-Reich* (Pennsylvania reports, or, collection of important news of the natural and spiritual world), Saur repeated a familiar pattern: he reported a story that offended the radical Protestant, freethinking sensibilities characteristic of German sects in Pennsylvania. In this case, he first cleared up the misunderstanding over which the preacher named "Bartholomä" had in fact lost his mind and attempted to stab his wife. Before telling the more salacious part of the story, however, Saur made sure to discredit his previous behavior as a minister; apparently, a Reformed minister with the *last name* Bartholomä had printed a sermon in which he "derided and ridiculed all other parties so abusively that only he and his own kind could claim the true faith." Saur concluded that this preacher had already been insane, for "only those who are crazy in their head, rather than faithful or wise," would judge an entire "party" based on the few bad or evil individuals present in any group.

After briefly retelling the story of Bartholomä stabbing his wife, Saur explained that the preacher's inability to preach gave rise to a controversy over who should pay his living—"his congregation or the township."[41] While pleading for his reader's sympathy, Saur scored one of his classic points against the paid ministry (which he called hireling ministers or

"Pfaffen") of the orthodox churches:[42] "And those can see themselves reflected in him who desire their listeners [congregation] to pay them a salary for the rest of their lives, for they do not know how soon God can and will make their proud heart and their false tongue useless. And among such listeners [this case] can serve as a warning that they should not promise a hireling preacher to keep him longer than he is sane and lives a Christian life."[43] Saur's words enraged professional, university-trained ministers such as Mühlenberg, who claimed that in exchange for their services parishioners owed them both deference and a salary.

For representatives of the orthodox, mainstream Protestant churches, the Nimrod epithet suggested a potent set of charges against the German printer Saur, equating his strong influence over his readers and his radical defiance of ministerial and civic authorities with both rebellion and tyranny. Yet the anonymous contributor and the "Evangelical preacher" writing for the *HDEG* hurled such damaging, even violent language at Saur that they themselves should be considered, by their own standards, Nimrods—tyrants, builders of towers, and confusers of language. Probably sensing the futility of continuing such a war of words, Saur tersely responded to the accusation in his own newspaper, the *Pensylvanische Berichte*, on February 1, 1752: "In the last Philadelphian newspaper[44] an anonymous lampoon was directed at Saur, which contained neither a single true word nor anything Christian; thus, Saur does not answer a single word. . . . To answer this and the previous [attack] there is not enough space in this newspaper, especially since 4000 people will not know what had been written in about 150 copies."[45] In this case, two numbers spoke more eloquently than many words: Saur's paper, he claimed, regularly sold 4,000 copies, whereas Franklin's *HDEG* sold a mere 150; if so few people knew of the charges against him, then defending himself would only call unnecessary attention to the matter.

Yet, by hiding behind the veil of anonymity, these "Nimrods" tease readers to speculate about their identity. Indeed, Mühlenberg had for years begged Gotthilf August Francke, his sponsor in Halle, as well as the Lutheran court preacher Friedrich Michael Ziegenhagen, to send him "a small printing press, namely, two sets of letters, so that we could print in two kinds of German characters."[46] Previously, Mühlenberg had already complained to Francke about "the German book publisher, Christoff Sauer, [who] had sought up to that time, both in private and in public, to defame both me and my office."[47] Apparently, Saur was retaliating for Mühlenberg's criticism of Saur's aforementioned Bible project, completed in 1743, which, Mühlenberg feared, might contain falsifications (a form of Babel) of scriptural language based on sectarian sensibilities, as well as numerous errors. Already knowing of Mühlenberg's ire against Saur, Francke warned against spending any time "editing printed books" and, more importantly, against accusing Saur unjustifiably of intentional falsifications of biblical language. In fact, Francke insinuated a slanderous intent (and thus another type of Babel) in Mühlenberg's words, asking whether he had in fact "discovered actual falsifications or additions to his newly printed Bibles." Otherwise, Francke cautioned, "it would not only be overhasty to accuse him of falsification on the basis of mere suspicions, but it would also have been better to take advantage of the opportunity for the people to obtain a Bible from him."[48] Perhaps blinded by a personal vendetta against Saur, Mühlenberg might be withholding God's word from the people—an action smacking of Catholicism and, thus, Babel. On May 24, 1747, Mühlenberg responded to Francke with a lengthy explanation of the controversy regarding Saur's Bible and asserted, with a bit of hurt feelings, that his "intention was never simply to set up a printing press in opposition to Mr. Sauer for the sake of quarreling and arguing."[49] Mühlenberg revealed that he had warned his congregations against Saur's Bible *before* it had even been printed, yet "after the Bible came out," Mühlenberg found that Saur "was faithful to Luther's version, except for a few phrases where he inserted another translation."[50] The mutual invectives between Saur and Mühlenberg continued, with the latter deriding the former's "wickedness," warning that Saur would further lead "the Germans [who are] scattered about in the seven provinces" through his "godless writings . . . into the thick darkness." Though Francke kept reminding Mühlenberg "not to get involved in controversies," the Lutheran minister continued to ask for a printing press and to squabble with Saur.[51]

Mühlenberg specifically evidenced his close attention to the affair concerning Pastor Bartholomä in a letter he wrote to Lutheran pastor Johann Martin Boltzius in Ebenezer, Georgia. Hard on the heels of Saur first breaking the story of the mad pastor stabbing his wife, Mühlenberg reported to his colleague Boltzius on November 23, 1751, that "Saur does not leave off maligning in coarse and subtle ways the pastoral office in his calendars and newspapers and instilling in people a revulsion toward them. The most scandalous pieces about godless pastors that he can hunt up he enthusiastically disseminates and always draws a conclusion from the particular to the universal." Mühlenberg even mentioned a specific issue discussed by the "Evangelical preacher" in the *HDEG* editorial: Saur's lampooning of the orthodox clergymen's black robes as "Satan's uniforms."[52] In the *HDEG*, the anonymous writer claimed that Saur said "the preachers in the churches wear black clothes, and therefore the preachers are Satan's servants."[53] Whether Mühlenberg was indeed responsible for the anonymous editorial lambasting Saur as a "freak of nature" is secondary: Mühlenberg's letter to Boltzius bespeaks an Old World minister troubled by a place he called "our confusing Pennsylvania." By contrast, he imagined Ebenezer as a pre-Babel unity where "shepherds and sheep are close together" and "only one church, religion, and constitution exists."[54] Locating Pennsylvania in a post-Babel world, Mühlenberg easily identified Saur as Nimrod—the instigator of linguistic confusion and religious heterodoxy.

Does Mühlenberg's own predilection for quarreling with Saur make him another candidate for the dubious honor of being called "Nimrod"? In his own estimation, Mühlenberg strove to restore a pre-Babel unity, while Saur continued to build towers of pride that challenged God and confused the minds, hearts, and words of the people. Yet Nimrod had never *intended* to confuse the languages and scatter the people; instead, he had tried to unite them in a singular, albeit maniacal pursuit—the building of the Tower. An enforced unity of purpose had ultimately defeated itself, creating the dispersion it so urgently tried to prevent. In that sense, Mühlenberg was perhaps a tragic Nimrod, trying to build a church that crumbled under the stress of multiple opinions and languages. Yet when he was thrust into a community split into several languages during his ministry to the Dutch, German, and English Lutheran Churches of New York, Mühlenberg embraced and mediated between these voices, thus creating a greater harmony than by enforcing a single authoritarian regime. Initially, Mühlenberg reported a failed Pentecost, with himself preaching—like the apostles in the Bible—in many languages, but the people *only* paying attention to the outward performance of the words rather than the inward, spiritual meaning. Although his diverse parish in New York perceived Mühlenberg's linguistic acumen as a Pentecost miracle, he himself rejected such a performance as empty signification.⁵⁵ Yet he somehow missed that his effort signified to his congregation that each language conveyed a spiritual message. On a later visit to the New York parish, Mühlenberg united the different languages in a polyglot hymn singing that emphasized a sense of community the people sorely needed.⁵⁶ Back in the Pennsylvanian congregations of New Hanover and Providence, he reported using the different languages represented in his parish instead of insisting on a single language.⁵⁷ Driven by a desire to unite the people, Mühlenberg had to abandon the authority of preaching in a single language, instead accepting the people's many voices and speaking to them on their own terms. Mühlenberg was thus less concerned with *linguistic* multiplicity than with the proliferation of *spiritual* opinions, supposedly spurred by the people's ignorance of sound Christian doctrine as well as the voices of nondenominational laymen like Saur, who publicly challenged clerical authority in both ministry and theology.

Unfortunately, Mühlenberg soon lent his voice to a design that was blatantly coercive. Michael Schlatter, Benjamin Franklin, and William Smith instigated the "Charity School" movement, an allegedly philanthropic system of nondenominational schools to educate German youths in Christian morals as well as the English language and civics. The "Charitable Scheme" and its advocates became tyrannical, ironically, by promoting an oppressive type of bilingualism. What did Mühlenberg do to support this scheme? More importantly, who were the Nimrods involved in this affair—an imperial design for suppressing German-immigrant language, culture, and political influence in the British colonies?

In the early 1750s, the German Reformed pastor Michael Schlatter began to lobby for sustained funding for education in Pennsylvania among the Reformed Church authorities in Holland. Schlatter published an influential tract—in Dutch and German—describing the situation of the churches in Pennsylvania and appealing for support to build schools, pay teachers, and provide instructional materials. David Thomson, an English pastor in Amsterdam, translated the tract as *True History of the Real Condition of the Destitute Congregations in Pennsylvania* and disseminated it in England.⁵⁸ Schlatter's "Appeal"—as it came to be known in England—apparently inspired individuals and institutions from King George II to the Pennsylvania proprietors and the Church of England to donate large sums for the relief of German Protestants in America, an effort that resulted in the establishment of the Society for the Promotion of the Knowledge of God Among the Germans. Schlatter was charged with the distribution of the funds and the establishment and oversight of schools among the German congregations. Once Thomson's translation of Schlatter's tract circulated in England, it turned the German Protestants in Pennsylvania into pitiable objects not only of English charity but of British imperial arrogance.[59] The reasons for the development of the Charity School movement from what Schlatter envisioned in his "Appeal" into a tool of imperial ideology can be found in Benjamin Franklin's assessment of the state of German immigrants and his broad influence on the language used to discuss the topic in England. Indeed, Benjamin Franklin and William Smith now appear on the scene as formidable contestants for the title of "Nimrod."

In a May 9, 1753, letter to his friend Peter Collinson in London, Franklin was almost at the point of despair over the Pennsylvania Germans. They seem, he argues, impervious to the core principle of civic society in eighteenth-century British America: the rule of reason, informed by an enlightened print culture.[60] Franklin is particularly concerned that Germans had established printing presses that usually published in the German language and were beyond the control of British authorities: "Few of their children in the Country learn English; they import many Books from Germany; and of the six printing houses in the Province, two are entirely German, two half German half English, and but two entirely English; They have one German News-paper, and one half German Advertisements intended to be general are now printed in Dutch and English; the Signs in our Streets have inscriptions in both languages, and in some places *only German*" (emphasis added).[61] According to Franklin, the Germans' ignorance, combined with their insistence on their language and the power of their presses, made it "almost impossible to remove any prejudices they once entertain." Describing the development of a bilingual society, though, Franklin can deliver no evidence that such a hybrid culture was not working. Instead, he quickly turns to scare tactics, conjuring up the terrifying possibility that German ignorance, a deterioration of the Protestant faith, and the pacifism of German sects would invite a French invasion. As possible remedies to break the influence of German language and culture, Franklin suggests "distributing"

German immigrants throughout the country, mixing "them with the English," establishing "English Schools where they are now too thick settled," and keeping shipowners from bringing impoverished individuals to the province.[62]

That Franklin's grievances made an impact in England first becomes evident in Collinson's reply. In a letter dated August 12, 1753, Collinson eagerly proposes a number of quite radical measures against the Germans "to Check the Increase of their Power," many of them directed against their ability to speak their own language. Among his proposals, the idea "To Establish More English Schools Amongst the Germans" ranks first. Other points include disqualifying German immigrants who do not speak English from public positions, prohibiting legal documents in German, "Suppress[ing] all German Printing Houses that print only German," and "prohibit[ing] all importation of German books."[63] Ultimately, Collinson argued that it might even be preferable to send German immigrants to other colonies altogether. Reading Collinson's proposal, Franklin realized that his first report might have been excessive; he even describes some of Collinson's suggestions, including the prohibition of German presses, as "too harsh."[64] Yet his mollifying words came too late, for William Smith's proposal for the establishment of the Charity School Society, drafted in December 1753, had already sought to address all of Franklin's gravest worries. In his proposal, Smith echoed almost verbatim Franklin's anxious objections against the influx of German immigrants, claiming that it was almost impossible to *"remove any prejudices they once entertain"* (emphasis added).[65] Smith turned Franklin's words and Schlatter's fundraising effort into a project on which the future of the British Empire hinged. Smith presented the true purpose of the Charity Schools: to make English citizens out of intractable foreigners and to suppress their language and identity. Smith forthwith made it his personal mission to unmask the threat posed by an allegedly confused and misguided German populace in Pennsylvania and target their supposed demagogue—the rebellious and antiauthoritarian Nimrod-printer Christoph Saur.

As an Anglican minister born in Scotland, Smith was still an outsider to the political landscape of Pennsylvania. While relying on the authority of Franklin's assessment, Smith and the Charity School movement needed something akin to a native informant—a Pennsylvania German authority figure who shared his exaggerated views of the situation, including Saur's supposed universal sway among German speakers in the province. This is where Mühlenberg comes back into the picture, unfortunately sacrificing his allegiance to fellow German immigrants to his towering hatred for Saur and his desire to shore up orthodox clerical authority. Since his calls for a printing press to counter Saur's influence had met with little approbation from his Halle sponsors, Smith's "Charitable Scheme" presented a unique opening for Mühlenberg to squelch Saur with his own print outlet and, hopefully, "reduce" his fellow Germans "to Order in Church and State."[66] In a "letter" read in his behalf "at the first meeting of the trustees of the Society for the Relief and Instruction of Poor Germans, held at William Allen's place at Mt. Airy, August 10, 1754,"[67] Mühlenberg lamented "the Riots, Disloyalty, and Irreligion which are nursed among his Countrymen by thus stirring them up against pious and regularly ordain'd Clergy, while vicious Vagabonds, coming in without Orders and Credentials are indulged, many of whom are justly suspected to be more in the French than British Interest." Behind the confusions, of course, lay his archenemy Christoph Saur, whom he styled "a professed Adversary to all regularly ordain'd Clergy." Notably, the Charity School organizers used translations from Mühlenberg's testimonials to incriminate Saur further, as "may be seen by the Extracts which are subjoin'd and literally translated from his Paper." The only "cure," accordingly, was to buy a "Press, and make a proper Interest to support a News Paper, Almanack &c."[68] I do believe that all Mühlenberg tried to gain from the Charity School movement was to counter Saur directly, to represent the orthodox position in print, and to provide more educational opportunities to an impoverished immigrant population (an education, albeit, with a strongly parochial quality). He never identified the German language or bilingualism as a problem to be stamped out by the "Charitable Scheme." Yet his overbearing concern with authority compelled him to counter any multiplicity of opinion as a type of rebellion. In the process, he was willing to subject the linguistic diversity of his parishioners to the supremacy of an Anglophone, British imperial agenda. In squelching Saur and many other Pennsylvania Germans who agreed with the printer, Mühlenberg acted like a Nimrod.

The English promoters and trustees of the "Charitable Scheme," especially William Smith and Benjamin Franklin, targeted the German language and linguistic proliferation in general as a problem undermining the integrity of the British Empire. Apparently, the linguistic multiplicity of the people made the tower of their political ambitions crumble. As Franklin complained in his letter to Collinson, the frequent bilingualism and sometimes even exclusive use of German in print, education, and public life represented a dangerous confusion of signifiers that removed a large portion of public discourse from imperial control. But why did Franklin's *HDEG*, as well as most publications and programs under the "Charitable Scheme," feature *both* English and German? Did the promoters of the "Scheme" recognize bilingualism as a conduit toward greater harmony between equal parts within Pennsylvanian society? In fact, the opposite was the case. Franklin's dismay over the development of a bilingual society in Pennsylvania—with German clearly gaining on English—proves that his use of both languages in the *HDEG* was anything but an attempt to promote linguistic mutuality. Rather, his nervous counting of the linguistic makeup of the province's printing houses explains the purpose of the side-by-side arrangement of German and English in his paper: pegging the former to the latter would balance the score and help prevent the condition Franklin feared the most—a society in which non–English speakers could become independent from the influence of the Anglophone majority.

Under the linguistic and civic regime envisioned by the "Charitable Scheme," bilingualism and translation functioned as tools of coercion and imperial reeducation. More than a tool for making German immigrants acquainted with the English language to create greater access to a common public sphere, the bilingualism promoted by the Charity School movement redefined the entire semiotic system of Pennsylvania, pursuing the dream of a common, imperial language. Short of being able to eliminate German and Germans from the landscape altogether, the promoters tried to establish a clear dependency of the German upon the English language, and, by extension, of the non-English immigrants on their more civilized, freer English superiors.

Franklin's *HDEG* had already taken an important step in disparaging the exclusive use of German in the province. The dual arrangement of German and English in the paper (fig. 1.1) was designed to accustom German-speaking readers to the dominant language of the province, especially its different visual appearance in print. Franklin's earlier venture into German-language newspaper printing—his *Philadelphische Zeitung*, edited by Louis Timothée—had failed in part because Franklin lacked the blackface or Gothic font Germans were used to reading and had thus printed the German paper in Roman (English) font.[69] In spite of its failure to appeal to German readers, the *Philadelphische Zeitung* signaled that an English font and the German language could speak in a unified voice. In the *HDEG*, such blending was once again straightened out. With the strict separation of English and German font *and* language also came a hierarchy that suggested English as superior and thus the appropriate replacement for German. Franklin made the anglicizing goal of the bilingual paper explicit in his English-only *Pennsylvania Gazette* of August 22, 1751: publishing "entertaining and useful Matters in *both Languages,* adapted to the Convenience of such as incline to learn *either.*" Certainly, English speakers could have used the paper to learn German, but Franklin's anxious letter to Collinson proved that his primary concern was to guide German-speaking immigrants to abandon an exclusive reliance on their mother tongue—especially if that language served the kind of infighting on display in the *HDEG*'s gossip columns and opinion pages.

That the peaceful enjoyment of one's liberty was a particularly *British* quality was made clear in the bilingual publication of William Smith's hallmark account of the Charitable School scheme, *Eine Kurtze Nachricht Von der Liebreichen Anstalt / A Brief History of the Charitable Scheme*, printed by Anthon Armbrüster and Benjamin Franklin in 1755 (fig. 1.3).[70] Superficially, the bilingual representation of the text was calculated to convey the spirit of mutuality and cooperation that prevailed between the German and English members of society and that characterized the "Charitable Scheme," which is also promoted in the text. Everything seemed fair and balanced: the schools erected by the organization would be established "for the pious Education of *German* Youth of all Denominations, as well as those *English* Youth that may reside among them"[71]; in those schools, "the Youth will be instructed in both the English and German Languages"[72]; and the schoolmasters had to be "acquainted with both the English and Dutch Languages, or willing to learn either of these Languages."[73] While stressing mutuality and balance, this bilingual arrangement would practically ensure that the German language was not taught *exclusively.* Anticipating objections, or at least questions,

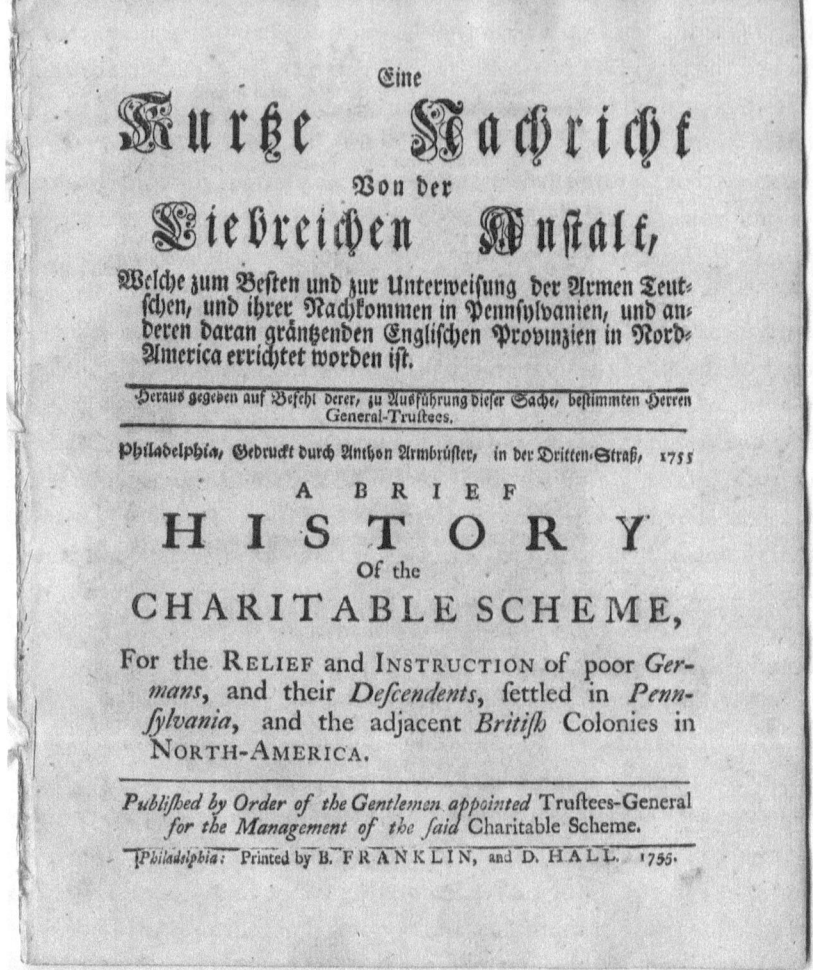

FIGURE 1.3 Bilingual title page of William Smith, *Eine Kurtze Nachricht Von der Liebreichen Anstalt /A Brief History of the Charitable Scheme* (1755).

about the utility of English instruction for German children, Smith first painted a picture of the full ascendancy of German immigrants to the privileges and opportunities of English society through language learning, which would "qualify the Germans for all the Advantages of native English Subjects" and allow them "to rise to Places of Profit and Honor in the Country. They will likewise be thereby enabled to buy or sell to the greater Advantage in our Markets; to understand their own Causes in Courts of Justice, where Pleadings are in English; to know what is doing in the Country round them; and, in a Word, to judge and act entirely for themselves, without being obliged to take Things upon the Word of others, whose Interest it may be to deceive and mislead them."[74] The air of opportunity and access, however, quickly gave way to a language of fearmongering and threats that articulated the hierarchical relationship between languages embedded in the seemingly equal and equitable bilingualism. The relationship between the German and the English language and people was one of subordination rather than coordination.

Certainly, being able to "judge and act entirely for themselves" sounded like a noble enterprise. Yet the quick segue into the language of deception and personal interestedness not only took a swipe at Saur's supposedly tyrannical sway among the German people but prepared for a barrage of threats and dire consequences arising from resistance to the "Scheme." Since "the chief Management [of the Charity Schools] is in the People themselves," any possible failure "must be entirely their own Fault."[75] Strategically, Smith cast any opposition as "repugnant to the Interests of Liberty, true Religion, and even of human Nature!" Quickly eliminating any options for disagreement, Smith painted the dire results of any abstention from educational opportunities offered by the promoters of the "Scheme":

> And shall they call you in vain?—GOD forbid!—If by any Infatuation, you should neglect the Means of Knowledge and eternal Happiness now offer'd you, think seriously what must be the Consequence. You will be accountable in the Sight of *Almighty* GOD, not only for your own sad Negligence, but for all that *Misery* and *Slavery*, which you may thereby entail upon your hapless Offspring to latest Generations. Your very Names will be held in Abhorrence by your own Children, if, for want of *Instruction*, their Privileges should either be abridged here, or they should fall a Prey to the Error and Slavery of our restless *Enemies*.[76]

The enemies included usual suspects such as "a *Popish* Enemy [who] has advanced far into our Country, even to your very Doors." Heightening the sense of dread or paranoia, Smith made the ignorance or "negligence" of German immigrants a liability to themselves and future generations.

He implied that German immigrants were becoming slaves to Nimrods or tyrants such as Christoph Saur, who were leading them astray and into their sectarian darkness.

Smith's fearmongering did not even serve the perhaps noble purpose of binding English and German members of society together against a common enemy. Rather, he made it clear that for the Germans citizenship and the protection it offered were tentative and had to be earned through proper submission as well as the learning of the English language and manners:

> It becomes you to exert yourselves for the calm Enjoyment of that Religion, for the Sake of which you crossed the stormy Ocean, and encountered the Horrors of the Desert. It becomes you to secure for your Children the *full* and *free* Possession of those fair Seats, which your own Hands have formed out of the vast Wilderness. Whatever unfavorable Notions you may apprehend the Government at Home may have fallen into concerning any Part of your Conduct, on account of the great Distance, you may now be sure, that while you do your Duty as good Subjects, we shall at all Times represent you in the most impartial Light to the honorable Society in *London*; and as this Society consists of some of the best and greatest Men in the *English* Nation, who have generously taken you and all your Concerns under their Protection, they will always be glad to recommend you in kind and acceptable Terms, to the Countenance of our most gracious Sovereign.[77]

We have to see past the repulsive bombast of Smith's rhetoric to appreciate its even more heinous subtleties. Rhetorically, Smith constructs a series of antitheses between signifiers imparting fear and dread and others referring to light, hope, and freedom. The Old World of Europe, the storms of the Atlantic, and finally even the "Horrors of the Desert" in America are all threats the immigrants have already braved or left behind, yet they linger and thus urge the fearful German settlers to turn toward the only source of salvation—"our most gracious Sovereign." Specifically, Smith insinuates that governments in the Old World may treat returning exiles as traitors, while membership in the British society of the American colonies was still provisional and very much depended on good behavior, including a *"calm* Enjoyment" of one's religion," fighting the "Popish Enemy," and performing their "Duty as good Subjects." Everything was still up in the air; everything depended on the goodwill of "the best and greatest Men in the *English* Nation, who have generously taken you and all your Concerns under their Protection." The "Charitable Scheme" and its instruction in English law, language, and morals was the path to full citizenship and even ensured one's property—"the *full* and *free* Possession of those fair Seats." Failure to follow Smith's instructions might result in the loss of a host of rights—civic and legal—ensured by the goodwill of the British Empire.

At last, Smith launched an only slightly veiled attack on the Nimrod behind the Pennsylvania Germans' alleged ignorance and deception— Christoph Saur. Though not mentioning his name directly, he clearly alluded to Saur as the deceiver and tyrant who compelled his readers to follow him blindly, turning them into his mindless slaves: "For whilst a People are incapable of knowing their own Interests, or judging for themselves, they can never be governed by *free* Principles, or by their own *Choice*; and tho' they should not be the immediate *Slaves* of the *Government* under which they live, yet they must be *Slaves* or *Dupes* to those whose Councils they are obliged to have Recourse to, and follow blindly on all Occasions, which is the most dishonourable Species of Slavery."[78] Though stated in the plural, "those whose Councils they are obliged to have Recourse to" unmistakably identified the German printer, whom Franklin and Mühlenberg had already lambasted as Nimrod. Smith's message was clear: though Saur offered German residents an ostensible freedom from the control of the government, he cunningly enslaved them under his own manipulative control instead. Saur and, by extension, the German language offered ignorance and thralldom, while Smith and the "Charity Schools" showed the path to knowledge, citizenship, and freedom. Ironically, Smith never allows for the possibility that Pennsylvania Germans listened to Saur because he understood their background and sensibilities, thus speaking *their* minds rather than telling them what to think. Alleging that their political and civic behavior was never a result of their own choices but rather a symptom of their enslavement proves that Smith (and the other minds behind the "Charitable Schools") could not conceive of the German population of Pennsylvania as anything but "*Slaves* or *Dupes*." The only thing that mattered was that they served the right master.

The relationship between the German and English portions of Smith's tract visually and linguistically cemented the proper order he envisioned. As much as the Germans' citizenship in the British Empire depended upon good behavior, it also depended on learning or even *ascending* to the English language. Here, Franklin's layout of Smith's book drew on and profited from generations of practice in print culture. American newspaper designer Edmund C. Arnold encapsulated the movement embedded in and cultivated by Western print culture in the "Gutenberg diagram." According to the diagram, the upper left-hand side of any text—in print or script—is the "primary optical area," from which the reader's attention gravitates diagonally to the lower right. The upper left, therefore, served to gain the immediate attention of the readers, gradually directing the focus to the lower right. This creation of reading gravity thus allows typesetters and printers to privilege information visually.[79] In Smith's *History*, the left-hand side's German language and Gothic font naturally captured the attention of the German readers, yet the gravitational pull of embedded reading practices would lead them toward the right-hand side, printed in English and Roman font (fig. 1.4). Though both German and English purportedly contained the same information, reading practices embedded in European traditions of print culture privileged the version set to the right, where the readers' attention was inevitably guided. Ultimately, I argue, Franklin and Smith envisioned a linguistic and cultural landscape where the attention-grabbing, German-language left could be eliminated in favor of the English right— the location of English imperial ascendency and dominance. In conjunction with techniques of book design and typesetting, translation and bilingualism thus functioned as tools of control, making linguistic and cultural assimilation the only paths to citizenship.

In decrying Saur, publicizing the alleged ignorance and enslavement of his readers, and pushing an imperialist assimilation program through the "Charity Schools," Franklin and Smith established themselves as the true Nimrods of the story. Smith's language of contingent citizenship and coerced assimilation could never provide true freedom, because it replaced thralldom to one side with fear and involuntary allegiance to the other. Smith and Franklin could not imagine a society—in Pennsylvania or the British Empire—in which one language, culture, and civic order did not rule over all others. Linguistic, social, and intellectual difference

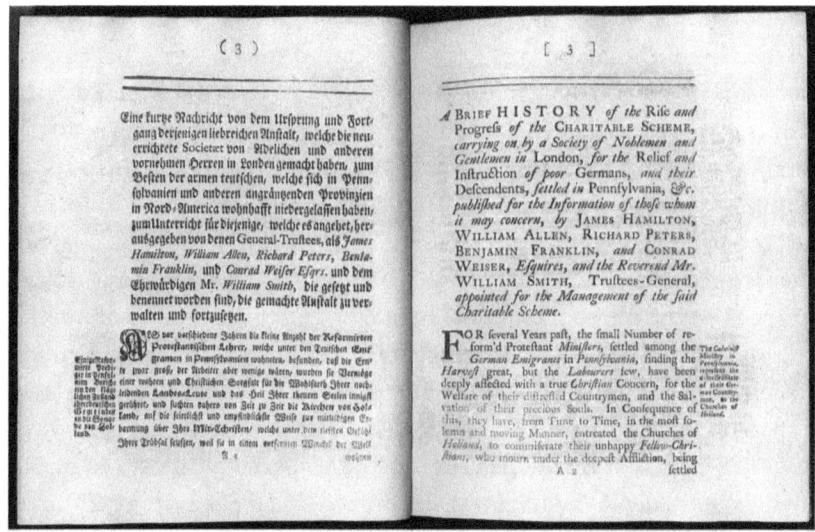

FIGURE 1.4 Bilingual double page in William Smith, *Eine Kurtze Nachricht Von der Liebreichen Anstalt /A Brief History of the Charitable Scheme* (1755).

could only be tolerated if it was submissive to the dominant order—all else was rebellion. As bilingualism offered an alternative or dissenting voice, it was considered a threat. Translation, in this case, was not a tool of social harmony but rather a form of linguistic and political imperialism. Exclusiveness in language and civic ideals was masked as rationalism and liberty, while dissent was labeled as confusion and rebellion. Rather than allowing Saur a potentially heroic position as a rebel against the establishment, Franklin, Smith, and also Mühlenberg cast him as a tyrant. They attempted to distract from their own uses and abuses of power by casting the stigma of tyranny upon the powerful mouthpiece of the German-speaking minority.

The identification of Nimrod with tyrannical power leads to an understanding of the Tower of Babel not merely as a monument of human pride and folly but also as a testament to the oppressive power some human beings exert over others. If we follow the insight that power and oppression mask themselves by blaming difference and dissent for internal or external threats, we see the story of Babel and Nimrod in a different light. What if Nimrod was not merely the tyrannical king responsible for the Tower, the enslaver of his people, and the confounder of language, but also a master propagandist in control of the message that whitewashed his abuses of power? Perhaps Nimrod spun a story that turned the people's many languages into the culprit for the fall of the Tower, a maniacal project conceived to undo an original pluralism into a single-minded and egotistical project and projection of imperial power. Monolingualism, in that interpretation, was not a prelapsarian linguistic unity but rather an enforced condition that threatened to fall apart in the face of human multiplicity. In this version, "Babel" could be a positive image—not of the confusion of languages but of the freeing of human cultures from oppressive monolingualism and other kinds of conformity. In colonial Pennsylvania, Mühlenberg, Franklin, and Smith desperately hoped to enforce spiritual and linguistic unison to shore up the power and dominance of orthodox religion and imperial political order. Yet their coercive deployment of translation and bilingualism does not automatically cast their most ardent critic, Pennsylvania German printer Christoph Saur, as the hero of anti-imperial resistance. Rather, their failure to reign in the divergent languages and opinions of colonial Pennsylvania proves that the edifices built to eliminate difference—be they towers or border walls—are inevitably doomed to crumble.

Notes

1. *Die Hoch-Teutsche und Englische Zeitung / The High Dutch and English Gazette*, January 1, 1751/52.

2. *Oxford English Dictionary*, 3rd ed., s.v. "Nimrod."

3. The following account of the traditions surrounding the Nimrod figure relies primarily on Arno Borst, *Der Turmbau von Babel: Geschichte der Meinungen über Ursprung und Vielfalt der Sprachen und Völker*, 6 vols. (Stuttgart: Anton Hiersemann, 1957–63), vol. 2, pt. 1 (1958).

4. "Nimrod," in *JewishEncyclopedia.com: The Unedited Full-Text of the 1906 Jewish Encyclopedia*, accessed March 8, 2014, www.jewishencyclopedia.com/articles/11548-nimrod.

5. Borst, *Turmbau*, 2:209–13.

6. Ibid., 399.

7. Ibid., 1063–64.

8. Ibid., 1432–43.

9. Ibid., 1567–68.

10. For scholarship on Pennsylvania's turbulent religious and political atmosphere in the eighteenth century, see Patricia U. Bonomi, "The Middle Colonies: Embryo of the New Political Order," in *Perspectives on Early American History: Essays in Honor of Richard B. Morris*, ed. Alden T. Vaughan and George Athan Billias (New York: Oxford University Press, 1973); Bonomi, "'Watchful Against the Sects': Religious Renewal in Pennsylvania's German Congregations, 1720–1750," *Pennsylvania History* 50 (1983): 273–83; Bonomi, *Under the Cope of Heaven: Religion, Society, and Politics in Colonial America* (New York: Oxford University Press, 1986); Donald F. Durnbaugh, "Pennsylvania's Crazy Quilt of German Religious Groups," *Pennsylvania History* 68, no. 1 (2002): 8–30; John B. Frantz, "The Awakening of Religion Among the German Settlers in the Middle Colonies," *William and Mary Quarterly* 33 (1976): 266–88; Sally Schwartz, "A Mixed Multitude": The Struggle for Toleration in

Colonial Pennsylvania (New York: New York University Press, 1987).

11. Patrick M. Erben, *A Harmony of the Spirits: Translation and the Language of Community in Early Pennsylvania* (Chapel Hill: University of North Carolina Press for the Omohundro Institute of Early American History and Culture, 2012).

12. In recent translation theory, the radical Protestant approach to Pennsylvania as a linguistic utopia and translation as a means for fleshing out an immanent spiritual script is most closely reflected in Walter Benjamin's "The Task of the Translator" and Lawrence Venuti's "Translation, Community, Utopia," in *The Translation Studies Reader*, ed. Lawrence Venuti (London: Routledge, 2000), 15–23. The best historical overview of this quasi-mystical view of translation and its function is Umberto Eco, *The Search for the Perfect Language*, trans. James Fentress (Oxford: Blackwell, 1995).

13. This essay is part of a larger reevaluation of Benjamin Franklin in recent historiography, which has labored to complicate his image from author of the American Revolution (an idea first promulgated in a letter by Benjamin Vaughan commonly inserted in editions of Franklin's *Autobiography*) to a British colonial subject who was, for much of his life, deeply invested in championing the imperial enterprise. See Carla Mulford, *Benjamin Franklin and the Ends of Empire* (Oxford: Oxford University Press, 2015); Gordon S. Wood, *The Americanization of Benjamin Franklin* (New York: Penguin Books, 2004).

14. Changes in translation theory from an early modern to Enlightenment model are best chronicled in Jonathan Sheehan, *The Enlightenment Bible: Translation, Scholarship, Culture* (Princeton, N.J.: Princeton University Press, 2005).

15. Eric Cheyfitz, *The Poetics of Imperialism: Translation from "The Tempest" to "Tarzan"* (New York: Oxford University Press, 1991); Stephen Greenblatt, *Learning to Curse: Essays in Early Modern Culture* (New York: Routledge, 1990), and *Marvelous Possessions: The Wonder of the New World* (Chicago: University of Chicago Press, 1992).

16. Cheyfitz, *Poetics*, 59.

17. Benjamin Franklin, *Plain Truth: Or, Serious Considerations On the Present State of the City of Philadelphia, and Province of Pennsylvania. By a Tradesman of Philadelphia* (Philadelphia: Franklin and Hall, 1747), 21; Franklin, *Die Lautere Wahrheit, Oder Ernstliche Betrachtung des gegenwärtigen Zustandes Der Stadt Philadelphia und der Provintz Pensylvanien. Von einem Handwercksmann in Philadelphia. Aus dem Englischen übersetzt durch J. Crell* (Philadelphia: Gotthard Armbrüster, [1747]).

18. Anna Brickhouse, *The Unsettlement of America: Translation, Interpretation, and the Story of Don Louis de Velasco, 1560–1945* (Oxford: Oxford University Press, 2015), 2–3, 17–20.

19. Christoph Saur's pamphlets responding to Franklin's *Plain Truth* include *Christliche Wahrheiten und Kurtze Betrachtung Über das kürtzlich herausgegebene Büchlein, Genannt: Lautere Wahrheit. Aufgesetzt zur Überlegung, Von einem Handwercksmann in Germanton* (Germantown: Saur, 1748); *Ein Gründliches Zeugnüß Gegen das kürtzlich herausgegebene Büchlein, Genandt: Plain Truth. Oder: Lautere Wahrheit. Von einem Teutschen Bauers-Mann in Pensylvanien* (Germantown: Saur, 1748); *Klare und Gewisse Wahrheit, Betreffend den eigentlichen Zustand, so wohl der Wahren Friedliebenden Christen und Gottesfürchtigen, als auch der verfallenen, Streit=oder Kriegs=Süchtigen, zusammt ihrer beyder Hoffnung und Ausgang. Schrifftmässig dargelegt von einem Teutschen Geringen Handwercks Mann* (Germantown: Saur, 1747). For Saur's translation and publication of the Charter of Privileges, see *Der neue Chaerter, oder Schrifftliche Versicherung der Freyheiten, welche William Penn, Esq. den Einwohnern von Pensylvanien und dessen Territorien gegeben. Aus dem englischen Original übersetzt* (Germantown: Saur, 1743).

20. Leonard W. Labaree et al., eds., *The Papers of Benjamin Franklin*, 41 vols. to date (New Haven, Conn.: Yale University Press, 1961–), 4:485.

21. For listings of Franklin's German-language newspaper ventures, see Karl John Richard Arndt and May E. Olson, *German-American Newspapers and Periodicals, 1732–1955: History and Bibliography* (Heidelberg:

Quelle und Meyer, 1961), 548–79. Also see Willi Paul Adams, "The Colonial German-Language Press and the American Revolution," in *The Press and the American Revolution*, ed. Bernard Bailyn and John B. Hench (Worcester, Mass.: American Antiquarian Society, 1980), 151–228; Ralph Frasca, *Benjamin Franklin's Printing Network: Disseminating Virtue in Early America* (Columbia: University of Missouri Press, 2006), 98–114.

22. See table I.i. in Aaron Spencer Fogleman, *Hopeful Journeys: German Immigration, Settlement, and Political Culture in Colonial America, 1717–1775* (Philadelphia: University of Pennsylvania Press, 1996), 2; for a discussion of ethnic identity and political culture in colonial Philadelphia and Pennsylvania, also see Fogleman, "Introduction: An Immigrant Story" and "Germans in the Streets: The Development of German Political Culture in Pennsylvania," in *Hopeful Journeys*, 1–12 and 127–48.

23. J. M. Duffin, "Introduction," in *Acta Germanopolis: Records of the Corporation of Germantown, Pennsylvania, 1691–1707*, ed. J. M. Duffin (Philadelphia: Genealogical Society of Pennsylvania, 2008), 19.

24. Fogleman, *Hopeful Journeys*, 138. For further scholarship on politics in colonial Pennsylvania and specifically the German-speaking immigrants' involvement, see Dietmar Rothermund, "The German Problem of Colonial Pennsylvania," *PMHB* 84 (1960): 3–21; Rothermund, *The Layman's Progress: Religious and Political Experience in Colonial Pennsylvania, 1740–1770* (Philadelphia: University of Pennsylvania Press, 1961); Alan Tully, "Englishmen and Germans: National-Group Contact in Colonial Pennsylvania, 1700–1755," *Pennsylvania History* 45, no. 34 (1978): 237–56; Tully, "Ethnicity, Religion, and Politics in Early America," *Pennsylvania Magazine of History and Biography* 107, no. 4 (1983): 491–536; Tully, *Forming American Politics: Ideals, Interests, and Institutions in Colonial New York and Pennsylvania* (Baltimore: Johns Hopkins University Press, 1994); Tully, "Politics and Peace Testimony in Mid-Eighteenth-Century Pennsylvania," *Canadian Review of American Studies* 13, no. 2 (1982): 159–77; Tully, *William Penn's Legacy: Politics and Social Structure in Provincial Pennsylvania, 1726–1755* (Baltimore: Johns Hopkins University Press, 1977); Hermann Wellenreuther, "Image and Counterimage, Tradition and Expectation: The German Immigrants in English Colonial Society in Pennsylvania, 1700–1765," in *America and the Germans: An Assessment of a Three-Hundred-Year History*, ed. Frank Trommler and Joseph McVeigh (Philadelphia: University of Pennsylvania Press, 1985), 85–105.

25. On Philadelphia as a multiethnic city during the mid-eighteenth century, see Edwin B. Bronner, "Village into Town, 1701–1746," in *Philadelphia: A 300-Year History*, ed. Russell F. Weigley (New York: W. W. Norton, 1982), 47; Gary B. Nash, *First City: Philadelphia and the Forging of Historical Memory* (Philadelphia: University of Pennsylvania Press, 2002), 34–44.

26. Marie Basile McDaniel, "Divergent Paths: Processes of Identity Formation Among German Speakers, 1730–1760," in *A Peculiar Mixture: German-Language Cultures and Identities in Eighteenth-Century North America*, ed. Jan Stievermann and Oliver Scheiding (University Park: Penn State University Press, 2013), 185.

27. Franklin, who regularly contributed anonymous letters to his own English paper, *The Pennsylvania Gazette*, and delighted in writing under pseudonyms both male and female (e.g., Poor Richard and Silence Dogood), was quite possibly more involved in the attacks on Saur than he was willing to admit. Franklin scholar J. A. Leo Lemay's *The Canon of Benjamin Franklin, 1722–1776: New Attributions and Reconsiderations* (Newark: University of Delaware Press, 1986) provides an excellent window into Franklin's anonymous and pseudonymous publications (mostly in periodicals such as his English paper *The Pennsylvania Gazette*). Also, Lemay offers extremely useful tools for scholars to consider other pieces that may or may not have been written by Franklin. Lemay notes in his introduction that "in the eighteenth century, authors rarely signed contributions to newspapers or magazines with their own names. Instead, they used pseudonyms or attached no signature to the piece" (15). The fact that the two pieces in the *HDEG* are anonymous, therefore, falls squarely within

the practice of the time and does not necessarily indicate Franklin's authorship. Lemay further notes, however, that Franklin "frequently writes an editorial disclaimer before his known compositions," and therefore "one must suspect any piece preceded by a disclaimer to be Franklin's" (23). Certainly Lemay has a more specific disclaimer in mind, but both introductions to the pieces in the *HDEG* explicitly point away from the editor/publisher of the paper as the author (one directly addresses "Mr. Fräncklin," and the other identifies an "Evangelical Preacher" as the author), which, I argue, counts as a disclaimer and thus indicates Franklin's authorship. If Franklin was responsible for the content of these pieces, the German translations could have been prepared by Joseph Crell, the translator of Franklin's *Plain Truth*, or Franklin's printing partners Gotthard and Anthon Armbrüster.

28. All translations are mine unless noted otherwise. "Nachbar Saur! Ihr habt in eurer letzten Zeitung eure Riesenstärcke, euren Löwenmuth, euren Fuchsverstand und Kriegeslist, eure Affenberedsamkeit und Tiegerlieder vereiniget; und als ein unbewöhnlicher Held, einen armen, schwachen, krancken, hülflosen und unter der Zucht Gottes stehenden Reformirten Pfarrer in Tolpehacken, besiget. Ist das vernünftig und Christlich? keinesweges!"

29. "Denn es sind noch Leute vorhanden, welche behaupten, daß Christoph Saur sein Weib vor Zeiten, für einen Haasen angesehen, weil sie nach Ephrata gelauffen war: Ja Christoph Saur hat seine Frau nicht mit dem Messer erstechen, sondern mit der Flinten erschiessen wollen; Und er ist wie ein Nimrod im Busch um Ephrata herum geloffen." Marie Christine Saur had indeed left her husband to join the cloister at Ephrata, founded by the German mystic Conrad Beissel, but the story about Saur's reaction cannot be corroborated. On Marie Christine Saur, see Stephen L. Longenecker, *The Christopher Sauers: Courageous Printers Who Defended Religious Freedom in Early America* (Elgin, Ill.: Brethren Press, 1981), 29–34.

30. See Donald F. Durnbaugh, *Fruit of the Vine: A History of the Brethren, 1708–1995* (Elgin, Ill.: Brethren Press, 1997), 88–89.

31. Bethany Wiggin covers the affair concerning Saur's wife as well as Saur's criticism of Beissel's hymnody in "Sister Marcella, Marie Christine Sauer (d. 1752), and the Chronicle of the Sisters at Ephrata," in *Mysticism and Reform, 1400–1750*, ed. Sarah Poor and Nigel Smith (South Bend, Ind.: Notre Dame Press, 2015), 295–320. Wiggin's essay also attends to complicated gender issues at work in the relationship between Maria Christina Saur, her husband Christoph, Conrad Beissel, and the celibate Sisters' house at Ephrata. My essay's focus on linguistic difference and problems of cultural and political authority precludes an adequate treatment of this relevant problem. Also see Samuel W. Pennypacker, "The Quarrel Between Christopher Sower, the Germantown Printer, and Conrad Beissel, Founder and Vorsteher of the Cloister at Ephrata," *Pennsylvania Magazine of History and Biography* 12, no. 1 (1888): 76–96.

32. "Daß ihr euren Pasquillenmäßigen fleischlichen Kützel an einen krancken und hülflosen Mann kühlet." A *Pasquille* is an anonymous lampoon or vitriol. Ironically, Saur's opponent, in fact, used just such a method in his own right. *Kützel* is an extreme sensual desire or voluptuousness. Thus, the anonymous writer was punning on Saur's supposedly heated writing as a form of self-gratification compensating for the absence of his wife.

33. "Und gebrauchet dabey eure Zunge und Feder zum Scepter und grossen Siegel."

34. For a treatment of Christoph Saur's religious notions, see Longenecker, *Christopher Sauers*; Longenecker, "Democracy's Pulpit: Religion and Egalitarianism Among Early Pennsylvania Germans" (Ph.D. diss., Johns Hopkins University, 1990). In addition to the orthodox denominations and their clergy, Saur also criticized radical religious dissenters, especially when he suspected their representatives—like the aforementioned Conrad Beissel or the leader of the Moravians, Count Nicholas Ludwig von Zinzendorf—of pursuing religious influence for the sake of personal gain and glorification. On Saur's criticism of Zinzendorf, see Donald F. Durnbaugh, "Christopher Sauer, Pennsylvania-German Printer: His Youth in Germany and Later

Relationships with Europe," *Pennsylvania Magazine of History and Biography* 82, no. 3 (1958): 316–40.

35. "Ihr aber habet viele Jahre her, ohne Beruf und Commißion[,] ... euren groben, lieblosen und ungesaltzenen pasquillanten Geifer über das Kirchen-Reich ausgestossen, und dem Satan nachgeahmt, der alles unter einander mischet und das Kind gerne mit dem Bade weg wirfft! ... Man rüget euch deßwegen nicht gerne, weil ihr (ob zwar eine Misgeburth:) doch von unserer teutschen Nation und Geblüte seyd." The German word *Misgeburth* (modern spelling: *Missgeburt*) connotes an abominable being but literally means a monstrous or misshapen birth.

36. "Sehet wie ruhig und ungekränckt unsere Englische Mitbürger leben und die Freyheit geniessen! Sie haben auch Buchdrucker, welche aber verständiger und weiser sind, als unser vorwitziger Sauer."

37. "Sind seine Seelen=Kräffte noch zu schwach / undeutlich und verwirret"; "undeutlichen und verwirreten Sätzen."

38. "Wenn wir nun gleich den Hr Sauer zum Richter über Kirchen Sachen beruffen wolten so fehlete ihm doch, 1.) die gründliche Erkenntniß von den Schätzen des Kirchen Reiches, denn er kan die Heil. Schrifft nicht in ihren ursprünglichen Sprachen nach dem Sinne des Heil. Geistes verstehen, ja nicht einmal die Confessionen der Protestanten in ihren Sprachen, folglich kan er nicht urtheilen, wie weit eines jeden Confession mit Gottes Wort überein stimmet, oder davon abgehet, &c."

39. *Biblia, Das ist: Die Heilige Schrift Altes und Neues Testaments, Nach der Deutschen Ubersetzung D. Martin Luthers, mit jedes Capitels kurtzen Summarien, auch beygefügten vielen und richtigen Parllelen* [sic]; *Nebst einem Anhang* [variant: *dem gewöhnlichen Anhang*] *des dritten und vierten Buchs Esrä, und des dritten Buchs der Maccabäer* (Germantown: Saur, 1743). Saur responded to the criticism by printing variant title pages that did not call the radical Pietist additions "the usual appendix" (dem gewöhnlichen Anhang) but simply "an appendix." On the controversy, see Durnbaugh, *Fruit of the Vine*, 132–35.

40. "Rebellen=und Pöbelmäßige Schreib= Art"; "unsere Christliche Hohe Obrigkeit."

41. "Ob ihn seine Gemeine ernehren soll, oder die Taunship?"

42. Shrewdly, Saur avoided naming specific preachers in his critiques, especially avoiding direct attacks on Mühlenberg. Nevertheless, Saur's delegitimizing of orthodox ministers implicated Mühlenberg all the same.

43. "Und es können sich diejenige an ihm spiegeln, die von ihren Zuhörern begehren sie sollen sie ihr Lebenlang besoldten, da sie doch nicht wissen wie bald ihnen Gott das hochmüthige Hertz und falsche Zunge untüchtig machen kan und wird. Und solchen Zuhörern kan er zur Warnung dienen, daß sie keinem Lohn=Prediger versprechen ihn länger zu behalten als er verständig ist, und Christlich lebt." *Pensylvanische Berichte, Oder: Sammlung Wichtiger Nachrichten aus dem Natur= und Kirchen=Reich*, November 1, 1751.

44. Saur's paper was published in Germantown, where he lived.

45. "Weil in der letzten Phil. Zeitung eine Pasquill an den Saur gerichtet, worinnen gar kein einziges reales Wort noch etwas Christliches war, so antwortet der Saur auch nicht auf ein Wort; was aber doch die Hauptsache seyn soll, das mögte er ein andermal beantworten: Dieses und Voriges (nicht nach ihrer weise, sondern mit Grund der Wahrheit) zu beantworten ist in der Zeitung kein Platz, zumal, dabey 4000 Menschen nicht wissen was etwa in 150 Stücken zu lesen war."

46. Mühlenberg to Gotthilf August Francke, March 6, 1745, in *The Correspondence of Heinrich Melchior Mühlenberg*, ed. and trans. John W. Kleiner and Helmut T. Lehmann, 4 vols. (Camden, Maine: Picton Press, 1986–93), 1:181. Original German: "Wenn es möglich wäre so wolte unsern lieben Vater Francken fragen, ob Sie mir könten zu einer kleinen Buchdruckerey verhelffen, nemlich 2 sets of letters [sic], daß man 2erley teutsche Schrifft könte drucken?" Heinrich Melchior Mühlenberg, *Die Korrespondenz Heinrich Melchior Mühlenbergs: Aus der Anfangszeit des deutschen Luthertums in Nordamerika*, ed. Kurt Aland et al., 5 vols. (Berlin: Walter de Gruyter, 1986–2002), 1:157.

47. Mühlenberg to Francke, March 6, 1745, in Mühlenberg, *Correspondence*, 1:173. "Unter die Prüfungen rechne 1) daß der teutsche

Buch Drucker Christoffer Sauer allhier mich und mein Amt Heimlich und öffentlich bis daher hat suchen zu prostituiren." Mühlenberg, *Korrespondenz*, 1:150.

48. Francke to Mühlenberg, June 16, 1745, in Mühlenberg, *Correspondence*, 1:195. "Bey dem, was Sie von dem teutschen Buchdrucker und Zeitungs Schreiber Sauer melden, vermuthe, daß Sie in seinen neugedruckten Bibeln wirckliche Verfälschungen oder Zusätze wahrgenommen, ob ich solches gleich nicht deutlich aus Ihren Worten ersehen können, denn außer solchem Fall wäre es nicht nur übereilt gewesen, dessen auf bloße Muthmasungen ihn zu beschuldigen, sondern es wäre auch besser gewesen, die Gelegenheit, daß die Leute bey ihm die Bibel hätten haben können, zu gebrauchen." Mühlenberg, *Korrespondenz*, 1:164.

49. Mühlenberg to Francke, May 24, 1747, in Mühlenberg, *Correspondence*, 1:336. "Die Buchdruckerey betreffend, so habe nur in generalen terminis davon geschrieben. Meine Absicht ist niemahls gewesen eine Druckerey nur um Zancken und Streitens willen in opposition zu H. Sauer anzurichten." Mühlenberg, *Korrespondenz*, 1:288.

50. Mühlenberg to Francke, May 24, 1747, in Mühlenberg, *Correspondence*, 1:337. "Nachdem die Bibel heraus gekommen, so gieng ich sie durch, fand daß er bey Lutheri Version geblieben, ausgenommen ein paar kleine Expressionen, wo er eine andere Translation zwischen geklammert." Mühlenberg, *Korrespondenz*, 1:289.

51. Francke to Mühlenberg, September 17, 1747, in Mühlenberg, *Correspondence*, 1:353. "Dabey ich denn nur erinnere, daß es nicht rathsam seyn möchte, sich in Controversien einzulassen." Mühlenberg, *Korrespondenz*, 1:303.

52. Mühlenberg to Johann Martin Boltzius, November 23, 1751, in Mühlenberg, *Correspondence*, vol. 2, 187, 187–88. "Saur höret nicht auf in seinen Calenders und Zeitungen auf grobe und subtile Weise das Predigt Amt zu verachten und den Leuten einen Eckel dargegen einzuprägen.... Nur einige Exempel anzuführen: unsere schwartze Prediger Kleider werden genant des Satans Montour." Mühlenberg, *Korrespondenz*, 1:460–61.

53. *HDEG*, January 1, 1752.

54. Mühlenberg to Johann Martin Boltzius, November 23, 1751, in Mühlenberg, *Correspondence*, vol. 2, 188. "O liebes Eben Ezer wie vielen Vorzug hast du vor Pennsylvania! Da ist einerley Religion, Kirche und Verfaßung! Da sind Hirten und Schaaffe nahe beysamen!" Mühlenberg, *Korrespondenz*, 1:461.

55. Heinrich Melchior Mühlenberg, *The Journals of Henry Melchior Muhlenberg*, trans. and ed. Theodore G. Tappert and John Doberstein, 3 vols. (Philadelphia: Evangelical Lutheran Ministerium of Pennsylvania and Adjacent States and Muhlenberg Press, 1942–58; repr., Camden, Maine: Picton Press, 1980), 1:279–80. The German originals of Mühlenberg's journals have not been published and are located at the Lutheran Archives Center in Philadelphia.

56. Ibid., 1:331.

57. Ibid., 1:357.

58. Michael Schlatter, *The Case of the German Protestant Churches Settled in the Province of Pennsylvania, and in North America* (London, 1753).

59. Whitfield J. Bell Jr., "Benjamin Franklin and the German Charity Schools," *Proceedings of the American Philosophical Society* 99 (1955), 381–87; Patrick M. Erben, "Educating Germans in Colonial Pennsylvania," in *"The Good Education of Youth": Worlds of Learning in the Age of Franklin*, ed. John H. Pollack (New Castle, Del.: Oak Knoll Press; Philadelphia: University of Pennsylvania Libraries, 2009), 122–49.

60. On Benjamin Franklin's evolving political ideology and philosophy of empire, see Carla J. Mulford, *Benjamin Franklin and the Ends of Empire* (Oxford: Oxford University Press, 2015); Lorraine Smith Pangle, *The Political Philosophy of Benjamin Franklin* (Baltimore: Johns Hopkins University Press, 2007); Gordon S. Wood, *The Americanization of Benjamin Franklin* (New York: Penguin Books, 2005), esp. chap. 1, "Becoming a British Imperialist," 61–104. Rather than assessing Franklin and Collinson's adherence to a specific eighteenth-century political party or orientation (such as Whigs vs. Tories), I argue that their ideology of empire—though evolving—always adhered to its fundamental Englishness.

61. Benjamin Franklin to Peter Collinson, Philadelphia, May 9, 1753, in Labaree et al., *Papers of Benjamin Franklin*, 4:484.

62. Ibid., 4:485.

63. Peter Collinson to "My Dear Friend" [Benjamin Franklin], August 12, 1753, in Labaree, *Papers of Benjamin Franklin*, 5:18–21.

64. Benjamin Franklin to Peter Collinson, [1753?], in Labaree, *Papers of Benjamin Franklin*, 5:158–60.

65. William Smith to Richard Peters and Benjamin Franklin, [February 1754], in Labaree, *Papers of Benjamin Franklin*, 5:214–15.

66. Henry Melchior Muhlenberg to Benjamin Franklin, August 3, 1754, in Labaree, *Papers of Benjamin Franklin*, 5:421.

67. Labaree, *Papers of Benjamin Franklin*, 5:418n6.

68. Henry Melchior Muhlenberg to Benjamin Franklin, August 3, 1754, in Labaree, *Papers of Benjamin Franklin*, 5:421–22.

69. *Philadelphische Zeitung*, no. I, May 6, 1732; no. II, June 24, 1732. On the failure of Franklin's first German-language newspaper, see Frasca, *Benjamin Franklin's Printing Network*, 104.

70. William Smith, *Eine Kurtze Nachricht Von der Liebreichen Anstalt / A Brief History of the Charitable Scheme* (Philadelphia: Anthon Armbrüster; Philadelphia: B. Franklin and D. Hall, 1755).

71. Ibid., 7.

72. Ibid., 9.

73. Ibid., 14.

74. Ibid., 14.

75. Ibid., 15.

76. Ibid., 16–17.

77. Ibid., 17–18.

78. Ibid., 15–16.

79. Edmund C. Arnold, *Designing the Total Newspaper* (New York: Harper & Row, 1981), 26.

CHAPTER 2

The Moravian Threat to the Old World Establishment

CRAIG ATWOOD

The Moravians provide an instructive example of why it is helpful to look at early American history from a transatlantic perspective.[1] The Moravians first developed their utopian vision of the New Jerusalem in a small village named Herrnhut on the fringes of the Holy Roman Empire in the 1720s and '30s, but within a few years they had established an extensive communication network throughout Protestant Europe and several British, Danish, and Dutch colonies.[2] Compared to the established Anglican, Lutheran, and Reformed Churches of Europe, the Moravians were not a large group. But they were organized, energetic, creative, and courageous, and they quickly became a focal point of controversy and even civil unrest on both sides of the Atlantic. By 1740, a type of anti-Moravian network was established to oppose them because their approach to race, gender, class, Christian doctrine, and church structures challenged many assumptions of European society.[3] As Aaron Fogleman has shown, when Moravians aggressively brought their form of radical Protestantism across the Atlantic, their opponents in Europe stepped up their campaign and agitated against Moravian work in British North America.[4] Although their opponents, and some modern historians such as Fogleman, may have overstated the actual threat that Moravians posed to the social order, there is little doubt that they offered a radically different vision of what the world could and should be.[5]

The leader of the Moravians was the quixotic Count Nikolaus Ludwig von Zinzendorf (1700–1760), a charismatic figure whose sermons and hymns highlighted the paradoxical and emotional aspects of Christianity.[6] Zinzendorf's ecumenical perspective challenged the confessional structure of Europe and the parochial system of European Protestantism, since his *Brüdergemeine* (or Moravian Brethren) welcomed people from every church and nation.[7] Moravians transgressed the confessional boundaries that usually kept theological disagreements out of the public arena. They also blurred national and ethnic boundaries. Although the Brethren's mission to the Six Nations of the Iroquois and to African slaves earned them admiration from many elites in Europe, it also generated hostility from slaveholders and those seeking to take native lands.[8] Despite some dramatic successes, such as obtaining recognition as a legitimate church from the British Parliament in 1749 and buying the Wachovia Tract in North Carolina, the Moravians were ultimately defeated in almost every arena in Europe and America. Rather than transforming Western Christian culture, the Moravians gradually adopted the mores of the "Old World" religious and social establishment.

The Moravians remained deeply connected to the world they had come from, but they believed that their mission communities, or *Gemeinen*, allowed them the opportunity to realize their vision of a Christian society in which people of different skin colors, cultures, and languages could worship the Savior in harmony. It would be a society governed by cooperation and self-sacrifice rather than competition and conquest. Moravian settlements were to be houses of peace and healing, harbingers of the millennial kingdom under the direct lordship of Christ, whom the Moravians elected as their Chief Elder. In Moravian settlements in America there were no gallows, brothels, or other signs of worldly corruption that Europeans brought with them to America. Although the Moravians were sometimes victims of violence, they did not engage in violence for religious purposes. During the French and Indian War, Moravians were willing to take up arms to defend themselves if attacked (unlike many Mennonites), but they were unwilling to serve in a militia or go on military campaigns against natives and the French. None of this endeared the Moravians in Pennsylvania to their non-Quaker neighbors.[9]

This chapter will argue that the social and religious life of Moravian religious communities represented an implicit and at times explicit challenge to the norms of the early modern period. The Moravians' ecumenism and multilingualism challenged the role of confessionalism and ethnic identity in the public order. Their work among enslaved Africans and indigenous peoples challenged European assumptions about race, and their feminized spirituality challenged gender norms. The Moravians began their radical experiment in Christianity in Germany, but they quickly carried their new ideas across the Atlantic, where they grew even more radical. This reached its peak in the Moravian commune of Bethlehem in Pennsylvania in the mid-eighteenth century.

Perhaps nothing symbolizes more clearly the Moravian effort to transcend cultural, racial, ethnic, and gender barriers than their practice of polyglot singing. Sometimes two different languages were sung at the same time in Bethlehem in the mid-eighteenth century, including tribal dialects. The Moravian Archives have preserved a manuscript with a single hymn, "Lamb, Lamb, O Lamb," translated into twenty-five languages that represented the church's global ambitions for such an occasion. The manuscript identifies the languages as German, Greek, Hebrew, Arabic, Latin, Italian, French, English, Czech, Danish, Swedish, Dutch, Hungarian, Estonian, Latvian, Spanish, "Brittish" (Welsh), Criole (Dutch Creole), Russian, Dörptisch (Tartu dialect of Estonian), Greenlandish, Wendish, Armenian, "Aoraish" (a Persian dialect), and Popoish (a West African dialect).[10] In these polyglot singing times, the tune was the same, but the words were different. Sometimes each language was sung sequentially; sometimes all at once by people who spoke that language. It must have been quite confusing, but Zinzendorf believed that "liturgical confusion is better than an enforced order."[11]

CONFESSIONALISM

To understand the conflict over Moravianism in the eighteenth century, it is helpful to review the religious situation of Europe. From the early 1400s until the mid-1700s, Europe experienced several periods of religious conflict, beginning with the Hussite revolution in Bohemia in 1419.

The Moravians in Herrnhut claimed to be the spiritual descendants of a radical Hussite church called the Unity of the Brethren (in Latin, Unitas Fratrum) that had been destroyed by war and persecution. The Peace of Westphalia ended the Thirty Years' War in 1648 and defined the confessional map of the imperial states, but it did not end religiopolitical violence in Europe. Until Joseph II's patent of toleration in 1781, Protestants in Habsburg lands faced fines, imprisonment, and most vividly, in the case of the Salzburg Lutherans, exile. Moreover, if a Catholic ruler took over a Protestant territory, the population could be forced to become Catholic, as happened when the French conquered the Palatinate in the late seventeenth century.[12] Beyond the Holy Roman Empire, sovereigns were free to manage the religious affairs of their subjects as they saw fit. Each established Protestant territorial church had a statement of belief, a *confessio*, that determined orthodoxy in that realm.[13]

The study of religious controversy in the eighteenth century is complicated because orthodoxy in Prussia or Sweden differed dramatically from orthodoxy in Holland, England, Geneva, or Massachusetts. The various religious confessions also marked national or ethnic identity and political loyalty. And conversely, religious dissent was generally seen as social and political dissent. Radical Protestant groups, most notably Anabaptists and the Unity of the Brethren, were excluded from the Peace of Westphalia and were typically described as heretics, schismatics, enthusiasts, *Schwärmer* (enthusiasts), or sectarians by religious and political authorities. These groups represented potential threats to public order because they refused to endorse the authority of the established churches and, by implication, the confessional identity of the realm. Since confessions of faith helped define national identity and ethnicity, religious dissent represented social disorder or even rebellion.

Against this background, we can appreciate why the tiny village of Herrnhut on the estate of Count Zinzendorf in Upper Lusatia could be perceived as a threat to the social order throughout Protestant Europe. Herrnhut was established by a small band of emigrants from Moravia who claimed to be members of the Unity of the Brethren.[14] The Brethren tended to be pacifist, and they avoided swearing oaths. They insisted that church membership should be voluntary and that the secular authorities should neither help nor hinder the church; but unlike the Anabaptists, they recognized the legitimacy of the Lutheran and Reformed Churches.

The Brethren had been remarkably ecumenical in outlook during this confessional age and played a key role in bringing Reformed and Lutherans together in Poland and Bohemia in the 1570s. But the Brethren in Moravia and Bohemia were politically weak, and in the 1620s they were forced to convert to Catholicism or go into exile.

In the early 1700s, the Lutheran Pietist revival spread to Silesia and Moravia. Pietism was a Protestant renewal movement in Germany that focused on increasing the piety of both the laity and the clergy by emphasizing the importance of being "awakened" or experiencing the New Birth.[15] Some of the German-speaking Czechs who were "awakened" in the revival belonged to families that had been part of the Unity of the Brethren prior to its suppression. A few of the "awakened" decided to leave Habsburg lands and found refuge on the estate of Count Zinzendorf in Saxony. There they established a village named Herrnhut just north of Berthelsdorf, which soon became a center of Pietist renewal under the leadership of Zinzendorf. Under Zinzendorf's leadership the remnant of a Czech Hussite church was transformed by the German Pietist movement into a distinctive and controversial missionary group.[16]

Like many German Pietists, Zinzendorf was strongly influenced by the English Philadelphian movement, associated with the mystic Jane Leade, who believed that the millennial age was dawning and would bring an end to religious divisions and conflicts.[17] The true Philadelphian church would emerge prior to the return of Jesus as Christians forgot their disputes and embraced each other in brotherly love. True to his Philadelphian perspective, Zinzendorf was one of the few European aristocrats in the early eighteenth century to grant partial toleration to religious dissenters on his land.[18] Zinzendorf's estates became a haven for the Moravian Brethren, Schwenkfelders, Behmists, radical Pietists, and Philadelphians. Zinzendorf tried to make Herrnhut into a Philadelphian community that he called the *Brüdergemeine*. Shortly before leaving for America in 1741, Zinzendorf expressed his ecumenism thus: "we are able to accept people from all kinds of denominations and sects into our *Gemeine* (congregation) without requiring them to change their denominational form."[19]

Zinzendorf and the residents of Herrnhut hoped to reclaim the spirit of the apostolic church. Members instituted offices and rituals of the early church that were viewed with suspicion in the established churches.[20]

These included the kiss of peace, the agape meal (or lovefeast), footwashing, and the practice of calling fellow believers "brother" and "sister." The Herrnhuters appointed both men and women to serve as elders, deacons, and evangelists. Significantly, they did not write a new confession of faith. Rather they officially adopted the Augsburg Confession, the defining document of Lutheranism; but they insisted that faith is primarily an inward disposition toward Christ rather than an outward subscription to a confessional statement.[21] In other words, they could affirm the Augsburg Confession because they did not think confessions were very important.

In 1727, Zinzendorf drafted a *Brotherly Agreement* that spelled out the rules of behavior for the community, and over the next decade the Herrnhuters created a new form of Christian community that combined Lutheran doctrine with many aspects of monastic discipline. For instance, single men and single women set up separate common households (called choirs), and no one was allowed to marry without permission of the elders.[22] In his efforts to resurrect the Unity of the Brethren as a Philadelphian religious fraternity within the religious framework established at Westphalia, Zinzendorf engaged in complex, confusing, and contradictory diplomacy.[23] In 1735, he arranged for one of the Moravian emigrants, David Nitschmann, to be consecrated as a bishop by a Prussian court chaplain named Daniel Ernst Jablonski, who was also one of the two last bishops of the Unity of the Brethren in Poland.[24] Two years later, Jablonski and Nitschmann consecrated Zinzendorf as a bishop even though he had recently been ordained as a Lutheran minister. His transconfessional stance meant that he could be an ordained pastor in the Lutheran Church and at the same time a bishop in the Unity of the Brethren. Zinzendorf insisted on the legitimacy of the episcopacy of the Unity of the Brethren when negotiating with other episcopal churches, most notably the Greek Orthodox Church, the Coptic Church, the Church of Sweden, and the Anglican Church.[25] It was a key aspect of their recognition by the British Parliament in 1749.

The question of what to call Zinzendorf's religious organization remained unsettled for years. For the most part, in German-speaking territories, it was called the *Brüdergemeine* or eventually the *Brüderkirche*. This was often translated as Brethren's Church or United Brethren in English, but the terms "Moravians" and "Moravian Brethren" were also used in English territories. The official name of the church in Latin was

Unitas Fratrum, which emphasized the putative connections to the old Unity of the Brethren. The Moravians themselves used different names for their organization in different contexts.[26] To some degree the diversity of names represented disagreement among the leaders of the church as to its true identity, but this confusion contributed to the controversy surrounding the Moravians. Were they the old Unity of the Brethren reborn, or a new (and illegal) Pietist sect? In the words of historian W. R. Ward, were the Moravians an "Ancient Church, New Sect or Interconfessional Movement?"[27] The short answer is that they were all three.

There was no precedent in law or practice for what Zinzendorf and the Moravians were creating in Herrnhut. Despite (or perhaps because of) the ecumenism of the Moravians, Herrnhut was embroiled in religious conflict from the beginning. In 1731, the Holy Roman emperor formally accused Zinzendorf of enticing his subjects away from Moravia and Bohemia by offering them religious toleration. Further emigration from Czech lands was forbidden. On two occasions, the Saxon government investigated Herrnhut to determine if the community was disrupting the Peace of Westphalia by introducing a new church outside the parish structure of the territorial (Lutheran) church. The authorities feared that Herrnhut could shred the religious patchwork quilt that defined early modern Europe. In 1736, Zinzendorf was banished from Saxony, but the Moravian emigrants were allowed to stay, so long as they did not disturb the peace. Zinzendorf embraced his exile as an opportunity to travel freely as a pilgrim evangelist. However, controversy followed Zinzendorf wherever he went during his exile.[28]

Despite the threat of banishment and exile, the Moravians expanded their activities beyond Herrnhut in the 1730s. In 1732, they sent their first missionaries to slaves on the island of St. Thomas, and three years later the first evangelists arrived in Greenland and Georgia. None of the established Protestant churches had attempted missions on the ambitious scale of the Moravians. Initially slaveholders were reluctant to let Moravians preach to slaves because they would tell them that they had souls and were loved by God.[29] For decades whites were afraid that Moravian missions would lead to widespread slave rebellions in the islands. Sometimes masters resorted to violence to impede the Moravians' work. The image of white Moravians calling Africans and Native Americans "brother" and "sister" and welcoming them into the church with the kiss of peace was profoundly unsettling to whites throughout the Atlantic world.[30]

Whereas most European Protestant churches were organized along national or ethnic lines, Zinzendorf created a multiethnic, international church. In addition to Czechs, the Unity of the Brethren included Danes, Poles, Swiss, Dutch, English, Scots, Swedes, French, and Latvians among its members. In 1745, the church adopted Zinzendorf's controversial "Tropus plan" as a way to affirm the Philadelphian ideal of a transconfessional fellowship without rejecting the historic confessions of faith and liturgies.[31] Members of the Brüdergemeine were divided into Moravian, Lutheran, and Reformed groups called *tropoi paedia*. Theoretically at least, this meant that most people in the Unitas Fratrum had dual church membership. The Brüdergemeine allowed people in different national churches or radical sects to join in common worship without rejecting their allegiance to another religious body. Interestingly, the "Moravian" tropus included Anabaptists and other pacifists.

While some twentieth-century historians praised Zinzendorf's tropus plan as a milestone of ecumenism,[32] it was profoundly disturbing in a time ordered by confessionalism. Zinzendorf's understanding of the tropoi paedia can be compared to the Moravian understanding of language as a medium for communicating religion.[33] Rather than defining the church in terms of a single language or nationality, the Moravians encouraged people to use their native tongues to sing distinctly Moravian hymns. German served as the common language for people who spoke a wide variety of European and non-European languages and dialects. The Brüdergemeine was a polyglot community.

The Moravian mission posed a serious threat to the religious status quo in the Atlantic world because it crossed national and colonial boundaries. Prior to 1749, when the British Parliament declared the Unitas Fratrum "an ancient and episcopal church," the church's status was uncertain. Was it a dissenter English church, a German church, or a mission society?[34] Did its missionaries have a right to preach, baptize, serve communion, perform weddings, and otherwise function as clergy without oversight from the locally established church? Compounding the problem of Moravian legitimacy was the fact that Moravians preached in regions that were under the jurisdiction of different established churches:

the Church of Denmark, the Dutch Reformed Church, the Church of England, the Russian Orthodox Church, the Coptic Orthodox Church, the Swiss Reformed Church, and the German Reformed Church. From time to time, Moravians ran afoul of ecclesiastical authorities. The missionary Georg Schmidt, for example, was banned from South Africa by Dutch authorities in 1743 after he established a church among the Khoi people.

The Philadelphian ecumenism that allowed the Moravians to work among different churches and within so many cultures heightened the impression that they were chameleons who could change their doctrine to suit their surroundings. In 1742, Henry Melchior Muhlenberg in Philadelphia asked Zinzendorf, "How is it that sometimes you can be a Moravian bishop and sometimes an inspector and a Lutheran pastor?"[35] The more successful the Moravians were in their missions, the greater the threat they posed to the confessional order. If the Greek Orthodox patriarch and the Coptic Orthodox patriarch could both affirm the Moravians as sound in doctrine and practice, how could Moravians assert that they were adherents of the Augsburg Confession? What was the point of allowing Moravians to convert slaves in Jamaica or Antigua if those converts did not then become active participants in the confessional order of the Church of England? In 1738, the Classis of Amsterdam sent a letter to all Reformed churches warning them about the Moravian Church. This had a negative impact on Moravian work in Africa and Pennsylvania and contributed to the riot in Philadelphia in 1742.[36]

The more successful the Moravians were, the more heated the opposition to them grew, especially among their chief rivals in the Pietist movement. Halle, in the new Prussian kingdom, was the center of a vast network of Pietist preachers and laymen who were promoting religious and moral revival.[37] The Halle Foundations included schools, a publishing house, and numerous other charitable organizations that promoted August Hermann Francke's vision of moral and religious reform. Zinzendorf studied at Halle under Francke, but he did not get along with Francke's son and successor, Gotthilf. The younger Francke saw Zinzendorf as a serious threat to his own initiative to revive religious life in Germany. The Halle-Herrnhut rivalry, sketched by Hans Schneider, was a transatlantic phenomenon, and many aspects of the Moravian controversy in America make sense from this perspective.[38]

MORAVIANS IN BRITISH NORTH AMERICA

From late 1741 to early 1743, Zinzendorf inspected Moravian work in British North America. He knew that the Moravians' situation in the Holy Roman Empire was insecure, and he looked to America as a possible place of refuge for the Czech members of the church. More importantly, America offered a unique opportunity to realize his millennial dream of uniting the different Protestant churches and sects in a Philadelphian fellowship he called the Church of God in the Holy Spirit.[39] And the Moravians would be able to evangelize slaves and native peoples in America. Unlike other radical German groups who came to Pennsylvania as refugees from European persecution, the Moravians came as missionaries with an extensive organization.[40] The church carefully selected hundreds of people with a variety of skills and resources to build the New Jerusalem in the American wilderness. About 20 percent of the Moravians who came to British North America were ordained ministers, many of whom had a university education. In fact, Moravian clergy in America generally had better credentials than clergy in other churches. The Moravians also sent bishops to the colonies so they would be able to ordain their own ministers in America as need arose. Of all the utopian visions that people have brought to the New World from Europe, Zinzendorf's was among the most ambitious and best organized. However, his plans for Pennsylvania also escalated the conflict with Halle.

The Moravians first came to America as part of General Oglethorpe's philanthropic venture in Georgia. The trustees granted the Moravians certain privileges, most notably an exemption from serving in the militia and swearing oaths. The Moravians planned to evangelize slaves and natives in Georgia, but had little success in either endeavor. A Halle-trained Lutheran pastor named Johann Martin Boltzius opposed their work among German-speakers, and many of the English colonists resented their exemption from military service. There was also internal dissent among the Moravians, and within five years it was clear the mission was doomed.[41]

Meanwhile, in Pennsylvania, three Lutheran congregations (sometimes called the United Congregations) in the Philadelphia area had requested that Francke in Halle send them a pastor. Francke did not act on the request until he received news that Zinzendorf himself was traveling to Pennsylvania. Francke chose to send a Halle graduate named Henry Melchior Muhlenberg to Pennsylvania as a pastor specifically to oppose Zinzendorf. Muhlenberg had been a chaplain on the estate of Zinzendorf's aunt, Henrietta Sophia von Gersdorf, who had become one of Zinzendorf's foes. When Muhlenberg finally met the count in December 1742, he informed him, "you are just what your aunt told me you were."[42] Unsurprisingly, before Muhlenberg assumed his duties in Pennsylvania, he traveled first to Georgia to confer with Boltzius about how to deal with the Moravians.[43] Francke used Muhlenberg as an agent to keep him informed of Moravian activity in the New World, and he published news about the Moravians within his network. The Halle-Herrnhut rivalry was a struggle between two competing understandings of Christianity and the role of the church in civil society. Muhlenberg hoped to create a sense of Lutheran identity among German immigrants in Pennsylvania, while Zinzendorf envisioned a new ecumenical Church of God in the Holy Spirit.[44]

In 1741, the Moravians began a settlement named Bethlehem on the Lehigh River north of Philadelphia. This was to be the anchor of the extensive American Plan Zinzendorf developed with August Gottlieb Spangenberg, the chief elder of the Moravians in North America.[45] There were four major components to the American Plan. First was an extensive mission to native peoples, especially the tribes in the Iroquois Confederation. Zinzendorf himself spent several weeks living in Shamokin, one of the major Iroquois settlements on the Susquehanna River, and the subject of an essay in this volume by Katherine Faull. The image of a white European aristocrat living among the Indians threatened natives and colonists alike because it challenged racial and class norms. The Moravians, on the other hand, mythologized this encounter through paintings and hymns, and the story was used to promote Moravian missions in Europe.

Of more lasting significance than Zinzendorf's visit was the fact that Moravian linguists learned several native dialects, produced grammars and dictionaries, and translated some of Moravian hymns, litanies, and Scripture passages into Delaware.[46] The Moravians were remarkably successful at blending European Christianity with native language and culture.[47] Since Moravians believed that Jesus was the redeemer of all nations, they did not insist that converts had to learn European languages and culture to be Christian. The Moravians were not free of the Europeans' assumption of cultural superiority over dark-skinned peoples, but they lacked the racial hatred that was characteristic of many colonists, especially after the French and Indian War.[48]

The Moravian work among the indigenous peoples did not win them many friends among the colonists. Much of the violence against the Moravians in the Middle Colonies can be traced to colonists' fear of the indigenous peoples. Violence between natives and colonists escalated during the Seven Years' War as the French and English fought for control of North America. Both sides enlisted natives as allies and armed them for battle. Even though the Moravians were pacifists who did not participate in the war, they were suspected of supplying firearms to the natives. When sixteen Moravian missionaries (including children) were massacred at the mission station of Gnaddenhütten in 1755, it generated some sympathy for the Moravians among white people, including Muhlenberg.[49] That sympathy was short-lived, however, and settlers grew suspicious when the Moravians tried to protect their Indian converts by establishing the village of Nain near Bethlehem. The fact that Moravians were willing to protect Indians and bring them closer to a white settlement confused and angered many of their neighbors.

After the Paxton Boys, a mob of white men, murdered several Conestoga Indians near Lancaster in 1763, the colonial government insisted that the Moravian Indians be brought to Philadelphia for their own safety.[50] Muhlenberg criticized the authorities for calling up the militia against the Paxton Boys, writing, "it seemed strange that such preparations should be made against one's own fellow citizens and Christians, whereas no one ever took so much trouble to protect from the Indians His Majesty's subjects and citizens on the frontier."[51] Muhlenberg ignored the fact that the Moravian Indians were indeed Christians. Despite their misgivings, Muhlenberg and the other Lutheran pastors agreed that Lutherans should obey the commands of the government. They instructed their parishioners "not to join the approaching rebels, but rather to stand on the side of the government."[52]

The second major feature of Zinzendorf's "American Plan" was evangelization of European colonists. Though the lack of churches and clergy in colonial America has often been exaggerated, established churches did have difficulty providing pastors in British North America.[53] Often colonists built their own churches and provided a semblance of religious life without ordained clergy. In the 1740s, the Moravians dramatically changed the religious landscape of the Middle Colonies by sending dozens of evangelists, teachers, and pastors to the New World. Already by 1742 two-thirds of the sixty pastors serving in German Reformed and Lutheran congregations were associated with the Moravians. Moravian evangelists were among the most active itinerants in the Great Awakening. Thought they preached primarily to German-speaking audiences, some preached in English and Swedish as well. By 1760, the Moravians had opened about two dozen schools that provided free education for poor students.[54]

This aggressive Moravian evangelistic effort during the Great Awakening became a source of great concern to Francke in Halle, especially since Moravians were preaching in Reformed and Lutheran congregations. In their correspondence, Francke and Muhlenberg agreed that the ecumenism of the Moravians threatened the very existence of the Lutheran and Reformed Churches in the New World. Muhlenberg reported to his superiors in Halle:

> Count von Zinzendorf had already been in the country with his people for one year when I came. He wanted to reform everything and bring the Lutherans, Reformed and all the rest into his Moravian polity. Among Lutherans he pretended he was an authentic Lutheran pastor, among the Reformed he said he was an authentic Reformed [pastor], and so on. As a result of his activities and crude proceedings, such confusion and chaos were created that one can see neither beginning nor end. Things are quite confused here now. They are scolding, blaming, slandering and fighting among and against one another so much that it is pitiful.[55]

Much of Muhlenberg's activity in the 1740s focused on stopping Moravian work among German Lutherans in Philadelphia, Lancaster, Tulpehocken, and elsewhere.[56] Several congregations were divided as Muhlenberg erected boundaries between his followers and the "Zinzendorfers." In at least three places (Philadelphia, Raccoon, and Lancaster), anti-Zinzendorf parishioners instigated riots against Moravian preachers. In every case Muhlenberg sided with the rioters.

Zinzendorf's third major goal was the creation of a Philadelphian organization in Pennsylvania that he called the Church of God in the Holy Spirit. It was to be a gathering of German-speaking Christians united in their love for Jesus rather than confessional statements and ecclesiastical structures. Henry Antes, a member of the German Reformed Church, arranged the first meeting of this ecumenical fellowship in Germantown. In addition to representatives of the Lutheran and Reformed Churches, celibates from the Ephrata Cloister, and even some Separatists came together to discuss the meaning of true Christianity. The flexibility of the Moravians was shown by the fact that they kept Saturday as a Sabbath rest (Sunday was a day of worship) so as not to offend Seventh Day Baptists. Only six meetings were held as one by one the different groups withdrew from the discussions, beginning with the Separatists and radical Pietists. Some of the participants felt that Zinzendorf was too overbearing; others suspected that he was merely trying to bring everyone into his Brüdergemeine. But the fear that Moravians were undermining the confessional identity believed necessary for social order was compounded by the Moravians' willingness to discuss theology with mystics and enthusiasts.

What most threatened pastors in Lutheran and Reformed Churches, especially Muhlenberg, was the Moravian transgression of the confessional structure transplanted from Europe. The perceived threat posed by the Moravians encouraged Lutherans and Reformed to rely on European confessions and liturgy to build a sense of ecclesiastical identity in American congregations. Muhlenberg looked to Halle to supply resources for his Lutheran congregations in Pennsylvania, and in turn, Halle requested that Muhlenberg keep them informed of what the Moravians were doing. On the one hand, Muhlenberg and his allies used the press and law courts to persuade people that the Moravians were dangerous radicals rather than genuine Lutherans. On the other hand, the Moravians were attacked for being too tied to the Lutheran Church by the separatist spokesman Christopher Saur and Conrad Beissel, leader of the Ephrata Cloister.[57] The opposition to the Moravians by the Lutherans, Reformed, and Separatists grew so intense that they gave up their ecumenical plans and scaled back their evangelical work among the white settlers after 1748. As Moravians withdrew from involvement with other German-speaking churches, the controversy subsided.

THE BETHLEHEM COMMUNE

The fourth major enterprise of the Moravians in the 1740s was the construction of the town of Bethlehem, which was to be the headquarters of the whole Moravian mission in North America. Bethlehem was part of a larger economic complex that included Christian Spring and Nazareth, which the Moravians bought from the British evangelist George Whitefield.[58] Bethlehem was on the western fringe of the global Moravian Church, but in many ways it represented the fullest expression of the Zinzendorfian ideal of a Christian community.[59] For about twenty years Bethlehem was a commune where residents worked without monetary payment and were guaranteed housing, food, and medical care. The central governing board, which included women, organized all aspects of life, even marriages. There was little distinction between secular and religious activities in Bethlehem since all work was considered sacred. Bethlehem had some of the most impressive buildings and prosperous industries in colonial Pennsylvania.

Bethlehem is a fascinating community to study from a transatlantic perspective. The Moravians brought a high level of European culture to Pennsylvania, particularly musical culture. They were renowned as instrument makers.[60] The English artist Valentin Haidt lived and painted in Bethlehem in the middle of the eighteenth century.[61] Well into the nineteenth century Bethlehem was under the authority of Moravians in Europe, and there was frequent visitation and correspondence between Bethlehem and the rest of the Moravian world. Although German was the dominant language in Bethlehem, the town was a cosmopolitan community with a multilingual population. This was celebrated through the occasional practice of polyglot singing in worship. The Moravians believed that they were overcoming the curse of the Tower of Babel through multilingualism.[62] Spirituality could unite people where language, nationality, culture, and even confessions of faith divided them. It should be noted, however, that the interconfessional, multilinguistic spirituality advocated by the Moravians was deeply rooted in Zinzendorfianism.

Most of the charges leveled against the Moravians in the popular press had a grain of truth, even if they were exaggerated. Insofar as Moravian communalism, ecumenism, pacifism, and egalitarianism represented a threat against the established order in Europe and America, the

Moravians were guilty as charged. However, as long as the Moravians confined themselves to their own congregations and did not transgress confessional lines, they could be tolerated as a religious sect. However, Moravian communalism threatened the class structure of Euro-American society. Muhlenberg and others across the confessional spectrum believed that Bethlehem's communal society was a rejection of Euro-American economic values and a threat to private property. They used the specter of the Anabaptist kingdom of Münster to warn people of the dangers of communalism and fanaticism.[63] Halle enlisted public figures such as the Indian agent Conrad Weiser to spread rumors that Moravians were trying to take property, wives, and children from their neighbors.[64] Even Americans who rejected the aristocratic structure of Europe were uncomfortable with aristocrats like Zinzendorf washing the feet of commoners or serving them tea in lovefeasts. Moravians even buried their dead without marking who was of high status and who was of low estate.

It is clear that the Moravians' unusual attitude toward gender was a source of particular concern in anti-Moravian publications. This has been argued most strongly by Aaron Fogleman, who asserts that what most frightened people about the Moravians was "female power run amok, which could be seen in the radical gospel of femaleness in the Trinity, women preaching, strange marriage and sex practices that undermined the patriarchal family."[65] Fogleman overstates the role that sexuality played in the opposition to the Moravians in America, particularly in the case of Muhlenberg, who makes little mention of the heterodox sexuality of the Moravians.[66] Most of the opposition to the Moravians involved confessional and racial issues, but that does not mean that sexuality played no role in the controversies. It is clear that the Moravians destabilized the patriarchal structure brought over from Europe.

Polemicists warned the public that Moravian elders and eldresses interfered in parents' right and duty to arrange marriages for their children. They claimed Moravians used a lottery to assign spouses, a misunderstanding of the Moravian practice of making decisions by consulting God through the lot. Moravians also allowed single women to live communally in the Single Sisters' House rather than getting married at a young age.[67] Women were allowed to hold leadership positions and even to preach and administer the sacraments, which seemed to threaten the patriarchal foundations of the family, church, and society.[68] Moravians taught women to read and write, and they endangered their safety by sending them out as missionaries among Indians and Africans. There was no precedent for this high level of women's leadership in Protestant culture. We should not exaggerate the level of gender equity in Moravian communities, but it is evident that women had higher status and a greater public role in Moravian communities than in other towns and villages in the New World or the Old. It should be noted that shortly after the death of Zinzendorf, the Moravians gradually adopted more traditional gender roles in their church.[69]

THEOLOGY

Many ecclesiastical figures in Europe and America argued that the true threat of the Moravians lay in their theology, which was the root of their social radicalism. Despite their different definitions of orthodoxy, pastors from different ecclesiastical and national backgrounds agreed that certain aspects of Zinzendorf's theology threatened traditional Christian understandings of God, the soul, and Christian morality. One reason it is hard to define what the Moravians believed is that their opponents found so many contradictory reasons to reject them.[70] It should be noted that the Moravian Church gradually turned away from some of these ideas in the decades after the Zinzendorf's death.[71] In fact, the church's historians were so effective at repressing the evidence of Zinzendorf's heterodoxy that it is only since the early 1990s that we have been able to discuss the true nature of Moravian spirituality and doctrine in the colonial era.[72]

Zinzendorf stressed doctrine of the full humanity and the full divinity of Christ to a degree shocking in Western Christianity. He asserted that the Creator was God the Son, not God the Father; therefore, it was the creator who was incarnate in Jesus Christ.[73] Moravians could sing about God being formed in Mary's womb and the creator dying on the cross. Zinzendorf was not shy about the fact that Jesus was fully human, either. He insisted that the incarnation had removed all of the shame associated with the human body.[74] Since Jesus had male sexual organs, there is nothing shameful about the male body. Since Mary gave birth to the Son of God through her uterus and vagina, there is nothing shameful about the female body. Even people sympathetic to the Moravians thought their hymns were in poor taste and an offense to public decency since they sometimes made reference to sexual organs. More disturbing was the way that this idea of the sanctity of the body was incorporated in Moravian society. The Moravians taught that sexuality was not shameful, but they did not endorse the type of promiscuous sexuality associated with the Mother Eva Society that had scandalized Germany in 1700.[75]

The wounds of Jesus, especially the wound in his side, were the second major motif of Zinzendorfianism.[76] The side wound was an object of special devotion because it was a portal into the heart of God that was torn open at the moment of redemption on the cross. Zinzendorf sometimes described the side wound as the birth canal of the regenerated soul. Just as God opened Adam's side to take a rib in order to form a woman, the side of Jesus was opened so that his bride, the church, could be born. Moravians on both sides of the Atlantic delighted in singing about the bleeding side of Jesus and their desire to crawl into his heart. Some of the most popular hymns translated into native languages were about the side wound of Jesus.[77]

This leads to the third prominent theme, namely the mystical marriage of the soul with Christ.[78] Zinzendorf believed that all souls are essentially feminine. Men and women alike were created to become the brides of Christ united in mystical union to him. He said in essence that Christian doctrine is summed up in two sentences: Your creator is your savior. Your savior is your husband.[79] Moravians drew on the long tradition of erotic mysticism in their hymnody and preaching, but what scandalized their opponents was the claim that sex within marriage was a sacramental act. Unlike the followers of Conrad Beissel at Ephrata Cloister, who believed that the mystical marriage of the soul with the divine required sexual abstinence, Zinzendorf taught that a man and his wife should engage in sex as a form of prayer that celebrates the mystical marriage of the soul to Christ.[80] The Moravians' sexual practices rarely resembled the salacious descriptions given in polemics against them, but there is no doubt that they believed that sex within marriage was equivalent to Holy Communion. Moravian marriage counselors were trained to help married couples with their sexual practices, which scandalized preachers across the theological spectrum.[81] The general attitude was that Moravians were encouraging immorality by proclaiming that sexual intercourse was sacred and good.[82]

Worshipping the bleeding wounds of Jesus, talking about his sexual organs, and proclaiming that sexual intercourse should be an act of religious devotion would have been threatening to most Christian pastors in every established church in the eighteenth century, but Zinzendorf went further. Almost as soon as he arrived in Pennsylvania, he proclaimed that the Holy Spirit should be adored as the Mother.[83] For about two decades the Moravians in Europe and America prayed to the Mother Spirit and sang praises to her. In the mid-1750s, they established an elaborate religious festival in honor of the Mother.[84] There was nothing overtly heretical about using the word "Mother" to describe the Holy Spirit, since that term had never been forbidden by an ecumenical church council, but nearly every branch of Western Christianity was committed to the notion that the Fatherhood of God establishes a social hierarchy with fathers ruling the household. By introducing a feminine aspect in the Trinity, Zinzendorf was implicitly challenging the patriarchal structure of Christendom. The idea that Moravian theology was a threat to traditional gender norms was strengthened by the fact that women held prominent leadership roles in Moravian communities.

CONCLUSION

The Moravians threatened European norms on both sides of the Atlantic in so many ways that it is surprising that there was not more opposition to them. Moravian preaching and hymn singing caused a few riots in a few places, and there were numerous polemics published against the church, but the Moravians were admired as well as hated. The church attracted thousands of followers from almost every level of European and American society, including members of the aristocracy. Muhlenberg often complained that wealthy and powerful people in Pennsylvania were more likely to join the Moravian Church than his "poor" Lutheran Church.[85] Thousands of people entrusted their sons and daughters to Moravian boarding schools in both Europe and America in the eighteenth century. Some were attracted to the Moravians because they shared their millennial hope for a better world; others were attracted to the beauty of Moravian worship and the high quality of pastoral care provided by the Moravians.[86] Outsiders frequently expressed admiration for the morality and integrity of Moravians while having reservations about their doctrine and hymns.

The transatlantic opposition to the Moravians was motivated primarily by the fact that the church was attractive to many people in the mid-eighteenth century. Elites such as the Anglican Archbishop Herring encouraged anti-Moravian publication because they feared the church's influence was growing.[87] Whenever Moravians competed successfully against established churches, the clergy argued that their theology and practices were heretical. When colonists felt threatened by Indians, foreigners, or their own slaves, Moravian religious ideas appeared to threaten the social order. If war or insurrection loomed, Moravians became objects of ridicule and violent attack. As the British and French Empires descended into the maelstrom of war, opposition to the Moravian religious and social experiment grew. As a result, the Moravians chose to retreat from the public arena and stop competing with the Lutheran, Anglican, and Reformed Churches. They withdrew their evangelists and carefully controlled what they published, reserving some of their most cherished beliefs and practices to private settings. Their once-aggressive mission was scaled back. Over time the Moravians in America became Americans in their attitudes and social practices. By the end of the nineteenth century the church forgot that Zinzendorf and his followers had once been religious and social radicals who shook the foundations of power.

Notes

1. Jon F. Sensbach, "Searching for Moravians in the Atlantic World," in *Self, Community, World: Moravian Education in a Transatlantic World*, ed. Heikki Lempa and Paul Peucker (Bethlehem, Pa.: Lehigh University Press, 2010), 35–53; Michele Gillespie and Robert Beachy, eds., *Pious Pursuits: German Moravians in the Atlantic World* (New York: Berghahn Books, 2007); Gisela Mettele, "Constructions of the Religious Self: Moravian Conversion and Transatlantic Communication," *Journal of Moravian History* 2 (2007): 7–35.

2. For more on the Moravians and Zinzendorf, see Dietrich Meyer, "Zinzendorf und Herrnhut," in *Geschichte des Pietismus*, ed. Martin Brecht and Klaus Deppermann, 4 vols. (Göttingen: Vandenhoeck und Ruprecht, 1995), 2:5–106.

3. Craig D. Atwood, "'The Hallensians Are Pietists; Aren't You a Hallensian?' Mühlenberg's Conflict with the Moravians in America," *Journal of Moravian History* 12 (2012): 47–92. Peter Vogt, "Spangenberg als Apologet des Grafen von Zinzendorf 1750–1752," *Unitas Fratrum* 61/62 (2008): 74–88, provides a graph

showing the increase in anti-Moravian polemics in the 1740s.

4. Aaron Spencer Fogleman, *Jesus Is Female: Moravians and Radical Religion in Early America* (Philadelphia: University of Pennsylvania Press, 2007).

5. Paul Peucker, review of *Jesus Is Female: Moravians and the Challenge of Radical Religion in Early America*, by Aaron Spencer Fogleman, H-German, H-Net Reviews, November 2007, https://www.h-net.org/reviews/showpdf.php?id=13909.

6. Peter Vogt, "Nicholas Ludwig von Zinzendorf, 1700–1760," in *The Pietist Theologians: An Introduction to Theology in the Seventeenth and Eighteenth Centuries*, ed. Carter Lindberg (Oxford: Blackwell, 2005, 207–23); John R. Weinlick, *Count Zinzendorf* (New York: Abingdon Press, 1956; repr., Bethlehem, Pa.: Moravian Church in America, 1989); Erich Beyreuther, *Die Große Zinzendorf Trilogy: Der junge Zinzendorf, Zinzendorf und die sich allhier beisammen finden, Zinzendorf und die Christenheit* (Marburg an der Lahn: Verlag der Francke Buchhandlung, 1988); Nikolaus Ludwig von Zinzendorf, *A Collection of Sermons from Zinzendorf's Pennsylvania Journey*, trans. Julie Weber, ed. Craig D. Atwood (Bethlehem, Pa.: Moravian Publication Office, 2002).

7. Giesela Mettele, "Identities Across Borders: The Moravian Brethren as a Global Community," in *Pietism and Community in Europe and North America, 1650–1850*, ed. Jonathan Strom, Brill's Series in Church History 45 (Leiden: Brill, 2010).

8. Jon F. Sensbach, "Slavery, Race, and the Global Fellowship: Religious Radicals Confront the Modern Age," in Gillespie and Beachy, *Pious Pursuits*, 223–36; Sensbach, "Don't Teach My Negroes to Be Pietists: Pietism and the Roots of the Black Protestant Church," in *Pietism in Germany and North America, 1680–1820*, ed. Jonathan Strom, Hartmut Lehmann, and James Van Horn Melton (Burlington, Vt.: Ashgate, 2009), 183–98; Krista Carmenzind, "Violence, Race, and the Paxton Boys," in *Friends and Enemies in Penn's Woods: Indians, Colonists, and the Racial Construction of Pennsylvania*, ed. William Pencak and Daniel K. Richter (University Park: Penn State University Press, 2004), 201–20.

9. Jared Burkholder, "Neither 'Kriegerisch' nor 'Quäkerisch': Moravians and the Question of Violence in Eighteenth-Century Pennsylvania," *Journal of Moravian History* 12 (2012): 143–69; Scott Paul Gordon, "Patriots and Neighbors: Moravians and the American Revolution," *Journal of Moravian History* 12 (2012): 111–42.

10. The hymn text in English: "Lamb, Lamb, O Lamb / With eyes of flame / so thoroughly mov'd / So griev'd and yet so lov'd / My hearts not mine, not mine / 'tis thine / My Lamb once slain / Thy cross thy Pain / Thy Blood thy toil / have claim'd it for their spoil." Poetry Collection, box 4, Moravian Archives, Bethlehem.

11. September 1, 1759, *Jüngerhaus Diarium*, Moravian Archives, Bethlehem.

12. On the role of religious persecution on emigration from the Rhine territories, see Gregg Roeber, *Palatines, Liberty, and Property: German Lutherans in Colonial America* (Baltimore: Johns Hopkins University Press, 1993); Stephen L. Longenecker, *Piety and Tolerance: Pennsylvania German Religion, 1700–1850* (Metuchen, N.J.: Scarecrow Press, 1994); and Donald F. Durnbaugh, "Radical Pietist Involvement in Early German Emigration to Pennsylvania," *Yearbook of German-American Studies* 29 (1994): 29–48. Aaron Spencer Fogleman, *Hopeful Journeys: German Immigration, Settlement, and Political Culture in Colonial America, 1717–1775* (Philadelphia: University of Pennsylvania Press, 1996), gives detailed immigration statistics and provides a good description of the economic pressures in the Rhineland following the French invasion.

13. R. Po-Chia Hsia, *Social Discipline in the Reformation: Central Europe, 1550–1750* (London: Routledge, 1989); Jonathan Strom, "Conversion, Confessionalism, and Pietism in Dargun," in *Confessionalism and Pietism: Religious Reform in Early Modern Europe*, ed. Fred van Lieburg (Mainz: Philipp von Zabern, 2006), 149–67; Heinz Schilling, *Die neue Zeit: Vom Chistenheitseuropa zum Europa der Staaten, 1250–1750* (Berlin: Siedler, 1999); Schilling, "Confessional Europe," in *Handbook of European History, 1400–1600: Late Middle Ages, Renaissance, and Reformation*, vol. 2, *Visions,*

Programs and Outcomes, ed. Thomas A. Brady, Heiko A. Oberman, and James D. Tracy (Leiden: Brill, 1995), 641–81.

14. According to the Moravian emigrants, their families had kept the Unitas Fratrum alive in secret after the church was declared illegal in Bohemia and Moravia, but there is scant historical evidence to validate this claim. Edita Sterik, *Mährische Exultanten in der erneuerten Brüderunität im 18. Jahrhundert*, Beiheft Unitas Fratrum 20 (Herrnhut: Herrnhuter Verlag, 2012), 1–89, provides a detailed examination of the founding of Herrnhut. A more skeptical view of this claim is provided by Joseph Müller, *Zinzendorf als Erneuerer der alten Brüderkirche* (Leipzig: Friedrich Jansa, 1900), 46–48. For more on the Unitas Fratrum, see Craig D. Atwood, *The Theology of the Czech Brethren from Hus to Comenius* (University Park: Penn State University Press, 2009).

15. Douglas Shantz, *An Introduction to German Pietism* (Baltimore: Johns Hopkins University Press, 2013).

16. Hans Schneider, "'Philadelphische Brüder mit einem lutherischen Maul und mährischen Rock': Zu Zinzendorfs Kirchenverständnis," in *Neue Aspekte der Zinzendorf-Forschung*, ed. Martin Brecht and Paul Peucker (Göttingen: Vandenhoeck und Ruprecht, 2006), 11–36, argues persuasively that Zinzendorf was a radical Pietist despite his claim that he was not a Pietist at all. For a discussion of Zinzendorf's views of Pietism, see Atwood, "'The Hallensians Are Pietists,'" 52–54.

17. Hans Schneider, *German Radical Pietism*, trans. George MacDonald (Lanham, Md.: Scarecrow Press, 2007).

18. Peter Vogt, "Zinzendorf's 'Philadelphian' Ecumenism in Pennsylvania, 1742: An Example of Cross-Cultural Dynamics in Eighteenth Century Pietism," *Covenant Quarterly* 62 (2004): 13–27; Hans Schneider, "'Philadelphische Brüder."

19. Nikolaus Ludwig von Zinzendorf, "Sermon Given in Heerendyk on August 16, 1741," in *A Collection of Sermons from Zinzendorf's Pennsylvania Journey*, trans. Julie Weber, ed. Craig D. Atwood (Bethlehem, Pa.: Moravian Publication Office, 2002), 7.

20. Paul Peucker, "The Ideal of Primitive Christianity as a Source of Moravian Liturgical Practice," *Journal of Moravian History*, 6 (2009): 7–29.

21. Nikolaus Ludwig von Zinzendorf, *Ein und zwanzig Discourse über die Augspurgische Confession*, in *Hauptschriften*, ed. Erich Beyreuther and Gerhard Meyer, 6 vols. (Hildesheim: Georg Olms, 1962–65), 6:203. For information on the establishment of the so-called Renewed Brethren's Church, see Joseph T. Müller, *Zinzendorf als Erneuerer der alten Brüderkirche* (Leipzig: Friedrich Jansa, 1900), 46–48. In 1732, the faculty of Tübingen agreed with Zinzendorf that the Moravians could maintain their own church discipline and remain in the Lutheran Church.

22. For more on the distinctive Moravian religiosocial system developed in Herrnhut and put into effect in several other communities, see Atwood, *Community of the Cross*; Beverly Smaby, *The Transformation of Moravian Bethlehem from Communal Mission to Family Economy* (Philadelphia: University of Pennsylvania Press, 1988); Hans-Walter Erbe, "Herrnhaag: Eine religiöse Kommunität im 18. Jahrhundert," *Unitas Fratrum* 23/24 (1988): 4–222; Helmut Erbe, *Bethlehem, Pa.: Eine Herrnhuter-Kolonie des 18. Jahrhunderts* (Herrnhut: Gustav Winter, 1929).

23. Müller, *Zinzendorf als Erneuerer*, 48–60.

24. Alexander Schunka, "A Missing Link: Daniel Ernst Jablonski as the Connection Between Comenius and Zinzendorf," in Lempa and Peucker, *Self, Community, World*.

25. Arthur Manukyan, *Konstaninopel und Kairo: Die Herrnhuter Brüdergemeine im Kontakt zum Ökumenischen Patriarchat und zur Koptischen Kirche: Interkonfessionelle und interkulturelle Begegnungen im 18. Jahrhundert*, Orthodoxie, Orient und Europa 3 (Würzburg: Ergon Verlag, 2011).

26. Craig D. Atwood, "Use of the 'Ancient Unity' in the Historiography of the Moravian Church," *Journal of Moravian History* 13 (2013): 111–12.

27. W. R. Ward, "The Renewed Unity of the Brethren: Ancient Church, New Sect, or Interconfessional Movement?," *Bulletin of the John Rylands Library* 70, no. 3 (1988): 77–92.

28. J. Taylor Hamilton and Kenneth G. Hamilton, *History of the Moravian Church: The Renewed Unitas Fratrum, 1722–1957*

(Bethlehem, Pa.: Interprovincial Board of Christian Education of the Moravian Church in America, 1967), 64–65.

29. Jon Sensbach, "Don't Teach My Negroes to Be Pietists: Pietism and the Roots of the Black Protestant Church," in Strom, Lehmann, and Melton, *Pietism in Germany and North America*, 183–98.

30. Jon Sensbach, "Race and the Early Moravian Church: A Comparative Perspective," *Transactions of the Moravian Historical Society* 31 (2000): 1–10; Sensbach, *A Separate Canaan: The Making of an Afro-Moravian World in North Carolina, 1763–1840* (Chapel Hill: University of North Carolina Press, 1998).

31. Müller, *Zinzendorf als Erneuerer*, 88.

32. Arthur James Lewis, *Zinzendorf, the Ecumenical Pioneer: A Study in the Moravian Contribution to Christian Mission and Unity* (Philadelphia: Westminster Press, 1962).

33. Patrick M. Erben, *A Harmony of the Spirits: Translation and the Language of Community in Early Pennsylvania* (Chapel Hill: University of North Carolina Press, 2012), argues that the Moravians played an important role in promoting translation and multilingualism in colonial Pennsylvania.

34. Ward, "Renewed Unity of the Brethren."

35. Henry Melchior Muhlenberg, *The Journals of Henry Melchior Muhlenberg*, trans. and ed. Theodore G. Tappert and John W. Doberstein, 3 vols. (Philadelphia: Evangelical Lutheran Ministerium of Pennsylvania and Adjacent States and Muhlenberg Press, 1942–58; repr., Camden, Maine: Picton Press, 1980), 1:77–78.

36. Hamilton and Hamilton, *History of the Moravian Church*, 70.

37. Atwood, "'The Hallensians Are Pietists,'" 49–63. For more on Halle Pietism, see Martin Brecht, ed., *Geschichte des Pietismus*, 4 vols. (Göttingen: Vanderhoeck und Ruprecht, 1992–2000); Jonathan Strom, "Problems and Promises of Pietism Research," *Church History* 71 (2002): 536–54.

38. Hans Schneider, "Die 'zürnenden Mutterkinder': Der Konflikt zwischen Halle und Herrnhut," *Pietismus und Neuzeit* 29 (2009): 43–53, 64–66.

39. Peter Vogt, *An Authentic Relation of the Occasion, Continuance, and Conclusion of the First Assembly of some Labourers out of most of the Christian Religions and other private religious People in Pensilvania kept in German Town 1st and 2nd January 1741/2*, Nikolaus Ludwig von Zinzendorf, Materialien und Dokumente, Reihe 2, Band 30 (Hildesheim: Georg Olms, 1976).

40. On the multiculturalism of early Pennsylvania, see Sally Schwartz, *"A Mixed Multitude": The Struggle for Toleration in Colonial Pennsylvania* (New York: New York University Press, 1987). On German immigration, see Aaron Spencer Fogleman, *Hopeful Journeys: German Immigration, Settlement, and Political Culture in Colonial America, 1717–1775* (Philadelphia: University of Pennsylvania Press, 1996), 136. Only 1 of the 830 Moravian immigrants died in transit to America, a mortality rate that was thirty-eight times lower than for all other German immigrants.

41. Aaron S. Fogleman, "The Decline and Fall of the Moravian Community in Colonial Georgia: Revising the Traditional View," *Unitas Fratrum* 48 (2001): 1–22.

42. Mühlenberg, *Journals*, 1:79.

43. Ibid., 1:63.

44. Walter Wagner, *The Zinzendorf-Muhlenberg Encounter: A Controversy in Search of Understanding* (Nazareth, Pa.: Moravian Historical Society, 2002); Karl-Otto Strohmidel, "Henry Melchior Mühlenberg's European Heritage," *Lutheran Quarterly* 6 (1992): 5–34.

45. Craig D. Atwood, "Spangenberg: A Radical Pietist in Colonial America," *Journal of Moravian History* 4 (2008): 7–27.

46. Julie Tomberlin Weber, "Translation as a Prism: Broadening the Spectrum of Eighteenth-Century Identity," in *Ethnographies and Exchanges: Native Americans, Moravians, and Catholics in Early North America*, ed. A. G. Roeber (University Park: Penn State University Press, 2008), 195–207.

47. Roeber, *Ethnographies and Exchanges*.

48. Amy C. Schutt, "Female Relationships and Intercultural Bonds in Moravian Indian Missions," in Pencak and Richter, *Friends and Enemies in Penn's Woods*, 87–103; Gregory T. Knouff, "Whiteness and Warfare on a Revolutionary Frontier," in Pencak and Richter, *Friends and Enemies in Penn's Woods*, 238–58.

49. Mühlenberg, *Journals*, 1:387.

50. Krista Carmenzind, "Violence, Race, and the Paxton Boys," in Pencak and Richter, *Friends and Enemies in Penn's Woods*, 201–20.
51. Mühlenberg, *Journals*, 2:19.
52. Ibid., 2:20.
53. Patricia Bonomi, *Under the Cope of Heaven: Religion, Society, and Politics in Colonial America* (New York: Oxford University Press, 1986); Mark Hälberlein challenges the assumption that lack of pastors meant lack of religiosity in Pennsylvania. Hälberlein, *The Practice of Pluralism: Congregational Life and Religious Diversity in Lancaster, Pennsylvania, 1730–1820* (University Park: Penn State University Press, 2009).
54. Fogleman, *Jesus Is Female*, 113.
55. Heinrich Melchior Mühlenberg, *The Correspondence of Heinrich Melchior Mühlenberg*, ed. and trans. John W. Kleiner and Helmut T. Lehmann, 4 vols. (Camden, Maine: Picton Press, 1986–93), 1:116; Heinrich Melchior Mühlenberg, *Die Korrespondenz Heinrich Melchior Mühlenbergs: Aus der Anfangszeit des deutschen Luthertums in Nordamerika*, ed. Kurt Aland et al., 5 vols. (Berlin: Walter de Gruyter, 1986–2002), 1:101.
56. Atwood, "'The Hallensians Are Pietists,'" 74–85; Fogleman, *Jesus Is Female*, 199–204; Hälberlein, *Practice of Pluralism*, 62–76.
57. For the conflicts between the Brethren and Moravians, see Donald Durnbaugh, *Brethren in Colonial America: A Source Book on the Transplantation and Development of the Church of the Brethren in the Eighteenth Century* (Elgin, Ill.: Brethren Press, 1967), 267–320; Christopher Saur, "Herrnhutiana. Bericht und Gegenbericht von einer durch den Herrn Grafen von Zinzendorf in Pensylvanien erhobenen Klage," *Acta historico-ecclesiastica* 41 (1743): 11/779–82.
58. Whitefield transported several Moravians from Georgia to Pennsylvania to build the orphanage on the Nazareth estate, but Whitefield and the Moravians had a falling out over the issue of predestination, and Whitefield forced them to leave his land. They then purchased the land that became Bethlehem, but in 1743 bought Nazareth from Whitefield.
59. Katherine Carté Engel, *Religion and Profit: Moravians in Early America* (Philadelphia: University of Pennsylvania Press, 2009).

60. Nola Reed Knouse, *The Music of the Moravian Church in America* (Rochester: University of Rochester Press, 2008).
61. Vernon Nelson, "Johann Valentin Haidt und Zinzendorf," in *Graf Ohne Grenzen: Leben und Werk von Nikolaus Ludwig Graf von Zinzendorf*, ed. Paul Peucker (Herrnhut: Unitätsarchiv im Verlag der Comeniusbuchhandlung, 2000), 152–58.
62. Erben, *Harmony of the Spirits*, 236–41.
63. Häberlein, *Practice of Pluralism*, 65.
64. Atwood, "'The Hallensians Are Pietists,'" 83–84.
65. Fogleman, *Jesus Is Female*, 219.
66. For one of the few references to suspicions of aberrant sexuality, see Mühlenberg, *Journals*, 1:167. Derrick R. Miller, "Moravian Familiarities: Queer Community in the Moravian Church in Europe and North America in the Mid-Eighteenth Century," *Journal of Moravian History* 13 (2013): 54–75.
67. Beverly Prior Smaby, *The Transformation of Moravian Bethlehem from Communal Mission to Family Economy* (Philadelphia: University of Pennsylvania Press, 1988).
68. Smaby, *Transformation of Moravian Bethlehem*, 13; Peter Vogt, "A Voice for Themselves: Women as Participants in Congregational Discourse in the Eighteenth-Century Moravian Movement," in *Women Preachers and Prophets Through Two Millennia of Christianity*, ed. Beverly Mayne Kienzle and Pamela J. Walker (Berkeley: University of California Press, 1998), 227–47; Katherine M. Faull, *Moravian Women: Their Related Lives* (Lewisburg, Pa.: Bucknell University Press, 1998).
69. On the Moravian retreat from women's leadership, see Beverly Smaby, "'No One Should Lust for Power': Dismantling Female Leadership Among Eighteenth-Century Moravians," in Gillespie and Beachy, *Pious Pursuits*, 159–75; and Smaby, "'Only Brothers Should Be Accepted into This Proposed Council': Restricting Women's Leadership in Moravian Bethlehem," in Strom, Lehmann, and Melton, *Pietism in Germany and North America*, 133–62.
70. John Wesley accused the Moravians of being quietist and antinomian because they rejected his idea of Christian perfection. Calvinists like Gilbert Tennant accused them of

universalism because they rejected predestination. Muhlenberg attacked them because they rejected the Pietist understanding of conversion as a painful spiritual process. Some accused them of being crypto-Catholic because they had bishops and their Single Sisters looked like nuns. Anglicans like Bishop Herring attacked them because their bishops were not really in apostolic succession. Others attacked the Moravians because they were too forgiving of sins and did not separate themselves from the unconverted.

71. Paul Peucker, "Selection and Destruction in Moravian Archives Between 1760 and 1810," *Journal of Moravian History* 12 (2012): 170–215.

72. Craig D. Atwood, "'Deep in the Side of Jesus': The Persistence of Zinzendorfian Piety in Colonial America," in Gillespie and Beachy, *Pious Pursuits*, 50–64; Atwood, "Interpreting and Misinterpreting the Sichtungzeit," in *Neuen Aspekte der Zinzendorf-Forschung*, ed. Martin Brecht and Paul Peucker, Arbeiten zur Geschichte des Pietismus 47 (Göttingen: Vandenhoeck und Ruprecht, 2006), 174–87.

73. Atwood, *Community of the Cross*, 79–85; Peter Zimmerling, *Gott in Gemeinschaft Zinzendorfs Trinitätslehre* (Giessen: Brunnen Verlag, 1991), 74–85.

74. Craig D. Atwood, "'He Has Carried You My Members': The Full Humanity of Christ and the Blessing of the Physical Body in Zinzendorfian Piety," in *Alter Adam und Neue Kreatur: Pietismus und Anthropologie*, ed. Udo Straeter (Halle: Franckeschen Stiftungen, 2009), 197–207.

75. Willi Temme, *Krise der Leiblichkeit: Die Sozietät der Mutter Eva (Buttlarsche Rotte) und der Radikale Pietismus um 1700* (Göttingen: Vandenhoeck und Ruprecht, 1998). For a discussion of Moravian views of marriage and sexuality within the context of German Pietism, see A. G. Roeber, *Hopes for Better Spouses: Protestant Marriage and Church Renewal in Early Modern Europe, India, and North America* (Grand Rapids, Mich.: William B. Eerdmans, 2013), 146–82.

76. Craig D. Atwood, "Understanding Zinzendorf's Blood and Wounds Theology," *Journal of Moravian History* 1 (2006): 31–47; Peter Vogt, "'Honor to the Side': The Adoration of the Side Wound of Jesus in Eighteenth-Century Moravian Piety," *Journal of Moravian History* 7 (2009): 83–106.

77. Rachel Wheeler, "'Der Schönste Schmuck': Mahican Appropriations of Moravian Blood and Wounds Theology," *Covenant Quarterly* 63 (2005): 20–34; Jane T. Merritt, "Dreaming of the Savior's Blood: Moravians and the Indian Great Awakening in Pennsylvania," *William and Mary Quarterly*, 3rd ser., 54 (1997): 723–46.

78. Peter Vogt, "'Ehereligion': The Moravian Theory and Practice of Marriage as Point of Contention in the Conflict Between Ephrata and Bethlehem," *Communal Societies* 21 (2001): 37–48; Craig D. Atwood, "The Union of Masculine and Feminine in Zinzendorf's Piety," in *Masculinity, Senses, Spirit*, ed. Katherine Faull (Lewisburg, Pa.: Bucknell University Press, 2011), 11–38; Atwood, "Sleeping in the Arms of Christ: Sanctifying Sexuality in the Eighteenth-Century Moravian Church," *Journal of the History of Sexuality* 8, no. 1 (1997): 25–51; Paul Peucker, "The Songs of the Sifting: Understanding the Role of Bridal Mysticism in Moravian Piety During the Late 1740s," *Journal of Moravian History* 3 (2007): 51–87.

79. Zinzendorf derives this formulation from Isaiah 54:5, "The one who has made you is your husband." *Gemeinreden*, reproduced in Zinzendorf, *Hauptschriften*, 4:123; Zinzendorf, *Nine Public Lectures on Important Subjects in Religion*, trans. and ed. George W. Forell (Eugene, Ore.: Wipf and Stock, 1998), 77–78.

80. Vogt, "'Ehereligion.'"

81. Paul Peucker, "In the Blue Cabinet: Moravians, Marriage, and Sex," *Journal of Moravian History* 10 (2011): 7–37; Peter Vogt, "Zinzendorf's 'Seventeen Points of Matrimony': A Foundational Document on the Moravian Understanding of Marriage and Sexuality," *Journal of Moravian History* 10 (2011): 39–67; Katherine Faull, "Instructions for the Married People's Choir," *Journal of Moravian History* 10 (2011): 39–67.

82. Henry Rimius, *A Candid Narrative of the Rise and Progress of the Herrnhuters, Commonly call'd Moravians or Unitas Fratrum: With a*

short Account of their Doctrines, drawn from their own Writings (London, 1753), 67.

83. Zinzendorf, *Collection of Sermons*, 21.

84. Craig D. Atwood, "The Mother of God's People: The Adoration of the Holy Spirit in the Eighteenth-Century Brüdergemeine," *Church History* 68 (1999): 886–909.

85. Mühlenberg, *Journals*, 1:109.

86. Colin Podmore argues this point most persuasively in *The Moravian Church in England, 1728–1760* (Oxford: Clarendon Press, 1998), 120–58.

87. Jonathan Yonan, "Archbishop Herring, Anti-Catholicism, and the Moravian Church," *Journal of Moravian History* 4 (2008): 28–43.

CHAPTER 3

Women, Migration, and Moravian Mission
Negotiating Pennsylvania's Colonial Landscapes

KATHERINE FAULL

In 1741, when Count Nikolaus Ludwig von Zinzendorf came to Philadelphia to execute his "Pennsylvania Plan," one of the less contentious meetings he conducted was with a twenty-one-year-old woman, Anna Margarethe Bechtel. In sharp contrast to the hubbub that surrounded his sermons at the Arch Street Church and his final contretemps with Heinrich Melchior Mühlenberg,[1] Zinzendorf's meeting with the daughter of Johannes Bechtel, lay preacher of the Reformed Congregation in Philadelphia, was marked only by her enthusiasm for him, his daughter Benigna von Zinzendorf, and his companion, Anna Nitschmann. Young Anna Margarethe was so convinced that the count was "a true child of God" that, in her memoir, she credited herself with bringing her father to Zinzendorf and the Moravians and eventually effecting Bechtel's removal from the Reformed congregation.

It did not take long for Anna Margarethe, through her involvement with the establishment of the Children's School in Germantown, to become drawn to the "Zinzendorfians," and soon the count personally invited her to join the fledgling community in Bethlehem.[2] With that entry into the *Gemeine* Anna Margarethe started her remarkable lifelong work among the American Indians of New York, Pennsylvania, and

Ohio. Anna Margarethe was to become one of the most successful Moravian missionaries of the colonial period, working with her husband, Johannes Jungmann, as well as David Zeisberger and the married couples Martin and Johanna Mack and Johann and Johanna Schmick.

While the literature on the Moravian mission and the activities of the male figures in this remarkable movement is large, critical study of women missionaries' roles in the Old and New Worlds has until very recently been overlooked by scholars. In recent years, the challenges and opportunities for cross-cultural exchange available to these women in the Moravian Church has become the focus of study for historians such as Jane Merritt, Amy Schutt, Gunlög Fur, Rachel Wheeler, and Alison Duncan Hirsch.[3] However, the majority of these studies focus on native women's roles in the negotiation of the contact between Euro-Americans and Native American cultures and cosmologies. This essay focuses on the Moravian missionary women who worked in the 1740s and '50s in Pennsylvania, which, as Jane Merritt has argued, constituted a very different moment in the "gender frontier."[4]

Fortunately, the growth in Moravian studies, spurred on by the increasing availability of translated manuscript materials, has led to explorations of the fascinating world of cultural exchange between Moravian sisters and Mohican, Delaware, and Iroquois women in what I, after James Merrell, am calling "Susquehanna country."[5] My own work editing and translating the Shamokin mission diaries has revealed a landscape of encounter in the 1740s and '50s that demonstrates how previously invisible Moravian women were agents of change and exchange.[6] The Shamokin diaries were written at the confluence of the North and West Branches of the Susquehanna River (at present-day Sunbury) and trace the movements of missionaries and native peoples along the river as they traveled between Shamokin and Gnadenhütten, and Bethlehem and the backcountry. These mission diaries reveal how, in prerevolutionary Pennsylvania, Moravian women formed a network both among themselves, as they communicated and traveled between the mission stations, and also with the native women who lived either in or nearby the missions.[7]

The spheres of activity of these Moravian women missionaries in the 1740s and '50s seem to differ significantly from those of the later decades, as Jane Merritt has recently argued.[8] This period marked a positive

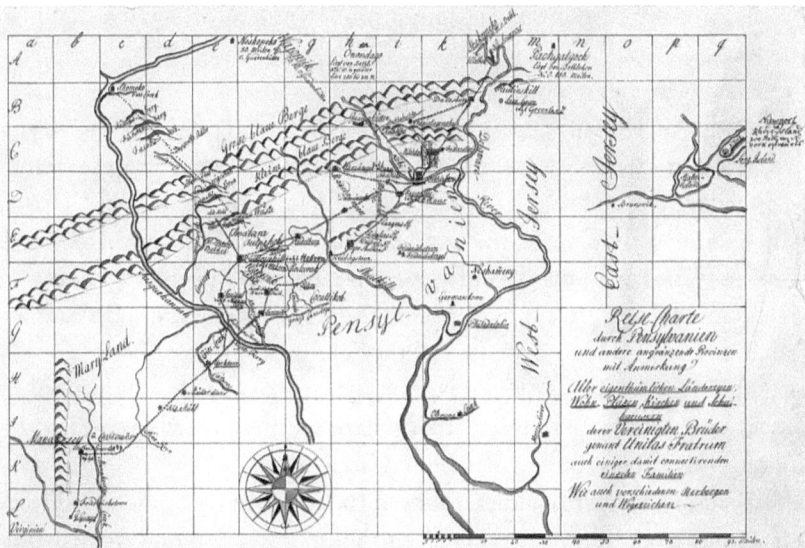

FIGURE 3.1 "Reise Charte durch Pennsylvanie und anderer angränzenden Provinzen," travel map of Pennsylvania, northern Maryland, and New Jersey, ca. 1750.

gender bias toward women in which women missionaries navigated the ethnographic and geographic frontiers with more agency than they would in the 1770s after Zinzendorf's death.[9] This essay examines the ways in which four women who worked in the Pennsylvania and New York mission field negotiated the Pennsylvania backcountry of the 1740s and '50s. Specifically, this essay considers how Jannetje Mack, Catharine Schmidt, Martha Powell, and Anna Margarethe Bechtel navigated the land before them. It also offers conceptions about these women's notions of space in the colonial world and how the experience of migration affected both European and native women's perceptions of Susquehanna country.

THE MORAVIAN CHURCH AND ITS MISSION IN NORTH AMERICA

The mission records for Pennsylvania in the prerevolutionary period identify the places and periods during which the Moravian women missionaries were active and reveal how they moved between missions, often accompanying their converts on arduous journeys to avoid persecution by suspicious and often murderous militia gangs, such as the Paxton Boys.[10]

These Moravian women missionaries were part of the remarkable movement of peoples across the Atlantic in the eighteenth century: a century that saw a vast emigration of Germans to America in search of financial wealth and religious and political freedom. In 1702, the Pietists, who had been persecuted in Saxony, called Daniel Falckner, a German who had lived in central Pennsylvania, where the problem of how to interact with the native inhabitants of the area was of paramount importance, to Halle to report on the viability of the province of Pennsylvania for possible settlement. August Hermann Francke posed 103 questions to Falckner on subjects ranging from where Germans settled to how the Indians might be subdued. Falckner described the Indians of Pennsylvania as simple, vengeful, akin to apes in the upbringing of their children, suspicious of capture, speaking an unsophisticated language consisting of "no more words than things," and adhering to a Manichaestic religion worshipping a god of both good and evil.[11]

Eight years after Falckner's report to Francke, Count Nicholas Ludwig von Zinzendorf, the future leader of the Moravian Church, entered Francke's *Pedagogium* in Halle (the subject of Overhoff's chapter 4 in this volume). During his six years there he met his first missionaries who had returned from the Danish colony of Tranquebar, today Tharamgambadi, in the Indian state of Tamil Nadu; at this time he most likely read Falckner's *Curieuse Nachricht von Pennsylvania*.[12] In 1732, even before he sent his own missionaries out into the field, Zinzendorf outlined his mission theology in a letter to Johann Ernst Geister, a missionary sent to Madras by the Stollberg *Konsistorium*. In this letter, Zinzendorf writes of the appropriate demeanor toward the non-Christian: "Show a happy and lively spirit and in external matters, do not rule over the heathen in the slightest fashion, but rather gain respect among them through the strength of your spirit, and in external matters humble yourself below them as much as possible."[13] From his contact with the Halle missionaries who had been in Tranquebar, Zinzendorf must have been well aware of the problems Protestant missionaries had already encountered in their contacts with other cultures. The tone of the letter to Geister suggests that he attributed the Protestant missionaries' problems to the attitude they adopted toward the non-Christians.[14] For example,

Zinzendorf professed that the refusal of some missionaries to mix with the non-Christians, or to live at their level of poverty, was contrary to the spirit of Christ. Missionaries and non-Christians alike, he claimed, should both show deference only to the invisible Savior.

Zinzendorf delineated both his understanding of the natural state of sin into which non-Christians had been born and their need for salvation from the inherently sinful characters of this state when he visited Moravian missions in the West Indies. Upon leaving the missions on St. Thomas, on February 15, 1739, Zinzendorf gave a farewell speech in Dutch Creole to the mission members:[15]

> A heathen should not have another reason to convert himself, than that he believes that Jesus God's son has died to pay for mankind's sin, and that he now truly lives so that man may live with him; A heathen cannot do by nature as much good, as any a human who has learned from childhood to do good, and does not get permission to do evil. Because a heathen is from childhood on used to doing evil, and not learned any better. But when a heathen gets the mercy of the Lord Jesus, that his sin is forgiven, and he is washed with Jesus's blood; so he receives the strength to leave all evil, and to do good and so he hates sin so much, as he had loved it before. Then he is one of Christ's people, so as your Master Martinus will teach you furthermore.[16]

For Zinzendorf, converting the non-Christian extended both the kingdom of God and also created another unique and unrepeatable *Vergegenwärtigung*, or a "making present" of Christ. This understanding of mission policy meant that baptisms, whether in the West Indies, North America, or Greenland, were individual and not performed en masse, and that the individual's path to salvation was charted by means of frequent "speakings" with spiritual helpers from the same national background as the candidate and the missionaries. Within the missions this meant that each convert was a member of a small group of people who came together regularly in the evenings to discuss their spiritual growth, exchange confidences about their personal problems, encourage and forgive each other, and help each other toward Christ.[17] This emphasis on the individual connection between missionary and convert as well as the importance of shared ethnicity would have significant importance for Moravian women missionaries in their exchanges with native women in Susquehanna country.

Such an individualistic approach to conversion had both benefits and drawbacks. The benefits showed themselves in the success of the missions. A drawback was that only small numbers of converts could enter into the kingdom of God. Zinzendorf, recognizing that each human being had his or her own particular form of religious life, became convinced that this individuality should be encouraged rather than eradicated and replaced with a foreign form. The individuality of each human being was balanced by the commonality of being born not only into a class, race, culture, or gender but also into humanity, and as such, born into the world spiritually. In terms of our physiognomy, Zinzendorf argued that the most significant mark that distinguishes us from all others is not skin color or gender, but the mark of the thorns on the brow.[18]

However, the fantasy of a universal brotherhood in Christ met with some challenges. In 1742, shortly after his voyage to the West Indies, Zinzendorf traveled to North America and met with native peoples. Arriving in Shekomeko, New York, a later Moravian mission settlement, he set out in his diary his intention to settle among the Indians. For example, rather than going directly to the villages and preaching, Zinzendorf explained to the Six Nations that he was already intimately acquainted with the Great Spirit and requested that he and his followers be permitted to live in their towns as friends until they had got to know each other better.[19] Zinzendorf believed that once the Indians observed the Moravians in their lives of faith and service, the call to convert would come to them through a personal connection with Christ. In his well-known "Methodus der Wilden Bekehrung" (Method for converting the heathen, 1743), Zinzendorf delineated a projected sequence of events that would lead to the moment of conversion: starting with the missionaries' everyday life of prayer and praise observed by the non-Christians, followed by the latter's questions about the "Lamb," explanations of salvation, discussions of the role of evil in the body and spirit, the transformation of desire (lust) into love, and then baptism.[20] Given the importance of the daily routine as a model of the Christian life for the nonheathen, the presence and activities of the women missionaries were paramount. And the person to speak to the native women about, for example, the relationship of body and soul had to be a woman.

THE MORAVIAN WOMEN MISSIONARIES

Analysis of the Pennsylvania mission map for the 1740s–70s reveals the presence of the women missionaries in this formative early period and demonstrates how their movements throughout the region created spheres of influence among the larger Moravian community and the native people with whom they interacted. For example, Jannetje Mack worked at Shamokin in 1745, moved to Gnadenhütten in 1746, and then returned to the Susquehanna in 1747 and 1748. In 1749, she moved back to Gnadenhütten, where she died in December of that year. While in Gnadenhütten, Mack labored alongside Margarethe Jungmann, who, although never at Shamokin, would have heard much about the mission and would have conducted Speakings with many of the native women who moved from mission to mission through Susquehanna country. In turn, Margarethe Jungmann worked at Gnadenhütten from 1746 to 1752, alongside Martha Büninger.[21] Martha worked both at Gnadenhütten and at Wechquetnach in Connecticut. Both women labored with an important missionary couple, Johann and Johanna Schmick, at Gnadenhütten, at the mission at Meniolagomekah, and, after the odyssey of the Moravian Indians from Nain to the barracks at Philadelphia, at Friedenshütten.[22] Mapping the work of these women highlights the strong networks they created between themselves and also with the native women among whom they were living.

In her work on the Moravians and the Indian Great Awakening in Pennsylvania, Jane Merritt has argued that the years 1749–50 saw the greatest number of Moravian conversions in Gnadenhütten, especially among the women: eighty-seven in just those two years.[23] Anna Margarethe Jungmann served the Gnadenhütten mission for six years, from 1746–52, ministering to the women and children of the mission congregation. From the Gnadenhütten mission diary we can glean an outline of her daily life, one punctuated by working in the school for the children, calling on the Delaware in their homes (by 1752 she was able to converse in Delaware), and holding Speakings and pastoral interviews with the widows, married women, and single Sisters. Her success as a missionary was due in no small part to her understanding of Mohican and Delaware worldviews that was gained through her Speakings with the women, her pastoral visits, and her counseling. Given her linguistic fluency, she was able to listen to and understand the women's concerns, their fears, and their dreams. She blessed their crops, helped to plant corn and squash, dispensed medicines and blessings to the sick, prayed over the dead and dying women and children, and guided them spiritually.[24] She was also able to translate the Moravian understandings of body and soul into a linguistic and cultural system that was mutually shared with the Native American women.

It is important to recognize that women are frequently considered to be the primary carriers of cultural meaning and, as such, can perhaps more easily translate the physical and natural world to each other: the acts of pounding corn, making moccasins, sewing a blouse, mending a shirt, and planting crops lie in an extralinguistic realm of mutual understanding. Contrary perhaps to the male-gendered spaces of building, damming, fencing, plowing, and blacksmithing, women's work can be mutually understood and successfully translated. Where women's acts stand in a shared liminal space between native and European worlds, it seems that more successful negotiations of meaning can take place.

Alison Duncan Hirsch expands this argument for the crucial role of women into the political realm. In her study of Susquehanna country, she claims that the presence and agency of women on the frontier were crucial to the maintenance of peace.[25] Speaking of the area around the confluence of the North and West Branches of the Susquehanna River, she argues, "With the reduction of interactions including women, the danger of interracial violence increased and led to even less cross-cultural contact, creating a vicious cycle that culminated in war. As long as women remained deeply involved at every level of social interaction, there was peace; as women disappeared, or were forced from such interaction, there was war."[26] A close reading of the 1750s Moravian mission map can reveal the powerful agency of Moravian women missionaries and their spheres of activity in Susquehanna country from 1747–55. The presence and activities of women missionaries can be understood not only as those of "brokers" or elusive "mediators," as Merrell has termed figures such as Andrew Montour,[27] but also as agents of translation. If Merrell describes the sense of Susquehanna country as "confusion," a veritable Tower of Babel, then the solution to such linguistic and cultural temporal multiplicity might lie in the act of translation, both linguistic and cultural. The translations performed by these women, while confusing to such historians as Merrell, produced moments in which Moravian missionaries, male and female, shared food, knowledge, labor, and hopes at a time of enormous political and social upheaval on the Pennsylvania frontier. Moravian women's quotidian actions became the dynamic equivalent of native women's lives, successfully translating where often language differences could not. However, with all of the potential agency for both Euro and native women, the Moravian mission movement also poses the question of whether these cultural negotiations were successful. Rachel Wheeler has wrestled with the assumption that Christian Indians did not adhere to an essential concept of "native" culture as identified by both Native and Anglo historians. In her book *To Live upon Hope*, Wheeler challenges traditional scholarly notions that Christianized Indians somehow betrayed their native identity. Wheeler's work points a way to a far more nuanced cross-cultural hermeneutic that we can also apply to the radical shifts in European women's identities too. As we will see below, the challenges that Martha Powell received to the authenticity of her Moravian faith, for example, might not be that different than the doubt that accompanies the conversion of a Mohican woman, or a Delaware, or even Anna Mack's pastoral conversations with Madame Montour.[28]

THE SHAMOKIN MISSION ON THE SUSQUEHANNA (1745–55)

Shamokin preexisted Moravian presence by many centuries, first as a Susquehannock town, then as a Delaware, Shawnee, and Iroquois settlement, finally overseen by the vice-regent of the Five Nations, the Oneida sachem Shikellamy. Initial attempts to establish a mission there proved difficult because the nature of the place, a traditional crossroads or confluence of trade and cultures, meant that there was no stable population. In his account of Shamokin, James Merrell describes the river confluence on the eighteenth-century Pennsylvania frontier as "a debatable land, a place marked by confusion and contention. . . . The Susquehannocks [had] been all but destroyed by their Iroquois neighbors in the late seventeenth century,"[29] leaving too few "natives" remaining there to serve as a charter group that could determine the character of life in the region.

By Merrell's account, Susquehanna country constituted a liminal space, where identities and spheres of activity and influence were fluid and contested. Zinzendorf describes the famous colonial interpreter Andrew Montour as paradigmatic of this confluence of peoples and cultures and languages. Dressed in "decidedly European" fashion and described by Zinzendorf as having a face broadly daubed with paint applied with bear's fat, his ears hung with pendants of brass and other wires plaited together, he was not considered anything particularly unusual.[30] Andrew Montour fits well with what Merrell calls the "sense of the Susquehanna Valley"; he is the first guide to Jannetje Mack and Catharine Schmidt, the Moravian women missionaries to the area. For Merrell, this Susquehanna confluence was a dark place, consisting of a "babel of voices, accents, dialects, and languages."[31] However, if focus is shifted to the everyday activities of the women, both Moravian and native, this "babel" becomes translatable: a multiplicity of languages and cultures that was not feared but welcomed.

Following this argument, my reading of Susquehanna country is not as dark as Merrell's. By taking a closer look at who was living at the confluence and what activities constituted its nature of place, then, we see a different picture emerging, one in which the Moravian missionaries were able to draw on their significant past experience to navigate this new world. In her monograph on Andrew Montour's mother, Madame Isabelle Montour, Simone Vincens describes the confluence that greeted Isabelle, her husband, Carondowana, and their children as they moved to Ostonwakin as relatively "cosmopolitan." Madame Montour's village, situated on a fertile flood plain at the point where the Loyalsock Creek runs into the West Branch of the Susquehanna River (at the site of today's Montoursville), was a mere ten miles from a Delaware Wolf clan village; fifteen miles from Shikellamy's Oneida village (at today's Milton); twenty miles from a Shawnee village at the mouth of Chillisquaque Creek and the West Branch; and just twenty-five miles from the confluence. Up the North Branch were many Delaware villages, and it was just five days' travel to the fertile Wyoming Valley, home to numerous Seneca villages. Downstream of Shamokin at the confluence were more Delaware villages.[32] There were also numerous traders around the confluence (at Chenastry on the Taylor map; see figure 3.2), where James Le Tort kept his store. It is to this dynamic environment that the Moravian women came and successfully navigated

WOMEN, MIGRATION, AND MORAVIAN MISSION 111

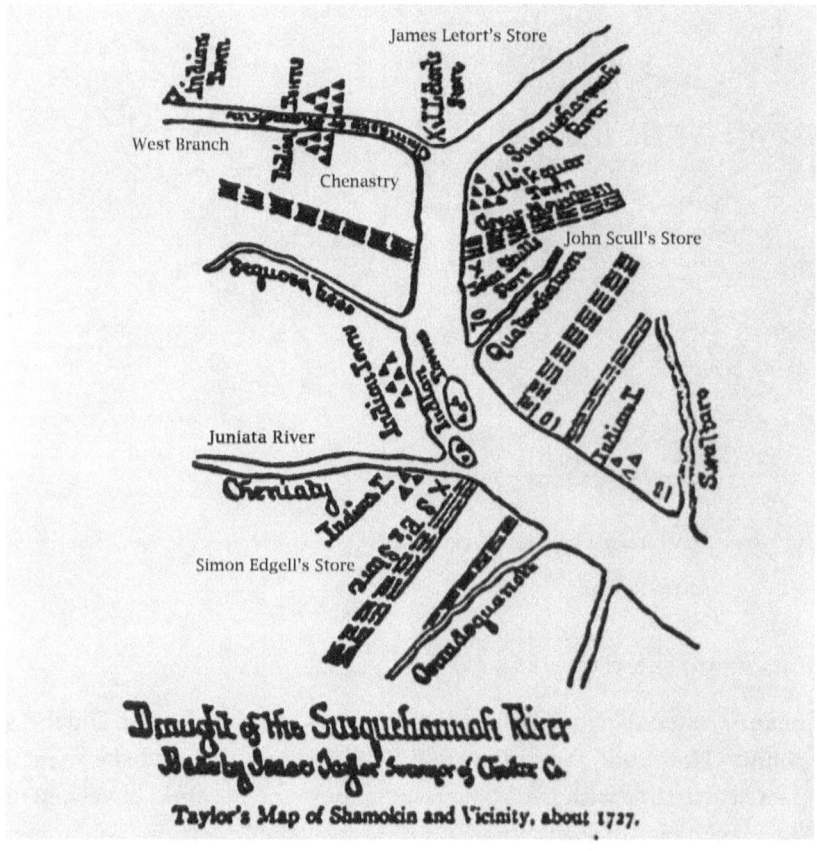

FIGURE 3.2 Taylor's map of traders at the confluence with annotations.

cultural, linguistic, and religious difference. These women's travels between Bethlehem and the missions in central Pennsylvania created a de facto cultural network that was temporal as well as geographical. The nature of this network makes any kind of linear biographical recounting of the women's experiences in the Moravian Church and with one another difficult, in that to tell one's story invokes the others. It is important, however, to delineate the lives of four of these women—Johanna Mack, Anna Schmidt, Martha Powell, and Anna Margarethe Jungmann—to demonstrate the complexity of their interconnectedness in the mission field over the course of the decade.

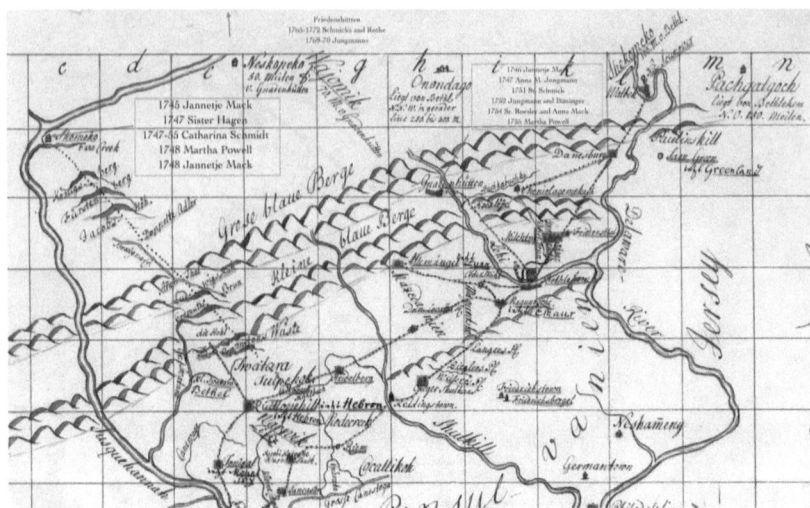

FIGURE 3.3 Detail of travel map (fig. 3.1) annotated with dates of Moravian women missionaries' service.

JOHANNA (JANNETJE) MACK (NÉE RAU/ROWE)

Johanna Mack, daughter of Johannes Rau, was born on a farm in Dutchess County, New York, two miles from Shekomeko. As a child she spent a great deal of time with her Mahican neighbors and became conversant in their language. In 1742, when Zinzendorf visited Shekomeko, he met Johanna there. She was invited to join the Moravians and returned to Bethlehem with Zinzendorf and his party. There she was married to Martin Mack and began her work in the missions. Over the next four years (in 1745, 1747, and 1748) she would focus her energies at the Shamokin mission. In 1746, she started the Gnadenhütten mission (present-day Lehighton), establishing it as a refuge for the Shekomeko Indians who had been expelled from New York with the Moravians following the New York ban on Moravians working among the Indians.[33]

In 1745, Johanna and Martin retraced Zinzendorf's journey from Bethlehem to Shamokin on foot, traveling by way of Tulpehocken, where she in all likelihood met Catharina Schmidt.[34] Accompanied by Andrew Montour, they arrived at the confluence on September 16, 1745. The Macks asked Andrew for lodging, but, there being no bark to build a hut, he took them to Shamokin Island. There they were greeted by

Andrew's mother, Madame Montour, who was now over eighty years old. Andrew left the Macks with his mother in order to visit his wife's family farther west into Ohio country. While he was away, Madame Montour told the Macks what she had heard about Bethlehem from her son and asked how the Delaware Indians were doing there. Johanna described the utopian community at Bethlehem, where the spiritual and material needs of all were met, irrespective of gender, race, or class. In response, Madame Montour bewailed the corrupt state of Shamokin, a place she described as consisting of nothing but drunkenness and dancing. Johanna attempted to explain why: "Anna explained to her how it is that the people still were forced to behave this way, because they did not believe in the Lord Jesus, and this was only the fruit of that."[35]

That first night in Shamokin served as proof of the old woman's words: "In the evening there was a great uproar because almost everyone who lived around here was drunk. Some even came into our hut who looked quite frightful and bellowed like cattle. The old mother gathered everything up and hid it in the bushes. We commended ourselves to the Lamb and to his eternal angels that they might keep watch over us and protect us."[36] The next day, the Macks crossed the river to visit with Shikellamy, but drunken Indians once again cut short their time.

This less than auspicious beginning of her stay in Shamokin was compounded by a bout of fever, but soon Johanna began to settle into a routine on the island, helping her neighbors and initiating pastoral visits with the Delaware women. As they traversed the river almost daily, the Susquehanna became an aquatic travelator, carrying Johanna back and forth across the confluence. Travel therefore proved difficult when the water was too high or the canoes were on the opposite shore. Shikellamy welcomed them into his house, offered them bread and meat, and even took Martin and Anna in to stay with him once Andrew Montour had to leave. Almost as confirmation of Zinzendorf's mission policy as outlined in his "Methodus der Wilden Bekehrung," especially as it pertained to allowing the native people to observe the missionaries' daily lives, Shikellamy told them, "I would not usually allow a trader or other white people to live with me, but because I know you a little and you have been living here a while I will allow it. My cabin is for me and for you and for your brethren; no one else."[37]

Johanna and Martin stayed at Shamokin for four months; it had been a time of famine at Shamokin, and Andrew Mack apologized to them for having had nothing but corn to eat for the previous seven weeks. They returned to Bethlehem before setting out in 1746 to found the Indian village of Gnadenhütten on the Lehigh River. There they worked with one of the most experienced women missionaries, Anna Margarethe Jungmann, as well as her husband, Johannes. Johanna and Margarethe had worked together before at Shekomeko, and that experience, plus their shared fluency in the Mahican and Delaware languages, resulted in great success working with the women at Gnadenhütten. As outlined above, after working at Gnadenhütten in 1746, Jannetke Mack returned to the Shamokin mission on the Susquehanna in 1747 and 1748. In 1749, she moved back to Gnadenhütten, where she died in childbirth in December of that year.

ANNA CATHARINA SCHMIDT (*NÉE RIEDT*)

Of all the Moravian woman missionaries, Catharina Schmidt lived longest among the Indians at Shamokin—on and off for seven years until the Penn's Creek Massacre in 1755. Born in 1727 in Heidelberg, Pennsylvania, Catharina was distinguished among the Moravians for her knowledge of the region and her facility with Indian languages.

Catharina grew up in the house of her cousin, Conrad Weiser. There, in 1742, she met Count Zinzendorf and his companion and later second wife, Anna Nitschmann, as they traveled to Shamokin. Like many other of the earliest woman missionaries, Catharina was personally invited by Zinzendorf to join the *Gemeine* in Bethlehem. In 1747, she was married to Anton Schmidt; soon thereafter, they were sent to Shamokin to set up the mission's smithy. Upon his appointment as blacksmith, Shikellamy gave Anton the Oneida name Rachwistonis to show that he was as much a part of the Iroquois project as he was of the Moravian one, and thus must answer to the Indians' needs as well as to those of the Moravians.

During her time at the mission, Catharina worked with Johanna Mack, regularly visiting the Delaware women on the island. She and Johanna were very successful at building the kind of relationships with the native women that Alison Duncan Hirsch describes as crucial to the peace project: when Catharina was leaving Shamokin for a brief visit to

Bethlehem, Shikellamy's daughter-in-law gave her a pair of moccasins to give to Johanna Mack, as "she loves her so much."[38] In 1748, Martin noted in the diary, "My [Annerl] wife and Sister Schmidt pounded corn for us to eat today on Shikellamy's pounding block. This pleased Shikellamy greatly and he was happy that our sisters could also pound corn."[39]

Although it is difficult to trace Catharina Schmidt's daily activities as closely as those of her husband (who was the crucially important blacksmith at Shamokin), Catharina's continued presence at the mission meant that native women could come to the house, be counseled on pastoral matters of children, marriage, and illness, and be offered refuge in times of trouble. When she was absent visiting Bethlehem, the women were usually turned away.[40]

Let us now move to two very different Moravian women missionaries, whose lives in the Old World were radically different from the colonial upbringings of Johanna Mack and Catharina Schmidt. Martha Powell and Margarethe Jungmann came to their life's work as Moravian missionaries from completely different European vantage points.

MARTHA POWELL (NÉE PRITCHETT) (1704–1774)

Martha Powell was born in the village of Norly near Oxford in England. According to her first-person memoir, her father was a member of the Church of England and "earnest in putting me to a Dancing School as also much delighted in seeing me Exercise and practise the same."[41] Martha's mother was raised a Quaker but converted to Anglicanism when she married Martha's father. Whatever more sobering Dissenter influence might have been conveyed to Martha was lost by the age of five when her mother died, and Martha was left in the care of her stepmother. Of the ensuing years Martha would write, "in my tender years I drank in the delights of the World as Dancing and Mirth with all the vigour yet often in Church I was dissolved in tears in hearing the Epistles and Gospels read and perticular such as mentioned the Passion and Suffering of our dear Saviour." Clearly delineating between her proclivity toward worldliness and her consciousness of its pitfalls, "at my 15th year I left them [her parents] hiering myself out from place to place in Oxford where on account of my fine aire in Dancing I was much esteemed by the rich gentry." Martha continued as a "professional dancer" for fifteen years; she wrote that at the age of thirty-one she "became at times trubilled and uneasy" and so discontinued her social lifestyle. This may have been in part a result of her regular attendance at meetings of the Methodist Society in Oxford. Though she was plagued by her vivid awareness of sinfulness (she described Satan as standing at the foot of her bed),[42] her reputation as a dancer resulted in pressure being brought on her to attend another ball.[43] Brother Gambold and Brother Kennchiss of the Society in Oxford helped her through this spiritual crisis.

Martha met Count Zinzendorf during his time in England. As with Catharina Schmidt, Zinzendorf personally invited her to go to Germany and join the *Gemeine*. Martha refused the offer, moving instead to London, where she became the spiritual leader of the young Moravian women living there. In 1742, at the age of thirty-eight, she married the merchant Joseph Powell; together they joined the first Moravian sea congregation to sail to America. It was not an easy voyage for Martha: "On this voyage I experienced much grief and sorrow principally occasioned thro' and by my sister in law whose mean origin I knew, we both being born and grown up in one Neighborhood but now on her coming from the Congregation in Herrendyk denyed that I knew her de[s]cent and thro her unconverted, wicked mind, earnestly endeavored every way practiable [sic] to blemish and hurt me."

Now that she was a member of the Moravian church and newly arrived in Philadelphia, the difficult sea journey and her sister-in-law's attempts to destroy her reputation seemed immaterial. At this time she most likely met Margarethe Bechtel (later Jungmann); Martha and Joseph Powell became the founding members of the first Moravian church in Philadelphia (her husband was a deed holder for the first Moravian church there), and soon became the first residents of Bethlehem. When Martha arrived in Bethlehem on August 1, 1742, she described the place as a "nether paradise," a utopian vision in the Pennsylvania forests. However, there was also trouble in paradise for Martha: apparently she did not get on with the other Sisters. Perhaps her outspoken ways were counter to expectations of Moravian married Sisters. Martha wrote, "I always found, when as it sometimes happened, that by some of my sisters I was accused for my over plainness." But her plainness and life experience served her well when, in 1748, she and Joseph traveled to Shamokin to take up their mission work.

The turbulence of the Susquehanna country that greeted Martha may have suited her better than the quiet introspection and order of Bethlehem. This world was dominated by the disorder and confusion occasioned by the rupture of worlds and the increase in interaction and trade along the river. In Shamokin from January to April 1748, Martha had much traffic with the non-Moravian women traders who made a living along the river, as well as the native women who lived around the confluence.[44] Almost as soon as Martha arrived at the mission, Shikellamy's daughter-in-law came to greet her. "With an other woman [I went] to visit Sister[;] she wept and tould the other woman it trubled her that she could not understand and speake with Sister Smith more."[45] Martha had not yet learned the Native American languages, and so it would seem that her role at the mission was to assist with negotiations with the female traders, including Mrs. Harris and Anna LeTort, who lived nearby, and the unidentified woman who lived across the river and whose main trade was in liquor.

The diary records the culture divide between missionaries and traders. Joseph Powell wrote, "Feb. 1 came two Traders down the river, Cal'd of Shikellame but came not to Us. We see that tho we behave friendly towards the Traders yet when one Happens to com in our house he's as a Fish out of water. Thank our Lord That they trouble us so little." The lives of the women traders were not easy, and so they called on the Powells for assistance. The diary entry for February 25, 1748, reveals that "Mrs Harris Sent Desiring we'ed immediately Both come over understanding by the Messenger that her Man William had beat Hir and wanted to rob hir of hir Skins. We refus'd to go telling him to speak About it to Shekellim. Shekellami and two of his Sons went. We Roth to hir thus: 'Dr. Mrs Harris. We are willing if Possible To Serve and help you, but in and with such a Matter we cannot meddle, then we are People of Peace and love living alone for Our Dear Lord in this World.'" Sisters Powell and Catharina Schmidt plowed the land around the mission to ready it for planting corn. They both negotiated with the female traders when the traders brought native men and women to the mission. The Sisters sought comfort from one another in the absence of the male missionaries when the Iroquois warriors returned from their wars with the Catawba and drank and caroused all night long. They provided bread for the Nanticoke who had moved upriver from the shores of the Chesapeake Bay, as the Nanticoke children had grown used to the food of the Europeans. The Sisters baked little loaves in the ashes of the fire as a treat on Christmas Day. Shikellamy acknowledged their importance to the mission by greeting both the Brothers and the Sisters in his addresses.

Martha and Joseph Powell did not stay at Shamokin long. After three months they returned to Bethlehem and began the first store there in 1752. After a brief spell in Gnadenhütten, the majority of Martha's mission work, from 1756–65, was performed in Jamaica. From Jamaica she wrote that "I loved and was loved by the poor dear Negro slaves for near 6 years when at last the heat of the country had so impared my dying boddy that had I stayed I should soon have been at home with my lord." Martha died in Bethlehem in 1774.

ANNA MARGARETHE JUNGMANN (NÉE BECHTEL, MARRIED NAME BÜTTNER) (1721–1793)

We already met Anna Margarethe Bechtel at the beginning of this essay. In many ways, her life best exemplifies the challenges and agency of Moravian women missionaries as they migrated to America and worked in the mission in North America. Born in Frankenthal in the Palatinate, the daughter of a Reformed father and a Huguenot mother, Margarethe emigrated to America in 1726 at the age of five. Her father bought a piece of land in Germantown, where he raised his children strictly according to pietistic principles, reading the Bible, Arndt's *Wahres Christentum*, hymnbooks, and prayer books, segregating his children from the influences of the outside world: "Every morning and evening we had our family worship when my father each time read us a chapter out of the Bible, and then fell on his knees and prayed aloud, often for a full hour, which several times made him faint."[46] This paternal piety had a strong formative effect on Margarethe, to the extent that she made herself ill. Perceiving her own lack of grace, she hungrily anticipated her time of conversion. As indicated earlier, in 1741 Count Nikolaus von Zinzendorf arrived in Philadelphia, and the twenty-one-year-old urged her father to accept the count's invitation to meet him. Reluctant at first, her father followed her encouragement, rode to see him, and then returned with Zinzendorf the next day. Margarethe was overjoyed and soon became fast friends with Anna Nitschmann and the count's daughter, Benigna von Zinzendorf. Margarethe, feeling abandoned back in Germantown, felt a strong desire to join the *Gemeine* in Bethlehem, and soon, after a few personal visits by Zinzendorf to her father, she was allowed to do so. Within a couple of months of becoming a member, Margarethe married a missionary, Brother Gottlob Büttner, and in 1742 they were sent to the Indian village of Shekomeko in upstate New York, near today's city of Poughkeepsie. In her memoir, composed much later in life, Margarethe wrote of her beginnings in the mission field:

> We set off and soon arrived. You can imagine how I felt. I did not yet myself really know what I wanted. I did not yet know the Saviour and the Congregation well enough to value them fully and was now to be a blessing to other souls! Not only that, but in my parents' house I had had everything I had wanted. Now I found myself placed in a situation of the utmost poverty. Many a day we hardly knew where we should find something to eat. And this and some other circumstances made me very unsettled. But I learned the language of the Indians very quickly and soon got a love for them and was loved by them in return; and this cheered me up again and made my course a great deal easier."[47]

Anna Margarethe Büttner immediately embarked on her work with the married women and children. From the Shekomeko mission diary we can see her conducting services for the women, calling on them in their homes, preaching to them to find a way into their hearts, and blessing women and children after their baptism.[48] Within a year she held her first address in Mohican and was soon loved by the Mohican women.[49] Rachel Wheeler has given a brief but vivid account of Margaretha Büttner's and Jannetje Mack's joint activities at the mission in her monograph study of the Mohican Indians' Christian villages.[50] Pointing to the "degree of sisterhood" between the women, Wheeler traces the way in which Moravian gendered structures of pastoral care afforded the Mohican women in the Christian village positions of agency that mirrored the Moravian women's actions. Mohican women were attracted to the religious and pastoral power granted them by being able to work as nurses and teachers to the Mohican children. And perhaps it was witnessing this mimetic desire among the native women that caused Zinzendorf to write about the mission theology of the Moravians the way he did in 1743.

Nearly three years after entering marriage and the mission field, Margarethe Büttner also became pregnant. But this was not a time of rejoicing for her. She describes the almost insurmountable pain of losing her husband, Brother Gottlob Büttner, to consumption when she was six months pregnant. Now widowed in the mission field, she had to make her way back to Bethlehem, accompanied by the Macks and their child, along with Sister Post and her child. On this trip, the Moravians were attacked by opponents, but she arrived safely in Bethlehem to deliver her son. Her pains were multiplied, as he only lived for three weeks. She wrote in her memoir, "That was yet another new trial. The Saviour's ways were still almost impenetrable to me, and I hardly knew what I should think about what had happened."[51]

Having returned to Bethlehem, after enduring the hostility of a suspicious mob in Esopus on the return journey and in line with Moravian practice with young widows, Margarethe married Johannes Jungmann a mere six months after her first husband's death.[52] Their first calling was to the Children's School in Falckner's Swamp and then, in 1746, to serve at the new mission village that had been started at Gnadenhütten, Pennsylvania, by her old coworkers, Martin and Jannetje Mack. Margarethe Jungmann worked among the native converts from the Shekomeko mission and also the Lenni Lenape from the area around the Blue Mountains along the Lehigh River for six years.

At Gnadenhütten, a three-day journey along the Nescopeck Path and then down the North Branch of the Susquehanna to Shamokin, there were many opportunities for exchange, visits, and comfort for Sisters Jungmann, Mack, Schmidt, and Powell. Margarethe continued the ministries to women and children that she had conducted at Shekomecko, this time also learning Delaware in addition to her skills in Mohican. According to the Gnadenhütten mission diary, by 1752 Margarethe was able to converse fluently in both languages (quite a linguistic feat, as they are from completely different language groups) and even began translating messages from the communicants to Zinzendorf.[53] Margarethe returned to Bethlehem twice during these years to deliver her daughter and son, and then in 1753 stayed there for a year before being dispatched again with her husband to Pachgatgoch in upstate New York. Praised for her skills, both linguistic and pastoral, she worked at that mission until 1757 and then returned to Bethlehem until 1769. After nine years making soap, her missionary skills were once again put to good use when she was sent up the Susquehanna to Wyalusing (Friedenshütten) and then Sheshequin, which lies a little farther north, until in 1772 she moved with Brothers Ettwein and Zeisberger to the Ohio country. In 1785, at the age of sixty-four, Margarethe returned to Bethlehem for the last eight years of her life. At her funeral, her remarkable accomplishments in the mission field were remembered, not least in the verses that were composed in her honor. Foregrounding her work among the Native Americans, the congregation imagined her joy at seeing the hosts of Mohicans, Wampanoag, Delaware, and Shawnee who would meet her in heaven. These converted native women from the missions she had worked with throughout her life would join her in the side wound of the Savior, the resting place she had told them about all her working life.[54]

CONCLUSION

Amy Schutt has argued, "Indian women relied in their relationships with Euro-American missionary women as well as with other Indian women to cope with drastic changes in their lives."[55] This chapter has attempted to reveal the perspective of the missionary women in this process. Embedded within the Moravian mission diaries we find the perspectives of the women missionaries, and evidence of native, *métis*, and Euro-American women's involvement in trade, care, and mission on an intimate level. Despite the dearth of official records of women's activities, speech, and agency, from these sources we are able to delineate women's experience as moving beyond the traditional notion of them as refugees for financial, religious, or ethnic reasons or as silent companions of fathers, husbands, masters, or maybe brothers. In the Moravian Church of the eighteenth century, the reasons why women moved across continents and oceans, through forests, and along rivers were not necessarily from any external necessity but from an internally generated, spiritual need—as an expression of a concept of God's will in their lives.

But representing these complex networks is difficult, not least because within the traditional historiography of this period, both native and Euro women's lives were simply elided. As has been pointed out here, more recently the focus has turned to native women in terms of their agency and mobility. However, what I hope this chapter has begun to show is how

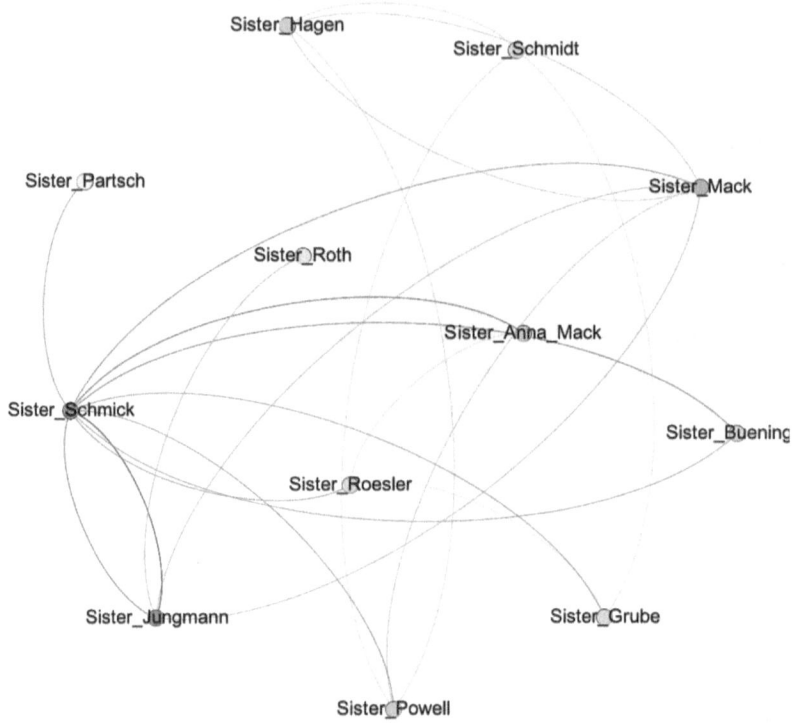

FIGURE 3.4 Visualization of strength of connections between Moravian women missionaries discussed in this chapter who were doing work at the Moravian missions mapped in figs. 3.1 and 3.3 in the mid-Atlantic states, 1747–75.

a group of women who were active as missionaries in the Moravian mission field of the eighteenth century brought with them their expertise from either Europe or the early settlements in New York State and Pennsylvania to effect a translation of culture and knowledge on the Susquehanna River.

The source materials for this chapter are predominantly unpublished or, if published, reside in eighteenth-century Fraktur imprints. Seemingly straightforward questions, such as birth dates and places, require lengthy investigations of manuscript sources or typed-up lists of information taken from the *Geburts- und Taufregister* of the Bethlehem community (also unpublished) or other missions. In this chapter, I have also wanted to map the way in which these women lived and worked (in German I would use the verb *agieren*) in the mid-Atlantic. I have tried to show how their lived lives became an integral part of the warp and weft of the environment of the Pennsylvania backcountry. But to do that I had to also delve into why they were here, what brought them to this place at this time. How did they translate the skills, experiences, concepts of self that had been learned in the Pfalz, Germany, or a village near Oxford, England, or a farm close by the Mohican villages in upstate New York to the banks of the Susquehanna or the Lehigh River? In an attempt to describe these complex movements, I have provided some annotated historical maps to accompany this chapter. However, these geospatial mappings do not represent visually the strength of relationships between the four women discussed in this chapter. A network analysis tool, however, renders visible what has been invisible to date, namely, the powerful network of women's lives in the history of this place.

Notes

1. Walter H. Wagner, *The Zinzendorf-Muhlenberg Encounter: A Controversy in Search of Understanding* (Nazareth, Pa.: Moravian Historical Society, 2002).

2. See Anna Margarethe Jungmann's (*née* Bechtel's) memoir in *Moravian Women's Memoirs: Their Related Lives*, ed. and trans. Katherine Faull (Syracuse: Syracuse University Press, 1997), 48–57.

3. Jane Merritt, "The Gender Frontier Revisited: Native American Women in the Age of Revolution," in *Ethnographies and Exchanges: Native Americans, Moravians, and Catholics in Early North America*, ed. A. G. Roeber (University Park: Max Kade German-American Research Institute Series and Penn State University Press, 2008), 165–74; Amy Schutt, "Female Relationships and Intercultural Bonds in Moravian Indian Missions," in *Friends and Enemies in Penn's Woods: Indians, Colonists, and the Racial Construction of Pennsylvania*, ed. William Pencak and Daniel Richter (University Park: Penn State University Press, 2004), 87–103; Gunlög Fur, *A Nation of Women: Gender and Colonial Encounters Among the Delaware Indians* (Philadelphia: University of Pennsylvania Press, 2009);

Rachel Wheeler, *To Live upon Hope: Mohicans and Missionaries in the Eighteenth-Century Northeast* (Ithaca, N.Y.: Cornell University Press, 2008); Alison Duncan Hirsch, "Indian, Métis, and Euro-American Women on Multiple Frontiers," in Pencak and Richter, *Friends and Enemies in Penn's Woods*, 63–86.

4. Merritt, "Gender Frontier," 167.

5. See James Merrell, *Into the American Woods: Negotiations on the Pennsylvania Frontier* (New York: W. W. Norton, 2000).

6. See also James Merrell, "The Other 'Susquehannah Traders': Women and Exchange on the Pennsylvania Frontier," in *Cultures and Identities in Colonial British America*, ed. Robert Olwell and Alan Tully (Baltimore: John Hopkins University Press, 2006), 197–219. In this chapter, Merrell explores much of the same geographical territory that is explored in this chapter. However, his focus is not on the connection between Moravian mission policy and social structure as conditions for women's agency on the frontier.

7. On extended family networks among Native women, see Schutt, "Female Relationships," and Wheeler, "To Live upon Hope."

8. See Merritt, "Gender Frontier."

9. Ibid., 167. See Beverly Smaby, "'No One Should Lust for Power . . . Women Least of All': Dismantling Female Leadership Among the Eighteenth-Century Moravians," in *Pious Pursuits: German Moravians in the Atlantic World*, ed. Michele Gillespie and Robert Beachy (New York: Berghahn Books, 2007) (Oxford: Berghahn, 2007), 159–75.

10. See Kevin Kenny, *Peaceable Kingdom Lost: The Paxton Boys and the Destruction of William Penn's Holy Experiment* (Oxford: Oxford University Press, 2011); and Katherine Faull, "The Nain Indian House," http://storiesofthesusquehanna.blogs.bucknell.edu/2014/01/24/the-nain-indian-house/.

11. Daniel Falckner, *Falckner's Curieuse Nachricht von Pennsylvania: The Book That Stimulated the Great Emigration to Pennsylvania in the Early Years of the XVIII Century*, ed. and trans. Julius F. Sachse (Philadelphia: printed for the author, 1905; repr., University Park: Penn State University Press, 2011), 132–33.

12. Falckner, *Falckner's Curieuse Nachricht*.

13. "Einen fröhlichen und munteren Geist zu zeigen und im geringsten nicht äußerlich über die Heiden zu herrschen, sondern mit Geisteskraft sich in Respekt bei ihnen zu setzen, dem äußern nach aber sich so viel als möglich unter sie zu demütigen." As quoted in [Nikolaus Ludwig von Zinzendorf,] *Texte zur Mission*, ed. Helmut Bintz (Hamburg: Friedrich Wittig Verlag, 1979), 37 (my translation).

14. For an extended examination of the mission to Tranquebar, see A. G. Roeber, *Hopes for Better Spouses: Protestant Marriage and Church Renewal in Early Modern Europe, India, and North America* (Grand Rapids, Mich.: William B. Eerdman's, 2013), especially chaps. 4 and 5.

15. The remarkable nature of this speech (its language and its occasion) was recognized during Zinzendorf's time, as the text can be found in *Büdingische Sammlung Einiger In die Kirchen-Historie Einschlagender Sonderlich neuerer Schrifften . . . : Nebst darzu gehörigen Registern* / [Nikolaus Ludwig von Zinzendorf], accessed February 16, 2014, http://digital.bibliothek.uni-halle.de/hd/content/pageview/628778/. It is highly likely that the speech was written for him by the missionaries on Saint Thomas, Friedrich Martin, Mattheus Freundlich, or Timothy Fiedler. For an analysis of Zinzendorf's Creole and a translation, see Cefas van Rossem and Hein van der Voort, *Die Creol taal: 250 Years of Negerhollands Texts*, accessed March 23, 2014, www.dbnl.org/tekst/ross026creo01_01/ross026creo01_01_0012.php. Much has been written in the last decade on the Moravian mission in the Caribbean. See especially Jon Sensbach, *Rebecca's Revival: Creating Black Christianity in the Atlantic World* (Cambridge, Mass.: Harvard University Press, 2011). Oldendorp's voluminous writings on the mission in the Caribbean are now also available in German. See Christian Georg Andreas Oldendorp, *Historie der Caribischen Inseln Sanct Thomas, Sanct Crux und Sanct Jan, insbesondere der dasigen Neger und der Mission der evangelischen Brüder unter denselben Erster und zweiter Teil: Kommentierte Ausgabe des vollständigen Manuskriptes aus dem Archiv der Evangelischen Brüder-Unität Herrnhut*, 2 vols. to date (Berlin: Verlag für Wissenschaft und Bildung, 2000–).

16. "Een Heyden no mo hab ander reden voor bekeer hem, als dat em geloov, dat Jesus Gods Zoon em a Herr voor betaal voor, de mens Zonde, en dat hem nu waar leevt voor mag de mens lev met hem: Een Heyden no kan du van natuur zoo veel goed, als wel meenig mens, die bin van kleens af geleerd voor du goed, en no kryg permissive vo du quaed. Want een Heyden bin vom klyn af gewent vor du bosheit, en na leer beter. Maar als een Heyden kryg die Genade van de Heer Jesus, dat zyn Zonde word vergeven, en em word gewaschen met Jesus Bloed; soo em kryg die kracht om al quaed te laten, en goed te doen, en em haat de zoned so veel, als em a had live tevooren. Dan em bin een van Christus sin Volk, zoo als yoe Bas Martinus zal leer yoe verder." Transcribed by Van Rossem and Van der Voort, *Die Creol taal*.

17. For a more detailed examination of the "Speakings" in the mission field, see Katherine Faull, "Speaking and Truth-Telling: Parrhesia in the Eighteenth-Century Moravian Church," in *Self, Community, World*, ed. Heikki Lempa and Paul Peucker (Bethlehem, Pa.: Lehigh University Press, 2010), 147–67. For a more general overview of Moravian theology, see Craig D. Atwood, *Community of the Cross:*

Moravian Piety in Colonial Bethlehem (University Park: Penn State University Press, 2004).

18. For a more detailed investigation of Zinzendorf's anthropology, see Katherine Faull, "Faith and Imagination: Nikolaus Ludwig von Zinzendorf's Anti-Enlightenment Philosophy of Self," in *Anthropology and the German Enlightenment: Perspectives on Humanity* (Lewisburg, Pa.: Bucknell University Press, 1995), 3–56.

19. According to the minutes of the synod at Hirschberg in 1743, Zinzendorf argues for a slow and gradual method of conversion. He writes, "Besser ist's, wenn fünf, sechs Jahr nichts aus der Heiden Bekehrung wir, und es schneidet hernach auf einmal durch" (It's better if nothing comes of the conversion of the heathen for five or six years and then suddenly there's a breakthrough). Zinzendorf, *Texte zur Mission*, 85.

20. "Methodus der Wilden Bekehrung," in ibid., 86.

21. For Martha's brief memoir, see Faull, *Moravian Women's Memoirs*, 30–32.

22. For an account of the Nain Indians, see the transcription of my lecture on "The Nain Indian House" on the Stories of the Susquehanna website, http://storiesofthesusquehanna.blogs.bucknell.edu/2014/01/24/the-nain-indian-house/.

23. Jane T. Merritt, "Dreaming of the Saviour's Blood: Moravians and the Indian Great Awakening in Pennsylvania," *William and Mary Quarterly*, 3rd ser., 54, no. 4 (1997): 737.

24. Ibid.

25. Hirsch, "Indian, *Métis*, and Euro-American Women," 65.

26. Ibid.

27. Merrell, *Into the American Woods*.

28. As Wheeler argues, speaking of the revisionist histories of the 1960s and '70s, "When native Christianity was considered, it was usually—with some important exceptions—depicted as a disingenuous mechanism of covert resistance or a course of last resort. Anthropologists and textual critics working in colonial discourse and postcolonial studies have also tended to interpret native Christianity as either a case of colonization of consciousness or masked resistance." Wheeler, *To Live upon Hope*, 10.

29. James H. Merrell, "'The Cast of His Countenance': Reading Andrew Montour," in *Through a Glass Darkly: Reflections on Personal Identity in Early America*, ed. Ronald Hoffman, Mechal Sobel, and Fredrika J. Teute (Chapel Hill: University of North Carolina Press, 1999), 20.

30. Quoted in ibid., 19.

31. James H. Merrell, "Shamokin, the Very Seat of the Prince of Darkness: Unsettling the Early American Frontier," in *Contact Points: American Frontiers from the Mohawk Valley to the Mississippi, 1750–1830*, ed. Andrew R. L. Cayton and Fredrika J. Teute (Chapel Hill: University of North Carolina Press, 1998), 16–59.

32. Simone Vincens, *Madame Montour and the Fur Trade (1667–1772)*, trans. and ed. Ruth Bernstein (Bloomington, Ind.: Xlibris, 2011), 199.

33. For an account of the troubles faced by the Moravians and the converts, see Philip Smith, *General History of Duchess County, 1609–1876* (Pawling, N.Y.: the author, 1877), 300–316. Smith's account includes a sketch of the Indian village.

34. See Rachel Wheeler, "Women and Christian Practice in a Mahican Village," in *Religion and American Culture: A Reader*, 2nd ed., ed. David G. Hackett (New York: Psychology Press, 2003), 144n62.

35. "Die Anna erzehlte ihr woher es käme, dass die Leute noch so thun müßten, weil sie nicht an den Herrn Jesum glaubten, und das wäre nur die Früchte davon." September 17, 1745, Shamokin diary, Moravian Archives, Bethlehem (hereafter MAB).

36. "Des Abends war überall ein großer Lärm, weil fast alles besoffen war, was hierum wohnte. Es kamen auch welche in unsre Hütte, die ziemlich fürchterlich aussahen und brülleten wie das Vieh. Die alte Mutter fasste alles zusammen und versteckte es im Busch. Wir befohlen uns dem Lamm und seinem leibigen Engelein das die uns bewachten und behüten wollten." October 17, 1745, Shamokin diary, MAB.

37. "Wenn ein Träder oder jemand ander von weisen Leuten wollte bey ihm wohnen dem wollte er's nicht erlauben. Aber uns thäte er's erlauben, weil er uns ein bischen kannte

und wir bey ihnen wohnen thäten.... Die Cabine wäre für ihn und für unsre Brüder und da sollte sonst niemand wohnen." November 3, 1745, Shamokin diary, MAB.

38. See Shamokin diary, 115.

39. "Meine Frau und Schwester Schmidt haben heute Welschkorn gestampfen in Shikellimis Stampf-Block vor uns zum essen. Es hat dem **Shikellimi** recht wohl gefallen, und hat sich gefreut, dass unsere Schwestern auch Welschkorn stampfen können." November 9, 1747, Shamokin diary, MAB.

40. The absence of a woman missionary at Shamokin could cause difficult situations. For example, on February 5, 1750, just over a year after Shikellamy's death, his son John came to the mission to talk to David Zeisberger about the conduct of his wife. "Den 5ten John besuchte uns, discurierte viel mit David.... David fragte ihn auch ob seine Frau nichts zu ihm gesagt hätte von uns? Er sagte, Ja, wir hätten zu ihr gesagt, sie sollte zu den Delawares gehen, es thäte sich nicht schicken, dass sie hier logierte, weil wir laute Mannsleute hier wären, u. des Schmidts seine Frau nicht da wäre. David sagte ihm wir hätten sie eine Nacht lassen hier schlafen, weil sie spät wäre hier gekommen u. sie auch ihre Füße erfroren hätte gehabt, dass sie sich nicht hätte können in seinem Hause Feuer machen. Er war wohl zufrieden damit u. sehr aufgeräumt" (On the 5th John visited us and discoursed at length with David.... David asked him also whether his wife had not said anything to him of us? He said, yes, we had told her she should go to the Delaware, it was not seemly that she lodge here with us because we are all men and the smith's wife was not here. David told him that we allowed her to spend one night here because she had come late and because her feet were almost frozen because she could not make fire in his house. He seemed quite satisfied with this and was very relieved). February 5, 1750, Shamokin diary, MAB.

41. All quotations are taken from her unpublished memoir (MemBeth 225, MAB).

42. "Once about the year [17]39 I had the most hellish Night wherein my eyes were never clos'd, Satan to all my Apprehension stood by my Bed continually suggesting that as I had serv'd him I was his property and belonged of Right to him." MemBeth 225, MAB.

43. Martha writes, "the Ball could not be properly carried on without me, on which I consented. But just in the beginning of this my last dance I was struck with such anguish, pain, and horrour that I with haste got out earnestly beseeching the Lord to bare and have mercy on me, in so great a sin against better knowledge—this was the heaviest night I as yet ever felt." MemBeth 225, MAB.

44. For a fuller, although somewhat dated, account of the traders in the area around Shamokin, see John H. Carter, "The Shamokin Indian Traders," *Proceedings of the Northumberland County Historical Society* 15 (1946): 5–24; repr., *The Shamokin Indian Traders* (Shamokin, Pa.: Northumberland County Historical Society, 1995). For a more recent study of Madame Montour and her extended family, see Vincens, *Madame Montour*, which originally appeared in French: *Madame Montour et son temps* (Montreal: Québec/Amérique, 1979). For the relationship between the Letorts and the Montours, see especially 199–200.

45. Shamokin diary, 86, MAB.

46. "Wir hatten alle Morgen u. Abende unsre Haus Andacht, da uns mein Vater jedesmal erst ein Capitel aus der Biebel vorlas, u. denn auf die Knie fiel u. da oftmals eine ganze Stunde laut betete, daß er mehrmalen drüber in Ohnmacht fiel." Faull, *Moravian Women's Memoirs*, 49.

47. "Gar manchen Tag wußten wir kaum, wo wir etwas zu essen finden würden, diese und gar manche andre Umstände machten, daß es bey mir sehr durcheinander ging. Weil ich aber die Sprache der Indianer hurtig lernte, auch gleich die Indianer sehr lieb kriegte, und wiederum von ihnen geliebt wurde, so hat mich das wieder aufgemuntert und mir meinen Gang sehr erleichtert.

"Ein paar Tage drauf wurde ausgemacht, daß wir unter die Indianer nach Schekomeko gehen sollten. Wir traten unsre Reise an und kamen auch bald daselbst an. Nun kann man sich aber doch vorstellen, wie mir zu muthe war (ich wußte selbst noch nicht recht, was ich wollte) den Heiland und die Gemeinde wußte ich noch nicht genugsam zu schäzen, und sollte andern Seelen zum Segen seyn, dazu kam noch dieses; in meiner Eltern Hause hatte ich alles, was ich begehrte, und nun sahe ich mich in die bitterste Armut versetzt." Ibid., 51.

48. See Shekomecko diary, October 1, 1742; October 4, 1742; October 24, 1742; box 111, Indian Records, MAB.

49. Shekomecko diary, February 18, 1743; November 13, 1743; box 111, Indian Records, MAB.

50. Wheeler, *To Live upon Hope*, 167–71.

51. Faull, *Moravian Women's Memoirs*, 52.

Als ich nun noch nicht ganz 3 Jahre hier gewesen, hatte ich den großen, mir fast unüberwindlich scheinenden Schmerz, daß mein lieber Mann, der schon lange an der Auszehrung krank gewesen, heimging, den 23ᵗ Februar 1745, da ich im sechsten Monat schwanger war. Im März reiste ich dann mit Geschwister Martin Macks u. ihrem Kind, der Schwester Postin und ihrem Kind zu unserem großen Schmerz, daß wir nun die liebe Indianer Gemeine verlassen mußten, von Schekomeko nach Bethlehem ab. Wir hatten unterwegs von feindlichen Leuten viel auszustehen, wie in der Indianer Historie etwas davon zu finden ist. Im Juni wurde ich glücklich von einem Söhnlein entbunden, aber 3 Wochen nachher nahm es der liebe Heiland schon wieder zu sich. Das war nun wieder eine neue Probe für mich. Ich konnte mich damals fast nicht in die Wege des lieben Heilands finden, und wußte kaum, was ich dazu denken sollte.

52. For a detailed examination of the pastoral care of widows, see Katherine Faull, "'You Are the Savior's Widow'": Religion, Sexuality, and Bereavement in the Eighteenth-Century Moravian Church," *Journal of Moravian History* 8 (Spring 2010): 89–115.

53. See Gnadenhütten diary, box 117, folders 1–3, MAB.

54. Margarethe Jungmann memoir, MAB. The transcription of the memoir can also be accessed at http://katiefaull.com/moravian-materials/umgang-mit-dem-heiland-leben slaufe-bethlehemer-schwestern/margarethe -jungmann-1721-1793/.

Wenn sie des Herren Wunden-Maal geküßt für ihre Gnaden-Wahl und sieht in obern Schaaren die Mahikander, Wampanosund Delawares u. Schawano die selig heimgefahren / o wie, wird sie, sich da freuen / mit den Reyhen der Erlößten / die sich liessen lehren und trösten. /// (In Chekameka und am Kent/dem Ort sonst Pachgatgoch genennt/an Beaver Creek, Muskingum, / an der Mahony, überall / wo sie in diesem Thränen Thal / mit ihrem Manne zog 'rum / O Ja, da, da, wird sie sehen / herrlich stehen, gantze Scharren / die fürs lamm geschlachtet waren.) / Ein jeder Indianer Stamm/wird schöne singen: {Gottes} L̶a̶m̶ ̶o̶ lam! / du bist für uns gestorben / und hast uns dadurch unseren Theil / an deinem unschätzbaren Heil / mit deinem Blut erworben / Amen! Deinem Namen / sey die Ehre, daß wir hörten deine Lehre! / Da stimet sie gewiß mit ein / und wird ganz hingenomen seyn / beym Singen solcher Lieder: / Sie siehet Gott in Seinem Sohn / und sinkt vor Seinem Herrnthron/beschämt voll Freude nieder /// Sonne, Wonne, Jubeltöne, alles Schöne / wird sie haben u. sich stets am Heiland laben.

55. Amy Schutt, "Female Relationships and Intercultural Bonds in Moravian Indian Missions," in Pencak and Richter, *Friends and Enemies in Penn's Woods*, 89.

PART 2

The Languages of Education and Established Religions

CHAPTER 4

Benjamin Franklin, the Philadelphia Academy, Halle, and Göttingen

JÜRGEN OVERHOFF

Academic histories of American higher education now generally agree that the first beginnings of the University of Pennsylvania are to be found in 1749.[1] On November 13, 1749, the trustees of the newly envisioned "Publick Academy in the City of Philadelphia" convened for the first time and elected the prominent printer, politician, and scientist Benjamin Franklin as their president. On the same day, Franklin drew up a set of "Constitutions" for this unprecedented institution of higher learning in Pennsylvania.[2] This Philadelphia Academy, styled a College in 1755 and the University of the State of Pennsylvania in 1779, became known in 1791 under its present name of the University of Pennsylvania. Because the Academy's trustees agreed on February 2, 1750, to take over responsibility for their city's "Charity School"[3]—projected in 1740 but never realized—later generations would refer to that year as the earliest founding date of the university.

That the Philadelphia Academy was thus organized from the outset by a large board of trustees, a group of twenty-four men with distinct ideas about education and from diverse religious backgrounds, is a striking feature of the early history of the institution, suggesting that it is misleading to depict the astonishingly talented Franklin—"a harmonious human multitude,"[4] as one of his biographers once famously called him—as the single (and almost mythical) founder of that institution. Clearly, Franklin was the Academy's *spiritus rector*—after all, he acted as president of its board of trustees. Yet, without the idealistic and financial support of the other trustees (and without a large amount of money pledged to the good cause by many more citizens of Philadelphia), the Academy would not have come into being. Therefore, it seems fair to say that the Philadelphia Academy was founded by a large body of public-spirited American gentlemen, even if, admittedly, Franklin was one of the most proactive citizens of Pennsylvania.[5]

For Walter Isaacson, who recently described the founding process of the Philadelphia Academy in his best-selling biography of Benjamin Franklin, the University of Pennsylvania is thus the result of an honorable public endeavor of which all Americans can be proud. Fittingly, when the original trustees of the Academy designed a new curriculum, it included classes on moral philosophy for the future citizens of a thriving American civil society. It was the trustees' explicit wish that the students of the Philadelphia Academy learn how to apply their knowledge of ethics to the political realities of their community. In academic debates, students were thus asked to field a wide range of questions about American law, politics, and economics—and they were strongly encouraged to study English, German, French, and Spanish, those being the most important of the modern European languages spoken on the North American continent. Multilingual merchants and tradesmen, the trustees held, would be more successful in their business. The classical languages, Latin and Greek, were not cherished in the same way. Students could simply ignore them. In this respect, the Academy's curriculum differed markedly from that of other colonial colleges.[6] Accordingly, Isaacson depicts the Philadelphia Academy—not Harvard or Yale—as the product of typical American virtues: community spirit and citizenship.[7]

FRANKLIN ON THE LOOKOUT FOR EUROPEAN MODEL UNIVERSITIES

It is tempting to see the Philadelphia Academy as a quintessential American institution, one designed exclusively for the needs of a flourishing American colony by a group of public-spirited Americans and easily able to operate without help or inspiration from Europe and its centuries-old university system. Yet the trustees were receptive to good educational ideas and methods from the academies and universities of Europe; they were indeed open to both British and continental models. What other models would they have had, after all? The president of the Philadelphia Academy's board of trustees, especially, was constantly looking for inspiration from abroad. On his many stays in France, Germany, England, Scotland, and the Netherlands, Franklin visited a number of European universities that he thought could serve as models for the Philadelphia Academy in more than just one aspect.

Thus, when he toured England and Scotland in 1758 and 1759, he took a close look at the academic proceedings and courses of study at the leading universities of Britain. First, in the spring of 1758, he traveled to Cambridge, where he met the physician and fellow of the Royal Society John Hadley, with whom he conducted several scientific experiments concerning the effects of extreme heat and cold.[8] But Franklin also talked to a number of other Cambridge dons, as he reported in a letter to his wife, Deborah: "[We] were present at all the ceremonies, dined every day in their halls, and my vanity was not a little gratified by the particular regard shown me by the chancellor and vice chancellor of the university, and the heads of colleges."[9]

He was flattered the more several months later when he visited the University of St. Andrews. At this venerable Scottish academy, founded in in 1413, he was awarded an honorary doctorate, allowing him to refer to himself thereafter as Dr. Franklin. He also visited the University of Edinburgh, a seat of learning since 1583 with an excellent reputation in the field of medical research. When medical courses were introduced in Philadelphia in 1765, the insights won during Franklin's stay at Edinburgh surely helped to shape the curriculum of the Philadelphia medical school. As Edward Potts Cheyney points out in his *History of the University of Pennsylvania*, "it was in Edinburgh that the foundation was laid for what proved to be the beginning of medical teaching at Philadelphia."[10] And the addition of the medical courses to the Philosophical School was not only important in itself, but justified calling the Philadelphia Academy afterwards a university.

One year after the founding of the medical school in Philadelphia, Franklin looked again for innovative aspects of academic life in Europe, this time in Germany. In 1766, during an extended summer vacation spent traveling through the northern and western parts of the German Empire,[11] he visited the bustling imperial cities of Frankfurt and Cologne, and he enjoyed fresh "Air and Exercise"[12] in the countryside near Hanover at the spa of Pyrmont in the principality of Waldeck, where he stayed for about a week. In Pyrmont, he certainly sought to recover from his exhausting duties as colonial agent in London, but the main reason for his trip to Germany was his wish to visit the University of Göttingen, one of the leading academies of the time, situated in the Electorate of Hanover, whose ruler was of course the British King George III.

As a letter from the Hanoverian minister Burchard Christian von Behr to Franklin indicates, the summer journey to Germany was planned months ahead.[13] Above all, as Franklin pointed out in a letter to a German friend, he wanted to talk to certain "professors at Göttingen."[14] Thus, only a few days after his arrival in the principality of Waldeck, Franklin left Pyrmont for Hanover, where Baron Gerlach Adolph von Münchhausen, King George's prime minister in his German homeland of Hanover, provided Franklin with a letter of recommendation for three professors in particular: Johann Stephan Pütter, historian and professor of German constitutional law; Johann David Michaelis, Lutheran professor of theology; and Gottfried Achenwall, professor of the history of the Roman-German Empire.[15]

When Franklin eventually arrived in Göttingen, where he stayed for almost two weeks until July 26, he first asked the librarian, writer, and scientist Rudolph Erich Raspe to guide him through Göttingen's university library. Raspe later rose to some prominence as the collector and publisher of the famous *Baron Munchhausen's Narrative of His Marvellous Travels and Campaigns in Russia*, tall tales about the life of Hieronymus Carl Friedrich von Münchhausen, a distant relative of the Hanoverian prime minister.[16] The university library came into existence in 1734, three years before the university itself was founded by Adolph Gerlach von Münchhausen in 1737.[17]

Because of its pioneering cataloguing systems and its large and regular financial income, fixed by a generous state budget, the university library of Göttingen was soon considered one of the leading research libraries in Europe. Franklin's visit to the library coincided with efforts by the trustees of the Philadelphia Academy to raise additional funds in

England so as to increase the collection of their own library beyond its modest origin: a donation of books from the Welsh surveyor and cartographer Lewis Evans in 1750.[18] A German student, Johann Matthäus Hassencamp, later head librarian at the University of Rinteln in the principality of Schaumburg, witnessed Franklin's tour through the university library and later recalled that the prominent visitor from America, the celebrated inventor of the lightning rod, had made a lasting impression on him. Contrary to the devout student's expectations, Franklin had not spoken and acted in an arrogant manner—obviously the way some German professors liked to behave—but had dealt with the young people in the library extremely affably.[19]

After his tour through the university library, Franklin made his long-awaited acquaintance with Pütter, Achenwall, and Michaelis, meeting with them repeatedly at the houses of Pütter and Michaelis for hour-long conversations in the afternoon and evening. Since Franklin could not speak German, the four men must have conversed in English, as confirmed by Achenwall's repeated introduction of English technical terms into the report he later wrote of their meeting. The report was first published in 1766 in a series of articles in the *Hannoverische Magazin* and again in 1769 as a small treatise bearing the title *Einige Anmerkungen über Nord-Amerika und über dasige Grosbrittanische Colonien: Aus mündlichen Nachrichten des Herrn D. Franklins* (Some observations on North America and her British colonies: from first-hand reports by Dr. Franklin).[20]

In the preface to his detailed report, Achenwall told his readers that the famous American had sought to learn as much as possible from the German professors about the organization of the University of Göttingen. This account was confirmed by Pütter, whose memories of Franklin's stay at his house form a fascinating part of his autobiography. Getting reliable firsthand knowledge of the structure of the courses taught at Göttingen was, as Pütter emphasized, Franklin's leading interest when he toured Germany. Pütter was so impressed by the American visitor's wish to learn about German academic history that he presented him with his history of the University of Göttingen, the *Göttingische Gelehrtengeschichte*, published in 1765.[21]

Achenwall also wrote about the German professors' intense interest in American institutions of higher learning, which they clearly articulated in conversation with Franklin. He told them that an academy had been founded in Philadelphia in 1749, that he himself had made the proposal and with great pains had brought it to pass. He also told them that the Philadelphia Academy had the right to create masters of philosophy, that in 1764 the medical faculty had been established, and that he hoped the academy would soon become a proper university endowed with the right to make doctors of medicine. Michaelis, the Lutheran university teacher, was stunned to hear from Franklin that the Philadelphia Academy had no professor of theology and that it would find it very difficult ever to establish one. The academy in Pennsylvania, as Franklin explained, was chartered by the assembly for the general good of the colony. As there were many religious faiths, all enjoying equal rights and none dominating, theology was excluded from the syllabus of the academy. Nevertheless, every pupil and every student remained free to be instructed in his own faith in the schools, churches, and synagogues of his own sect.[22]

FRANKLIN'S INTEREST IN THE PAEDAGOGIUM REGIUM IN HALLE

Franklin's trip to Germany in 1766; his conversations with Pütter, Achenwall, and Michaelis; and his own abiding interest in the departmental structure, organization, and management of the University of Göttingen have been recent topics of investigation.[23] Virtually unknown, however, is that at some point in the early 1750s, from the beginning of the process leading to the founding of the Philadelphia Academy, Franklin and the other trustees were already on the lookout for European models for a well-functioning academy. They showed particular interest in the development of the best universities and academies of Germany. The most adequate German institution of higher learning that came into their focus was the Pietist school in the Prussian university town of Halle, the Paedagogium Regium.

The Paedagogium Regium, founded at the end of the seventeenth century through the influence of the leading Pietist August Hermann Francke and by special privilege of the Brandenburg elector Friedrich III (who was soon to become Friedrich I, king of Prussia, in January of 1701), was an educational institution with a boarding school for boys of the upper class, especially of the nobility. It was an outstanding academy for the distinguished worldly and practical education for future Prussian officers and state employees. The subjects taught were French, German stylistics, history, geography, mathematics, physics, and philosophy. In another area, called recreation exercises, courses in botany, economics, mineralogy, and anatomy were offered. Students were also invited to visit artisans' workshops, and they practiced glass cutting. The ratio of students to teachers was quite favorable: eighty-two students were taught by thirty-six teachers.[24]

It was the flamboyant Methodist evangelist George Whitefield, one of the most widely recognized public preachers in colonial America, who first suggested that Franklin take a close look at the Halle Pietist school syllabus. As a student at Pembroke College, Oxford, Whitefield had been an associate of the evangelical-Pietist Holy Club, run by the Wesley brothers, John and Charles, where Whitefield was introduced to the work of Francke. After being ordained in 1736, he started to preach in London to large congregations, often in the open air, to tremendous success. John Wesley then asked this promising young preacher to act as a missionary in North America, in the new colony of Georgia,[25] where Whitefield was charged with laying the foundations, metaphorically and literally, for a home for orphans modeled on the prototype of Francke's orphanage at Halle.[26]

Whitefield had made Franklin's acquaintance in Philadelphia in the 1740s, at a time when the preacher repeatedly and very successfully collected money for the orphanage in Georgia. In his friendly exchange with Franklin, the preacher-entrepreneur Whitefield referred to the Paedagogium Regium in a letter of February 26, 1750. This letter was designed as a direct response to Franklin's little pamphlet *Proposals Relating to the Education of Youth in Pennsylvania*, which spelled out the educational goals of the Philadelphia Academy.[27] Franklin had composed and printed it in mid-October 1749, only a few weeks after he had first announced the need for an "ACADEMY or college in this province" in the influential and widely read *Pennsylvania Gazette*, which he had edited since founding it in 1729.[28] Copies of the *Proposals* were sent by its author to a large number of friends, pedagogues, scientists, and school experts whom he encouraged and invited to comment on his programmatic thoughts on education.

In his letter, Whitefield first excused himself for having been so slow to respond; then he congratulated Franklin on his formidable plan:

> Ever since I received your last kind letter, I have been endeavouring to redeem some time to answer it, but till now have not had opportunity. Indeed even now a multiplicity of business obliges me to be much more brief than otherwise I should. However, I cannot help informing you, that I am glad that the gentlemen of Philadelphia are exerting their efforts to erect an academy. I have often thought such an institution was wanted exceedingly; and if well-conducted, am persuaded it will be of public service. Your plan I have read over, and do not wonder at its meeting with general approbation. It is certainly well calculated to promote polite literature.[29]

But then Whitefield added a caveat; he complained that Franklin had not given Christian religion a proper place in the Academy's curriculum. "I think," he remarked, "there wants *aliquid Christi* in it."[30]

Indeed, Franklin and the other trustees had agreed to teach Christian religion not as a subject in its own right nor according to a denominational fashion, but rather as part of classes in history and morality. The study of history, Franklin held in his *Proposals*, would "afford frequent opportunities of showing the necessity of a *public religion*, from its usefulness to the public; the advantage of a religious character among private persons."[31] Lectures in morality, on the other hand, would demonstrate that "the glory and service of God" is "only the same thing in other words" as benevolent behavior toward other humans, since "*doing good to men* is the *only service of God* in our power."[32]

Franklin's redefinition of religious education as a mere subdiscipline of history and morality set his *Proposals* strictly apart from the regular course of studies offered in the other colleges of British North America. The training of clergymen was the explicit goal of such colleges as Harvard, Yale, William and Mary, and the College of New Jersey—which is why these colleges placed such a heavy emphasis on theology and on the study of the biblical languages, Hebrew and Greek. Students of the nondenominational Philadelphia Academy could do without proper theological training. Instead, they benefited from a sound knowledge of the modern languages. According to Franklin, the ability to master the German language—or, for that matter, to speak French or Spanish fluently—would do Philadelphia's students infinitely more good than belief in controversial and mysterious Christian dogmas like the Trinity. Therefore, it does not come as a surprise that Whitefield feared there could not be any good foundation of the instruction of the languages, arts, and sciences without a proper Christian religious education. He expressed his concerns in his letter to Franklin clearly, and it is well worth quoting them at length:

> It is true, you say, "The youth are to be taught some public religion, and the excellency of the Christian religion in particular:" but methinks this is mentioned too late, and too soon passed over. As we are all creatures of a day; as our whole life is but one small point between two eternities, it is reasonable to suppose, that the grand end of every Christian institution for forming tender minds, should be to convince them of their natural depravity, of the means of recovering out of it, and of the necessity of preparing for the enjoyment of the supreme Being in a future state. These are the grand points in which Christianity centers. Arts and sciences may be built on this, and serve to embellish and set off this superstructure, but without this, I think there cannot be any good foundation.[33]

Accordingly, Whitefield thought it worthwhile to send Franklin a little book about a well-ordered Christian school in Germany written in German. Whitefield wondered, "Whether the little Dutch book I have sent over, will be of any service in directing such a foundation, or how to build upon it, I cannot tell. Upon mentioning your desire [to found an academy] to the King's German chaplain, a worthy man of God, he sent it to me, and thought, if translated, it might be of service. Glad should I be of contributing, though it was but the least mite, in promoting so laudable an undertaking."[34] The well-respected Lutheran chaplain of the Hanoverian King George II, who sent "the little Dutch"[35] book over to his friend Whitefield, was the German Reverend Friedrich Michael Ziegenhagen. He was born in Pomerania in 1694, had earned a bachelor's degree at All Souls College Oxford, and, beginning in April 1714, continued his academic training as student of Lutheran theology in Halle, where he was strongly influenced by August Hermann Francke. In 1722, Ziegenhagen was appointed court preacher at St. James's Palace in London.[36] That the royal chaplain took a genuine interest in Franklin's ambitious plan for a new academy in Philadelphia does not come as a surprise: Ziegenhagen was deeply interested in all kinds of foreign missions.

In 1737, he had helped those unfortunate Lutherans from Salzburg, expelled from their homeland in southern Germany by the intolerant Roman Catholic Archbishop Leopold Anton von Firmian, to reach the distant American shores of Georgia, where they sought to live their Protestant faith unmolested and in peace in a settlement above the Savannah River referred to as New Ebenezer. There, the Salzburger emigrants were furnished with pastors from Halle. Ziegenhagen had also acted as sort of unofficial bishop to the Pennsylvania congregations, who had asked him to get them a qualified Lutheran minister. Through Gotthilf August Francke, the director of the Paedagogium Regium of Halle, Ziegenhagen secured the services of Heinrich Melchior Mühlenberg, who visited him in London before departing for America in 1741. Still in the British capital, Ziegenhagen prepared Mühlenberg for his future responsibilities in North America.[37]

To date, the enigmatic "little Dutch book" Ziegenhagen gave Whitefield for Franklin has been mentioned in the academic histories of the University of Pennsylvania only in the footnotes. And there is a reason for its neglect by generations of Franklin scholars: they simply did not know what to make of it. Accordingly, in 1961, the general editor of Franklin's papers, Leonard W. Labaree, laconically stated in his commentary to Whitefield's letter of February 26, 1750, "The little German book [Ziegenhagen] gave Whitefield for B[enjamin] F[ranklin] has not been identified."[38] And there the matter rested until recently.

Fortunately, the trustees of the Philadelphia Academy commissioned an English translation of the little German book, and the original manuscript of that translation has been kept in the archives of the University of Pennsylvania, preserved as an attachment to the trustees' minutes of their meeting of September 10, 1751.[39] During the course of that meeting, the trustees found it necessary to discuss new "Rules for the better Regulation" of their academy, as they confessed having real "Difficulties in that Matter."[40] To come up with fresh ideas, they discussed the English translation of the German booklet in detail. Franklin explained to his colleagues that this manuscript, originally "written in the German Language" and sent to him by Whitefield, contained the "Rules and Orders" of a "celebrated School at Hall in Saxony" in Germany.[41] But which school, exactly?

After careful comparison of a great variety of school ordinances (*Schulordnungen*) printed in Halle in the first half of the eighteenth century, it is now certain that the English manuscript, bearing only the vague title "Observations for the Explication of the Foregoing Accounts,"[42] is in fact a translation of Gotthilf August Francke's *Kurtzer Bericht von der gegenwärtigen Verfassung des Paedagogii Regii zu Glaucha vor Halle* (Brief report about the present constitution of the Paedagogium Regium at Glaucha in Halle) of 1734, a detailed description of that school's rules and regulations. The coauthor of Francke's *Kurtzer Bericht* was Johann Anastasius Freylinghausen, one of the most influential theologians of the Pietist Halle School, its second director, and Gotthilf August Francke's brother-in-law.

COMMON FEATURES AND DIFFERENCES BETWEEN THE PAEDAGOGIUM
REGIUM IN HALLE AND THE PHILADELPHIA ACADEMY

What could Franklin and the other trustees of the Philadelphia Academy have learned from reading the English translation of Gotthilf August Francke's brief report? First, Francke made it clear that there could not be good education of youth without a proper instruction in the fundamental tenets of Christianity. Francke's emphasis on Christian religion as the foundation of all worldly philosophical and educational endeavors and of all lasting achievements in the realm of the arts and sciences was obviously why Ziegenhagen and Whitefield strongly recommended the *Kurtzer Bericht* to Franklin.

Secondly, the trustees in Philadelphia were made aware that the students at the Pietist Halle school were instructed in a great variety of subjects: not only religious education, history, and the classical languages, but also modern languages, physics, economics, and even some crafts. Students were not only prepared for the enjoyment of the Supreme Being in the afterlife, but also trained for a great variety of vocational fields and callings in their present earthly life.

And, thirdly, pupils at Halle would learn discipline. The school day began early in the morning, lessons were considerable in number, and misconduct of students would be sanctioned immediately and sometimes quite severely. Although the teachers were asked to conduct their classes in the Christian spirit of love and patience, they were entitled to harshly admonish those students who stubbornly resisted the demands of fairness, logic, efficiency, and good learning. If willful pupils proved to be incorrigible or inveterate, they were expelled from the Paedagogium Regium.[43]

Unfortunately, it is impossible to say to what degree the rules and regulations of the Paedagogium Regium influenced the Philadelphia trustees directly and immediately. The minutes of their meetings are silent on the matter. All that can be said is that the board of trustees *did* discuss Francke's brief report during their meeting of September 10, 1751. As we have already heard, the minutes indicate that the trustees felt the need to find new "Rules of the better Regulation" of the Philadelphia Academy; they admitted to having "Difficulties in that matter."[44] Thus, they found it very useful to have the translation of the Halle ordinance at hand. After all, they had formally commissioned a translation of the *Kurtzer Bericht*—and they had paid for it. Johann Friedrich Vigera, a talented German teacher and *Sprachmeister* of Philadelphia, produced the commissioned translation;[45] the trustees were obviously satisfied with his work.

Although a direct influence cannot be substantiated, some general remarks can be made about the importance of the Paedagogium Regium in Halle for the Philadelphia Academy. Clearly, the close study of the rules and orders of the famous school at Halle in Germany helped the trustees to understand that strict discipline was important for an institution of higher education.[46] Thus, when the Philadelphia Academy was turned into a college in 1755, the trustees drew up a set of severe new rules for the better regulation of the college. According to these rules, which remained in effect until 1779, the schedule maintained a clear distinction between work and play and accustomed boys to life by the clock. Teachers were entitled to admonish students more harshly, or inflict "Punishments on Delinquents."[47] Backed by punishments, the schedule also set routines that enabled teachers to monopolize the students' time. The rules also required the students to stay inside the college yard while they attended the Academy, and the trustees offered prizes for excellence in schoolwork and used their corporate funds for this purpose. This was the kind of educational ideal cherished by the leaders of both the Paedagogium Regium and the Philadelphia Academy. And, generally, the trustees of the Philadelphia Academy must have liked the broad curriculum of the school at Halle, since it was very similar to the one they adopted themselves in 1749.

A striking similarity between Philadelphia and Halle was the fact that the training in the use of modern languages was held in the highest esteem by teachers of both institutions. Franklin defended the prevalence of English, German, French, and Spanish—and the marginalization of Latin and Greek—throughout his life. In 1789, a year before he died, he published extremely derisive remarks about the classical languages. In his *Observations relative to the Intentions of the Original Founders of the Academy in Philadelphia*, he wrote that the Latin and Greek languages were to be seen in no other light than as "the *Chapeau bras*" of modern literature.[48] In other words, they were as useless as the decorative hats that went by that name in France—"a Man of fashion is not thought dress'd without having one, or something like one, about him, which he carries under his Arm."[49] Franklin's mocking description of Latin and Greek and his insistence on the value of the modern languages was clearly put forward in contrast to the founding purpose of William and Mary, Harvard, and Yale.

On the other hand—and here the schools at Halle and Philadelphia continued to differ—the Philadelphia Academy remained a nondenominational school without proper classes on Christian religion. A look at the religious affiliation of the academy's students reveals that Anglicans clearly outnumbered members of other denominations and confessions, yet Presbyterians, Quakers, and Baptists were also represented in fair numbers. The first Jewish boys to attend classes in the Philadelphia Academy were David Judah and the brothers Moses and Nathan Levi, who enrolled in the 1760s. The trustees deliberately wanted to keep their academy open for students (and teachers) from all sorts of confessional backgrounds.[50]

This background explains why, when Franklin, in his conversation with the professors of the University of Göttingen in 1766, explained that the new College of Philadelphia would do perfectly well without a professor of theology, the German scholars marveled at what they heard. They were simply hesitant to believe him. Although not Pietists themselves but inclined toward an enlightened philosophy, they thought it wrong not to teach Christian religion at an institution of higher learning. They immediately recognized that the Philadelphia Academy was an institution unparalleled by any university they knew or had heard of.[51]

Meanwhile, in Philadelphia, even religious people began to accept that a college without a professor of theology did not necessarily pave the way to irreligion and immorality. After all, six days a week, before the actual classes began, a morning hour was prescribed for daily prayers. And when they had stayed in the Academy for at least eight hours, the teachers and their pupils concluded a long day with more prayers. In addition, the students were actively encouraged to take part in the religious life of their various denominations: on Sundays, each student was required to attend the church of his choice. Thus, in the 1760s, even German Lutheran community leaders sent their sons to the Philadelphia Academy, including the Halle-trained Heinrich Melchior Mühlenberg, whose son Peter, later elected to the U.S. Congress as a representative from Pennsylvania and, in 1801, to the U.S. Senate, matriculated in 1761.[52]

Notes

1. See Ann D. Gordon, *The College of Philadelphia, 1749–1779: Impact of an Institution* (Philadelphia: University of Pennsylvania Press, 1975), 27; David B. Brownlee and George E. Thomas, *Building America's First University: An Historical and Architectural Guide to the University of Pennsylvania* (Philadelphia: University of Pennsylvania Press, 2000), 17.

2. "Constitutions of the Publick Academy in the City of Philadelphia," in *The Papers of Benjamin Franklin*, ed. Leonard W. Labaree et al., 41 vols. to date (New Haven, Conn.: Yale University Press, 1961–), 3:422.

3. University of Pennsylvania Archives, Minutes of the Board of Trustees, vol. 1, 1749 to 1768, February 2, 1750, University of Pennsylvania Archives.

4. Carl Van Doren, *Benjamin Franklin* (1938; repr., Harmondsworth: Penguin Books, 1991), 782.

5. See Jürgen Overhoff, "Franklin's Philadelphia Academy and Basedow's Dessau Philanthropine: Two Models of Non-denominational Schooling in Eighteenth-Century America and Germany," *Paedagogica Historica: International Journal of the History of Education* 43 (2007): 808.

6. See Gordon, *College of Philadelphia*, 149.

7. Walter Isaacson, *Benjamin Franklin: An American Life* (New York: Simon and Schuster, 2003), 146–48.

8. Henry Williams Brands, *The First American: The Life and Times of Benjamin Franklin* (New York: Doubleday, 2000), 286.

9. Benjamin Franklin to Deborah Franklin, September 6, 1758, in Labaree et al., *Papers of Benjamin Franklin*, 8:133.

10. Edward Potts Cheyney, *History of the University of Pennsylvania, 1740–1940* (Philadelphia: University of Pennsylvania Press, 1940), 98.

11. See Jürgen Overhoff, "Benjamin Franklin, Student of the Holy Roman Empire: His Summer Journey to Germany in 1766 and His Interest in the Empire's Federal Constitution," *German Studies Review* 34, no. 2 (2011): 277–86.

12. Benjamin Franklin to Deborah Franklin, June 13, 1766, in Labaree et al., *Papers of Benjamin Franklin*, 13:315.

13. See Burchard Christian von Behr to Benjamin Franklin, June 10, 1766, in Labaree et al., *Papers of Benjamin Franklin*, 13:300.

14. Benjamin Franklin to Rudolph Erich Raspe, September 9, 1766, in Labaree et al., *Papers of Benjamin Franklin*, 13:409.

15. See Jürgen Overhoff, *Benjamin Franklin: Erfinder, Freigeist, Staatenlenker* (Stuttgart: Klett-Cotta, 2006), 225–26.

16. Raspe published Münchhausen's surprising adventures in 1785. A loose German translation by Gottfried August Bürger appeared in 1786 in Göttingen under the title *Wunderbare Reisen zu Wasser und Lande, Feldzüge und Lustige Abentheuer des Freyherrn von Münchhausen, wie er dieselben bey der Flasche im Cirkel seiner Freunde selbst zu erzählen pflegt.*

17. Overhoff, *Benjamin Franklin*, 226.

18. See Cheyney, *History of the University of Pennsylvania*, 38.

19. See *Johann David Michaelis ehemaligen Professors der Philosophie zu Göttingen ... Lebensbeschreibung von ihm selbst abgefasst, mit Anmerkungen von Hassencamp* (Leipzig: Barth, 1793), 103: "Gerade damahls ... studirte ich in Göttingen, und hatte Gelegenheit [Franklin] kennen zu lernen. Franklin, das erinnere ich mich noch wohl, war mir, ich weiß selbst nicht warum, weit interessanter ... und sehr leutselig."

20. The report was first published in *Hannoverisches Magazin*, nos. 17, 18, 19, 31, 32 (February 27, March 2, March 6, April 17, April 20, 1767): 257–96, 482–508. In 1769 and 1777, two further versions of the text appeared in print. In this chapter I quote from *Einige Anmerkungen über Nord-Amerika und über dasige Grosbritannische Kolonien ... verfaßt von Hrn. D. Gottfried Achenwall* (Helmstedt: Kühnlin, 1777).

21. Johann Stephan Pütter, *Versuch einer academischen Gelehrtengeschichte von der Georg-Augustus-Universität zu Göttingen* (Göttingen: Vandenhoek, 1765). In his autobiography, Pütters writes about Franklin's visit to Göttingen:

> Ein litterarischer Besuch, der im Herbste 1766 unserer Universität auf einige Tage den Aufenthalt des berühmten Fränklins ... verschaffte, macht auch mir noch eine angenehme Erinnerung dieser Zeit. Fränklin gieng damals damit um, die Errichtung einer Americanischen Universität zu Philadelphia befördern zu helfen. Das war mit einer von den Bewegungsgründen, die ihn veranlaßten, einige Tage sich bey uns zu verweilen, um die innere Einrichtung unserer Universität näher kennen zu lernen. Ob er gleich der Teutschen Sprache nicht mächtig war, schien es ihm doch ganz gelegen zu kommen, daß er meine Göttingische Gelehrtengeschichte mitnehmen und über dessen Inhalt mit mir und anderen sich hier unterreden konnte. Ich hatte das Vergnügen, daß [er] in Gesellschaft einiger anderer hiesiger Gelehrten einen Nachmittag und Abend bey mir zubrachten.

Johann Stephan Pütters Selbstbiographie zur dankbaren Jubelfeier seiner 50jährigen Professorenstelle zu Göttingen (Göttingen: Vandenhoeck und Ruprecht, 1798), 490–91.

22. See Achenwall, *Einige Anmerkungen*, 29–30:

> Zum Unterricht in den Wissenschaften ist schon vorlängst eine hohe Schule in Boston, der Hauptstadt in Massachusetsbey, angelegt, und seit 1749 ist eine andere in Philadelphia, als der Hauptstadt in Pensilvanien, errichtet. Herr Franklin hat solche in Vorschlag, und durch viele Bemühungen zu Stande gebracht, und ist also der Stifter davon. ... Diese Universität bestehet aus einem Präsidenten, als dem Haupte derselben, welcher 250 Pfund stehenden Gehalts hat, und vier Professoren. ... Diese hohe Schule hat das Recht Magistros philosophiae zu creiren. Im Jahr 1764 ist auch eine medicinische Profeßion angelegt, und Herr Franklin hoft für diese Universität auch das Recht auszuwürken, Doctores der Arzneywissenschaft creiren zu können. Einen öffentlichen Lehrer der Rechte hat sie noch nicht, und einen Professor der Gottesgelahrtheit dürfte sie wohl schwerlich jemals erhalten. Denn weil diese Universität von den Landständen zum allgemeinen Landesbesten errichtet ist, der Religionen aber im Lande verschiedene sind, welche alle gleiche Gerechtsame genießen, und deren keine die herrschende ist: so bleibt die Theologie ausgeschlossen, und jeder läßt sich in Schulen seiner Glaubensgenossen in seiner Religion unterrichten.

23. Overhoff, *Benjamin Franklin*, 223–29; Overhoff, "Benjamin Franklin, Student," 277–86.

24. Hanno Schmitt, "On the Importance of Halle in the Eighteenth Century for the History of Education," *Paedagogica Historica: International Journal of the History of Education* 22, no. 1 (1996): 88–89.

25. See Edward J. Cashin, *Beloved Bethesda: A History of George Whitefield's Home for Boys, 1740–2000* (Macon, Ga.: Mercer University Press, 2001), 9.

26. On Whitefield's life, see the excellent standard biography: Harry S. Stout, *The Divine Dramatist: George Whitefield and the Rise of Modern Evangelicalism* (Grand Rapids, Mich.: William B. Eerdmans, 1991).

27. Benjamin Franklin, *Proposals Relating to the Education of Youth in Pennsylvania* (1749), in Labaree et al., *Papers of Benjamin Franklin*, 3:397–421.

28. The *Gazette*'s article was published on August 24, 1749; it has been reprinted in Labaree et al., *Papers of Benjamin Franklin*, 3:385–88.

29. George Whitefield to Benjamin Franklin, February 26, 1750, in Labaree et al., *Papers of Benjamin Franklin*, 3:467.

30. Ibid.

31. Franklin, *Proposals*, 336.

32. Ibid., 342.

33. George Whitefield to Benjamin Franklin, February 26, 1750, in Labaree et al., *Papers of Benjamin Franklin*, 3:468.

34. Ibid.

35. "Dutch" is here used as a synonym for "German," as was common in eighteenth-century Pennsylvania.

36. See Norman J. Threinen, "Friedrich Michael Ziegenhagen (1694–1776): German Lutheran Pietist in the English Court," *Lutheran Theological Review* 12 (1988): 56–94; Threinen, "Friedrich Ziegenhagen: The London Connection to India and America," in *Halle Pietism, Colonial North America, and the Young United States*, ed. Hans-Jürgen Grabbe (Stuttgart: Steiner, 2008), 113–34.

37. See Heinrich Melchior Mühlenberg, *The Journals of Henry Melchior Muhlenberg*, trans. and ed. Theodore G. Tappert and John Doberstein, 3 vols. (Philadelphia: Evangelical Lutheran Ministerium of Pennsylvania and Adjacent States and Muhlenberg Press, 1942–58; repr., Camden, Maine: Picton Press, 1980), 1:18–22. Mühlenberg left Germany on April 8, 1742, never to return. On June 13, 1742, he sailed to America; see Theodore E. Schmauk, *A History of the Lutheran Church in Pennsylvania (1638–1820)* (Philadelphia: General Council Publishing House, 1903).

38. Labaree et al., *Papers of Benjamin Franklin*, 3:468.

39. The first hint of the existence of such a manuscript was given to me by University of Pennsylvania archivist J. M. Duffin. I owe him my thanks.

40. Minutes of the Board of Trustees, vol. 1, 1749 to 1768, September 10, 1751, University of Pennsylvania Archives.

41. Ibid.

42. "Observations for the Explication of the Foregoing Accounts," attachment to the trustees' minutes of September 10, 1751, University of Pennsylvania Archives).

43. Gotthilf August Francken and Johann Anastasio Freylinghausen, *Kurtzer Bericht von der gegenwärtigen Verfassung des PAEDAGOGII REGII zu Glaucha vor Halle, Zum Dienste derer, welche Nachfrage zu thun pflegen, in Druck vorgeleget Von den DIRECTORIBVS desselben* (Halle: Im Waisenhaus, 1734), chap. 5, 50.

44. Minutes of the Board of Trustees, vol. 1, 1749 to 1768, September 10, 1751, University of Pennsylvania Archives.

45. Ibid.

46. See Minutes of the Board of Trustees, vol. 1, 1749 to 1768, July 11, 1755, University of Pennsylvania Archives. See also Gordon, *College of Philadelphia*, 181.

47. Rules and Statutes of the College, Academy, and Charity School [of Philadelphia], July 11, 1755, in Labaree et al., *Papers of Benjamin Franklin*, 6:103.

48. Benjamin Franklin, "Observations Relative to the Intentions of the Original Founders of the Academy in Philadelphia," in *Benjamin Franklin on Education*, ed. John Hardin Best (New York: Columbia Teachers College Press, [1962]), 174.

49. Ibid.

50. Overhoff, "Franklin's Philadelphia Academy," 811.

51. See Overhoff, *Benjamin Franklin*, 227.

52. See Overhoff, "Franklin's Philadelphia Academy," 811.

CHAPTER 5

German or English?
Halle's Pastors in Pennsylvania and the Search for the Right Language, 1742–1820

WOLFGANG FLÜGEL

> It is still our comfort and joy . . . that we can enjoy God's Word in our pure mother tongue, for the sake of our soul's edification, although we indeed carry out our bodily occupation and our civil dealings in the usual language of the land. It would have been a hard trial for us, if we had to do without the German language in worship.
> —HEINRICH MELCHIOR MÜHLENBERG

These words are from a sermon that Pastor Heinrich Melchior Mühlenberg delivered in 1766, almost twenty-five years after his arrival in Pennsylvania.[1] They inform us, first, about the language use of a Lutheran pastor from Germany—which language he used in which situations. In addition, they shed light on the ambivalences involved in the acculturation process for immigrants, while pointing to the central significance that language plays, for various reasons, in this process. This significance springs from the fact, repeatedly demonstrated by sociologists in recent years, that language, like religion, represents a mark of ethnic and national belonging and hence a cornerstone of the cultural identity of immigrants. Language and religion are intertwined.[2] An example is the German Lutherans and the Anabaptists in America. The Moravians as a global community, however, regarded the German language as a less important sign for their identity and belief.[3] Fundamentally, immigrants' use of their mother tongue works to establish a group in two ways: on the one hand, it produces shared identity (*Zusammengehörigkeit*) within the group; on the other hand, it represents a strong mark of distinction that outwardly signals differentiation from other demographic groups and thus influences how the immigrant group is perceived in the surrounding society (*Aufnahmegesellschaft*).[4] As Mühlenberg's words clearly show, the second or local language represents, as the medium of daily communication, the central resource for immigrants' participation in the social, economic, and political life of their new home. Knowledge of the second language is a prerequisite for the social advancement of immigrants. However, because the mastery of language requires not only lexical background knowledge but also specific cultural background knowledge, knowledge of the local language serves as an indicator for the level of acculturation on the part of the immigrant.[5] At the same time, their inclination to speak, like Mühlenberg, either the first ("mother tongue") or the second language, depending upon the situation, permits further conclusions regarding the establishment of the cultural identity of immigrants.

Proceeding from these reflections, the focus in the following is on the group of pastors around Mühlenberg, Johann Christoph Kunze, and Justus Heinrich Christian Helmuth—thus, on the pastors who between 1742 and 1786 were sent by the Francke Foundations in Halle (Saale) to North America, where they worked until 1820. As the most important leaders of opinion and part of the elite—as "religious leaders, ethnic spokesmen, cultural brokers, social critics, political observers, . . . [and] champions of charity and education"—these men shaped the German Lutheran congregations (*Gemeinden*) in North America and brought them together into the continent's first Lutheran church system (*Kirchenwesen*), still in existence today.[6] In this context, it is important to remember that in America at that time Lutheranism represented a German denomination (apart from a few Swedes) and therefore that the Lutheran Church formed a special stronghold of German ethnicity.[7] Because of this constellation, the Halle pastors became, as founding fathers of this church, especially important agents in the acculturation process of German Lutherans. In this context, the following aspect should be emphasized: throughout this acculturation process the German pastors, as well as their congregations, opened themselves up to the receiving community and adopted its cultural patterns. This observation may sound trivial, but different examples show that this behavior is not self-evident; other migrant groups have denied a cultural opening and been skeptical about any kind of integration.[8]

Against this backdrop, this chapter shows how the Halle pastors shaped this acculturation process. How did they use both the German and the English language as instruments for the construction and stabilization of the German Lutheran Church in Pennsylvania? How did they bind together language and confession for this purpose? How did they deal with the ambivalences of the acculturation process—ambivalences arising from the tension between, on the one hand, attempts to form a German Lutheran immigrant church in an English context and, on the other hand, the increasing Americanization of the German immigrants? Put another way, how did the pastors promote, on the one hand—for instance, through a special commitment to schooling—the acquisition of the local language and thus the integration process, and how did they attempt, on the other hand, to preserve the German mother tongue in a society of change?

BETWEEN GERMAN AND ENGLISH: GERMAN IMMIGRANTS
IN PENNSYLVANIA

During the period under investigation, Pennsylvania went through a social, political, and cultural transformation. In the middle of the eighteenth century, the influence of the little group of English Quakers who had shaped the colony since the seventeenth century waned as a mass of English, Scotch, Irish, and Germans, as Anglicans, Lutherans, and members of other denominations, immigrated, settled down, and deeply transformed the host society. Finally, political and military conditions after American independence led to greater homogenization and Americanization.

Among the immigrants to Pennsylvania in the eighteenth century, the Germans occupied a unique place: approximately one hundred and twenty thousand German settlers—about half of them Lutherans—constituted roughly one-third of the entire population of the land and thus the most significant ethnic minority.[9] The overall population had increased explosively at the beginning of the period, when the first wave of immigration reached its high point: in the 1740s and '50s, the ratio of German-speaking to English-speaking immigrants who settled permanently in Pennsylvania fluctuated between 2:1 and 3:1.[10] Thus, German was frequently heard in Pennsylvania, and its ubiquity brought two consequences. First, within the English environment of Pennsylvania, German immigrants attracted more attention as aliens than other groups because of their language and numerical size. The increased visibility of an "alien" ethnic group elicited, among the English-speaking majority, the anxious and defensive responses often characteristic of such situations.[11] Benjamin Franklin's remarks are paradigmatic: "Advertisements intended to be general are now printed in Dutch and English; the signs in our streets have inscriptions in both languages, and in some places only German. They begin of late to make all their bonds and other legal Writings in their own language which are allowed good in our Courts."[12] Franklin concluded that Pennsylvania "will in a few years become a German colony" and that, very soon, the Germans would "be so numerous as to Germanize us instead of our Anglifying them."[13]

Secondly, because of the constellation described above, many Germans fell into an "ethnic mobility trap." This concept refers to the phenomenon—applicable to all immigrant groups—that with increasing size and autarchy comes a reduction in pressure on the group to open itself to the society of the new land and to master the language spoken by the majority of the population. Conversely, there is an increase in the group's inclination to cut itself off from the surrounding world and to hold fast to the first language, with the consequence that social advancement may be hindered.[14] Franklin's remarks reveal that many Germans in Pennsylvania preferred to live together in relatively closed German settlements, such as Germantown, or formed their own neighborhoods in cities such as Lancaster and Philadelphia. There they cultivated social contacts chiefly with one another and kept their distance from the surrounding English-dominated society as well as from English-speaking denominations.[15] In doing so, they managed to preserve their cultural peculiarities and their German language.[16] Even in 1780, Kunze commented, "there are entire counties in the land where only Germans live, whose children do not understand a single word of English," thus confirming Franklin's observation.[17]

Certainly, this separation pertains to only a part of the German settlers. On the one hand, already in the years around 1750, separation could be maintained neither on the "frontier" nor in places where the pressure of a rapidly growing population led to an intermixing of settlement areas and thus to a babbling Babel (*babylonisches Sprachgewirr*). Furthermore, members of the educated elite, as well as social climbers, were, at least in principle, bi- or trilingual. Along with the language, these people also adopted the cultural practices of the English-speaking population.[18] Bearing witness to this development is a fictional conversation, published in the *High German American Calendar* of 1754, between a "newcomer" (*Neukommer*) and a German who had already lived in Pennsylvania for some time. In the course of this dialogue, it is observed that "the Germans will soon be half English"—a remark on their at least rudimentary knowledge of the English language and cultural practices.[19]

On the other hand, the shared experience of military and political events such as the French and Indian War, the Revolutionary War, and the domestic development of the new nation in the 1790s had a homogenizing effect and led to processes of integration and Americanization for all groups of the population. Over the course of these processes, many German immigrants, especially those of the second and third generations, found their place more and more in the surrounding society.[20] An index for this change is the increasing use of the English language in these generations, which sometimes led to intergenerational conflict:[21] Already in 1751, Mühlenberg noted in his journal that the languages were sometimes mixed in daily life, but many immigrants of the first generation were displeased to hear their children speak English.[22]

Here we see a tension that increased as the influx of new German immigrants came to an almost complete standstill in the final third of the eighteenth century, due to political events in Europe and North America. As a consequence, the distinct German identity was actually imperiled, at least until German mass immigration began again in the 1820s. For many German Americans in these decades, the continued existence of the German language represented a sign of hope for the survival of an independent German ethnicity in North America.[23] This ambivalence between hope and trepidation finds expression in a short article in a

German-language pocket calendar from 1786, according to which the laws of the United States would, one day in the not-too-distant future, be published in the German language as well.[24] Helmuth thought similarly in 1813: in forty years, according to his vision, Philadelphia could become a German city, and Lancaster and York, German administrative districts (*Verwaltungsbezirke*).[25] Certainly these prognoses were not without shadows. The essay in the pocket calendar limits its vision with the caveat "If then they [the Germans] want."[26] Helmuth expressed it more clearly, underlining the constitutive significance of language. He asserted that already in the present "no people on earth" could "surpass the German residents of Pennsylvania" if the "Germans remained German and maintained also German language and morals."[27]

LANGUAGE CHOICE ACCORDING TO NECESSITY:
HEINRICH MELCHIOR MÜHLENBERG

Like Martin Luther, who regarded language as the edge of the sword of spirit and the most important tool for spreading God's word,[28] the Halle pastors, at the beginning of the time period under consideration, adopted a pragmatic position on the language question, as we saw clearly in Mühlenberg's words at the beginning of this essay. Already in the 1740s, Mühlenberg and his colleague, Peter Brunnholtz, expressed in their diaries and correspondence the considerable significance of the English language and confessed that they still had to improve their own language abilities.[29] This estimation was directed both to the general requirements for living in an English-speaking environment—where, for instance, the English language was necessary in order to draft legally binding documents—and to the demands of their pastoral occupation.[30] Of course, the pastors preached in the German mother tongue to the Lutheran congregations that had established themselves, such as St. Michael and Zion in Philadelphia, in the pockets of German settlement. Likewise, if they published their sermons, they published them in German. Things were different in the hinterlands, however, where pastors increasingly also made use of the second language for ministerial tasks (*Seelsorge*).[31] Thus, Mühlenberg described the case of a young woman who had lived since childhood in a Quaker community. There she had "entirely forgotten the German language and had grown up in such a way that she knew nothing of Christian teaching. I had to instruct her in the teaching of the faith in the English language."[32] Similarly, pastors Brunnholtz and Johann Friedrich Handschuh also reported that they had to resort to the English language—for example, if they preached during their visits to Swedish-Lutheran congregations or congregations of English-speaking denominations.[33]

In addition, Mühlenberg purposefully used the English language for events that involved an official interest, even if they were the affair of a Lutheran congregation. In a solemn ceremony, he reported to Halle, "we laid the first foundation stone for the first Lutheran church in Providence. There was also a huge crowd of people in attendance, both English and German ... afterwards held a German oration. ... After that held also an English oration."[34] Through his language selection, Mühlenberg sought not only to reach the members of his own church, but also to launch a charm offensive at the English people and win new church members in the marketplace of religion.[35] Thus, his language selection was dictated not by concern for the continued existence of the German language, but exclusively by the requirements of the conversion of individuals and the preservation of Lutheranism. In view of religious relations in Pennsylvania, the existence of Lutheranism appeared acutely endangered to Mühlenberg. He repeatedly detected a "decline among our poor Lutheran people," which had led to the almost "complete ruin of our Lutheran Church."[36] As Mühlenberg weighed his priorities in view of this situation, he wrote in 1755 that if he were a "worshipper or bigot of the German language ... I might fear its gradual disappearance. Meanwhile, it seems to me to be all the same with regard to the languages, if only our Protestant-evangelical teaching is preserved and the power of divine salvation is promoted and propagated."[37] In a situation in which the aforementioned tensions shaped the relationship between German and English settlers, Mühlenberg, with his stance, ultimately promoted linguistic openness vis-à-vis the English-speaking environment. In so doing, he came near to the wishes of Franklin, for instance, and simultaneously contributed to the integration of German Lutherans. Similar to Francis Daniel Pastorius a generation before, Mühlenberg regarded language as above all a medium for orienting oneself in a multiethnic society.[38]

ATTEMPTS AT INTEGRATION: LANGUAGE AND INSTRUCTION
IN SCHOOLS

Against the backdrop of the freedom of religion guaranteed in Pennsylvania, and the religious competition that resulted from it, Mühlenberg believed that the school possessed fundamental significance—alongside the pastor's ministerial work—for the preservation of Lutheranism.[39] As in Germany, so also in America, responsibility for the schools rested with the pastors. In these parochial schools, pastors like Brunnholtz or catechists like Johann Helfrich Schaum—also sent from Halle—imparted to children basic knowledge about religion as well as reading, writing, and arithmetic; instruction was in German.[40] To be sure, Mühlenberg complained repeatedly that in many places there were no suitable pastors or schoolmasters, or the quality of education was poor.[41] It was above all the German-speaking Moravians, regarded by the Halle pastors as their chief adversaries, who were in position to fill the resulting gaps. At least in the decades at midcentury, the Moravians successfully competed against the Halle pastors; this success was founded upon their missionary zeal, their ecumenical and thus multilingual initiatives, and their personal strength.[42]

In this situation, Mühlenberg's desire to contribute through schooling to the general and the religious education of German Lutherans—and in so doing to stabilize their Lutheran identity—collided with the interest of the English-speaking majority in anglicizing the German settlers. To this end, the Society for Promoting Religious Knowledge and the English Language Among the German Emigrants in Pennsylvania (also known as the Society for the Promotion of the Knowledge of God Among the Germans), founded in London in early 1753, established and financed charity schools in Pennsylvania after the English model, as Patrick M. Erben discusses in the present volume.[43] Against the backdrop of the simmering quarrels between England and France and the fear that the German immigrants would sympathize with the French, the Germans in these charity schools were to be molded into loyal British subjects through an education shaped by Anglicanism.[44] Franklin was a supporter of the plan and turned to Mühlenberg for assistance in the summer of 1754. The pastor, who viewed himself as a loyal subject of King George II, and who also discerned substantial common ground between

Anglicans and Lutherans, reacted positively. Next to his personal disposition, the decisive factor for Mühlenberg was that the children were supposed to be instructed in the English and German languages, and also—most importantly—to learn the catechism of their own denomination, which strengthened religious identity as Mühlenberg conceived of it.[45] In other words, Mühlenberg used charity schools as structural instruments for stabilizing Lutheran identity. Like his language selection shown above, this decision was dictated not by concern for the continued existence of the German language, but exclusively by the requirements of the conversion of individuals and the preservation of Lutheranism. Thus he took advantage of the opportunity and placed the schoolhouses of the New Providence and New Hanover communities at the disposal of the charity schools.[46]

Nevertheless, a large number of German settlers rejected the project, even though they did not have to pay to attend the charity schools—something they often had to do for the community schools.[47] Unlike Mühlenberg, moreover, the communities in Providence and New Hanover feared that the charity schools would not advance integration in a positive sense, but were a tool of forced assimilation that would contribute to the complete suppression of the German language and culture.[48] This fear was stoked through numerous pamphlets by (Johann) Christoph Saur, the first German printer in North America. However, Saur's rejection of the English schools was not motivated by a rejection of the English language: already in 1751 Saur had published *Beyhülfe Vor die Teutschen Um Englisch zu lernen* (Aid for the Germans to learn English), one of the first language-instruction books of its kind.[49] In fact, there were two different causes. First, Saur's reproach that charity schools turned on "wehrlose Sekten" pointed to a sense of affront. Only Lutherans and Calvinists constituted the administration board, with no members of other German denominations. Second, a political motive must be emphasized: to protect Pennsylvania against armed attacks by France, Franklin had tried since the 1740s to establish a colonial volunteer army according to the pattern of other colonies. But Quakers, who still held a majority in the assembly, voted against this scheme, asserting that military operations were against God's commandments.[50]

As a devoted separatist, Saur supported the Quakers. In this context, his rejection of charity schools should be understood within the pluralistic colonial society as an attempt to sway newcomers religiously and to convince them to support the Quakers politically.[51] It should be noted, finally, that for Mühlenberg the charity schools were only a temporary necessity.[52] He was sure that the English would cease supporting the schools as soon as war with France resulted in predominance over France. And in fact, the British stopped their financial support of charity schools after the outbreak of the French and Indian War. In addition, Mühlenberg, who had had very bad experiences at English schools, rejected further cooperation. He deemed English private schools "highly dangerous for our German children [because] nothing has been taught about Christ. Instead, all sorts of bad habits and vanities were allowed."[53]

His efforts were directed chiefly at furnishing communities more and more with their own pastors and catechists in order to hand down Lutheran thought as shaped by Halle. In view of the increasingly divergent cultural development of America and Europe, these future Lutheran clergymen should, ideally, no longer come as aliens (*Landesfremde*) from Germany to Pennsylvania, as Mühlenberg and his colleagues had done. Instead, they should be born in America and thus be very familiar with the local conditions. In order to educate these persons, Mühlenberg recommended to Gotthilf August Francke in Halle—albeit in vain—that a seminary be founded in Pennsylvania, taking Halle as its model.[54] Revealing here is the accepted deacademization of future pastors, compelled by the fact that for Lutherans in eighteenth-century North America—unlike in Germany—theological studies at a university were not yet possible. On the one hand, basic academic knowledge, which the Halle pastors could impart locally, appeared sufficient for pastoral service in Pennsylvania, even if in Germany the equivalent knowledge only permitted one to attain the office of catechist. On the other hand, the double knowledge of the "mother and local tongues" was an absolute necessity.[55]

This deacademization has a contradictory relationship with the anti-intellectualism intertwined with the Great Awakening.[56] Like the influential partisans of John and Charles Wesley, Pietists stressed the importance of emotionally laden sermons and contrasted them with the traditional sermons of Lutheran orthodoxy. Complaints from parishioners about sermons held by Handschuh and Schaum prove, however, that the church communities in general were open to the lively performance of revivalist preachers.[57] This setting corresponds with the importance of the practical hands-on abilities that proved so necessary for survival in many parts of the New World. In order to guarantee basic religious care in the new circumstances of America, the pastors needed abilities and soft skills different from those that they were taught in Germany. For these reasons, pastors criticized university education, not academic training as such. In contrast to revitalists, the Halle pastors rejected lay preachers in favor of academically trained pastors.

An academic expansion of theological education was first ventured by representatives of the younger generation of Halle pastors who, like Kunze or Helmuth, arrived from Halle around or after 1770. At this time, foundational work had already been completed in Pennsylvania. It was Kunze, substantially, who now in 1773–74 again took up and put into practice Mühlenberg's idea of a German *Seminarium* as an "attempt at a small beginning of a German university [*Hochschule*]."[58] The foundation of the seminary also responded to Kunze's observation that the Germans in Pennsylvania by no means attained the educational level of their fellow countrymen in Europe. To remedy this situation, German immigrant children at Kunze's seminary were to be prepared to attend academies and colleges. This seminary has thus been considered an "academy..., in which promising children would receive, step-by-step, a good foundation for the preaching office, school service, and notarial and clerical occupations."[59] This orientation toward integration and upward social mobility had consequences for the preferred language of instruction: "In the instruction of German youth,... the intention should always be directed to English, nevertheless in such a way that the German method of teaching [*Lehrart*] should prevail in the presentation of all subjects [*Wissenschaften*], excepting only English language and rhetoric."[60]

Work on the *Seminarium* was interrupted by the war in 1777–78, and in 1779 the institution was integrated as a department within the newly organized University of Pennsylvania. Subsequently, a partial reorientation in the area of language training occurred. That Kunze (between 1780 and 1784) and Helmuth (between 1784 and 1794) each held the post of professor of philology—that is, professor of Oriental and German languages—reveals that German also could be learned next to the classical languages in this institute of higher education.[61] This offer, to be sure, was directed not at native German speakers, but rather at English-speaking students, as well as German Americans who no longer had mastery of German.

However, the attempt to broaden knowledge of the German language in local society attained only slight success: "There are but a few boys remaining in the German School who are learning to read and write the German language before they begin to learn Latin."[62] Following the intention of Luther's pamphlet *An die Ratsherren aller Städten*, ideally all Christians should have some knowledge of classical languages in order to read biblical texts in their original version. But here the offer to learn Latin was targeted at future pastors.

GERMAN AND ENGLISH: TWO MOTHER TONGUES

The failure of the *Seminarium* corresponded with a change in the linguistic behavior of the German residents of Pennsylvania that began in the years around 1780. Kunze commented, "[The] ability to speak German is slight among those born here.... Most Germans do not speak German," and if they did, they spoke it in a "dialect that no learned person could be compelled to use, even by torture."[63] This linguistic development, to be sure, can be understood as an index for the positive course of the integration process, especially among second- and third-generation immigrants. The Halle pastors around Mühlenberg, Brunnholtz, and Handschuh helped to facilitate this process *nolens volens*. Nevertheless, it is important to ask how the pastors around Kunze and Helmuth handled the changed situation.

Kunze especially, who in 1779 followed his father-in-law in the office of elder *Senior* of the Philadelphia community, took a clear stance in demanding bilingualism: The "sensible Germans do not despise the English language and honor their mother tongue. The former they speak when they must and the latter when they can."[64] English, he continues, "is and will remain the mother tongue here. But any German who turns his back on the German language for this reason, must have either made his reputation foul in Germany, or neither there nor here conceived of much that is reasonable in any language."[65] Interesting is Kunze's unequivocal statement, in which he essentially follows Mühlenberg's position: "In business and trade, necessity teaches us English: but in worship, altering the language would reveal a terrifying spiritual condition and constrict devotion and openheartedness.... Thus we speak German here, and the second and third generation, which perhaps still would like to maintain religion and worship, will continue to speak German in matters of worship."[66] Depending on the situation, Kunze viewed both English (for trade, economic dealings, and academics) and German (for religion) as his mother tongue.[67] Consequently, he later published his academic treatises in English.[68]

A similar position with respect to the bilingualism of German Lutherans was taken by Helmuth, who assumed Kunze's office in the Philadelphia community after the latter's departure for New York in 1784 and who remained head of the Lutherans in Philadelphia until 1820. Helmuth was, to be sure, distinct from Kunze and above all from Mühlenberg in doggedly devoting himself, for programmatic reasons, to the preservation of the German language. In Helmuth's eyes, the German language was less a functional means of communication and much more the central precondition for the future survival of Lutheranism. Regardless, he urged that the German settlers acquire the necessary skills—for instance, knowledge of the English language—for daily life in American society.[69]

With recourse to Halle though, Helmuth and other pastors sought to establish a comprehensive educational system by which German settlers would learn the German language and skills for daily life.[70] After their own plans could not be realized, however, Helmuth participated, along with Gotthilf Heinrich Ernst Mühlenberg, in the founding in 1786 of Franklin College in Lancaster. Franklin College still exists as Franklin and Marshall College.[71] Entirely in accord with the intentions of the two pastors, the educational aim of Franklin College was to impart the knowledge and skills necessary for the benefit of religion and the republican system and thereby to enable the Germans to participate equally in public life. The curriculum included, in addition to religion, mathematics, and moral and natural philosophy, the German and English languages, as well as Latin and Greek.[72] In their opening address, the trustees—including the two pastors—pointed out multiple times that, next to sound education, knowledge of English was the key to the social advancement of Germans, for instance in the hierarchy of administration or in politics.[73]

Nevertheless, there were other reasons why the curriculum of Franklin College included German as a mother tongue—one that immigrants used only a little for life in the new land.⁷⁴ On the one hand, it helped to generate acceptance for the college in the German community, cutting down an initial barrier to acceptance among the immigrants. This was necessary because of a skepticism about education that was connected with the social standing of the German settlers; such skepticism strengthened the effects of the ethnic mobility trap. Indeed, the immigrants were mostly craftsmen or farmers, and, following the usual practice in Germany, they often provided for their children only an elementary education, such as was offered in the community schools. To address this point, the trustees suggested that the knowledge provided at Franklin College would also be useful for nonacademic professions.⁷⁵ On the other hand, as the quote from Kunze at the beginning of this section confirms, competent bilingualism was an exception in the migrant communities.⁷⁶ In this context, the curriculum was able to rescue the German language from extinction or corruption, insofar as it was now correctly taught.⁷⁷

In addition to his involvement with schooling, Helmuth pursued linguistic and theological education along still other avenues, through which he was also able to reach adults. Anthony Gregg Roeber has identified Helmuth as a co-initiator of the Mosheim Society, founded in 1789. This was an adult literary society founded chiefly by members of the second and third generations of the most acculturated German Americans in order to cultivate the German language and culture.⁷⁸ Between 1811 and 1817, moreover, Helmuth founded and edited the *Evangelical Magazine*, seeking to address the loss of knowledge of the German language and what he saw as the underlying cause of this loss, the decline of the Lutheran confession.⁷⁹

LANGUAGE AND WORSHIP AS PILLARS OF CULTURAL IDENTITY

In the early nineteenth century, in many German Lutheran congregations in Pennsylvania and New York, the reality of bilingualism produced many disputes about which language future worship services should be held in. Two parties emerged. First were the Germanizers under the leadership of Helmuth, Smith, and, initially, Kunze, who accepted English for use in daily life but strictly rejected it for worship services.⁸⁰ Against them were the Americanizers, primarily members of the generation born in Pennsylvania, among them Mühlenberg's sons, Friedrich August and Gotthilf Heinrich. They demanded that English be used in Lutheran worship services alongside German or that a purely English service be offered on regular occasions.[81] But this did not entail a rejection of the German language in general. On the contrary, many Americanizers, such as Mühlenberg's sons, were members of the Mosheim Society.

The quarrels were triggered by the following contradiction: On the one hand, until the early nineteenth century, Lutheran worship services in Pennsylvania were a stronghold of the German language. But on the other hand, many second- and third-generation German Americans had less and less command over their mother tongue and could not understand worship in German. From this rose a danger, recognized by Germanizers as well as Americanizers, that English-speaking German Americans would lose their Lutheran faith and thereby endanger their own salvation. The loss of parishioners, then, posed a threat to the ongoing existence of Lutheran parishes in general. To work against this, both Germanizers and Americanizers developed strategies.

Helmuth, as a Germanizer, countered the decline of the German language in various ways, as shown, and he strictly forbade the use of English in Lutheran worship services. His chief argument was that German life, and with it, Lutheran faith, could be preserved in America only if German was spoken. He offered two particular reasons for refusing English services: First, he feared that English worship services would lead to the loss of the German language in America, and suggested that this would lead to the inability to read Lutheran prayer literature.[82] In fact, this argument was justified because the central Lutheran writings were in German, not English. Many pastors deemed English far too poor ("viel zu arm") to capture the wide range of Lutheran devotional literature, and German-language devotional literature thus went untranslated.[83] Furthermore, if Mühlenberg Jr. preached in English, he could use the *Book of Common Prayer* as an Anglican reverend would. It should also be noted that Helmuth felt the German language helped protect Lutheranism: in his mind, German served as a barrier that would keep rationalism, revivalism, and other ideas promoted by English denominations away from Lutheran parishes.[84]

Secondly, Helmuth feared that many English-speaking German Americans would not stay in Lutheran parishes providing English-language services but would drift into English, non-Lutheran denominations. Thus, a development that Mühlenberg had observed already in 1751 among the Dutch Reformed communities in New York City would repeat itself.[85] In this case, along with the German language, the Lutheran confession as a second pillar of an immigrant's identity would be changed. The consequences of this had also been perceived on the religious level, as one clergyman indicated: "To their worship the German Americans owe most of their peculiar character, and only this worship perpetuates their language . . . in worship and in churches, the German origin is obvious."[86]

This observation shows that for the generation that immigrated from Germany, language was connected both with their cultural identity as Germans and with their religious self-conception as Lutherans. Helmuth likened their situation to that of the Jewish people: being a minority, they survived as a nation because they kept their own language and worship service. With this stance, Helmuth positioned himself against the opinion given by John Jay in Federalist Paper no. 2, according to which all members of one nation were to speak the same language. At the same time, he touched indirectly upon a question of considerable public interest since the colonial period: is knowledge and use of the English language a necessary precondition for full citizenship?[87]

As Helmuth stuck with German-language worship services, pastors like Kunze, Friedrich August Mühlenberg, and Christian Endress—a German born in America and an active member of the Mosheim Society—accepted language change and tried to keep a common worship service as the congregation's "bond of unity."[88] They argued that with the decline of the German language, German worship also had declined.[89] Thus, whoever wanted to preserve Lutheran worship—and on this central concern both parties agreed—must offer it in English as well. Such was the conclusion of Friedrich August Mühlenberg.[90] In 1795, Kunze took the logical step and edited a *Hymn and Prayer-Book*.[91] He pointed to the altered language habits of the Germans. Contradicting his earlier statements, in which he had fused together the German language and Lutheran worship as a unified whole, Kunze's book opened up Lutheran theology to the English language.

A new justification and redefinition of language, religion, and national affiliation as pillars of immigrant's cultural identity is indicated by the fact that the proponents of English-language worship, such as Pastor Endress, expressly underlined their pride in being German and in being not German subjects, but American citizens.[92] Accordingly, they pleaded for worship in English—the language of the land—in order to preserve the faith of their forefathers for their children.[93] They supported their stance through references to the authority of Luther and his translation project. Luther had introduced the German language into worship because it seemed to him absolutely necessary in view of the language situation in Germany.[94]

In essence, Kunze stressed that holding a Lutheran worship service in a language that could not be understood by all parishioners violated the very nature of Lutheranism. Thus, the Americanizers could understand themselves as being guardians of their German heritage just as much as the Germanizers were, even if the decision to provide English Lutheran services looks like a reaction to an emergency situation. Just before he died in 1807, Kunze wrote, "On the force of religion, you can have no reasonable objection to the use of the English tongue, because it is undoubtedly as proper as the German for the conveyance of religious instruction to your children. The German may be studied as a secondary useful language."[95]

Ultimately, the two parties did not come to an agreement. In Philadelphia in 1805, some members left the German-speaking St. Michael and Zion community in order to found the English-speaking St. John's Lutheran Church.[96] A similar development took place in Lancaster and New York. In the following years, however, Lutheran pastors increasingly addressed their congregations in both German and English, or translated their sermons into English for publication.

The splitting of parishes also signaled social and political conflict. Friederike Baer emphasizes that the struggle for the right language mirrored an internal social differentiation of German Lutherans and their participation in public life.[97] Social developments produced political fragmentation of parishes in the 1790s.[98] Thus, the leaders of Americanizers and Germanizers belonged to different political parties: Peter Muhlenberg supported Thomas Jefferson and the Federalists, while Helmuth rejected them.

Increasingly, German Lutherans found themselves divided into prosperous and poorer social strata, with the dividing line mirroring linguistic divisions.[99] As many pastors and supporters of Franklin College in the 1780s had predicted, a working knowledge of the English language increased the chance of upward mobility. Associated with this development was ethnic segregation creating a social distinction between wealthy and poor neighborhoods. The use of English became more and more a sign of participation in the new political order and in economic prosperity. In fact, English-speaking Germans, as members of a higher social class, described their German-speaking compatriots as "rabble," while German-speaking Germans labeled the English-speaking "silly snobs."[100]

In light of this background, for those immigrant groups for whom the German-language service was an important hotspot, the introduction of English-language worship came across as an attack on a central institution of their own existence and on their cultural identity. This attack was also regarded as having a political element, inasmuch as it was a challenge to the fundamental right to religious freedom, including the right to a German service, as well as their own status as free individuals. Therefore, Germanizers refused any modification of their "deutsch-lutherischen" congregations.

In contrast, the Americanizers understood English-language worship as an adaptation to the prevailing social circumstances.[101] That did not mean a change of cultural identity, but a rebalancing effort within the coordinate system of the three pillars of immigrants' identity. This group kept their German identity as well, but they did not affix it any longer to language, but to culture and tradition. Their Lutheran confession remained, regardless of the language, a German denomination, and as such constituted an important pillar of their German Lutheran cultural identity.

Thus, from the late eighteenth century on, the self-designation "German" relates less and less often to language and more and more to ethnic origin and cultural identity. The word "German" is found with growing frequency in church names, whether as "deutsch-lutherisch" or as "German Lutheran." In the private sphere, the same development led to the anglicizing of German names, which accelerated the decline of the significance of the German language as a unifying force for all Americans with

German roots. Consequently, the opportunity arose for second- and third-generation German Americans—among whom fewer and fewer had command of their old mother tongue—to preserve their Lutheran identity, because Kunze, Muhlenberg Jr., and Endress opened up the Lutheran faith to the English language. Evidence of an attempt to preserve a distinctly German English-language Lutheranism is provided by Riordan, who reports that in 1802 Endress translated Luther's catechism into English and that in 1857 this book reached its 73rd edition. Additionally, 80 percent of the Lutheran certificates of baptism and other such printed matter from the first half of the nineteenth century were printed in Fraktur, a typical German typeface, but in the English language.[102] This implies that typical German Lutheran devotional rites and liturgy differing from other denominations, such as child baptism, survived in an English-language and non-Lutheran cultural background.[103]

Notes

This project has been funded by a generous Fellowship at the Horner Library given by the German Historical Institute Washington together with the German Society of Pennsylvania.

1. The original German reads, "Es ist noch immer unser Trost und Freude ... , daß wir Gottes Wort in unserer reinen Muttersprache zu unserer Seelenerbauung geniessen dürfen, ob wir wol unsern leiblichen Beruf und bürgerlichen Geschäfte in der landes-üblichen Sprache verrichten, und wäre uns daher eine harte Versuchung geworden, wenn wir der Deutschen Muttersprache bey dem Gottesdienst hätten entbehren müssen." Heinrich Melchior Mühlenberg, *Ein Zeugniß von der Güte und Ernst Gottes gegen sein Bundesvolk in alten und neuern Zeiten und des Volks Undankbarkeit gegen Gott, den höchsten Wohltaeter abgelegt aus 5 B. Mosis 32:1–6. vor der Evangelischen St. Michaelis- und Zions-Gemeine in Philadelphia, an dem Beth- und Dank-Feste, so von einigen Evangelischen Gemeinen in Pennsylvanien, und benachbarten Provinzen wegen Aufhebung der Staempel-Acte, x. und Abwendung anscheinender Gefahr, den 1sten August, 1766, feyerlich gehalten, und auf Begehren schrifftlich verfasset worden* (Philadelphia: Müller, 1766), 43.

2. On the various aspects of cultural identity, see Lothar Krappmann, *Soziologische Dimensionen der Identität: Strukturelle Bedingungen für die Teilnahme an Interaktionsprozessen*, 9th ed. (Stuttgart: Klett-Cotta, 2000); Werner Gephart, *Religion und Identität im Horizont des Pluralismus* (Frankfurt am Main: Suhrkamp, 1999). For the significance of religion, language, and ethnic/national belonging in the identity formation of immigrants, see the introduction to *Migration und Religiöse Dynamik: Ethnologische Religionsforschung im transnationalen Kontext*, ed. Andrea Lauser and Cordula Weisskoppel (Bielefeld: Transcript, 2008), 7–32. For Pennsylvania in general, see Patrick M. Erben, *A Harmony of the Spirits: Translation and the Language of Community in Early Pennsylvania* (Chapel Hill: University of North Carolina Press, 2012), 301ff. For German immigrants in Philadelphia around 1800, see Friederike Baer, *The Trial of Frederick Eberle: Language, Patriotism, and Citizenship in Philadelphia's German Community, 1790 to 1830* (New York: New York University Press, 2008), 1–21.

3. See Gisela Mettele, *Weltbürgertum oder Gottesreich: Die Herrnhuter Brüdergemeinde als globale Gemeinschaft, 1727–1857* (Göttingen: Vandenhoeck und Ruprecht, 2009), 124–29.

4. Hartmut Esser, *Migration, Sprache und Integration*, Arbeitsstelle Interkulturelle Konflikte und gesellschaftliche Integration / Wissenschaftszentrum Berlin für Sozialforschung, January 2006, accessed March 4, 2014, https://www.ssoar.info/ssoar/bitstream/handle/document/11349/ssoar-2006-esser-migration.pdf?sequence=1; see also Achim Trunk, "Eine Sprache für Europa, zwei oder viele? Die Sprachenfrage in der frühen europäischen Integration," in *Die kulturelle Integration Europas*, ed. Johannes Wienand (Wiesbaden: Verlag für Sozialwissenschaften, 2010), 173.

5. See Thomas Marx, "Über mentale Probleme des Sprachkontakts unter dem Aspekt kultureller Fremdheit," in *Sprache und Kommunikation im Kulturkontext: Beiträge zum Ehrenkolloquium aus Anlaß des 60; Geburtstages von Gotthard Lerchner*, ed. Volker Hertel, Irmhild Barz, Regine Metzler, and Brigitte Uhlig (Frankfurt: Peter Lang, 1996), 185–88.

6. On the role of the pastors, see Wolfgang Splitter, "*Divide et impera*: Some Critical Remarks on Halle Missionaries' Formation of a Lutheran Church in Pennsylvania," in *Halle Pietism, Colonial North America, and the Young United States*, ed. Hans-Jürgen Grabbe (Stuttgart: Franz Steiner, 2008), 46; E. Brooks Holifield, *God's Ambassadors: A History of the Christian Clergy in America* (Grand Rapids, Mich.: William B. Eerdmans, 2007), 72–73; Hermann Wellenreuther, "Die atlantische Welt des 18. Jahrhunderts: Überlegungen zur Bedeutung des Atlantiks für die Welt der Frommen im Britischen Weltreich," in *Transatlantische Religionsgeschichte: 18–20. Jahrhundert*, ed. Hartmut Lehmann (Göttingen: Wallstein-Verlag, 2006), 19; A. G. Roeber, *Palatines, Liberty, and Property: German Lutherans in Colonial British America* (Baltimore: Johns Hopkins University Press, 1993), 3; as well as, generally, Andreas Gestrich, *Absolutismus und Öffentlichkeit: Politische Kommunikation in Deutschland zu Beginn des 18. Jahrhunderts* (Göttingen: Vandenhoeck und Ruprecht, 1994); Luise Schorn-Schütte, "Zwischen 'Amt' und 'Beruf': Der Prediger als Wächter, 'Seelenhirt' oder Volkslehrer; Evangelische Geistlichkeit im Alten Reich und in der schweizerischen Eidgenossenschaft im 18. Jahrhundert," in *Evangelische Pfarrer: Zur sozialen und politischen Rolle einer bürgerlichen Gruppe in der deutschen Gesellschaft des 18. bis 20. Jahrhunderts*, ed. Luise Schorn-Schütte and Walter Sparn (Stuttgart: Kohlhammer, 1997), 1–35, esp. 5, 19.

7. On the importance of the churches in immigrant communities, see Ralf Roloff, "Religion und regionale Identität: Zur Bedeutung der Religion als Faktor regionaler Kooperation und Integration," in *Religion—Staat—Politik: Zur Rolle der Religion in der nationalen und internationalen Politik*, ed. Manfred Brocker (Wiesbaden: Westdeutscher Verlag, 2003), 339–51; Lucian Hölscher, "Der Raum des Religiösen: Semantische Strukturen des religiösen Lebens im 19. Jahrhundert—eine problemgeschichtliche Skizze," in Lehmann, *Transatlantische Religionsgeschichte*, 118.

8. For example, the Huguenots in Brandenburg-Piussia; see Ulrich Niggemann, *Hugenotten* (Cologne: Böhlau, 2011); Susanne Lachenicht, *Hugenotten in Europa und Nordamerika: Migration und Integration in der Frühen Neuzeit* (Frankfurt am Main: Campus Verlag, 2010), 384–88, 405–15.

9. See Hans-Jürgen Grabbe, *Vor der großen Flut: Die europäische Migration in die Vereinigten Staaten von Amerika, 1783–1820* (Stuttgart: Steiner, 2001).

10. See Carla Mulford, "Benjamin Franklin, Pennsylvania Germans, and the Ethnic Origins of Nations," in Grabbe, *Halle Pietism*, 151. This ratio does not reflect immigration; rather, it is the result of the fact that many of the incoming English left Pennsylvania for other colonies, while the Germans preferred to remain in Pennsylvania. Immigration is addressed also by the Halle pastors; for instance, Brunnholz, August 21, 1750, Archives of the Francke Foundation, Halle, Mission Archive (hereafter AFSt/M) 4C3: 48, p. 269— according to which, in the fall of 1749, 25 ships with a total of 1049 Germans arrived in Pennsylvania.

11. See Hartmut Esser, *Sprache und Integration: Die sozialen Bedingungen und Folgen des Spracherwerbs für Migranten* (Frankfurt am Main: Campus Verlag 2006), 159.

12. Franklin to Peter Collison, May 9, 1753, in *The Papers of Benjamin Franklin*, ed. Leonard W.

Labaree et al., 41 vols. to date (New Haven, Conn.: Yale University Press, 1961–), 4:484.

13. The first citation is Franklin to James Palmer, March 20, 1751, in *Papers of Benjamin Franklin*, 117; the second is Benjamin Franklin, *Observations Concerning the Increase of Mankind* (Boston: S. Kneeland, 1755), para. 23; see also Arthur Dundore Graeff, *The Relations Between the Pennsylvania Germans and the British Authorities (1750–1776)* (Philadelphia: Norristown Herald, 1939), 24, 31; Glenn Weaver, "Benjamin Franklin and the Pennsylvania Germans," *William and Mary Quarterly* 14 (1951): 537; Mulford "Ethnic Origins," 154. For additional authors with similar assessments, see Charles Henry Glatfelter, *Pastors and People: German Lutheran and Reformed Churches in the Pennsylvania Field, 1717–1793*, vol. 2, *The History* (Breinigsville, Pa.: Pennsylvania German Society, 1980), 309–10; Wolfgang Splitter, *Pastors, People, Politics: German Lutherans in Pennsylvania, 1740–1790* (Trier: Wissenschaftlicher Verlag, 1998), 114.

14. See Esser, *Sprache und Integration*, 160–61.

15. Regarding this phenomenon generally, see Werner K. Blessing, *Staat und Kirche in der Gesellschaft: Institutionelle Autorität und mentaler Wandel in Bayern während des 19. Jahrhunderts* (Göttingen: Vandenhoeck und Ruprecht, 1982), 5. For America specifically, see Beate Rese, *Texas—Ziel deutscher Auswanderung im 19. Jahrhundert* (Pfaffenweiler: Centaurus-Verlags-Gesellschaft, 1996), 133. This is shown also through the example of marital ties by Mark Häberlein, "The Integration of German Immigrants in 18th-Century North America: The Case of Lancaster, Pennsylvania," in *Atlantic Migrations: Regions and Movements in Germany and North America / USA During the 18th and 19th Century*, ed. Sabine Heerwart and Claudia Schurmann (Münster: Lit, 2007), 141; George M. Marsden, *Religion and American Culture* (San Diego: Harcourt Brace Jovanovich, 1990), 63; Martina Löw, *Deutsches Luthertum in "amerikanischer Wildnis": Eine religionssoziologische Studie über die Akkulturation deutscher Lutheraner am Beispiel der Kolonie New York* (Marburg: Tectum-Verlag, 2003), 27–33.

16. See Hermann Wellenreuther, *Ausbildung und Neubildung: Die Geschichte Nordamerikas vom Ausgang des 17. Jahrhunderts bis zum Ausbruch der Amerikanischen Revolution 1775* (Münster: Lit, 2001), 466–67; Splitter, *Pastors*, 63.

17. Cited per Carl Frederick Haussmann, *Kunze's Seminarium and the Society for the Propagation of Christianity and Useful Knowledge Among the Germans in America* (Philadelphia: Americana Germanica Press, 1917), 82: "das ganze Countees (Grafschaften) im Lande sind, wo lauter Deutsche wohnen, deren Kinder kein Wort Englisch verstehen."

18. On the multilingualism of the pastors, with the example of Francis Daniel Pastorius, see Erben, *Harmony of Spirits*, 147ff.

19. "Die Teutschen werden bald halb englisch." *Der Hoch-Deutsch Americanische Calender auf das Jahr 1754* (Germantown, Pa.: Christoph Saur, 1754), n.p. Regarding the rapid multilingualism of residents of the frontier, see Graeff, *Relations*, 16–17; Weaver, *Franklin*, 538.

20. See Karsten Lehmann, "Religion und Integration—Spezifika der politischen Debatte und Perspektiven der Forschung," in *Religion und Migration*, ed. Hega Nagel and Mechthild Jansen (Frankfurt am Main: VAS, 2007), 29–44. On America specifically, see Anne Aengenvoort, *Migration—Siedlungsbildung—Akkulturation: Die Auswanderung Nordwestdeutscher nach Ohio, 1830–1914* (Stuttgart: Steiner, 1999), 242–52; Löw, *Luthertum*, 21–23. Indicators include participation in political life, the adoption of English legal traditions, and the increasing number of German-English intermarriages; see Owen S. Ireland, *Religion, Ethnicity, and Politics. Ratifying the Constitution in Pennsylvania* (University Park: Penn State University Press, 1995), 244ff.; Roeber, *Palatines*.

21. Glatfelter, *Pastors*, 26.

22. Heinrich Melchior Mühlenberg, *The Journals of Henry Melchior Muhlenberg*, trans. and ed. Theodore G. Tappert and John Doberstein, 3 vols. (Philadelphia: Evangelical Lutheran Ministerium of Pennsylvania and Adjacent States and Muhlenberg Press, 1942–58; repr., Camden, Maine: Picton Press, 1980), 1:287, June 9, 1751.

23. See Baer, *Trial*, 1–21.

24. "Der Zustand der Deutschen in Pennsylvanien. Wenn sie wollen," in *Der Hoch=Deutsche*

Americanische Calender, Auf das Jahr 1786... (Germantown: Leibert u. Billmeyer, 1785), n.p.; see Splitter, *Pastors*, 309–10.

25. "Dritter Zuruf an die Deutschen in Amerika," *Evangelisches Magazin unter der Aufsicht der Deutschen Evangelisch=Lutherischen Synode* 2, no. 3 (1813): 174–77.

26. "Wenn sie [die Deutschen] denn wollen."

27. "Kein Volk auf der Erde die Deutschen Bewohner von Pennsylvanien übertreffen [wenn die] Deutsche Deutsch geblieben und auch Deutsche Sprache und Sitten beybehalten hätte." Justus Heinrich Christian Helmuth, *Die Spuren der Güte Gottes in der Deutschen Evangelisch Lutherischen Gemeinde in Philadelphia* (Germantown: Billmeyer, 1791), 9.

28. "Scheide, *darin dies Messer des Geistes steckt*." Martin Luther, "An die Ratsherren aller Städte deutschen Landes, daß sie christliche Schulen aufrichten und halten sollen" (1524), in *D. Martin Luthers Werke*, 120 vols. (Weimar, 1883–2009), WA 15, 38, 8–9.

29. Brunnholtz to Francke, August 28, 1744, AFSt/M 4A2:39; Heinrich Melchior Mühlenberg, *Die Korrespondenz Heinrich Melchior Mühlenbergs: Aus der Anfangszeit des deutschen Luthertums in Nordamerika*, ed. Kurt Aland et al., 5 vols. (Berlin: Walter de Gruyter, 1986–2002) (hereafter *KM*), Nr. 186, March 3, 1759, 2:372.

30. For instance, there is mention of a bill of sale, drafted in English, for a Lutheran church. *KM*, Nr. 165, December 2, 1755, 2:266ff.

31. On the communication with Presbyterians in Raritan, see *KM*, Nr. 72, November 16, 1748, 1:317ff.

32. "Die deutsche Sprache gantz verlernet und war so aufgewachsen daß sie nichts von der Christlichen Lehre wusste. Ich muß ihr die Glaubens Lehre in der Englischen Sprache beybringen." *KM*, Nr. 17, March 17, 1743, 1:71.

33. See Brunnholtz to Francke, July 12, 1749, AFSt/M 4C3:24, 113; *KM*, Nr. 93, June 15, 1751, 1:415. See also *Nachrichten von den vereinigten deutschen evangelisch-lutherischen Gemeinen in Nord-America, absonderlich in Pensylvanien: Mit einer Vorrede von D. Johann Ludewig Schulze, Halle, Waisenhaus 1787*, ed. Wilhelm Julius Mann, B. M. Schmucker, and Wilhelm Germann, vol. 1 (Allentown, Pa.: Probst, Diehl, 1886), 163; vol. 2 (Philadelphia: Eisenhardt, 1895), 12 (hereafter *HN*). Preaching in a foreign language was not unusual, as the example of Swedish Lutherans shows. See *KM*, Nr. 23, August 12, 1743, 1:100.

34. "Legten wir den ersten Grundstein zu der ersten lutherischen Kirche in Providence. Es war auch eine gewaltige Menge Volcks zugegen, sowohl Englische als Deutsche.... hernach hielt eine deutsche Rede.... Nach Vollendung derselben hielt auch eine Englische Rede." *KM*, Nr. 19, June 6, 1743, 1:88.

35. See Glatfelter, *Pastors*, 261. Cf. *HN*, 1:16.

36. "Verfall unter unsern armen Lutherischen Leuten," which had led almost to the "völligen Ruin unserer Lutherischen Kirche." *KM*, Nr. 23, August 12, 1743, 1:101. He grounded his stance in the claim that every individual could "in religious matters ... do and ... omit what he wants." *KM*, Nr. 17, March 17, 1743, 1:59–60.

37. "Anbeter oder Bigot der teutschen Sprache ... so mögte deren algemäligen Abgang befürchten. Inzwischen deucht mir es gleichviel zu seyn mit den Sprachen, wenn nur unsere Protestantisch=Evangelische Lehre erhalten und die Krafft der Gottseligkeit promovirt und propagirt wird." *KM*, Nr. 159, May 29, 1755, 2:242. Cf. *HN*, 1:16. Similarly, Pastorius had asserted that all languages are suited for the praise of God. See Erben, *Harmony of Spirits*, 154.

38. Erben, *Harmony of Spirits*, 155–56.

39. On the fundamental significance that Mühlenberg ascribed to schools, see, for instance, *KM*, Nr. 25, August 22, 1743, 1:107; *KM*, Nr. 76, December 20, 1749, 1:341; Patrick M. Erben, "Educating Germans in Colonial Pennsylvania," in *"The Good Education of Youth": Worlds of Learning in the Age of Franklin*, ed. John H. Pollack (New Castle, Del.: Oak Knoll Press; Philadelphia: University of Pennsylvania Libraries, 2009), 141–42.

40. See Charles Lewis Maurer, *Early Lutheran Education in Pennsylvania* (Philadelphia: Dorrance, 1932), 34–37, 201–11; John H. Pollack, "Introduction: Worlds of Learning in the Age of Franklin," in Pollack, *"Good Education,"* 16–20; Patrick M. Erben, "Educating Germans in Colonial Pennsylvania," in Pollack, *"Good Education,"* 123–49; *HN*, 2:171; Carl

Frederick Haussmann, *Kunze's Seminarium and the Society for the Propagation of Christianity and Useful Knowledge Among the Germans in America*, Americana Germanic 27 (Philadelphia, Pa. 1917, 11.

41. See, for instance, *KM*, Nr. 255, April 22, 1763, 3:60–61.

42. *KM*, Nr. 14, December 3, 1742, 1:42; *KM*, Nr. 17, March 17, 1743, 1:71; *KM*, Nr. 19, June 6, 1743, 1:89. On the language use of the Moravians, see Erben, *Harmony of the Spirits*, 301ff.

43. See Glatfelter, *Pastors*, 308–10; Samuel Edwin Weber, *The Charity School Movement in Colonial Pennsylvania, 1754–1763: A History of the Educational Struggle Between the Colonial Authorities and the German Inhabitants of Pennsylvania* (Philadelphia: Press of G. S. Lasher, 1905), 41ff.; M. G. Jones, *The Charity School Movement: A Study of Eighteenth Century Puritanism in Action* (Cambridge: Cambridge University Press, 2013), 36–41. On Will Smith, a leading figure in this undertaking, see George W. Boudreau, "Provost Smith and His Circle: The College of Philadelphia and the Cultural Transformation of Pennsylvania," in Pollack, "*Good Education,*" 168–84. On the language use of the Moravians, see Erben, *Harmony of the Spirits*, 301ff.

44. See Graeff, *Relations*, 16; Weber, *Charity School*, 38–39; Weaver, "Benjamin Franklin," 541. Mühlenberg also pointed to the connection between the foundation of the charity schools and the fear that Germans in Pennsylvania might adopt a pro-French position in the British-French conflict; see *KM*, Nr. 186, March 3, 1759, 2:374.

45. On the use of one's own catechism, see *KM*, Nr. 165, December 2, 1755, 2:266ff.; see also *KM*, Nr. 186, March 3, 1759, 2:374. Here Mühlenberg confirms that the Germans retained a free hand in religious instruction.

46. See Glatfelter, *Pastors*, 314; Elizabeth Lewis Pardoe, "Poor Children and Enlighted Citizens: Lutheran Education in America," *Pennsylvania History* 68, no. 2 (2001): 166; Horace W. Smith, *Life and Correspondence of William Smith* (Philadelphia: Ferguson Bros., 1877), 57–58; Weber, *Charity School*, 34.

47. Additionally, the project ran into financial difficulties: Only eleven of the twenty-five schools originally planned could be opened, and these had to cancel instruction after Great Britain stopped financial support as a consequence of the French and Indian War. See Maurer, *Early Lutheran Education*, 212–20.

48. See *KM*, Nr. 165, December 2, 1755, 2:266ff. By contrast, Francke commented in a positive sense that it was the political and Christian aim of the charity schools to integrate Germans into English society. See *KM*, Nr. 169, June 24, 1756, 2:291ff.

49. Christoph Saur, *Eine nützliche Anweisung oder Beyhülffe vor Deutsche um Englisch zu lernen: Wie es vor Neu-Ankommende und andere im Land gebohrne Land- und Handwerksleute, welche in der Englishcne Sprache erfahrene und geübte Schulmeister und Praeceptores ermangeln* . . . (Germantown: Saur, 1751).

50. Wellenreuther, *Glaube und Politik in Pennsylvania, 1681–1776: Die Wandlungen der Obrigkeitsdoktrin und des "Peace Testimony" der Quäker*, Kölner historische Abhandlungen 20 (Cologne: Böhlau Verlag, 1972), 199–269; Brunnholz, November 29, 1745, AFSt/M 4C4:14.

51. Erben, "Educating Germans," 138–39.

52. Mühlenberg was convinced that as soon as the English got the upper hand in the clashes with France, their commitment to the charity schools would wane. See *KM*, Nr. 186, March 3, 1759, 2:374.

53. "Höchst gefährlich für unserer teutsche Kinder [weil] nichts von Christo beigebracht, dafür alle möglichen Unarten und Eitelkeiten erlaubt." *KM*, Nr. 255, April 22, 1763, 3:60.

54. See *KM*, Nr. 112, February 18, 1752, and Francke's negative answer, in *KM*, Nr. 124, September 13, 1752, 1:531. See Karl Otto Strohmidel, "Turning Confessionalist: Heinrich Melchior Mühlenberg und das Luthertum im pluralistischen Pennsylvania," *Amerikastudien: Eine Vierteljahresschrift* 38 (1993): 391.

55. "Mutter- und hiesige Landes-Sprache." See *KM*, Nr. 364, June 6, 1766, 3:375ff.; *KM*, Nr. 409, September 12, 1767, 3:541n12.

56. See Michael Hochgeschwender, *Die Amerikanische Revolution: Geburt einer Nation 1763–1815* (Munich: C. H. Beck 2017), 352–54; Hochgeschwender, *Amerikanische Religion: Evangelikalismus, Pfingstlertum und Fundamentalismus* (Frankfurt am Main: Suhrkamp, 2007), 77–116.

57. For Handschuh, see Kurt Aland, "Einleitung" to *KM*, 2:17; Johann Nicolas Kurz to his colleagues, April 4, 1753, AFSt/M 4C6:13.

58. See Hausmann, *Seminarium*, 89; Pardoe, "Poor Children," 177–78; Aland "Einleitung" to *KM*, 4:12–13; *KM*, Nr. 602, February 21, 1773, 4:483.

59. See Aland, "Einleitung" to *KM*, 4:12–13; Hausmann, *Seminarium*, 29.

60. Quote from Hausmann, *Seminarium*, 99: "Beym unterricht der deutschen Jugend, . . . soll allzeit die Absicht aufs Englische gerichtet werden, doch so, dasz beym Vortrag aller Wissenschaften, nur die Englische Sprache und Redekunst ausgenommen, die deutsche Lehrart herrschen soll." The concept of a "German *Lehrart*" represents a demarcation vis-à-vis the English *Lehrart*, here described as non-Christian. See *KM*, Nr. 255, April 22, 1763, 3:60–61, according to which English academies and private schools are dangerous for German children because "nothing of Christ" is taught in them.

61. Hausmann, *Seminarium*, 17; Saul Sack, *History of Higher Education in Pennsylvania* (Harrisburg: Commonwealth of Pennsylvania, Pennsylvania Historical and Museum Commission, 1963), 113.

62. Sack, *Higher Education*, 113.

63. "Fähigkeit, Deutsch zu sprechen, ist in hier geborenen gering. . . . Die meisten Deutschen reden nicht deutsch," and if they do, they speak it in a "Mundart, zu deren Gebrauch ein Gelerter durch keine Foltern zu bringen wäre." Johann Christoph Kunze, *Von den Absichten und dem bisherigen Fortgang der privilegierten Deutschen Gesellschaft zu Philadelphia in Pennsylvanien: In einer vor der Gesellschaft gehaltenen Rede* (Philadelphia: Steiner, 1782), 35 and 48.

64. "Verständigen Deutschen . . . verachten die englische Sprache nicht und ehren ihre Muttersprache. Jene sprechen sie, wo sie müssen, und diese, wo sie können." Ibid., 35.

65. "Ist hier und wird die Muttersprache bleiben. Aber welcher Deutsche die Deutsche dabei vernachlässigen heist, mus sein Andenken entweder in Deutschland stinkend gemacht, oder weder dort noch hier in irgend einer Sprache viel vernünftiges gedacht haben." Ibid., 37.

66. "Im Handel und Gewerbe lert uns die Notwendigkeit Englisch: aber im Gottesdienst würde die Veränderung der Sprache eine wunderbare Gemütsfassung anzeigen und Andacht und Offenherzigkeit hemmen. . . . Wir reden also hier Deutsch, und das zweite und dritte Geschlecht, das etwa noch auf Religion und Gottesdienst halten möchte, wird in gottesdienstlichen Dingen noch Deutsch reden." Ibid., 43.

67. See ibid., 35, 37.

68. John Christopher Kunze, *A Table of a New Construction for Calculating the Great Eclipse Expected to Happen on the 16th of June, 1806* (New York: T. and F. Swords, 1806); Kunze, *A New Method of Calculating All the Lunar and Solar Eclipses, and New and Full Moons, from the Creation of the World: Grounded upon the Scripture Chronology* (New York T. and J. Swords, 1806).

69. Helmuth and Johann Friedrich Schmidt, for example, raised with Johann Ludwig Schulze the demand for imparting skills for daily life. Philadelphia, October 8, 1789 (AFSt/M 4 D 2: 17). On the multifaceted engagement of Helmuth, see Anthony Gregg Roeber, "The von Mosheim Society and the Preservation of German Education and Culture in the New Republic, 1789–1813," in *German Influences on Education in the United States to 1917*, ed. Henry Geitz, Jürgen Heideking, and Jürgen Herbst (Washington, D.C.: German Historical Institute; Cambridge: Cambridge University Press, 1995), 157–76; Roeber, "J. H. C. Helmuth, Evangelical Charity, and the Public Sphere in Pennsylvania, 1793–1800," *Pennsylvania Magazine of History and Biography* 121, nos. 1–2 (1997): 77–100.

70. See Roeber, "J. H. C. Helmuth," 84ff. (here at length).

71. See Glatfelter, *Pastors*, 495–511.

72. Regarding the contents of instruction, see *Freyheitsbrief der Deutschen Hohen Schule (College) in der Stadt Lancaster, in dem Staate Pennsylvanien nebst einer Anrede an die Deutschen dieses Staats, von den Trusties der besagten Hohen Schule* (Philadelphia: Melchior Steiner, 1787), 2.

73. See *Anrede* (= Anhang am *Freyheitsbrief*), 11, 14. See generally, in addition, Esser, *Migration*, 4. As an example *ex negativo*, it should be

noted that the pastors often had to function as translators, for instance of legal documents. See Erben, *Harmony of Spirits*, 145–46.

74. On the significance of the mother tongue—usually slight at best—for social advancement in the new land, see Esser, *Migration*, 2–3.

75. See *Anrede*, 14.

76. See Esser, *Migration*, 2.

77. See Sack, *Higher Education*, 116.

78. On the Mosheim Society, see Roeber, "Mosheim Society," 165–68, as well as "Abhandlungen der Mosheimischen Gesellschaft in Philadelphia, Erster Teil 1790/91," Joseph Horner Memorial Library, GERMAN AMER. COL, Ms. Coll. AE 1380. In addition to various pastors and graduates of the University of Pennsylvania, members of the society included the future congressman Henry Muhlenberg, a grandchild of Johann Melchior Mühlenberg, and a son of pastor Schmidt who later became a justice of the Supreme Court of Pennsylvania.

79. On the purpose of the magazine, see *Evangelisches Magazin* (1811): 1–4.

80. "Wenn man die Kinder blos englisch lernen ließe, und vollkomme englisch (d.h. nur Sprache lernen ohne die Sitten zu übernehmen); dagegen könnte kein Venünftiger etwas sagen—ihre zeitlich Wohlfahrt in diesem Lande macht es notwendig." See *Evangelisches Magazin* (1813): 67.

81. Gotthilf Heinrich Ernst Mühlenberg to Johann Friedrich Nebe, January 21, 1807, AFSt/M 4D6:17.

82. See Diary of Helmuth, PH48 A1803–1810, January 17, 1805; Baer, *Trial*, 58.

83. Heinrich Melchior Mühlenberg had already complained about this situation. See HN, 2:12. See *Evangelisches Magazin* (1813): 67–68: "alle gründlichen Erbauungs-Bücher, welche sie nun in ihrer Muttersprache nicht mehr lesen können, den deutschen Ernst im Gottesdienst, der doch in keiner englischen Kirche so biblisch rein ist."

84. On this fear, see Baer, *Trial*, 16.

85. See Mühlenberg, *Journals of Henry Melchior Muhlenberg*, 1:283, May 31, 1751; and *Evangelisches Magazin* (1813): 67–68.

86. "Ihrem Gottesdienst verdanken Deutsche Amerikaner den größten Theil ihres eigenthümlichen Charakters, und nur dieser erhält ihre Sprache.... im Gottesdienst und in den Kirchen ist die deutsche Abkunft unübersehbar." See *Amerikanische Ansichten von dem Gottesdienst und anderen Eigenheiten der Deutschen: Der Mosheimischen Gesellschaft in Philadelphia zugeeignet, und monatlich herausgegeben von Pastor Plitt*, no. 1 (January 1820): 1–2.

87. See Friederike Baer, "Speaking American," *American History* 42, no. 3 (2007): 62.

88. Kunze letters, May 12, 1807, Lutheran Archives Center at Philadelphia: PK 96, "Band der Einigkeit."

89. *Bemerkungen an die Mitglieder der Deutsch=Lutherischen Gemeine in und um Philadelphia, darüber daß nur Deutsch gepredigt wird, und deshalb ihre Gemeine in Verfall geräth* (Philadelphia: Zentler, 1815).

90. Friedrich August Mühlenberg, *Rede vor der incorporierten Deutschen Gesellschaft in Philadelphia, im Staat Pennsylvanien, am 20. September, 1794* (Philadelphia: Steiner u. Kämmerer, 1795), 14.

91. John Christopher Kunze, ed., *Hymn and Prayer-Book: For the use of such Lutheran Churches as use the English Language* (New York: Hurtin and Commardinger, 1795). For 1782, see Kunze, *Von den Absichten*, 36; for 1792, see Kunze, preface to *Hymn and Prayer-Book*.

92. Parallel to this linguistic development, the pastors also undertook a positive reinterpretation of their new home. While Mühlenberg and other pastors of the older generation described America as the "abendländische Wüste" (western desert), the younger Kunze, after the War of Independence, saw the country as "Gottes Haus," as a "Pforte des Himmels," and thus as the new promised land: "Hier ist Eben Ezer" (God's house; a gateway to heaven; Here is Ebenezer). For the negative view, see *KM*, Nr. 76, December 20, 1749. For the positive interpretation, see Johann Christoph Kunze, *Eine Aufforderung an das Volk Gottes in Amerika zum frohen Jauchzen und Danken. An dem von einem Erlauchten Congres wegen erhaltenen Friedens und erlangter Unabhängigkeit auf den 11ten December, 1783, ausgeschriebenen Dankfeste in der Zions-kirche zu Philadelphia vorgestellt, und auf Verlangen*

verschiedener Zuhoerer dem Druck übergeben nebst dem Anhange einer anderen Predigt aehnlichen Inhalts, und an dem Dank- und Bettage des Jahres 1779 gehalte (Philadelphia: Steiner 1784), 45, 76. On the sermon, see Wolfgang Flügel, "Das Beste aus zwei Welten. Geschichtskonstrukte hallescher Pastoren im Pennsylvania des 18. Jahrhunderts," in *Konstruktion von Geschichte: Jubelrede—Predigt—protestantische Historiographie*, ed. Klaus Tanner (Leipzig: Evangelische Verlagsanstalt, 2012), 188–91.

93. See *Eine Adresse an die Glieder der Deutschen Lutherischen Gemeine in und bey Philadelphia* (Philadelphia, n.d.); *Adresse der [sic] Committee, bestimmt von einer großen Anzahl Glieder der deutschen Lutherischen Gemeine, in Philadelphia, an die Corporation derselben, nebst ihrer Antwort* (Philadelphia: Geyer, 1805), 1; on pride at being simultaneously German and American by birth, see David F. Schäffer, *Bußtags=Predigt, gehalten Donnerstags, den 5ten August, 1813, an dem, durch die Synode anempfohlnen Buß und Bät=tag, in der Evangelisch=Lutherischen Kirche in Friedrichstaun* (Friedrichstaun: Melcheimer, 1813), 4.

94. See *Adresse Committee*, 5.

95. Lutheran Archives Center at Philadelphia: PK 96, Kunze letters: "Die Sprache verhält sich zur Herzensreligion gleichgültig, außer insofern, dass die eine mehr Erbauungsmittel enthält als die andere. Die deutsche ist hierinn gewiss die reichste in der Welt, und wo nicht absolute Nothwendigkeit den Zwang ... legt, unsere Kinder in einer anderen Sprache zum Christenthum anzuführen, sollte es unsere Herzenslust sein, dieselbe Erziehung [zu geben, die wir genossen]." Similarly, see Joseph Hutchins, *A Sermon preached in the Lutheran Church, on the opening of Franklin College, in the borough of Lancaster, Pennsylvania, July 17th, 1787* (Philadelphia, 1806), 17: "On the force of religion, you can have no reasonable objection to the use of the English tongue, because it is undoubtedly as proper as the German for the conveyance of religious instruction to your children. The German may be studied as a secondary useful language."

96. See H. Georg Anderson, "The Early National Period, 1790–1840," in *The Lutherans in North America*, ed. Eugene Clifford Anderson (Philadelphia: Fortress Press, 1980), 95–97; see also Splitter, *Pastors*, 314.

97. See Baer, "Speaking American," passim.

98. See Splitter, *Pastors*, 314.

99. See Baer, *Trial*, 14ff.

100. Ibid., 111, 117.

101. Ibid., 117–18.

102. See Liam Riordan, *Many Identities, One Nation: The Revolution and Its Legacy in the Mid-Atlantics* (Philadelphia: University of Pennsylvania Press, 2007), 157, 161–63; and Arthur Christian Repp, *Luther's Catechism Comes to America: Theological Effects on the Issues of the Small Catechism Prepared in or for America Prior to 1850* (Metuchen, N.J.: Scarecrow Press, 1982), 103.

103. See Riordan, *Many Identities*, 171.

PART 3

The Languages of Race and (Anti-)Slavery

CHAPTER 6

Writing Against Slavery
Germantown, Quakers, and the Ethnic Origins of Early Antislavery Thought

KATHARINE GERBNER

When William Penn advertised the Pennsylvania Colony to German- and Dutch-speaking Protestants in the Rhineland and Palatinate, slavery was far from his mind. In his *Account of the Province of Pennsylvania in America*, translated by Penn's agent Benjamin Furly into Dutch and German, Penn offered prospective emigrants five thousand acres of land for £100 and guaranteed freedom of worship to all in what was touted as the "Holy Experiment."[1] By March of 1683, less than a year later, three men from Krefeld, a town near the border of present-day Germany and the Netherlands, had purchased a total of fifteen thousand acres of land from Furly. They were joined by a group of Quakers from Krisheim, who immigrated to Pennsylvania in 1685. These settlers, along with the Pietist lawyer Francis Daniel Pastorius, settled the town of Germantown, Pennsylvania, about a half-day's walk from Philadelphia. While not all of the German immigrants converted to Quakerism, there were enough German- and Dutch-speaking Quakers to found a preparatory meeting in Germantown, Pennsylvania.[2]

In 1688, the Germantown Meeting authored a protest against slavery, the first of its kind written in the American colonies. The German and Dutch Quakers rejected both slave trading and slaveholding and argued that freedom of conscience should be matched by freedom of body. This type of antislavery stance differed from the prevailing English and Welsh Quaker thought of the same period. While the Germantown protest argued for an end to slavery in Pennsylvania, English and Welsh Quakers tended to accept a limited form of slaveholding, but they rejected the presence of slaves when they threatened the Quaker family. Linguistically, the Germantown protest was also unusual. It did not follow the typical format of a Quaker document sent between meetings. It addressed itself to "Christians" rather than "Friends" and, with minor exceptions, did not include biblical references and never mentioned Jesus Christ—all unusual practices for a Quaker text in the late seventeenth century. In its direct approach to the question of slavery, the Germantowners also omitted the salutary introduction to Friends that was customary for epistles sent between meetings.

This essay situates the Germantown Quaker protest within the complex linguistic, political, and social world of late seventeenth-century Pennsylvania, paying close attention to the conflicts and conversations between German, Dutch, English, and Welsh Quakers in Penn's "holy experiment."[3] It shows how ethnic and linguistic differences between seventeenth-century Quakers shaped early debates about slavery. Quakers from the Rhineland, Wales, and England developed different ideas about slaveholding based on their experiences in Europe, their transatlantic networks, and their ideals of community. While Germantown Quakers emphasized the rights of the enslaved, Welsh Quakers in Pennsylvania tended to focus on the dangers of slave owning for Friends. But the majority of Quakers in the late seventeenth century were not antislavery. Quaker immigrants from Barbados were influential in popularizing a "conversion ethic" that sought to reconcile slavery with Quaker practice.

Rather than looking forward to the Quaker abolitionist movement of the eighteenth century, this chapter seeks to demonstrate the diversity of early Quaker ideas about slavery. Like Jean Soderlund, I recognize that antislavery views came in many varieties—some emphasized the rights of the enslaved, while others focused on the dangers of slave owning for Friends. Yet I also argue that antislavery thought must be examined within the context of the prevailing Quaker acceptance of slavery. I expand on Kristen Block's analysis of Quaker slave owning in Barbados and Pennsylvania to demonstrate the wide range of pro- and antislavery positions that existed in late seventeenth-century Quaker Pennsylvania. Finally, my argument builds on Brycchan Carey's study of Quaker antislavery rhetoric by emphasizing the significance of early Quaker conversations about slavery. Yet my interpretation departs from Carey's in two ways: first, I emphasize the importance of ethnicity in early Quaker antislavery thought. Second, while Carey sees Quaker evangelization in Barbados as part of the movement toward antislavery, I argue that the Quaker "conversion ethic" should not be linked to antislavery beliefs, because it signaled an attempt to reconcile Quaker theology with slaveholding. Instead, I contend that the German and Dutch authors of the Germantown protest introduced a new perspective on slaveholding to an English and Welsh Quaker community that was in the midst of its own struggle to reconcile slavery with the Quaker peace testimony.[4]

PENNSYLVANIA AND THE WEST INDIAN CONVERSION ETHIC

The Quaker conversation about slavery began well before the founding of Pennsylvania. It was in Barbados, rather than Penn's Quaker colony, that Friends were first confronted with a booming slave society that was increasingly dependent on enslaved Africans for economic prosperity.[5] In the 1660s and '70s, Barbados was one of the primary destinations for Quakers in the Americas. Richard Dunn has estimated that hundreds of Friends lived on Barbados, and the vast majority of them were slave owners.[6] Indeed, slave owning was extremely common among seventeenth-century Quakers, and most did not see a conflict between slavery and their Quaker beliefs.

The first individual publicly to question the meaning of slave owning for Friends was the Quaker leader George Fox. While Fox addressed slavery as early as 1657, it was not until he visited Barbados in 1671 that he addressed the issue at length. After spending a month on the island, he advised Friends to "consider . . . if you were in the same Condition as the Blacks are," and to "do you for and to them, as you would willingly have them or any other do unto you, were you in the like slavish Condition." While Fox did not advocate an end to slavery, he encouraged Friends to preach to the enslaved men and women in their families and to "let them have two or three Hours of the Day once in the Week . . . to wait upon the Lord."[7] While some scholars have argued that Fox demonstrated a protoabolitionist stance, I have argued elsewhere that Fox was instrumental in developing and articulating a "conversion ethic" that sought to reconcile the Quaker conscience with slaveholding.[8] Fox encouraged Friends to evangelize to the slaves in their families, and there is evidence that at least some Barbadian Quakers attempted to do so.[9]

When Penn founded Pennsylvania in 1682, the Quaker colony relied on its connection to Barbados for shipping and economic ties.[10] Furthermore, many Barbados Quakers decided to immigrate to Pennsylvania, since Quakers were persecuted for their beliefs on Barbados. As a result, there was a strong contingent of slave-owning West Indian Friends in seventeenth-century Quaker Philadelphia. As Kristen Block has argued, these Barbadian immigrants brought with them a comfort with African slavery and a conversion ethic based on Fox's *Gospel Family-Order*. Wealthy slave-owning Quakers like Lewis Morris, who relocated from Barbados to the Middle Colonies, worked to silence the doubts that non–West Indian Quakers had about slavery. Morris, as Block writes, was "part of an effort in the Americas and Britain to establish ideals for 'godly' slaveholding. He and other West Indian Quaker leaders aimed ... to ease the consciences of individual masters, to create a consensus among the Society's members, and to help Friends in the colonies build up a stock of moral capital to be used against their non-Quaker peers."[11] West Indian Quakers introduced an ideology that reconciled slavery with the Quaker conscience and provided a robust economic incentive to accept African slavery.

QUAKER SLAVERY IN THE MIDDLE COLONIES AND UPPER SOUTH

In addition to immigrants from Barbados, the Middle Colonies were already home to a number of Quaker communities in the colonies both to the east—in East and West Jersey—and south, in Maryland and Virginia. Unlike the Quakers on Barbados, the first Friends to settle in the Middle Colonies did not encounter a massive slave regime. Still, over the second half of the seventeenth century, black laborers slowly replaced white indentured servants in many families. Friends participated in this shift and sought to integrate enslaved Africans into their households. Like Barbadian Quakers, they struggled to bring slavery in line with their religious discipline. While records are minimal, there are some sources that reveal how Quakers in Pennsylvania, Jersey, and the Chesapeake adapted to slaveholding.

In Maryland, Quakers congregated in Annapolis, Somerset, and what is now known as Talbot County.[12] Many of the Friends who settled on the Eastern Shore had worked the favorite Quaker circuits of the day. Wenlock Christison, one of the most influential leaders of Maryland Friends, had spent time in Barbados and had been sentenced to hang in Boston before he settled in Maryland. Given his past, it is not surprising that Christison used his Barbados connections to send "some negroes... out of Barbadoes."[13] While there is no indication of Christison's further thoughts about slavery, his comments make it clear that slaveholding was seen as an economically wise pursuit among at least some Maryland Friends.

While Maryland Quakers used their West Indian connections to import slaves, Friends in Virginia struggled to reconcile slaveholding with their peace testimony. In 1699, Nathan Newbie, a member of the Chuckatuck Meeting in Lower Virginia, was accused of beating his slave to death. In a letter addressed to the men's and women's meetings at Chuckatuck, he defended himself: "Whearas There hath been many Scandalous Reports that I have been the death of my negroe: this is to satisfie all persons that will belive the truth of the matter that I doe solemly declare in the presence of God that I never intended his death neither did I give him any Blow wch I thought might Take his life but this I must Confese that not many days before hee died I did Correct him sharply hee giveing mee great occation for the same."[14] Newbie's letter speaks to an aspect of Quakers and slavery that is rarely discussed: the problem of violence within the slave-owning Quaker family. Since most scholars interested in Quakers and slavery focus on antislavery, the experiences of Quaker slave owners, which include the difficulty of keeping a peace testimony while disciplining slaves, are rarely mentioned.[15] It seems that Friends tolerated a certain amount of violence within households but that Newbie crossed the line: the death of his slave, just days after he had been "corrected," meant that he had gone too far.

Newbie claimed to be sorry for what he had done, though he seemed more sorry that his name had been sullied: "[S]orrow did Arise in mee wch was not easily Removed. Upon this the Enemy of mens soul came in like A flood and sharp Triall I and greauicus [grievous] Temptations for A Long Time I was Under hee indeavering by his Craft to begett mee into deadnes and Coldnes this and the black Clouds of infamous Reports wch hanged over mee."[16] It was the "infamous Reports" of his actions that bothered Newbie more than the death of his "negroe." Still, it is clear that he had been too brutal in his treatment of his slave, and the members of his meeting presumably disciplined him (the minutes do not include systematic information on discipline). Yet despite his transgressions, Newbie remained a Friend. In 1707, eight years after writing his letter of defense, he became a traveling minister. Even then, he had problems with his reputation. Though the minutes do not say why, they do record that "some friends [were] Disattisfied as concern[s] Nathan Newby's testimony."[17] Eventually, Newbie was approved for the ministry, but other Friends continued to have doubts about him.

The Newbie episode sheds light on the difficulties that Quakers had even when they accepted slavery. How, for example, should an enslaved person be treated within the Quaker household? How should slaves be disciplined? And how could the Quaker community maintain its peace testimony in a slave society? These questions followed Quakers into Pennsylvania. As new settlers set up households, farms, and shops in the Delaware Valley, enslaved men and women became a common presence in Pennsylvania Quaker households. Quaker meeting minutes rarely mentioned slaves or servants, but again, one anomaly provides insight into one Quaker community in newly founded Pennsylvania. In April 1693, the Dublin Monthly Meeting noted, "The business conserning John Gilberts Commiting adultery with ye Widdow fforres Negro, as is Comonly reported, being debated & several circumstances appearing of his bad behaviour with other women, The judgment of ye Meeting is, that he is not a clear man: and therefore is requested to give forth a paper of Condomnation for ye clearing of truth & ffriends and till such tim[e] as he do it ffriends can have no Unity with him."[18] This disciplinary minute represents the only reference to a specific enslaved or free black in the entire minute book for the Dublin Monthly Meeting. It shows that John Gilberts was disowned by the meeting for "bad behaviour" with women. The first proof of his bad behavior was that he had committed "adultery with ye Widdow fforres Negro," a woman who is never named in the record. Though the note did not mention the legal status of this woman, it is clear that she belonged to the widow Ffores, implying that she was enslaved. The minute then revealed that Gilbert's relation with the widow's slave had been "debated" by members of the meeting. Only then was it mentioned that Gilberts had also behaved badly with "other women." The meeting deemed him out of unity, but it is clear that his relations with the "ye Widdow fforres Negro" were of the greatest concern to Friends. This imbalance in reporting suggests that the Dublin Friends were uncomfortable with the place of enslaved men and women in their households and communities. They condemned all types of adultery, but adultery with an enslaved woman was more threatening to the community because it undermined the patriarchal family and transgressed an unwritten, still-evolving racial boundary.

THE GERMAN ORIGINS OF RIGHTS-BASED ANTISLAVERY THOUGHT

As English, Welsh, and West Indian Quakers in the Middle Colonies struggled to integrate enslaved men and women into their households, a new wave of immigrants from the Rhineland, Palatinate, and other regions in current-day Germany added a new social and cultural constituency to Pennsylvania Quaker society.[19] The Germantown Quakers, most of whom had been Mennonites before their conversion, hailed from the borderlands between modern-day Holland and Germany.[20] Their experience of persecution during and after the Thirty Years' War, along with their firmly held nonconformist principles, made the prospect of immigrating to the "holy experiment" of Pennsylvania an attractive option. Yet despite a number of overlapping beliefs, the founders of Germantown arrived in Pennsylvania with a distinctive culture and a desire to create their own separate community.[21] The Germantowners consistently set themselves apart from the rest of the immigrant population in Pennsylvania. Upon his arrival in 1683, Francis Daniel Pastorius, a pietist lawyer, insisted—against William Penn's preference—that the Dutch and German settlers be given land together, rather than in dispersed pockets around Philadelphia. In 1689, the Germantowners were granted the first charter to become a borough, the only one of its kind ever to be issued in Pennsylvania. This political freedom lent Germantown such an air of independence that in 1701, the town argued that it should be exempt from Pennsylvania taxes.[22]

The Germantowners' conviction to remain autonomous, together with their lack of acquaintance with English Quaker conventions, presented them with a unique perspective on Quaker slave ownership in Pennsylvania. Their normative place within the Quaker meeting hierarchy, meanwhile, gave them a moral and religious voice with which to speak to the English Quakers. In 1688, the Germantown Meeting created what has become, in the past two centuries, a defining symbol of Quaker abolitionism. The Germantown protest, written in 1688 and submitted to the Dublin Monthly Meeting for consideration, conceived of blacks as the social and spiritual equals of whites. The Germantowners argued that there was "no more liberty" to have blacks as slaves than there was to have "other white ones," and in their phrasing of the Golden Rule, the Germantowners added the stipulation that no difference should be made based on "generation, descent, or colour."[23]

The Germantown Quakers built on their experiences as a persecuted religious minority in central Europe to develop their antislavery arguments. They compared the oppression of blacks in Pennsylvania to the oppression of Quakers and Mennonites in Europe, noting that "there are many oppressed for Conscience sacke" in Europe, while "here there are those oppressed, wch are of a black colour." Since the oppression of Quakers and Mennonites was not only religious, but also political and social, this suggests that the Germantowners believed that blacks, like Quakers in Europe, deserved to be treated as political citizens, not slaves.

The Germantowners also used the specter of Turkish and North African slavery to support their claims. They began their protest with a reminder that Christians—including Quakers—were often enslaved by Turks "and sold for slaves into Turkey." Appealing to the common fear of piracy and captivity in the Atlantic, they reminded their readers that Europeans are often "fearful and faint-hearted . . . [at] sea, when they see a strange vessel—being afraid it should be a Turk, and they should be taken." The reminder of Islamic slavery was apt, as many Quakers had been taken captive in North Africa, and Quaker epistles regularly updated Friends on the status of their enslaved brethren.[24] For the Germantown Quakers, it was hypocritical for Christians to do "as Turks doe," and they chided their coreligionists, concluding that slaveholding was "worse for them, which say they are Christians."[25]

Aside from building on their own persecution and the widespread fear of Islamic enslavement, the Germantowners emphasized the conflict between the Quaker peace testimony and the violent nature of slaveholding. What would happen, they asked, if these "stubbern men should joint [sic] themselves, fight for their freedom and handel their masters & mastrisses, as they did handel them before"? Would Friends "tacke the sword at hand & warr against these poor slaves"? The inherent violence of slaveholding was problematic for Friends, and the Germantown Friends utilized this discomfort to their advantage, suggesting that enslaved men and women had "as much right to fight for their freedom, as you have to keep them as slaves."

Finally, the Germantowners played to Friends' desire to attract new immigrants to the Quaker colony. At three separate points, the authors noted that their friends and acquaintances were hesitant to immigrate to a land with slaves. The "marketable" aspects of Pennsylvania were its inexpensive land, its unobtrusive government, and its religious liberty. The institution of slavery—with its potential for slave rebellion—worked against this image. For the Germantowners, who were desperate to attract more settlers from their own homelands, this was a major concern. But their primary concern, and the core of their argument, remained humanitarian. The Germantown Quakers thoroughly rejected the "traffik of men-body" and called for "liberty of ye body" to accompany "liberty of conscience." By doing so, they made a rights-based argument against slavery that insisted that all individuals should have liberty of both "body" and "conscience."

The Germantowners presented their protest to the Monthly Meeting at Dublin, where it was deemed too "weighty" an issue and referred to the Philadelphia Quarterly Meeting. The members of the Quarterly Meeting again deferred judgment and sent the Germantown protest to the Yearly Meeting, the reigning meeting in Pennsylvania. The scribe for the Yearly Meeting was careful to note the ethnicity of the petitioners, commenting that "some German fr[ien]ds" had presented a paper "Concerning the Lawfullness and unlawfullness of Buying and keeping of Negroes." After some discussion, the motion was rejected for having "so General a Relation to many other Prts [sic]."[26]

While the Germantown protest did not succeed in convincing Philadelphia Friends to give up their slaves, its arguments resonated with at least some men and women in Pennsylvania. It is impossible to quantify its exact influence, but many of the ideas articulated in the Germantown protest can clearly be seen in the first printed protest against slavery, *An Exhortation and Caution to Friends Concerning Buying or Keeping of Negroes* (1693). The *Exhortation* was authored by the Christian Quakers, a group of English, Welsh, and German Friends who rallied around the Quaker schismatic George Keith in the early 1690s. Like the Germantown protest, the *Exhortation* condemned slavery and called on all Christians to recognize that "Negroes, Blacks, and Taunies are a real part of Mankind, for whom Christ hath shed his precious Blood, and are capable of Salvation, as well as White Men."[27] While other Quaker antislavery texts of the seventeenth century based their arguments against slavery on the dangers of having blacks in the Quaker household and only marginally included a moral opposition to the slave trade, both the *Exhortation* and the Germantown protest argued that bodily freedom should accompany spiritual freedom.[28] Because the document was associated with Keith, orthodox Quakers never formally considered the ideas presented in it. Yet the antislavery ideas articulated in the Germantown protest and the *Exhortation* did not disappear.

WELSH QUAKERS AND FAMILY ORDER IN SEVENTEENTH-CENTURY PENNSYLVANIA

While German and Dutch Quakers in Germantown developed an antislavery ethic that combined humanitarian and pragmatic concerns, another group of immigrants from Wales and Cheshire (in northwestern England) worked to develop their own solution to the problem of slavery in colonial Pennsylvania. Like the German Quakers, these migrants settled apart from Philadelphia to protect both their language and their culture from foreign influence. The Welsh and Cheshire Quakers settled what became known as the "Welsh Tract" in southwestern Pennsylvania, which included Chester, Merion, Radnor, Haverford, Darby, and Marple. Barry Levy has shown that these Cheshire and Welsh Quakers were "familial radicals" who "inverted the ideals and purposes of their old regions' family system." Their ideal of their family, Levy has written, demanded "the thorough spiritualization of marriage, the granting of spiritual authority to women comparable with that of men, painful self-discipline in childrearing, and the creation of enormous amounts of wealth to give households the resources to accomplish such tasks."[29]

In the last decades of the seventeenth century, some Welsh and Cheshire Quakers began to purchase enslaved men and women to work on their land. As they did so, however, they questioned whether enslaved Africans could be fully integrated into their families and worried that these "strangers" would corrupt their households.[30] Cadwallader Morgan, a Welsh Quaker from Merion, articulated these fears in a paper that he presented to the Yearly Meeting in 1696.[31] Morgan's letter, which was either transcribed or translated from Welsh into English, was an intensely personal reflection on slavery.[32] He began by addressing "ffriends" before revealing, "there was Something before me Concerning the buying of Negroes." Due to the "Scarcity of hands here," Morgan continued, he was considering purchasing slave labor. But further thought led him to doubt this impulse. While a "good" slave "would be Some help," a "bad one of them" would disrupt his household. Morgan asked, "[What] if I should have a bad one of them, that must be Corrected, Or would Run away, Or when I went from home & leave him with a woman or Maid, and he Should desire or Seek to Comitt Wickedness, If Such a thing happened that it would be more Loss and Trouble to me, Then any outward Gain could Countervail." After further reflection, Morgan wrote, "[the Lord] made it known unto me, That I should not be Concerned with them, And afterwards I had no ffreedom to buy or take any of them upon any account." Morgan clarified that his decision did not have a bearing on other Friends: "I can Say," he wrote, "that I have nothing in my heart against any particular that buys them."[33]

Unlike the Germantown Quakers, who founded their argument against slavery on a declaration of the rights of men, Cadwallader Morgan posed slave ownership as a problem for the Quaker household. There would be nothing wrong with slave ownership if all slaves were "good," he implied, but the possibility of a bad slave could disrupt familial order. Morgan specified the sexual threat that an enslaved man posed to both servants and wives. Secondly, Morgan did not apply his personal revelation to other Friends, but he did ask his peers to consult their own consciences. In doing so, he tied slave ownership to "worldly gain."

Morgan's use of the word "worldly" was poignant in the context of 1690s Pennsylvania. In the wake of the Keithian schism, Friends yearned for unity, and the Yearly Meeting had begun a campaign to purge "worldly" things from their midst. In 1694, the Yearly Meeting specifically condemned "the worlds language" as well as "Loosnes and vanity in youth," but the meeting made no explicit connection between slave ownership and worldliness. Cadwallader Morgan's decision to deem slave ownership a "worldly" activity, combined with his reflective, nonbinding decision to abstain from slavery, had a significant effect on the members of the Yearly Meeting. While the meeting had rejected the Germantown protest outright for having "so general a relation to many other parts," Morgan's paper elicited a positive response from the meeting. In a 1696 minute, the Yearly Meeting advised Pennsylvania friends to "be Careful not to Encourage the bringing in of any more Negroes, and that such that have Negroes be Careful of them, bring them to Meetings, or have Meetings with them in their Families, and Restrain them from Loose and Lewd Living as much in them lies and from Rambling abroad on First Days or other Times."[34] The Yearly Meeting minute lacked Morgan's careful introspection but reiterated his concern about the effect of slaves on the Quaker household. This minute has been used as proof of the developing ethic of antislavery within late seventeenth-century Quakerism, but it is better described as an expression of Quaker tribalism.[35] When Morgan defined slaveholding as "worldly," he excluded slavery from the realm of the ideal Quaker household and contributed to a rising strain among Pennsylvania Quakers of defining the importation of slaves as a disorderly threat.

GEORGE GRAY AND THE WEST INDIAN CONVERSION ETHIC

While Cadwallader Morgan and the Yearly Meeting's 1696 minute represent the emergence of "tribalist" antislavery in Pennsylvania, a paper by George Gray—which was probably presented to Friends some time between 1696 and 1700—demonstrates the continued influence of West Indian Quaker thought in the Middle Colonies. Gray had lived in Barbados from the 1660s to the early 1690s, where he worked as a shopkeeper and planter.[36] He, like the majority of Barbadian Quakers, owned slaves, and he maintained a strong ethic about Quaker slaveholding that he brought with him to Pennsylvania in 1692. When Pennsylvania Quakers debated the role of enslaved men and women in their society in the mid-1690s, Gray articulated the Quaker ideals of conversion and reform that had prevailed in the West Indian Quaker community.

Instead of excluding blacks from the household, Gray proclaimed that it was "the Duty of every Master & Mistress" to keep "Nigro[s] as Servants untill they are in Some Measure brought into a Christian Life." Like George Fox in *Gospel Family-Order*, Gray was ambiguous about when or if Christianized slaves should be freed, but unambiguous in his conviction that Christianization was the duty of masters. He developed his argument with a lengthy biblical defense built on Leviticus 24, Ephesians 6:9, Exodus 21:5–6, and Joshua 24:15. Gray believed that blacks were "Heathen by Nature," and pleaded with masters to "bring [their blacks] unto Christianity or a Christian Life that [they] may be free m[e]n Indeed & in Truth." His ideas about Christian practice emphasized behavior over belief. Masters needed to encourage blacks to keep "family Meetings" and to discourage them from "rude[ness,]" "danc[ing], drink[ing] & hav[ing] Merry Meetings [that] are bad examples to all people." He accused blacks of disrupting First Days and "provokeing one another to doe Wickedly," and he urged Quaker masters to keep their slaves busy during the week so they did not have "Liberty to flock & go abroad in Company," which allowed for the opportunity to "do Mischeif & plott & Contrive."

Gray was perfectly aware that his ethic of Christian slavery was nearly identical to the stance of George Fox, and he invoked the Quaker founder directly: "[I]t Could be Well to take the advice of that ancient and faithfull Servant of the Lord G F [George Fox] to have & keep Meetings with them [i.e., the blacks], and it is not only his advice but the advice of many faithfull Servants of the Lord More, as William Edmundson and William Dewsbury." Gray also knew that he had the strength of precedence on his side. For decades, Quakers in the West Indies had integrated slavery into their religious practice by advocating for conversion and family meetings. The Quaker conversion ethic placed pressure on the "Rulers of familyes" to take responsibility for their entire household and to teach blacks, who were "heathen by Nature," truth about "the Kingdome of God & their everlasting happiness."[37]

George Gray's Barbadian past made him part of a sizable contingent of new Pennsylvania residents, and these slave-owning Quakers continued to voice their support for evangelization and slavery.[38] J. William

Frost has argued that the influence of Gray and other Quaker slave owners resulted in the Yearly Meeting's decision to reprint George Fox's *Gospel Family-Order* in 1701.[39] By pointing to Fox's proevangelization statements, these Friends aimed to make benevolent slave owning the orthodox Quaker position in colonial Pennsylvania.

"BLACK NEGROES AND POTTS": ROBERT PILES'S 1698 ANTISLAVERY STATEMENT

While George Gray advocated for a "conversion ethic" that would integrate slaves into the Quaker household, a Welsh Quaker named Robert Piles (also Pile or Pyle) combined elements of the Germantown Quakers' humanitarian concerns with the more "tribalist" arguments of Cadwallader Morgan. Piles's letter suggests that some of the ideas articulated by the Germantowners had percolated throughout the Quaker community in Pennsylvania, but that fears about protecting the Quaker family remained the most poignant and influential argument against slaveholding in Quaker Philadelphia.

Piles's letter, like Morgan's, was a personal reflection about slaveholding. While Piles initially had "sum inclination upon my mind to buy a negro, or negroes," he later questioned "ye lawfulness theyr of under ye Gospel ministration." Piles's original reasons for purchasing a slave provide insight into the mindset of a seventeenth-century Quaker landowner: slaves could be held for life, and they could replace English servants who had completed their indenture. Despite these beneficial aspects of slavery, Piles balked, asking himself whether slaveholding truly lived up to that "command of Christ Jesus, Do unto all men as ye would have all man doe unto you." After reflecting on this question, Piles came to the conclusion that "wee would not willingly ... be slaves [for a] tearm of life."[40] Piles's interpretation of the Golden Rule is significant because it resembled the reasoning of the Germantown Quakers more than that of Barbadian Quakers like Gray. Piles and the Germantown Quakers interpreted the Golden Rule in a radical way that implied not merely good treatment for slaves, but also social equality.

Apart from his radical interpretation of the Golden Rule, Piles's argument resembled the Germantown protest in a number of other interesting ways. Just as the Germantown Quakers claimed that "the negers are brought hither against their will and consent, and . . . many of them are stolen," Piles wrote that he had "heard" that "sum [were] stoln from their country." He asked whether purchasing slaves did not "incurredg rather than discurredg [slave traders] in that wicked work." Also like the Germantown Quakers, Piles worried that slaves "might rise in rebellion and doe us much mischief," and he reminded Friends that they did not "keep a malisha" because it was "against our principles." He, like the Germantown Quakers, even suggested that if the slaves *did* "doe us harm," it would be justified.

Unlike the Germantown Quakers, however, Piles focused on the reflections that had caused him to come to his antislavery position, and he pointed to a dream as the most significant factor in his own decision to abstain from slavery. In his dream, which has attracted a significant amount of attention from scholars, Piles saw himself and a friend walking down a road when he noticed a black pot.[41] Piles picked up the pot and, in a selfish gesture, refused to share it with his friend. He then went a "little farther" down the road and saw "a great ladder standing exact upright, reaching up to heaven." Desiring to go up the ladder, Piles feared that if he continued to hold the pot, he would not be able to ascend. So in order to climb the ladder, he chose to "la[y] ye pot at ye foot of ye ladder." There he saw a "man that gave those that goeth up this ladder sumthing to refresh them." He asked this man what the ladder was, and the man replied that it was "ye light of Christ Jesus, and whoever it bee that his faith bee strong in ye lord, God will uphold that it shall not fall." When Piles awoke, he concluded to "lett black negroes or pots alone."

In his dream, Piles used the adjective "black" only twice. At the beginning of the dream, he saw a "black pott" that he selfishly kept for himself, refusing to share it with his friend. At the end, he transferred the adjective from "pot" to "negroes," thereby linking the two nouns. The implication was that "negroes," like the black pot in the dream, caused selfish behavior and made it impossible for Friends to follow "ye light of Christ Jesus," represented by the ladder. So while Piles's initial attack on slavery resembled the arguments of the Germantown Quakers, his use of dreams set him apart from the arguments of the German and Dutch Friends in two important ways. First, his dream did not concern the spiritual status of the slave, but rather the spiritual status of Piles himself. By connecting "negroes" to the "black pott," he defined a slave as a spiritual barrier, not an individual. In fact, the linkage of pots and Negroes reinforced the idea that Negroes were commodities that could be owned or discarded. Just as Piles left the black pot at the "foot of the ladder," he chose to "leave black negroes . . . alone." Secondly, the use of the dream as a vehicle for argument connected Piles with a well-established tradition of Quaker dreaming.[42] By articulating his antislavery statement as a dream rather than a straightforward set of arguments, Piles made his perspective less menacing to Friends who owned slaves. While the Germantown Quakers were direct in their attack on slavery, Piles—while acknowledging and supporting the arguments of the German Quakers—proceeded in a more ambiguous manner that emphasized both his belonging to the tradition of Quaker dreamers and his self-reflective criticism.

Piles further distanced himself from the Germantown Friends by carefully considering how to discourage slaveholding among Friends. He suggested that enslaved men and women should be taught to "read English" and encouraged to "goe to meetings," suggestions that aligned with George Fox, George Gray, and Cadwallader Morgan. He also failed to specify if or when slavery should be ended. Instead, he included a series of obstacles that would have to be overcome before manumission was possible. It would have to "please ye lord," he wrote, "to open theyr understanding, and bring them measurably to bee obedient" before "ye quarterly meetings [could] bee proper Judges in setting them free." He also added the caveat that manumission should not be too much of a loss to masters. The long list of hurdles preceding manumission shows that Piles was a member of a community that had at least partially accepted slaveholding into its midst. It also suggests that Piles had considered and internalized the arguments of slave-owning Quakers like George Gray. Unlike the Germantown Quakers, Piles was sympathetic to the concerns of slave owners and was cautious, careful, and pragmatic in offering a vision for gradual manumission within the Quaker community. In the decades after Piles's antislavery statement, Welsh Quakers in Chester would put increasing pressure on the Philadelphia Yearly Meeting to halt the importation of more slaves, suggesting that Welsh Quaker leaders like Piles were successful in convincing members of their own communities to reject slavery.

ANTISLAVERY AND THE PHILADELPHIA QUAKER CAMPAIGN AGAINST WORLDLINESS

Piles's antislavery text was, like Morgan's, well received in Quaker Philadelphia. In 1698, the Philadelphia Monthly Meeting continued its debates about family order and the slave trade. At the Philadelphia Monthly Meeting on the 30th day of the 7th month, 1698, Penticott Teage criticized the slave auctions taking place "at the publick market" and convinced Friends that they "ought not to sell them after this manner." Piles's antislavery text may have been read and discussed at the same meeting, though it is not mentioned in the minutes.[43] What is known is that a month later, the meeting noted, "It is the sense of this Meeting that all masters of families among friends do endeavour to bring their Negros to the publick Meetings of worship on first days, and those that do not come to Meetings, may be restrained or prevented from Meeting together in Companies."[44] Both of these minutes showed a strong sense of concern for the behavior of enslaved men and women, the disorder of the slave trade, and the lack of discipline in slave-owning families.

It was the fear of disorder that led the members of the Philadelphia Monthly Meeting to oppose the slave trade—not the humanitarian reasons developed by the Germantown Quakers and the Keithians. On the 30th day of the 8th month, 1698, two days after the Philadelphia Monthly Meeting composed their minute concerning the lack of meetings among slaves, a group of nine Friends composed a letter "To the General Meeting off ffriends In Barbadoes" in which they begged their coreligionists to "put a stop to the importing of them." As they informed the Barbadian Quakers, "many negroes in these parts may prove prejudissial several wayes to us and our posterity," and contrary to their desire, "many negroes [were] brought in this last summer."[45] There is no evidence that the Barbadian Quakers received or responded to the request from the Philadelphia Monthly Meeting, but the correspondence illustrates the growing significance of Pennsylvania Friends within transatlantic Quaker discourses about slavery.

The debates about slaveholding in the Philadelphia Monthly, Quarterly, and Yearly Meetings must be understood within the context of the rising concern for discipline within the Pennsylvania Quaker community as a whole. The 1696 minute, which had critiqued slaves as being "loose" and "lewd," for example, fit into the more general criticisms about youth and servants in the middle colonies. In 1698/99, the Philadelphia Quarterly Meeting noted that newly arrived English children "prove loose and Disorderly to ye Reproach of Truth and Trouble to Friends."[46] "Loose[ness]" was not just a sin of slaves, but of disorderly children and servants.

The overlap between familial reform and antislavery activism was not confined to linguistic similarities. Around 1700, a number of Friends in Philadelphia became concerned not only about slaveholding and misbehaving children, but also about the new English fashions that were starting to appear in colonial Pennsylvania.[47] The Friends who led the campaign against the slave trade were the same Friends who denounced superfluity of apparel and fashionable furniture. Penticott Teage, the Philadelphia Friend who criticized the disorder of slave auctions, and William Southeby, one of the first English Friends to testify against slaveholding, were among a group of six Friends who drew up a paper to "Prevent Superfluous furniture in houses & supporfluous apparel" at the Philadelphia Quarterly Meeting in 1701/2.[48]

As the seventeenth century came to a close, Friends continued their campaign against disorderly behavior, culminating in the creation of the first Book of Discipline in 1704. The Book of Discipline, written by the Yearly Meeting and distributed to all Quarterly and Monthly Meetings in Pennsylvania and East and West Jersey, urged Friends to recall the order of the primitive Church—the true "Gospel Order." Gospel Order was a key term for English and Welsh Friends, and their Books of Discipline, which were updated every decade or so, demonstrate evolving ideas about proper living. The 1704 Discipline, which was the first book-length Discipline written by the Philadelphia Yearly Meeting, reaffirmed the predominance of the Yearly-Quarterly-Monthly Meeting system, defined the punishments for misbehavior, and advised Friends on how to manage their families, singling out children and servants for special attention: "Training up and preserving friends, children and servants in the way of ye lord, We cannot but Earnestly press all parents Guardiens Masters & Mistrises to take early Care of them . . . to keep them out of all Hurtfull erronious & unchristian principles & by counsel or correction whilst they have command over them to restrain them from all loosness

& wantonness."[49] Like the Yearly Meeting minutes and the papers by George Gray and Cadwallader Morgan, the Book of Discipline avoided the word "slave" by referring to all subordinates within a family as either "children" or "servants." Yet the language of the Discipline was strikingly similar to the minutes regarding slaveholding. In 1696, for example, the meeting urged masters to "Restrain" their slaves from "loose and lewd living as much in them lies," while the 1704 Discipline told masters to "Restrain [servants and children] from all loosness and wantonness." In both cases, masters were expected to be constantly vigilant of their inferiors, whether white servants, black slaves, or their own children. Furthermore, sexual transgression was highlighted as an overriding fear that challenged the power of masters, regardless of which subordinate committed it.

The Anglo-Welsh Quaker concern for properly ordered families wove its way through all of the major "issues" confronting Friends at the turn of the eighteenth century. Luxury and slavery were both defined as threats to the family. Yet family order did not just have to do with behavior—it had to do with institutional control. By setting boundaries on what a Quaker family could be, the Philadelphia Yearly Meeting aimed to regulate its members by purifying and protecting the Quaker family.

When slave-owning Friends first settled on Barbados, George Fox had responded by envisioning a "Gospel family order" that included slaves within the household. With the founding of Pennsylvania and the gradual decline of the Quaker community on Barbados, the Quaker discourse on slavery began to change. While German and Dutch Friends introduced a rights-based antislavery argument, it was the tribalist antislavery of English and Welsh Quakers like Cadwallader Morgan and Penticott Teage that moved the Philadelphia Yearly Meeting to oppose the slave trade. Their opposition did not have an immediate effect, but it was significant. In 1715, after persistent lobbying by the Welsh Quakers in Chester, the Philadelphia Yearly Meeting finally wrote to the London Yearly Meeting about the practice of slave trading. They requested that "all merchants & Traders Professing Truth . . . write to their Correspondents that they send no more negroes" and complained that "traders . . . have

Increased and Multiplyed Negroes amongst us to ye grief of divers ffriends." The Philadelphia Yearly Meeting asked whether London Friends could take the issue into their "weighty Consideration."[50] The London meeting responded cautiously. In their first statement about the slave trade, London Friends agreed that "importing them from their Native Country... by ffriends is not a commendable nor allowed practice and we hope ffriends have been carefull to avoid ye same." They also acknowledged that "ye Multiplying of negroe slaves among you may be of dangerous consequence considering ye Peaceable Principle," but they deferred any final judgment on slavery until they had "advised with other Plantations."[51] In other words, London Friends were sympathetic with the Philadelphia Yearly Meeting, but they were aware that Friends in other colonies—such as Barbados—would not concur.

The correspondence between the Yearly Meetings in Pennsylvania and London marked the beginning of a new international Quaker discourse on slavery and Christianity. While this discourse emerged from a desire to protect the Quaker household, the rights-based antislavery arguments articulated by the Germantown Quakers were not forgotten. German and Dutch Quakers remained a crucial influence on the developing Quaker conversation about slavery in the eighteenth century. In 1715, the early Quaker abolitionist John Hepburn praised "the German-Quakers who live in German Town" for keeping "their Hands clean from that vile Oppression and inriching Sin of making Slaves of their fellow Creatures, the Negroes."[52] Later abolitionists such as Anthony Benezet, who—as Maurice Jackson discusses in greater detail in this volume—spent several years living in Germantown and working at the Saur press, also built on the rights-based arguments of the Germantown Quakers as he cultivated support for his transatlantic crusade against slavery.

Today, Quakers are most often associated with the humanitarian arguments of Quaker abolitionists such as Benezet and John Woolman. Yet the emergence of Quaker abolitionism was far from inevitable. From a late seventeenth-century perspective, the West Indian "conversion ethic" would have seemed more likely to prevail within the international Quaker community than the humanitarian approach of the Germantowners. The development of rights-based antislavery must be seen within the broader context of Quaker thought about slavery, much of which sought to reconcile slaveholding with the peace testimony. It was in the ethnically and linguistically diverse world of early Pennsylvania—where Welsh, English, German, and Dutch Quakers came into conversation—that a new dialogue about the role of enslaved men and women in Quaker families was forged.

Notes

1. William Penn, *A Brief Account of the Province of East-Jersey in America* (London: Printed for Benjamin Clark, 1682); Rosalind J. Beiler, "Dissenting Religious Communication Networks and Migration, 1660–1710," in *Soundings in Atlantic History: Latent Structures and Intellectual Currents, 1500–1830*, ed. Bernard Bailyn and Patricia L. Denault (Cambridge, Mass.: Harvard University Press, 2009), 210–36.

2. The Germantown preparatory meeting was incorporated into the meeting hierarchy of the Society of Friends. It was a constituent of the Abington/Dublin Monthly Meeting, the Philadelphia Quarterly Meeting, and the Philadelphia Yearly Meeting. William Isaac Hull, *William Penn and the Dutch Quaker Migration to Pennsylvania* (Philadelphia: Patterson and White, 1935), 290–92. For the history of Germantown, see Harry Marlin Tinkcom and Margaret B. Tinkcom, *Historic Germantown: From the Founding to the Early Part of the Nineteenth Century* (Philadelphia: American Philosophical Society, 1955); Stephanie Grauman Wolf, *Urban Village: Population, Community, and Family Structure in Germantown, Pennsylvania, 1683–1800* (Princeton, N.J.: Princeton University Press, 1980); James M. Duffin, *Acta Germanopolis: Records of the Corporation of Germantown, Pennsylvania, 1691–1707* (Philadelphia: Colonial Society of Pennsylvania, 2008).

3. I have written elsewhere about the Germantown protest, and parts of this chapter have been adapted from previous writings. For more on a linguistic analysis of the 1688 Germantown protest, see Katharine Gerbner, "'We Are Against the Traffik of Men-Body': The Germantown Quaker Protest of 1688 and the Origins of American Abolitionism," *Pennsylvania History* 74, no. 2 (2007): 149–72. For the Atlantic/Caribbean dimensions of the early Quaker debates on slavery, see Gerbner, *Christian Slavery: Conversion and Race in the Protestant Atlantic World* (Philadelphia: University of Pennsylvania Press, 2018), chap. 3, and Gerbner, "The Ultimate Sin: Christianising Slaves in Barbados in the Seventeenth Century," *Slavery and Abolition* 31, no. 1 (2010): 57–73. For the relationship between the Germantown settlers and the Keithian controversy, see Gerbner, "Antislavery in Print: The Germantown Protest, the 'Exhortation,' and the Seventeenth-Century Quaker Debate on Slavery," *Early American Studies* 9, no. 3 (2011): 552–75.

4. Jean R. Soderlund, *Quakers and Slavery: A Divided Spirit* (Princeton, N.J.: Princeton University Press, 1985); Kristen Block, "Cultivating Inner and Outer Plantations: Property, Industry, and Slavery in Early Quaker Migration to the New World," *Early American Studies* 8, no. 3 (2010): 515–48; Block, *Ordinary Lives in the Early Caribbean: Religion, Colonial Competition, and the Politics of Profit* (Athens: University of Georgia Press, 2012); Brycchan Carey, "'The Power That Giveth Liberty and Freedom': The Barbadian Origins of Quaker Antislavery Rhetoric, 1657–76," *Ariel* 38, no. 1 (2007): 27–47; Brycchan Carey, *From Peace to Freedom: Quaker Rhetoric and the Birth of American Antislavery, 1657–1761* (New Haven, Conn.: Yale University Press, 2012).

5. For more on the Quaker community in Barbados, see Barbara Ritter Dailey, "The Early Quaker Mission and the Settlement of Meetings in Barbados, 1655–1700," *Journal of the Barbados Museum and Historical Society* 39 (1991): 24–46; Larry Gragg, *The Quaker Community on Barbados: Challenging the Culture of the Planter Class* (Columbia: University of Missouri Press, 2009); Block, *Ordinary Lives*, pt. 4.

6. Richard S. Dunn, *Sugar and Slaves: The Rise of the Planter Class in the English West Indies, 1624–1713* (Chapel Hill: University of North Carolina Press, 2000), 104–5. Dunn notes that all but four of the Friends he identified were slave owners. Collectively, Barbadian Friends owned at least 1,626 slaves in 1680. See also Gragg, *Quaker Community on Barbados*, 124–25.

7. George Fox, *Gospel Family-Order, Being a Short Discourse Concerning the Ordering of Families, Both of Whites, Blacks and Indians* ([London], 1676).

8. See Gerbner, "Ultimate Sin"; Gerbner, *Christian Slavery*, chap. 3.

9. John Stubbs to Margaret Fox, December 2, 1671, Friends Historical Library, London, Abraham Mss. 15; Joan Vokins, *God's Mighty Power Magnified as Manifested and Revealed in His Faithful Handmaid Joan Vokins, Who Departed This Life the 22d of the 5th Month, 1690, Having Finished Her Course, and Kept the Faith: Also Some Account of Her Exercises, Works of Faith, Labour of Love, and Great Travels in the Work of the Ministry, for the Good of Souls* (London: Printed for Thomas Northcott, 1691), 43; Joseph Besse, *A Collection of the Sufferings of the People Called Quakers*, vol. 2 (London: Printed and sold by Luke Hinde, 1753), 310–11.

10. Darold D. Wax, "Quaker Merchants and the Slave Trade in Colonial Pennsylvania," *Pennsylvania Magazine of History and Biography* 86, no. 2 (1962): 143–59; Wax, "The Negro Slave Trade in Colonial Pennsylvania" (Ph.D. diss., University of Washington, 1962); Block, "Cultivating Inner and Outer Plantations."

11. Block, "Cultivating Inner and Outer Plantations," 519.

12. Quakers settled in Maryland as early as 1658. Like their coreligionists in Barbados, they were quickly persecuted for their refusal to take oaths and support the militia, but they were not persecuted for any attempts to convert their slaves. On Quakerism in Maryland, see Kenneth L. Carroll, "Maryland Quakers in the Seventeenth Century," *Maryland Historical Magazine* 100, no. 1 (2005): 81–96.

13. July 2, 1681, Third Haven Monthly Meeting Minutes, 1676–1871, HV, Haverford Quaker and Special Collections, Haverford, Pa., film 73; SW box 132.

14. August 11, 1699, Lower Virginia Monthly Meeting Minutes, 1673–1723 (Carbon Copy), HV 1116 / box HW-43.

15. For book-length studies that focus on the antislavery views of seventeenth-century Quakers, see Thomas Drake, *Quakers and Slavery in America* (New Haven, Conn.: Yale University Press, 1950); Sydney V. James, *A People Among Peoples: Quaker Benevolence in Eighteenth-Century America* (Cambridge, Mass.: Harvard University Press, 1963); David Brion Davis, *The Problem of Slavery in Western Culture* (Ithaca, N.Y.: Cornell University Press, 1966); J. William Frost, ed., *The Quaker Origins of Antislavery* (Norwood, Pa.: Norwood Editions, 1980); Soderlund, *Quakers and Slavery*; Christopher Leslie Brown, *Moral Capital: Foundations of British Abolitionism* (Chapel Hill: University of North Carolina Press, 2006); Brycchan Carey, *From Peace to Freedom: Quaker Rhetoric and the Birth of American Antislavery, 1657–1761* (New Haven, Conn.: Yale University Press, 2012). A few newer studies have begun to look more closely at the relationships between Quakers and slaves. See, for example, Block, *Ordinary Lives*.

16. August 11, 1699, Lower Virginia Monthly Meeting Minutes, 1673–1723, HV 1116 / box HW-43.

17. August 9, 1707, Lower Virginia Monthly Meeting Minutes, 1673–1723, HV 1116 / box HW-43.

18. January 27, 1693. Abington Monthly Meeting (Mens) Minutes, 1682–1746, HV film 138A.

19. Parts of this section have been adapted from Gerbner, "'We Are Against the Traffik'"; Gerbner, "Antislavery in Print."

20. Over the past three centuries, scholars have disagreed over the ethnic, national, and religious identities of these original settlers. What must be taken into account is that ethnic, national, and religious boundaries were not defined as they are today. It is clear, however, that nearly all of the Krefelders and Krisheimers were Quakers when they arrived in Pennsylvania (see Hull, *William Penn*, appendix 4) and had practiced Quakerism in their native lands. The majority had been Mennonites before Quaker missionaries such as William Ames and William Penn arrived in

the Netherlands and Germany in the mid-seventeenth century. See ibid., 285. For more information, see Duffin, *Acta Germanopolis*, 3–13.

21. For more on the Pietist, Mennonite, and Quaker networks in Holland and Germany during the seventeenth century, see Beiler, "Dissenting Religious Communication."

22. Tinkcom and Tinkcom, *Historic Germantown*, 7; Duffin, *Acta Germanopolis*, 17–32.

23. The original Germantown protest is housed at the Quaker and Special Collections at Haverford College, Haverford, Pa. A digital version of the text is available online at http://triptych.brynmawr.edu/cdm/ref/collection/HC_QuakSlav/id/5837.

24. See, for example, Epistle No. 366, March 17, 1682, cited in William C. Braithwaite, *The Second Period of Quakerism* (London: Macmillan, 1919), 431. For more on Quaker captivity in North Africa, see [Samuel Tuke], *Account of the Slavery of Friends in the Barbary States, towards the Close of the 17th Century* (London: E. Marsh, 1848).

25. On the Germantowners' astute appeal to the fear of capture and enslavement by Islamic ships, see also Bethany Wiggin, "Slavery in Translation: German Baroque Figurations of African Enslavement in the Americas," in *Opening Spaces: Constructions, Visions, and Depictions of Spaces and Boundaries in the Baroque*, ed. Karin Friedrich (Wiesbaden: Harrassowitz, 2014), 723–40.

26. Minutes of the Philadelphia Yearly Meeting, 1688, repr. in Frost, *Quaker Origins*, 74.

27. *An Exhortation and Caution to Friends Concerning buying or keeping of Negroes* (New York: Printed by William Bradford, 1693).

28. For an in-depth comparison on the Germantown protest and the Exhortation, see Gerbner, "Antislavery in Print"; Carey, *From Peace to Freedom*, 85–95.

29. Barry Levy, "From 'Dark Corners' to American Domesticity: The British Social Context of the Welsh and Cheshire Quakers' Familial Revolution in Pennsylvania, 1657–1685," in *The World of William Penn*, ed. Richard S. Dunn and Mary Maples Dunn (Philadelphia: University of Pennsylvania Press, 1986), 215; Barry Levy, *Quakers and the American Family: British Settlement in the Delaware Valley* (New York: Oxford University Press, 1988), 21.

30. Levy, *Quakers and the American Family*, 137–39.

31. Morgan's paper was one of several presented to the Yearly Meeting "Relating to the keeping and bringing in of Negroes." While most have since been lost, one paper, written by William Southeby, was recently rediscovered. It has been reprinted, along with an important explanatory essay, in Nicholas Wood and Jean Soderlund, "'To Friends and All Whom It May Concerne': William Southeby's Rediscovered 1696 Antislavery Protest," *Pennsylvania Magazine of History and Biography* 141 (2017): 177–98. I am grateful to Nicholas Wood for alerting me to this important new piece of evidence. While the Southeby text came to my attention too late to be fully integrated into this chapter, it suggests that the humanitarian antislavery ideals present in the 1688 Germantown protest and Keithian *Exhortation* continued to circulate in seventeenth-century Pennsylvania. Southeby's ethnic origins are unknown. He was born a Roman Catholic and lived in Maryland before moving to Pennsylvania in 1686. Kenneth L. Carroll, "William Southeby, Early Quaker Antislavery Writer," *Pennsylvania Magazine of History and Biography* 89, no. 4 (1965): 416–27; Wood and Soderlund, "'To Friends,'" 180.

32. Carey, *From Peace to Freedom*, 97.

33. Morgan's letter is reprinted in Frost, *Quaker Origins of Antislavery*, 70. The original is available online at http://triptych.brynmawr.edu/cdm/ref/collection/HC_QuakSlav/id/19.

34. Philadelphia Yearly Meeting Minutes, 1696, reprinted in Frost, *Quaker Origins of Antislavery*, 74.

35. In using the term "tribalism," I am following Jean Soderlund's analysis of early Quaker antislavery views. Soderlund argues that the Quaker embrace of antislavery came in two forms: the idealistic and humanitarian approach of Anthony Benezet and John Woolman and the "tribalist" approach of many Quakers who were concerned about maintaining a tight-knit and exclusive community structure. Soderlund, *Quakers and Slavery*.

36. J. William Frost, "George Fox's Ambiguous Anti-slavery Legacy," in *New Light on George Fox, 1624–1691*, ed. Michael Mullett (York, UK: Ebor Press, 1994), 69–88.

37. George Gray's paper is reprinted in Frost, "George Fox's Ambiguous Anti-slavery Legacy."

38. While there are no exact figures on slave imports in late seventeenth-century Pennsylvania, Gary Nash has calculated that "about one in fifteen Philadelphia families owned slaves" between 1682 and 1705. Gary B. Nash, "Slaves and Slaveowners in Colonial Philadelphia," *William and Mary Quarterly* 30, no. 2 (1973): 226.

39. Frost, "George Fox's Ambiguous Antislavery Legacy."

40. Piles's text is reprinted in Frost, *Quaker Origins of Antislavery*, 71–72.

41. For other scholarly interpretations of Robert Piles's antislavery statement, see Soderlund, *Quakers and Slavery*, 19–20; Gary B. Nash and Jean R. Soderlund, *Freedom by Degrees: Emancipation in Pennsylvania and Its Aftermath* (Oxford: Oxford University Press, 1991), 44–45; Mechal Sobel, *Teach Me Dreams: The Search for Self in the Revolutionary Era* (Princeton, N.J.: Princeton University Press, 2002), 55–56; Carla Gerona, *Night Journeys: The Power of Dreams in Transatlantic Quaker Culture* (Charlottesville: University of Virginia Press, 2004), 21–27; Carey, *From Peace to Freedom*, 99–103.

42. For an analysis of Piles's statement within the context of Quaker dreams, see Gerona, *Night Journeys*, 23–27.

43. If Piles's text was not discussed at the meeting in September, it was most likely circulated and debated soon afterwards, since it is included in the meeting's papers relating to 1698.

44. Philadelphia Monthly Meeting Minutes, 1698, reprinted in Frost, *Quaker Origins of Antislavery*, 73.

45. "To the Generall Meeting off ffriends in Barbadoes: These from our Monthly Meeting at Philadelphia, the 30th of 8th mo., '98," reprinted in Frost, *Quaker Origins of Antislavery*, 72.

46. January 6, 1698/9, Philadelphia Quarterly Meeting (Mens) Minutes, 1682–1711.

47. See also Bethany Wiggin, "Globalization and the Work of Fashion in Early Modern German Letters," *Journal of Early Modern Cultural Studies* 11, no. 2 (2011): 35–60.

48. January 2, 1701/2, Philadelphia Quarterly Meeting (Mens) Minutes, 1682–1711. Southeby's 1696 and 1712 antislavery texts are both reprinted in Wood and Soderlund, "'To Friends.'"

49. Philadelphia Yearly Meeting, Book of Discipline, 1704, HV 976, box 1.

50. Philadelphia Yearly Meeting to London Yearly Meeting, 1712, Friends Historical Library, London, Epistles Received 2.132.

51. London Yearly Meeting to Philadelphia Yearly Meeting, 1713, Friends Historical Library, London, Epistles Sent 2.195.

52. John Hepburn, *The American Defence of the Christian Golden Rule, or an Essay to Prove the Unlawfulness of Making Slaves of Men* (1715), reprinted in Frost, *Quaker Origins of Antislavery*.

CHAPTER 7

"Ein schrecklicher Zustand"
Race, Slavery, and Gradual Emancipation in Pennsylvania

BIRTE PFLEGER

When Lutheran minister Henry Melchior Muhlenberg arrived in Charlestown in 1742, enslaved African Americans were among the first people he encountered in British North America. Muhlenberg described them as "black heathens who are sold as slaves to the white Christian people." The German pastor saw "many slaves here who are only half black" and condemned the "white Sodomites who commit fornication with their black slave women." Worst of all, in the minister's mind, whites refused to introduce slaves to Christianity because they feared that "the blacks would kill them all and make themselves masters of Carolina." Muhlenberg dismissed this explanation, concluding that "the so-called Christians lead a more evil life than the heathen, and for this reason they are not willing to let blacks acquire knowledge so that they will not be punished or disturbed in their sin." The pastor condemned this "horrible state of affairs," predicting that it would "entail severe judgment."[1]

Thirty-two years later, Muhlenberg, who traveled frequently and extensively throughout the British colonies over the course of his long life, returned to the South. On this trip, he deemed keeping black people enslaved a normal and expected aspect of life in America. While lodging with a German pastor who held over thirty African Americans in bondage,

Muhlenberg "strolled with Reverend R. and observed the establishment of his plantation and his Negro slaves." He praised the minister's gentle treatment of his slaves and only wished "that all Negro slaves would be kept so well as the few are kept here."[2] Two months earlier, during the same stay with Rappenhorst, Muhlenberg noted the death and burial of a "Negerin" whom a Salzburger man had bought for forty pounds and commented that it was "a difficult occurrence for a young beginner."[3] Muhlenberg lamented not the demise of the woman, but the loss of a valuable asset for the young man who owned her.

This normalizing of human bondage and at the same time recognition that slavery was a foreign (i.e., not German) institution in Muhlenberg's mind is also visually evident in his handwriting.[4] Muhlenberg wrote Kurrent, the traditional German script, and used German spelling for terms associated with African slaves in the 1740s; yet he used Latin script and anglicized spelling in reference to slavery by the 1770s (figs. 7.1 to 7.3). When the clergyman was not yet familiar with slavery upon arriving in 1742, he recorded enslaved people as "Schlaven" in Kurrent.

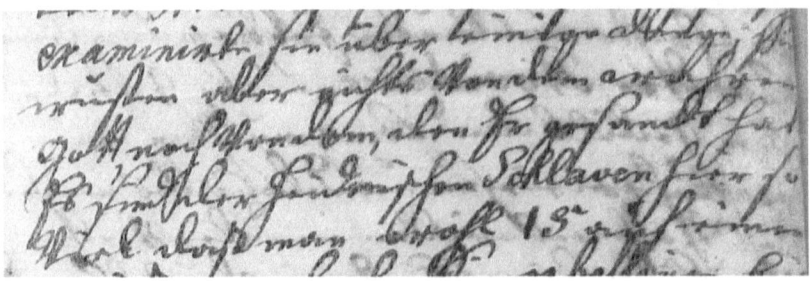

FIGURE 7.1 Journals of Henry Melchior Muhlenberg, September 23, 1742.

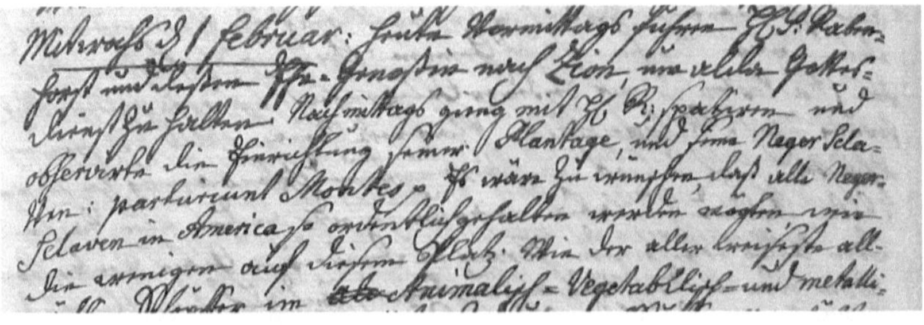

FIGURE 7.2 Journals of Henry Melchior Muhlenberg, February 1, 1775.

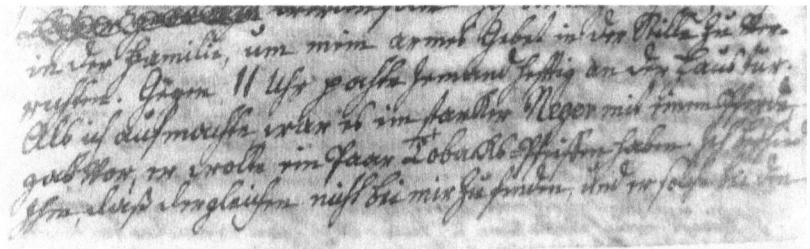

FIGURE 7.3 Journals of Henry Melchior Muhlenberg, March 8, 1778.

Thirty-two years later, as Muhlenberg had become not only linguistically fluent in the language of his adopted homeland, but also culturally proficient, he wrote about slaves as "Neger Sclaven," acknowledging to himself on the one hand the Anglo origin of the institution, but perhaps also the foreignness of human bondage: educated German speakers wrote Latinate terms or what they considered foreign words (*Fremdwörter*) in Latin script.[5]

The shift in Muhlenberg's assessment of Africans, African Americans, and slavery typifies the general change in many eighteenth-century German speakers' attitude toward the enslavement of black people. In the early years of German immigration to Pennsylvania, Muhlenberg and other German speakers did not automatically equate blackness with slavery but considered the heathenness of Africans the cause of their enslavement. Not unlike the English and Welsh Quakers discussed by Katharine Gerbner in this volume, German Lutheran and Reformed Church members considered blacks eligible candidates for conversion to Christianity, which might, by implication, lead to an end of their subjugation by whites. However, by the late eighteenth century the separation of Christians and heathen had turned into an unbridgeable gulf between blacks and whites in the minds of most German speakers, who were now made up mostly of Lutheran and Reformed Church members. By 1775, there were more Lutheran congregations in Pennsylvania than any other religious denomination, followed by German Reformed churches with 126 congregations.[6] When Pennsylvania's legislature debated the abolition of slavery in 1780, a majority of Lutheran and Reformed Germans voted against it, with only a handful of German Quakers, Presbyterians, and Sectarians supporting abolition.[7] While this development was in part due to new ideas about race in Western thought, German speakers' evolution—from advocacy of evangelization and rejection of slavery to a de facto if not more active support of the institution—can only be explained fully within the framework of their own struggle for equality in an Anglo-dominated world.[8]

This essay shows that Muhlenberg and his fellow German speakers in the mid-Atlantic region learned but also shaped the emerging American etiquette of race and slavery at the same time that they underwent their own metamorphosis in the eyes of Anglo colonists from "tawny" or "swarthy" to "white" people. They filtered the meaning of slavery, servitude, and freedom through the context of American experiences and the discussions there about indentured servants, freemen, and slaves. By 1780, German speakers' support of slavery at the very moment when Anglo-Pennsylvanians moved toward abolishing permanent, racially based, hereditary servitude was a sign of their anxiety to be recognized as free, white American citizens and an emblem of their economic success.[9]

Historians of slavery have generally focused on the southern colonies, leaving the mid-Atlantic region, as well as New England, on the margins of slavery historiography.[10] Most scholarship on race-based bondage in Penn's Woods has centered on the ways Quakers struggled with the institution for almost a century.[11] Starting with the famous Germantown protest of 1688, as Katharine Gerbner argues in her contribution, Quaker Yearly Meetings first condemned the slave trade in 1696 and again in 1715. Pennsylvania Quakers inched toward becoming the most important European American abolitionists by the end of the eighteenth century, including of course Anthony Benezet, as Maurice Jackson discusses in this book. They spoke out against the slave-labor system in 1758 and finally excluded any Friend from their congregation who still owned slaves in 1773.[12] While Jackson's superb work on Anthony Benezet shows us the far-flung network of antislavery sentiments beyond Quakers, he does not find significant numbers of German speakers among those who worked to abolish slavery.[13] Benezet's erstwhile employer and family friend and neighbor, newsman Christoph Saur, provides a notable exception. While many historians have explored the ideological constructions of race in eighteenth-century North America, the history of slavery in Pennsylvania outside the Quaker community has not been examined in depth.[14]

This chapter draws on scholarship about conceptualizations of race and slavery and seeks to connect it with the story of how Pastor Muhlenberg and many of his fellow German-speaking settlers in Pennsylvania became German Americans by the end of the eighteenth century. I argue that Germans were in a precarious position in terms of both their racial identity and their ability to claim the rights of freemen. As both Anglo and German settlers in prerevolutionary Pennsylvania slowly moved toward each other in the male and public sphere of politics and business, German speakers adopted increasingly rigid ideas about race and actively supported the institution of slavery. In adopting an increasingly racialized view, they strongly resembled their Anglo neighbors. At the same time, Pennsylvania lawmakers granted German speakers the right to claims of whiteness and self-ownership that accompanied the privilege of being white by enacting laws protecting German immigrants from the worst abuses prevalent in the redemptioner trade. The American Revolution bolstered German assertions of citizenship through their military service and support of Revolutionary ideology. Yet German speakers' continued uncertainty about their own claims to citizenship in the early republic contributed to hardening ideas of race and a desire to keep African Americans enslaved. This gradual shift from racial difference as a fluid concept to an innate permanent feature with negative meanings was evident among Americans of European descent overall during this time period, but German speakers' path toward it was unique to their own road toward whiteness and civic equality. African American Pennsylvanians thus paid the price for German speakers' quest to be accepted as equal members in a white American nation.

I begin with an overview of published German-language descriptions of Pennsylvania that reveal German speakers' ideas about color. Germans saw the darkness of African Americans early on as a permanent marker of difference. By the late 1700s, however, German speakers moved toward considering darker skin color an innate characteristic that was inferior to paleness.[15] In the process of becoming white Americans, German speakers also became racists like their Anglo neighbors. Next I explore the complicated ways in which German speakers understood the overlaps of slavery and indentured servitude in early Pennsylvania. Pennsylvania Germans objected to being associated with or treated like people of African descent, both de facto and de jure. We can see German speakers' insecurities about their own status in the publicly voiced outrage over being even mentioned in the same context as African Americans. I also attempt to reconstruct Germans' interactions with African Americans. Henry Muhlenberg's experiences and observations serve as sources for those interactions, and his evolving thoughts about slavery and African Americans provide a case study for German speakers' ideas in general.[16] What emerges most clearly in late eighteenth-century Pennsylvania is Germans' conviction that the federal government protected the institution of slavery, since slaves were above all else property.[17] Moreover, German speakers were convinced that the slave-labor system of Pennsylvania was benign and therefore different from the plantation slavery practiced south of Penn's Woods. For that reason, Muhlenberg and others could condemn slavery in Georgia or South Carolina while they did not question or even openly acknowledge the practice in Pennsylvania.

SLAVES AND SERVANTS

For at least the first half of the eighteenth century the hue of their skin did not make people of African descent automatically slaves in Germans' perception. In the early 1750s, Gottlieb Mittelberger described "innumerable negroes, or blacks" in Pennsylvania, and explained that they "have to serve all their lives as slaves."[18] Similarly, Peter Kalm clarified that blacks "are in a manner slaves; for when a negro is once bought, he is the purchaser's servant as long as he lives."[19] In other words, the mere presence of blacks did not immediately signal their enslavement in Mittelberger's or Kalm's minds. Germans were also not quite clear about what being of African descent meant. Just as the term "race" was not widely used until the early nineteenth century, the category of race also did not exist. This might explain why a mid-eighteenth-century discussion of Pennsylvania's religious landscape mixed the categories of race and religion by listing "Lutherans, Reformed, Catholics, Quakers, . . . Freethinkers, Jews, Mohammedans, Pagans, Negroes and Indians" together.[20] Similarly, the printer Christopher Saur referred to different "nations" when he discussed religious groups.[21]

Beyond the malleable meaning of race, religion, and nation, German speakers were ambivalent about slavery. As Jon Sensbach shows in his exceptional work, German Moravians in eighteenth-century North Carolina initially rejected slave labor in part because they feared using slaves would lead to their own laziness. When they did hire and eventually purchase a few slaves, German Moravians offered these bondsmen and women spiritual equality by inviting them to convert to their faith. Although only a few dozen black Moravians lived in Bethabara, Wachovia, Salem, and Hope, they nevertheless represented what Sensbach called "a moment of flickering hope in the maelstrom of American race relations."[22] However, as early as 1792, welcoming slaves as brethren, washing each other's feet, and exchanging the kiss of greeting became unacceptable to many white Moravians, who began to request racially segregated seating in church and ten years later separate worship altogether. Similarly, German speakers outside of the Moravian community did not expressly voice moral opposition to enslaving Africans and purchasing them. Still, many subscribed to a nascent free soil ideology that saw slavery as devaluing free men's labor and as detrimental to their own chances for economic upward mobility.[23]

While concerns about their economic advancement shaped German speakers' attitudes toward slavery, they could not completely escape minimal engagement in the institution. Even the Pietist Christopher Saur Sr. was entangled in the dilemma of opposing slavery while feeling pressure to support the institution. While the printer openly voiced his moral outrage over slavery and the mistreatment of all unfree laborers, he also accepted advertisements for runaway slaves and servants and announced the sale of at least one slave.[24] Although Saur at times included commentaries suggesting that better treatment of servants and slaves would make runaway advertisements obsolete, he did not refuse out of hand to print them.[25]

Overall, however, advertisements for runaway servants far outnumbered advertisements regarding slaves. While the disparity applied to both the *Pennsylvania Gazette* and the *Pensylvanische Berichte*, and reflected European Pennsylvanians' general preference for white indentured servants, the near absence of advertisements regarding slaves in Saur's newspaper indicates that German speakers stood at the margins of the slave-labor market. Between 1739 and 1757 Saur printed two advertisements for runaway slaves and one announcing the sale of a slave. During the same period his newspaper included ninety-four notices for runaway servants and six ads announcing the sale of servants.[26] In comparison, nearly every issue of the *Pennsylvania Gazette* between 1739 and 1755 included at least one advertisement for slaves who had run away or were for sale.[27] In other words, the commerce of human chattel largely took place in the English-language press, and German-language readers were usually not asked in their native language to be complicit in securing runaway slaves.

The overall distance of German speakers from the slave-labor market was also closely connected to the cost of slaves. Prices for all labor rose in the eighteenth century: in 1730, the average price for an indentured servant was £10 for five years of service, while slaves could usually be purchased for £20. By midcentury, indentured servants cost £14 for four years of service and slaves were valued between £40 and £100, a price beyond the budget of most Pennsylvanians, and certainly the vast majority of German speakers.[28]

Although Pennsylvania Germans prospered over the course of the eighteenth century, and a few even chose to replace their white servants with black slaves, economic considerations are not enough to explain why German speakers opposed the abolition of slavery in 1780. The number of German-speaking slaveholders was never in proportion to the strong support for the slave-labor system among them. In 1767, 26 out of 555 slave owners in Philadelphia were German. This number increased to 34 by 1780, while slave ownership in the city overall declined to 396.[29]

Instead we must comprehend how German speakers understood their own role in Pennsylvania's labor market in relation to Africans' place. Anglo-Pennsylvanians' treatment of European servants and African slaves also played a role in Germans' perception of themselves and blacks. It was not that Anglo settlers generally treated indentured servants like slaves, nor that they failed to appreciate the color difference and the accompanying issue of purchasing "civilized" versus noncivilized laborers. Instead, it was German speakers' perception of Anglo treatment of and discourse about German servants that made them particularly sensitive to being compared to and perhaps even thought of as interchangeable with black slaves.

At least until the mid-eighteenth century, German speakers' fears of being on par with Africans were not completely unfounded. Many newspaper advertisements for runaway indentured servants of German descent described the absconded persons' skin color as "tawny" or "swarthy." While these adjectives were at times also used for Irish runaways, they were generally not found in descriptions of English laborers.[30] Clearly, Anglo colonists did not consider German speakers to be quite as white as they were. Even Benjamin Franklin found that intrinsic differences of color separated Germans from Anglo-Pennsylvanians when he asserted that German immigrants could never "acquire our complexion." In his famous 1751 essay "Observations Concerning the Increase of Mankind," Franklin found that only the English and Saxons "ma[de up] the principle body of White People on the Face of the Earth." He feared that Germans, Africans, and all other nonwhites would "darken its [America's] People."[31] Since skin color was increasingly seen as an innate trait that signaled differences in degree of civilization, Germans together with Africans were not only considered inherently different from Englishmen but also deemed inferior to them.

In addition to the presumed visible marker of "complexion" that separated German speakers from Anglo settlers, the treatment of all unfree laborers separated them from free men, which increasingly meant Anglo-Americans. Indentured servants and redemptioners shared the fact that they were, in the words of one historian, "temporary chattels," who were someone's legal property and could be sold during their servitude.[32] In addition, poor people also shared another reality with black Americans: the danger of being mistaken for a runaway. Any person without a permanent home could be seized on suspicion of having stolen him- or herself from the rightful owner. Without being able to prove that they were free, poor people found wandering were arrested and advertised as runaways. They were sold to the highest bidder when no one claimed them to cover the prison charges.[33] Benjamin Franklin told of his own experience of being suspected as a runaway during his journey as a seventeen-year-old from Boston to Philadelphia in the fall of 1723.[34] Visible poverty could be read as a sign of servitude in similar ways as blackness.

Moreover, German redemptioners in particular shared an added characteristic with blacks that seemed to render Germans slaves.[35] Indentured servants, generally from the British Isles, contracted themselves for a fixed number of years before embarking upon the transatlantic voyage and were sold off to the highest bidder upon arrival. On the other hand, redemptioners, typically of German and Swiss birth, agreed with the captain on a specific sum for their freight to America but did not learn until they were auctioned off how long they would have to serve a master who agreed to pay their passage. Thus, German speakers felt that they had especially little control over the length of their bondage and other terms of their servitude. This arrangement seemed to leave many German speakers, even more so than people with indentures, at the mercy of their masters and contributed to their perception that they were treated like slaves.[36]

Not only were there de facto instances that might have given German-speaking servants the impression that they were similar to slaves, but in the legal realm the two groups were briefly treated the same. For nearly one year in the late 1720s, two separate laws decreed that imported unfree laborers of African and German descent were to be taxed at the same rate. While the first law established an import tariff of forty shillings on "Negroes," a second bill established the same amount for "Foreigners" but only twenty shillings for each Irish servant brought to the colony.[37] The two laws were repealed within a year, and the reasons for their passage and repeal were not at all connected with any intent to put Germans on par with African slaves. Nevertheless, German speakers were deeply offended by laws that suggested even remotely that they had anything in common with Africans. Even more than a half-century after the acts had been revoked, members of the German Society of Pennsylvania (GSP) still noted their outrage as a prelude to a long list of alleged wrongs done to Germans in Pennsylvania.[38]

These tax laws and other legal measures pertaining to unfree laborers were scrutinized on a regular basis by the GSP, a mutual aid organization founded in 1764.[39] The organization's assistance to their newly arrived countrymen, especially in the legal realm, illustrates German speakers' efforts to reinforce the distinction between themselves and people of African descent. The GSP counted among its first successes the passage of a law regulating the treatment of German passengers coming to Pennsylvania. Enacted in 1765, it was a revision of earlier rules and specified more clearly the minimum dimensions of space for each passenger on board transatlantic ships.[40] While the very real abuses in the immigrant trade made the change necessary, it also represented the GSP's efforts to distinguish the business of bringing German immigrants to Pennsylvania clearly from the slave trade. Temporarily unfree white German passengers had to fare better during their voyage to the New World than a cargo of black human chattel.[41]

GSP officers continued their quest to ensure the differentiation of redemptioners and lifelong bondsmen in connection with property rights and the sanctity of marriage. Nearly a decade after the assembly had passed An Act for the prohibiting of German & other Passengers in too great Numbers in any one Vessel, Lewis Weiss, a founding member of the GSP, wrote to Governor John Penn complaining that German immigrants were still often deprived of their property during the voyage:

> Passengers having Goods of any value on board of the same ship in which they transport themselves hardly ever take Bills of Lading for such Goods, the Merchants, Captains, or their Subordinates persuading them that it could do them no Good but rather involve them into Difficulties at their arrival. If they leave any Goods in the Stores ... they will now & then take a little Note "that the Merchant has such Chests, Casks, Bales, &c.," to the person who deposited such Goods with him. The Passenger puts the note in his Pocket Book, he has also the Invoice of his Goods, and his Money he has sowed up in his old Rags or in a Belt about his Waist. But on the voyage he or his Wife or some of his Family, or all of them grow sick. Then the plunder upon the sick or dead begin, and if the old ones recover or small Children survive the Goods are gone, and the proofs that they had any are lost.[42]

This description firmly established the rights of arriving Germans and the wrongs committed by unscrupulous traders. The GSP officer emphasized that German immigrants were not single men but brought their wives and children with them, which clearly differentiated them from slaves arriving from the Caribbean or Africa. Moreover, Weiss portrayed German immigrants as property owners who were apparently too trusting, while captains and merchants were dishonest and took advantage of passengers' illness or death. In tackling the issue of property rights, GSP members addressed frequent complaints, but they also chose a moment in history when insisting on the security of a man's possessions was a central aspect in claiming the rights of Anglo-American citizenship. Moreover, even though many German-speaking immigrants of this period arrived as unfree laborers, the GSP insisted that redemptioners nevertheless retained the right to their belongings, unlike the slaves who were sold in Pennsylvania.

Similarly, the GSP sought already in 1765 to prohibit the separation of spouses due to sale without their consent. In a petition to the assembly, the GSP proposed the following measure: "That no Master of any Vessel or Merchant . . . shall under Penalty of _____ be contriving, aiding or abetting, to part that sacred Oeconomy and State of Husband and Wife, subsisting between any such Passengers, by selling or disposing of the Husband without his Wife, or of the Wife without her Husband."[43]

Although they were unfree laborers, German redemptioners insisted on rights only freemen could traditionally claim. Germans' assertion that the bond between husband and wife was inviolable even for those who were at least temporarily held in bondage stood in direct opposition to the fact that servants could marry only with permission of their masters and that slave marriages had no legal validity at all.[44] Without mentioning the institution of slavery, the GSP consistently asked Pennsylvania lawmakers to regulate the immigrant trade not only to address widespread mistreatment but also to differentiate redemptioners from slaves. In granting many of the petitions and establishing a system of supervision after 1764, however flawed it was, the Pennsylvania assembly, in turn, assented to the fundamental difference between slaves of African descent and German-speaking servants. In agreeing to extend some protections for redemptioners, lawmakers clearly recognized even poor, unfree German speakers as future freemen who were expected to become settlers contributing to Pennsylvania's growth and prosperity. Acknowledging redemptioners' rights to property and marriage also meant that "swarthy" Germans had become white by the time the American Revolution began.

While Pennsylvania lawmakers recognized and underscored the contrast between servants and slaves starting in the 1760s, the two categories of unfree laborers were often used interchangeably throughout the colonial period and into the early republic. In part this was due to the continuous need for labor that led William Penn to observe already in 1685 that "it were better that they [servants] were blacks, for then we might have them for life."[45] Only the lighter color of their skin prevented the permanent bondage of indentured servants and redemptioners. A century and a revolution later, George Washington also was not concerned about the ethnic origin of the joiner and bricklayer he sought in 1784. In the instructions to his overseer, Washington recommended looking for skilled tradesmen among newly arrived Germans in Baltimore. At the same time, the founding father "would not confine [his overseer] to Palatines. If they are good workmen, they may be of Asia, Africa or Europe. They may be Mahometans, Jews or Christian of any Sect, or they may be Atheists." Useful skills, not ethnicity, race, or religion, determined the eligibility for employment in the judgment of the nation's first president. Similarly, when Washington resided in postrevolutionary Philadelphia, he used black and white, permanent and temporary unfree labor with similar interchangeability. In part to assuage abolitionists, the nation's first president replaced some of his African American slaves with German redemptioners.[46]

The interchangeability of white and black unfree laborers became especially obvious during the French and Indian War. When the Quaker-dominated assembly once again balked at assisting the Crown in military affairs in 1756, British general Shirley reneged his earlier assurance not to enlist indentured servants and redemptioners. In light of the fact that few free Pennsylvanians enlisted voluntarily, and due to the urgency of the situation, Shirley argued that the rights of the sovereign superseded the property rights of individuals.[47] According to the general, it was up to the assembly to legislate appropriate compensation for masters whose servants enlisted. Through newspaper notices in both the English- and German-language press, the assembly announced that masters should report any servants who had enlisted to their local assemblyman and should bring the original indenture as proof of how much time was still owed.[48] Throughout the war the assembly appropriated money to numerous petitioners.

With the resupply of unfree European laborers restricted due to the war and the stock of available indentured servants and redemptioners dwindling as a result of rising numbers of runaways, white Pennsylvanians turned to slave labor.[49] Based on the tremendous increase in advertisements for runaway servants after 1755, the lure of freedom was strong. Of all advertisements for runaway servants published in Saur's newspaper between 1739 and 1757, 40 percent appeared between 1755 and 1757.[50] At the same time, the number of imported slaves increased as the number of European and especially German immigrants decreased. While human cargoes from the Caribbean and Africa arriving in Philadelphia rose fourfold between 1750 and 1760, from 283 to 1,148, voluntary immigrants departing Amsterdam for the city of brotherly love declined almost fourfold, from 30,374 to 8,058.[51] In Chester County in 1760, 231 enslaved blacks outnumbered 149 white indentured servants. Philadelphia's enslaved population nearly doubled between 1750 and 1760, from 787 to 1,481.[52]

Employing black slaves in favor of white unfree laborers was publicly criticized. Among those who had objected to the practice long before the French and Indian War were self-described poor European immigrants who petitioned Pennsylvania legislators to prohibit slaveholders from hiring out their human property "to do all or most of the servile work in and about the City of Philadelphia." Enslaved people of African descent allegedly prevented "the Petitioners from being employed, to the utter Ruin of themselves and Families."[53] By 1751, the *Pennsylvania Gazette* reported that blacks who were hired out and thus enjoyed a degree of independence disturbed the public peace.[54] In other words, slave labor was unwelcome competition for poor white workers. In seeking relief from the assembly, poor immigrants, many of whom were German speakers, claimed the rights of free white men. The continued practice of hiring out slaves, however, shows that economic concerns overrode the desire of poor European settlers to amplify the distinctions between white servants and black slaves.[55]

The interchangeability of white and black unfree laborers was a reality for all early Americans.[56] The way German speakers in Pennsylvania understood that reality, however, contributed to their opposition to emancipating slaves. Since their own position, first as subjects in a British colony and then later as citizens in the new republic, continued to be challenged because of their ethnicity and language differences, many Pennsylvania Germans saw the continued enslavement of blacks as an affirmation of their status as freemen. They feared that if black people were allowed to be free and to own property, the difference between people of African and German descent would be reduced to skin color—a mark that had been decreed as an important badge of difference by the late eighteenth century, but that still did not seem distinguishing enough to Germans.

European observers and critics of Quaker abolitionism echoed German speakers' concern about the potentially disrupting consequences of ending slavery. One contemporary charged the Society of Friends with hypocrisy when they supported the abolition of slavery but had "not the least objection to buying an Irishman or Dutchman, and chaffer... to get him indented at about the eighth part of the wages they would have to pay a *country born*"(emphasis in original).[57] Others agreed that the way indentured servants and redemptioners were sold resembled the slave trade. William Priest, an Englishman traveling in late eighteenth-century Pennsylvania, described "a few particulars of what is here emphatically called a *white Guinea man*." He continued to explain that indentured servants and redemptioners were "liable to be *resold*, at the death or caprice of their *masters*."[58] Lord Sheffield, another English traveler, reported that two Irishmen had been bought by a free black man and added with dismay that "Irishmen [were] just emancipated in Europe," only, upon arrival in Pennsylvania, "to become the slaves of a Negro."[59] According to some late eighteenth-century critics, allowing for the possibility of white men being owned by black men was the ultimate danger of emancipating slaves.

It was exactly this line of reasoning that postrevolutionary-era German speakers espoused in their opposition to ending slavery and in their assent to republican ideology: the rights of white Americans had to supersede black Americans' claims to freedom. In a lengthy discussion of Quaker petitions to Congress for the abolition of slavery, a German-language newspaper published in Philadelphia laid out the case against federally mandated emancipation in 1790.[60] While the author, Karl Christoph Reiche, praised the intent to ease the suffering of fellow human beings, he explained that any attempt by Congress to interfere with slavery violated the Constitution and endangered the survival of the republic.[61] Since slaves were property just like horses and cattle, Congress had no right to free the slaves, as that would deprive citizens of their possessions. Alluding to a possible conspiracy to broaden federal powers, Reiche argued that the issue did not pertain only to plantation societies in Georgia or South Carolina, but affected the entire nation and every citizen. If Congress "has the power to take away the property of Carolinians or Georgians, [Congress] also has the power to take it away from Pennsylvanians and others."[62] The issue was now not about "mere humaneness" but about "the property of citizens," and as such it would not be "equitable" if the rights of "perhaps half a million blacks in all states" took precedence over the rights of whites, who outnumbered blacks "six times."

The next issue of Reiche's newspaper continued the discussion and found that if anything at all was to be done about slavery, Quakers and other abolitionists should turn to the individual states but even then should proceed with "great caution."[63] Using a biblical analogy, this German-language newspaper suggested that just as the good Samaritan could not heal the wounded instantly, "good, loving laws [passed] in the best interest of the Negro" would at least ease the pain of slavery.[64] In the final analysis, slavery was allegedly comparable to original sin—both were brought on by the devil, but both also could never be eradicated. Blacks had to "drink from the bitter cup of slavery," and it would be wrong if, in the process of getting rid of the cup, whites were injured.

Reiche's discussion of slavery and the pitfalls of trying to abolish the institution made it clear that German speakers saw themselves as citizens who had a stake in the outcome of the debate. Although Reiche recognized people of African descent as fellow humans, he considered them inferior people who were first and foremost property. As such, blacks could not claim Revolutionary equality and had to submit to the rights of citizens.[65]

Reiche's writings were in tune with other Pennsylvania proslavery arguments in English published shortly before the Revolution. These divided Africans into a hierarchy of five classes, with blacks at the top, above "Ourang Outangs, Apes, Baboons and Monkeys." In conjunction with the pecking order established by eighteenth-century naturalists, this line of reasoning established firmly that blacks were not equal to whites and thus should remain enslaved.[66]

Nearly two decades after this justification of slavery and ten years after Pennsylvania had passed its gradual emancipation law, the issue of slavery seemed no longer pressing in Pennsylvania. It was in reaction to Quaker efforts to seek abolition at the federal level that Reiche's newspaper addressed the topic. As a Pennsylvanian, the publisher and author considered himself affected by slavery only within the context of property rights. South Carolina and Georgia, where planters depended on black laborers to grow rice and indigo, were the places where the issue of emancipation mattered most.

Although over 3,700 slaves were registered in 1790 in Pennsylvania and 301 in Philadelphia alone, German speakers and other Pennsylvanians discussed the issue primarily as a southern problem.[67] Excluding Pennsylvania as a place where owning slaves was a daily reality limited white Pennsylvanians' moral culpability and minimized the extent to which slavery continued to exist in the state after the gradual abolition law was passed in 1780. Framing slavery as a southern issue allowed white Pennsylvanians to herald themselves as champions of freedom without granting equality to blacks. As a result, residents of Pennsylvania and other northern states erased slavery from their past and present without actually abolishing it completely.

The observations of Hector St. John de Crèvecoeur in his *Letters from an American Farmer* illustrate how white Pennsylvanians rewrote their history of slavery. Although the French immigrant voiced the hope that Pennsylvania slaves would be emancipated eventually, he found that their lives were fundamentally different from the fates suffered by their southern brethren. In terms that somewhat resemble the southern pro-slavery argument of the nineteenth century, Crèvecoeur alleged that Pennsylvania slaves

> enjoy as much liberty as their masters; they are as well clad and as well fed; in health and sickness, they are tenderly taken care of; they live under the same roof and are, truly speaking, a part of our families.... They are the companions of our labours, and treated as such; they enjoy many perquisites, many established holidays, and are not obliged to work more than white people. They marry where inclination leads them, visit their wives every week; ... in short, they participate in many of the benefits of our society without being obliged to bear any of its burthens.... They think themselves happier than many of the lower class of whites.[68]

According to this description, slavery in Pennsylvania existed miraculously without enslavement. Enslaved African Americans might even be freer than their masters since blacks enjoyed liberty, marriage, education, and the companionship of whites without any civil, social, and economic obligations. In a cultural climate that proclaimed the happiness of those kept in bondage, German speakers' opposition to emancipation was allowed to go largely unnoticed and thus did not cause rifts between Anglo- and German Pennsylvanians. Contemporary observers usually did not focus on the ethnicity of those who opposed abolition, and even historians have often categorized the opposition according to the arguments made by each group but not their backgrounds. As Owen Ireland points out, this argument-driven approach has led to a "three-pronged explanation of anti-abolition feeling." Slaveholders constituted the first group, those who could not move beyond their conviction of the sanctity of private property made up the second, and those who predicted complete economic and moral chaos if blacks were freed composed the third group.[69] In overlooking that German speakers voted and acted as an ethnic group when it came to the issue of slavery in the early republic, Anglo-Pennsylvanians incidentally recognized the citizenship rights of German settlers. Only citizens were allowed to take a stand, and only as Americans could they justly demand that their property was safe. As Pennsylvanians, they would conveniently forget that slavery still existed in the state after 1780.

HENRY MUHLENBERG AND SLAVERY

When Crèvecoeur published his observations in 1782, Henry Melchior Muhlenberg would have agreed with the Frenchman's characterization of northern slavery as benign and benevolent. The pastor's ideological journey from critic of slavery to silent supporter of the institution is evident in his extensive journals. Muhlenberg only specifically noted his thoughts about slavery when he wrote about the American South, a region he visited occasionally during his extensive travels. At the same time, his records of day-to-day interactions with people of African descent reveal how familiar he was with a world that relied on the labor of slaves, redemptioners, and indentured servants. His journals clearly show that he believed in the spiritual equality of blacks and whites, free and unfree in the eyes of God. However, he accepted the enslavement of African Americans in this world as divinely ordained, and thus distrusted free blacks. Although Muhlenberg himself never owned slaves, he came into contact with enslaved African Americans almost on a daily basis as a pastor and through the slaves owned by his friends and family members.[70] By the time Muhlenberg's adult son John Peter Gabriel Muhlenberg, a

Revolutionary War general, brought his family's slaves to the old man's home in the 1780s, Henry Muhlenberg had integrated the institution of slavery into his universe without question or comment.

Throughout his career as a clergyman, Muhlenberg, like most other Lutheran ministers in early America, was happy to baptize and catechize blacks and believed them to be as qualified to attain salvation as whites.[71] In some cases, Muhlenberg suggested that blacks were more devout than his white congregates. On one of his frequent trips to New Jersey in 1752, Muhlenberg praised "a Negro slave who diligently comes to our Dutch and English services and puts many nominal Christians to shame by her life." The slave woman was apparently very devoted to Muhlenberg, since she cried "bitterly" (bitterlich) when she heard that he was leaving. Moved by her sincerity, the pastor confessed that "the poor worm broke my heart."[72] Even black heathens who had committed the cardinal sin of murder were eligible candidates for conversion and salvation. Muhlenberg reported with pride the accomplishments of his colleague the Reverend Wrangel in rescuing "the poor soul" of a black man "from darkness and damnation" before he was hanged for murdering a child.[73]

Nearly a decade before the Declaration of Independence proclaimed the equality of all men, and before a proposal to abolish slavery was brought before the Pennsylvania legislature, Muhlenberg found it remarkable that free blacks could become equal members within a white community. When the pastor recorded the presence of "a mulatto" (i.e., half black from birth) among a group of confirmands, Muhlenberg approvingly noted that the man had purchased his freedom, had learned a trade, and spoke the German language.[74] Muhlenberg baptized and confirmed the former slave Thomas Wilkison after his church member neighbors vouched for his good character. While the pastor recognized Wilkison's individual worthiness and welcomed him into the Christian community, Muhlenberg recorded the presence of blacks more frequently within the context of slavery.[75]

Using the terms *Neger* and *sklaven* interchangeably and never using individual enslaved people's names, Muhlenberg often noted in passing when friends, family members, and other visitors brought their slaves to his home. Within this context, slaves appeared to him as faithful servants whose loyalty was secure and whose service the pastor appreciated. Reverend Wrangel's slave, for example, often drove the coach that transported Muhlenberg to and from visits to his colleague, and the pastor usually recorded these occasions. Similarly, a Pennsylvania German merchant in Philadelphia regularly sent his slave to the pastor's home for deliveries. Muhlenberg never hesitated to open the door to this man or to entrust money to him as payment for the goods he brought on behalf of his master.[76]

The clergyman was also delighted when, in 1763, he found an opportunity to improve relations between a master and a slave. Just outside of Philadelphia, Muhlenberg lodged with a German Anabaptist innkeeper who "was very embarrassed that he could not understand the Negro language" of the man he had just purchased. The multilingual pastor learned in a conversation held in "African, French, Spanish, and English" that the man had been kidnapped and baptized by the French in Africa, then captured by the English, and finally sold in Philadelphia to the innkeeper. When Muhlenberg inquired "whether he was satisfied with his present condition," the nameless slave only asked for some "warm clothing," which the "honest innkeeper" was happy to supply.[77] When African Americans were enslaved, Muhlenberg seemed perfectly at ease with them and concerned himself about their souls, noting with pleasure when they became part of the Lutheran community. He could also accept a free mulatto's conversion in the 1760s as long as he was well known for his good behavior in the community, as the Thomas Wilkison example illustrates. Yet the pastor became more concerned about the potential danger of blacks during the American Revolution. While he feared God's retribution for wrongs many slave owners committed against their slaves, he was also afraid of some blacks themselves.

Already in 1774 Muhlenberg noted that the news about his friend Pastor Rappenhorst's plantation was akin to messages that came to Job: a fire had destroyed the winter wheat harvest that was supposed to feed the livestock, a male slave was injured by a falling tree, a female slave was seriously ill, and a calf had been found dead. Muhlenberg concluded that "it is burdensome, expensive, and hardly profitable to exist with Negroes, and then one is not safe in one's existence."[78] In 1777, Muhlenberg found that Virginia's governor, Lord Dunmore, was to blame for the city of Norfolk being reduced to ashes, since he had spoiled everything by declaring the Negroes free.[79]

A year later the pastor and his family had left tumultuous Philadelphia for their quiet farm in Providence. Muhlenberg's distrust of blacks he did not know is obvious in his detailed recording of a very brief encounter with a "strong Negro" who knocked on the pastor's door late in the evening. Muhlenberg recalled that the man pretended he "wanted a couple of tobacco pipes." The man left quickly when the pastor told him that "he needed to look for them [the tobacco pipes] at the shopkeeper's." Yet Muhlenberg wondered "whether he had an ambush in mind or what he was up to." At a time of great uncertainty and war, at night and in a place where Muhlenberg did not know everyone as well as he did in Philadelphia, a black man without an apparent master seemed threatening to him. He attributed the fact that his family had "as yet suffered no evil" to "the most gracious protection of the Savior." God had stopped the strange black man from hurting Muhlenberg or his family, and the pastor admonished himself, "if I could only be more thankful."[80]

In the end, Muhlenberg advocated not owning slaves as the best solution for avoiding the quandary entailed by keeping people enslaved. During his travels in South Carolina in 1774, the pastor praised a German Lutheran planter who cultivated his land without slaves, proving "that a man can live and find food and clothing without the use of slaves, if he be godly and contented and does not desire to take more out of the world than he brought into it."[81]

None of Muhlenberg's reservations about slavery, however, prevented him from complaining bitterly about the alternative source of labor: German redemptioners. Muhlenberg's first experience with his German "house servant," whose service cost the pastor £15 for a five-year term, turned sour within nine months. Supposedly the man "was suborned by malicious people and demanded either his freedom or another master." When Muhlenberg's "jealous neighbors" bought the servant, the man added insult to injury by initially refusing to accept the clothing Muhlenberg offered to give him "because the jacket was not the same color as the coat." Muhlenberg blamed this insolent behavior on the weak position of clergymen in Pennsylvania.[82] At the same time, Muhlenberg was aware of other masters who had been cheated or otherwise abused by their servants. He became concerned that Germans' reputation was suffering because "now so many rotten people are coming into the country and acting so wickedly that the name [German] has begun to stink."[83] In the end Muhlenberg might have seen slaves as more reliable sources of labor than German redemptioners. At least he never noted the kind of disobedience and rebelliousness by slaves that he experienced as the master of a German servant. When his son and daughter-in-law brought their slaves to his home in Philadelphia in the 1780s, the pastor never voiced disapproval of the slave-labor system or the slaves themselves. The practice of holding blacks in bondage had become in his mind an unremarkable and expected part of life.

Between his arrival in the New World in 1742 and his death in 1787, Henry Melchior Muhlenberg had not only become the father of the Lutheran Church in Pennsylvania, a well-off landowner, and father of the Revolutionary War hero Peter Muhlenberg, he had also become a supporter of slavery. While he recognized blacks' spiritual equality and condemned the worst abuses, allegedly committed only by southern, Anglo-American slave owners, he came to deny blacks the humanity he had granted them when he first encountered enslaved African Americans in Charlestown. In the process of becoming a German American, he had also come to accept the institution of slavery. Keeping humans enslaved had become such an expected part of life in America that he rarely even acknowledged the presence of slavery in his own household and never commented on it within the context of life in postrevolutionary Pennsylvania.

Muhlenberg's contemporary German speakers underwent a similar metamorphosis. They learned with their Anglo neighbors that blackness signaled enslavement. As it became increasingly clear to them that all nonwhites were inherently inferior, Germans concentrated on their efforts to be seen as white and to ensure the enactment of laws that plainly differentiated German redemptioners from African slaves. Because of the imagined and real precariousness of their claims to American citizenship, postrevolutionary German speakers opposed the abolition of slavery in large part because the enslavement of blacks promised to ensure their own unequivocal assertion of the rights of free men. If people of African descent were inferior and not equal to whites, the place of Pennsylvania Germans as rightful members of the American nation seemed more secure.

Notes

1. "Schwartzen Heiden, die als Schlaven an die weißen Christe Leute verkauft sind"; "viele Schlaven hier welche nur halb schwartz sind"; "weißen Sodomiten... die mit Ihren schwartzen Schlavinnen Unzucht treiben"; "die Schwartzen würden sie alle umbringen und sich von Carolina Meister machen"; "die sogenannten Christen leben ärger wie die Heiden, deswegen wollen sie die Schwartzen nicht gerne zur Erkenntniß kommen laßen, damit sie nicht bestrafet und in Ihren Sünden gestöhret werden"; "erschrecklicher Zustand"; "schwehre Gerichte nach sich ziehen." Journals of Henry Melchior Muhlenberg, PM95A (1742), Lutheran Archives Center at Philadelphia. I am indebted to John Peterson and James Ziebell at the Lutheran Archives Center for providing digital images of the journal. I also consulted the published English translation of the journal. All translations are mine. They are also the same as Tappert and Doberstein's published translations, unless otherwise noted. *The Journals of Henry Melchior Muhlenberg*, trans. and ed. Theodore Tappert and John Doberstein, 3 vols. (Philadelphia: Evangelical Lutheran Ministerium of Pennsylvania and Adjacent States and Muhlenberg Press, 1942; repr., Camden, Maine: Picton Press, 1980), September 23, 1742, 1:58.

2. "Ging mit Hochwürden R. [Rappenhorst] spazieren und observierte die Einrichung seiner Plantage und seiner Negersklaven"; "dass alle Negersklaven in America so ordentlich gehalten werden mögen wie die wenigen auf diesem Platz." Journals of Henry Melchior Muhlenberg, PM95A (1774, 1775); *Journals of Henry Melchior Muhlenberg*, December 2, 1774, 2:638; February 1, 1775, 2:674. The translation by Tappert and Doberstein is slightly different: "I wished that all Negro slaves in America might be as well supported and provided with necessary food and clothing as those in this place."

3. "Ein harter Fall für einen jungen Anfänger." Journals of Henry Melchior Muhlenberg, PM95A (1774); *Journals of Henry Melchior Muhlenberg*, December 2, 1774, 2:638.

4. Scholars date the connections between script, handwriting, and identity to the eighteenth century. Tamara Plakins Thorton, *Handwriting in America: A Cultural History* (New Haven, Conn.: Yale University Press, 1998). For an argument that writers and printers purposefully chose multiple scripts, see Katherine Ellison "Millions of Millions of Distinct Orders: Multimodality of Seventeenth-Century Cryptography Manuals," *Book History* 14 (2011): 1–24.

5. "Both 'Schlave' and 'Sclave/Sklave' are derived from the Latin word's(c)lavus,' which was borrowed into Middle High German as 's(c)lave.' An important consonant change between Middle High German and New High German is what is known as the 'palatalization of /s/,' whereby 's' became 'sch' before most consonants, including 'l.' 'Schlave' would not have struck German speakers like Muhlenberg as 'fremd' since there were many other native Germanic words starting with 'schl-,' hence his writing of the word in Kurrent. 'Sclave/Sklave,' on the other hand, contains a series of consonants [skl] that is unusual for German: in fact there are no other German words that start with this combination. Thus, when using this variant, which by 1775 would have been the more commonly accepted written form, Muhlenberg would have recognized it as being 'fremd' on the basis of its sound shape and thus written it accordingly." I am indebted to Mark Louden, Professor of German at the University of Wisconsin–Madison, for sharing his expertise on the history of Kurrent and Latin script. Personal communication, April 27, 2017.

6. For the complete table of religious denominations in Pennsylvania in 1775, see *Pennsylvania: A History of the Commonwealth*, ed. Randall Miller and William Pencak (University Park: Penn State University Press, 2002), 136.

7. Owen Ireland, "Germans Against Abolition: A Minority's View of Slavery in Revolutionary Pennsylvania," *Journal of Interdisciplinary History* 3 (Spring 1973): 685–706. The ethnic makeup of opponents of abolition in the Pennsylvania General Assembly in 1779–87 was as follows: unknown: 35 percent (28 total); English: 12 percent (3); Welsh:

29 percent (2); Scotch: 67 percent (4); Scotch-Irish: 36 percent (14); Irish: 17 percent (1); German: 50 percent (15); others: 100 percent (1). Religious affiliation of opponents of abolition: Unknown: 37 percent (31); Anglican: 24 percent (4); Quaker: 9.5 percent (2); Presbyterian: 37 percent (5); Lutheran: 83 percent (5); Reformed: 64 percent (7).

8. As Jon Sensbach and others have argued, German speakers' rejection of slavery was based largely on their fear of what slavery would do to themselves, that is, that slaves would turn hardworking Germans into lazy people, leading to sinful behavior. Jon Sensbach, *A Separate Canaan: The Making of an Afro-Moravian World in North Carolina, 1763–1840* (Chapel Hill: University of North Carolina Press, 1998). Wolfgang Splitter's quantitative analysis of Muhlenberg's writings reminds us that Muhlenberg was a pragmatic preacher sent to America to tend to the spiritual well-being of German-speakers. Since his mission did not include the conversion of blacks or other heathens, one looks in vain for "theoretisch-systematischen Gedankenentwürfen" (theoretic-systematic thought designs) in his writings. Splitter also finds that Muhlenberg was mostly "indifferent" (neutral) when he mentioned slaves. At the same time, Splitter notes that Muhlenberg never expressed opposition to slavery and that his attitude toward the institution was "situativ und empirisch geprägt" (situational and based on experience). See Wolfgang Splitter, "'Neger,' Miterlöste,' 'Nebenmenschen': Heinrich Melchior Mühlenberg über die afroamerikanische Ethnie und die Sklaverei," *Amerikastudien / American Studies* 45, no. 3 (2000): 293–323.

9. "An Act for the gradual abolition of slavery," in *The First Laws of the Commonwealth of Pennsylvania*, comp. John Cushing (Wilmington, Del.: 1984), 282–87. The law, enacted on March 1, 1780, freed any child born to a slave after this date. The child did, however, have to serve a master to age twenty-eight and was to be treated like other servants.

10. For an exceptional new study on slavery in New England, see Allegra di Bonaventura, *For Adam's Sake: A Family Saga in Colonial New England* (New York: Liveright, 2013).

11. For the most recent discussion of Quaker antislavery, see Brycchan Carey, *From Peace to Freedom: Quaker Rhetoric and the Birth of American Antislavery, 1657–1761* (New Haven, Conn.: Yale University Press, 2012). For biographies of important Quaker leaders, see Thomas P. Slaughter, *The Beautiful Soul of John Woolman, Apostle of Abolition* (New York: Hill and Wang, 2008); Geoffrey Plank, *John Woolman's Path to the Peaceable Kingdom: A Quaker in the British Empire* (Philadelphia: University of Pennsylvania Press, 2012) For an early history of slavery in Pennsylvania, see Edward Turner, *The Negro in Pennsylvania: Slavery, Servitude, Freedom, 1639–1861* (Washington, D.C.: American Historical Association, 1911); Jerome Wood Jr., "The Negro in Early Pennsylvania: The Lancaster Experience, 1730–90," in *Plantation, Town, and Country: Essays on the Local History of American Slave Society*, ed. Elinor Miller and Eugene Genovese (Urbana: University of Illinois Press, 1974), 441–52; Jean Soderlund, *Quakers and Slavery: A Divided Spirit* (Princeton, N.J.: Princeton University Press, 1985). For a brief but useful overview, see Gary Nash, "Slaves and Slaveowners in Colonial Philadelphia," *William and Mary Quarterly*, 3rd ser., 30, no. 2 (1973): 223–56; Gary Nash and Jean Soderlund, *Freedom by Degrees: Emancipation in Pennsylvania and Its Aftermath* (Oxford: Oxford University Press, 1991), chaps. 1 and 2.

12. "Germantown Friends' Protest Against Slavery, 1688," reprinted in Samuel W. Pennypacker, "The Settlement of Germantown, and the Causes Which Led to It," *Pennsylvania Magazine of History and Biography* 4 (1880): 28–30. Leroy Hopkins, "The Germantown Protest: Origins of Abolitionism Among the German Residents of Southeastern Pennsylvania," *Yearbook of German-American Studies* 23 (1988): 19–29.

13. Maurice Jackson, *Let This Voice Be Heard: Anthony Benezet, Father of Atlantic Abolitionism* (Philadelphia: University of Pennsylvania Press, 2009). For an older, unpublished examination of slavery in Pennsylvania, see Merle Brouwer, "The Negro As a Slave and as a Free Black in Colonial Pennsylvania" (Ph.D. diss., Wayne State University, 1973).

14. The foundational work on the ideologies of race is Winthrop Jordan, *White over Black: American Attitudes Toward the Negro, 1500–1812* (Chapel Hill: University of North Carolina Press, 1968). Since Jordan's work, scholars have revised and broadened his ideas. For a great overview of more recent scholarship, see "Constructing Race," special issue, *William and Mary Quarterly*, 3rd ser., 14, no. 1 (1997). For studies on whiteness and blackness, see David Roediger, *The Wages of Whiteness: Race and the Making of the American Working Class* (New York: Verso, 1991); Noel Ignatiev, *How the Irish Became White* (New York: Routledge, 1995); Joanne Pope Melish, *Disowning Slavery: Gradual Emancipation and "Race" in New England, 1780–1860* (Ithaca, N.Y.: Cornell University Press, 1998). For recent works pointing to the intersections between ideas about race and gender, see Kathleen Brown, *Good Wives, Nasty Wenches, and Anxious Patriarchs: Gender, Race, and Power in Colonial Virginia* (Chapel Hill: University of North Carolina Press, 1996); Kirsten Fischer, *Suspect Relations: Sex, Race, and Resistance in Colonial North Carolina* (Ithaca, N.Y.: Cornell University Press, 2002). For a study of German-speaking slaveholders in North Carolina, see Sensbach, *Separate Canaan*.

15. The history of German speakers' relationships with Native Americans is beyond the scope of this chapter. For that reason, I limit my discussion to the ways in which ideas about Indians affected German concepts of skin color and race.

16. Although Muhlenberg was not representative of most German-speaking colonists because of his educational background, illustrious connections to important people, and not least of all his enormous success, anecdotal evidence suggests that his encounters with slaves and his reflections upon the institution expressed the sentiments of Pennsylvania Germans in general.

17. For a thorough discussion of German speakers' understanding of property, see A. G. Roeber, *Palatines, Liberty, and Property: German Lutherans in Colonial British America* (Baltimore: Johns Hopkins University Press, 1993).

18. Gottlieb Mittelberger, *Reise nach Pennsylvanien im Jahr 1750 und Rükreise nach Teutschland im Jahr 1754* (Stuttgart: Gottlieb Friderich Jenisch, 1756), 106–7.

19. Peter Kalm, *Peter Kalm's Travels in North America: The English Version of 1770*, new ed. (New York: Dover, 1987), 206.

20. Mittelberger, *Reise nach Pennsylvanien*, 54.

21. See, for example, *Der Hoch-Deutsch Americanische Calendar, 1751* (Germantown: Christopher Saur, 1752).

22. Sensbach, *Separate Canaan*, xvii.

23. Sensbach gives credence to the stereotype of the diligent German worker and discusses its origins as well as Germans' free-soil ideas. See Sensbach, *Separate Canaan*, 48–53.

24. *Pensylvanische Berichte*, May 16, 1746. In this case, Saur actually acted as a slave broker since the ad directed interested parties to "inquire with the printer of with B. Franklin." It is likely that Franklin owned the slave and that Saur was printing the ad as a professional courtesy to another printer.

25. See, for example, *Pensylvanische Berichte*, October 16, 1745. At the same time, Saur and later his son, Christopher Saur Jr., wrote antislavery articles. See *Pensylvanische Berichte*, November 16, 1754; February 13, 1761. According to Gary Nash, Saur refused to print ads for runaway slaves more often than other printers. See Gary Nash, *Forging Freedom: The Formation of Philadelphia's Black Community, 1720–1840* (Cambridge, Mass.: Harvard University Press, 1991).

26. These figures do not include the number of times advertisements were repeated. The first runaway servant ad appeared on July 16, 1744, five years after the first issue of Saur's newspaper was published.

27. For the complete table, see David Waldstreicher, "Reading the Runaways: Self-Fashioning, Print Culture, and Confidence in Slavery in the Eighteenth-Century Mid-Atlantic," *William and Mary Quarterly*, 3rd ser., 16, no. 2 (1999), 250, table I. Waldstreicher does not offer the total number of advertisements in each category, but calculated averages from looking at the first issue of each month for each year. According to Billy Smith and Richard Wojtowicz, 1324 runaways were advertised in Franklin's newspaper from 1728 to 1790. See Billy Smith and

Richard Wojtowicz, *Blacks Who Stole Themselves: Advertisements for Runaways in the "Pennsylvania Gazette," 1728–2790* (Philadelphia: University of Pennsylvania Press, 1989), 5.

28. Nash and Soderlund, *Freedom by Degrees*, 19–20; Cheesman A. Herrick, *White Servitude in Pennsylvania: Indentured and Redemption Labor in Colony and Commonwealth* (Philadelphia: John Joseph McVey, 1926), 201–2.

29. See Nash and Soderlund, *Freedom by Degrees*, 81, table 3–1. The table differentiates by religious affiliation. Since about 90 percent of German speakers in Philadelphia belonged to either the Reformed or the Lutheran Church, the number of slaveholders belonging to these churches is representative of ethnic affiliation as well.

30. See, for example, *Pennsylvania Gazette*, December 16–23, 1729.

31. Benjamin Franklin, "Observations Concerning the Increase of Mankind," in *The Papers of Benjamin Franklin*, ed. Leonard W. Labaree et al., 41 vols. to date (New Haven, Conn.: Yale University Press, 1961–), 4:225–34.

32. Herrick, *White Servitude in Pennsylvania*, 3. See also Sharon Salinger, *"To Serve Well and Faithfully": Labour and Indentured Servants in Pennsylvania, 1682–1800* (Cambridge: Cambridge University Press, 1987).

33. Herrick, *White Servitude in Pennsylvania*, 105–12.

34. *The Autobiography of Benjamin Franklin*, ed. J. A. Leo Lemay and P. M. Zall (New York: W. W. Norton, 1986), 19. Franklin described himself as "thoroughly soak'd and . . . tir'ed" when he entered a "poor Inn." He noted that "I cut so miserable a Figure too, that I found by the Questions ask'd me I was suspected to be some runaway Servant, and in danger of being taken up on that Suspicion."

35. For a more detailed discussion of the differences, see Herrick, *White Servitude in Pennsylvania*, 2–8.

36. German Society of Pennsylvania officers dealt with many cases in which redemptioners complained about the terms of their servitude.

37. The lower tariff on Irish imported servants might have been due to the fact that Ireland was part of the British Empire.

38. The tax on African slave imports was rejected by the Board of Trade and Plantations because it interfered with the lucrative English slave trade. The GSP was equally offended by the Convict Act of 1729, which required the mayor of Philadelphia to record the sale of all arriving servants. The GSP noted that it was clearly a sign of "opressing the Germans" when they "are ranked with the Convicts." "Petition of the German Society contributing for the Relief of distressed Germans in the State of Pennsylvania," GSP Minutes, 1770–1802, March 18, 1785.

39. For a short history of the GSP, see Birte Pfleger, *Ethnicity Matters: A History of the German Society of Pennsylvania* (Washington, D.C.: German Historical Institute, 2006). Henry Keppele, founding member and longtime president of the GSP, was involved both in the slave trade as well as in the business of bringing German-speaking redemptioners to Pennsylvania. For more information on Keppele as a businessman, see "John Henry Keppele (1716–1797)," accessed September 4, 2015, http://www.immigrantentrepreneurship.org/entry.php?rec=7.

40. See also Marianne Wokeck, *Trade in Strangers: The Beginnings of Mass Migration to North America* (University Park: Penn State University Press, 1999), 130–31.

41. For recent scholarship on the slave trade, ships, and the Atlantic voyage, see Marcus Rediker, *The Slave Ship: A Human History* (New York: Penguin Books, 2007); Stephanie Smallwood, *Saltwater Slavery: A Middle Passage from Africa to American Diaspora* (Cambridge, Mass.: Harvard University Press, 2007).

42. Lewis Weiss to Governor John Penn, January 1774, *Pennsylvania Archives*, 1st ser., vol. 4, 473.

43. "A Petition from sundry Germans, Freeholders and Inhabitants of the City of Philadelphia . . . ," *Votes and Proceedings*, January 11, 1765.

44. Although there was no written law that explicitly prohibited slaves from marrying each other, the concept of slave marriage was a legal impossibility. Since slaves were legally considered chattel, they did not have the ability to make any legal contracts such as marriage. For a discussion of this issue, see Hendrik Hartog, *Man and Wife in America:*

A History (Cambridge, Mass.: Harvard University Press, 2000), 93; Margaret Burnham, "An Impossible Marriage: Slave Law and Family Law," *Law and Inequality* 5 (July 1987): 187–225; Leslie Patrick-Stamp, "Ideology and Punishment: The Crime of Being Black (Pennsylvania, 1639–1804)" (Ph.D. diss., University of California, Santa Cruz, 1989).

45. William Penn to his steward at Pennsbury (1685), as quoted in Herrick, *White Servitude in Pennsylvania*, 79.

46. George Washington to Tench Tilghman, March 24, 1784, in *The Writings of George Washington from the Original Manuscript Sources, 1745–1799*, ed. John C. Fitzpatrick, vol. 27, *June 11, 1783–November 28, 1784* (Washington, D.C.: U.S. Government Printing Office, 1938), 367. Archeological evidence of the presence of slaves in the nation's first "White House" was discovered in Philadelphia during the construction of the new building for the Liberty Bell. This unleashed a controversy about the representation of slavery at a site celebrating the founding of the nation. See Dinitia Smith, "Slave Site for a Symbol of Freedom," *New York Times*, April 20, 2002; Edward Lawler Jr., "The President's House in Philadelphia: The Rediscovery of a Lost Landmark," *Pennsylvania Magazine of History and Biography* 126, no. 1 (2002): 5–96. For a recent discussion of the interchangeability of all types of laborers in the early republic, see Seth Rockman, *Scraping By: Wage Labor, Slavery, and Survival in Early Baltimore* (Baltimore: Johns Hopkins University Press, 2008).

47. General Shirley to Governor Morris, February 29, 1756, *Pennsylvania Archives*, 1st ser., vol. 2, 587–92. When the need for recruits arose again at the beginning of the Revolutionary War, the Pennsylvania Council of Safety resolved "That indentured Servants & apprentices ought not to be inlisted in the Flying Camp of this State, without Consent of their Masters & Mistresses in writing, and that all who have been inlisted heretofore, shall be discharged on the application of their Masters & Mistresses for that Purpose." *Colonial Records*, vol. 10, 723–24.

48. For these notices, see, for example, the *Pennsylvania Gazette*, November 11, 1756; *Pensylvanische Berichte*, December 25, 1756.

49. According to one scholar, in 1760 there were no advertisements announcing the sale or newly arrived servants in the *Pennsylvania Gazette*. In addition, "the record of arrivals of foreigners gives no ship for 1760." Herrick, *White Servitude in Pennsylvania*, 94n70. According to Waldstreicher, the number of advertisements for runaway servants increased with the start of the French and Indian War. At the same time, the number of advertisements selling slaves also increased.

50. This does not mean that all servants who ran away during the French and Indian War joined the military. As the Pennsylvania assembly noted, "many [left] their masters on pretence of going to inlist, and not being pursued.... They often [went] quite off without inlisting." "Address of the Assembly," February 13, 1756, *Colonial Records* [*Minutes of the Provincial Council of Pennsylvania*], vol. 7 (Harrisburg, Pa.: Theo. Fenn, 1851), 38.

51. Susan Klepp, "Encounter and Experiment: The Colonial Period," in Miller and Pencak, *Pennsylvania*, 61.

52. Ibid., 94; Nash and Soderlund, *Freedom by Degrees*, 5, table 1–1.

53. *Votes and Proceedings*, November 22, 1722.

54. *Pennsylvania Gazette*, March 5, 1751.

55. Advertisements announcing the availability of slaves for hire appeared sporadically in the *Pennsylvania Gazette*. For examples, see *Pennsylvania Gazette*, April 5, 1770; November 29, 1770.

56. Ira Berlin, *Many Thousands Gone: The First Two Centuries of Slavery in North America* (Cambridge, Mass.: Belknap Press of Harvard University Press, 1998).

57. "Rowan's Letter of 1797 from Wilmington, Del.," quoted in Herrick, *White Servitude in Pennsylvania*, 98n89.

58. William Priest, *Travels in the United States of America: Commencing in the Year 1793, and Ending in 1797* (London: J. Johnson, 1802), 144.

59. John Sheffield, *Observations on the Commerce of the American States* (London, 1784), 243–44.

60. *Der General-Postbothe an die Deutsche Nation in America*, April 9, 1790. For a discussion of the national debate over slavery and petitions to Congress for abolition, see Jordan, *White over Black*, 325–31.

61. One historian has described Reiche as having had an "unsettled career as clergyman, teacher, and author." Reiche died within months of the last issue of his newspaper and within weeks of working as editor for Melchior Steiner's *Neue Philadelphische Correspndenz*. See Robert Cadzden, *A Social History of the German Book Trade in America to the Civil War* (Columbia, S.C.: Camden House, 1984), 2, 26n52.

62. "Slave Trade in Congress of the United States," *Der General-Postbothe an die Deutsche Nation in America*, April 9, 1790.

63. "Fortsetzung," *Der General-Postbothe an die Deutsche Nation in America*, April 13, 1790.

64. Reiche was probably referring to Luke 10:30–36, in which a Samaritan helped an injured man after two other men, a priest and a Levite, had passed the man in need. Samaritans were despised by Jews.

65. For a discussion of the issue of equality in the antislavery movement in the early republic, see Jordan, *White over Black*, 372–74.

66. *Personal Slavery Established, by the Suffrages of Custom and Right Reason: Being a Full Answer to the Gloomy and Visionary Reveries, of All the Fanatical and Enthusiastical Writers on that Subject* (Philadelphia: John Dunlap, 1773), 18–19.

67. For the number of slaves in Pennsylvania, see Nash and Soderlund, *Freedom by Degrees*, 5, table 1–1; 7, table 1–2. For a discussion of postrevolutionary New England discourse on slavery and the resulting silence and erasing of slavery from New England history, see Melish, *Disowning Slavery*.

68. J. Hector St. John de Crèvecoeur, *Letters from an American Farmer and Sketches of Eighteenth-Century America* (1782), ed. Albert E. Stone (New York: Penguin Books, 1986), 170. For a discussion of the nineteenth-century proslavery arguments, see Drew Gilpin Faust, ed., *The Ideology of Slavery: Proslavery Thought in the Antebellum South, 1830–1860* (Baton Rouge: Louisiana State University Press, 1981); Faust, *A Sacred Circle: The Dilemma of the Intellectual in the Old South, 1840–1860* (Baltimore: Johns Hopkins University Press, 1977).

69. Ireland, "Germans Against Abolition," 685n3.

70. One of Conrad Weiser's sons, Muhlenberg's brother-in-law, owned several slaves, as did the pastor's son John Peter Gabriel Muhlenberg. *Journals of Henry Melchior Muhlenberg*, 3:213. Muhlenberg performed a wedding ceremony for a black man "who formerly belonged to my brother-in-law." Ibid., July 25, 1783, 3:552; the entry for this day notes a letter from his son and a list of his property that includes three slaves.

71. For examples, see ibid., July 22, 1753, 1:367; September 9, 1763, 1:669; May 20, 1770, 2:439. Lutherans were almost the only Protestant denomination that admitted African Americans into their congregations a regular basis. For a discussion of Lutherans and African Americans within the context of a sexual scandal, see Graham Russell Hodges, "The Pastor and the Prostitute: Sexual Power Among African Americans and Germans in Colonial New York," in *Sex, Love, Race: Crossing Boundaries in North American History*, ed. Martha Hodes (New York: New York University Press, 1999), 60–71.

72. "Eine Mohren Sklavin welche fleissig mit in unsere Niederdeutschen und Englischen Versammlungen ging und mit ihrem Wandel viele Nahmen Christen beschämte"; "der arme Wurm brach mir mein Herz." Journals of Henry Melchior Muhlenberg, PM95A (1752). Tappert and Doberstein translate "Wurm" as "woman." *Journals of Henry Melchior Muhlenberg*, July 26, 1752, 1:342.

73. "Die arme Seele"; "aus der Finsternis und Verdammung." Journals of Henry Melchior Muhlenberg, PM95A (1764); *Journals of Henry Melchior Muhlenberg*, January 14, 1764, 2:10–12.

74. *Journals of Henry Melchior Muhlenberg*, October 18, 1768, 2:362.

75. Gary Nash estimates that there were about 150 free blacks in Philadelphia in 1770, while 1,392 were enslaved in 1767, declining to 1,270 in 1769. See Gary Nash, "Slaves and Slave Owners in Colonial Philadelphia," *William and Mary Quarterly* 30, no. 2 (1973): 223–56.

76. See, for example, *Journals of Henry Melchior Muhlenberg*, November 22, 1776, 2:759; February 6, 1777, 3:12.

77. "War sehr verlegen, dass er die Negersprache nicht verstehen konnte"; "ob er mit

seinem gegenwärtigen Stande vergnügt wäre"; "warme Kleider"; "ehrliche Wirt." Journals of Henry Melchior Muhlenberg, PM95A (1763); *Journals of Henry Melchior Muhlenberg*, December 16, 1763, 1:721–22.

78. "Hiobs Botschaften"; "es ist mühsam, kostbar und wenig profitable mit Negern zu hausen, und dann ist man des Lebens nicht sicher." Journals of Henry Melchior Muhlenberg, PM95A (1774). Tappert and Doberstein translate this last part differently: ". . . hardly profitable business managing a place with Negro slaves, especially when one tries to maintain them in a Christian or at least humane manner." *Journals of Henry Melchior Muhlenberg*, November 30, 1774, 2:637.

79. "Die Zustände verdorben, weil er die Neger frei erklärte." Journals of Henry Melchior Muhlenberg, PM95A (1777); *Journals of Henry Melchior Muhlenberg*, February 7, 1777, 3:13.

80. "Starker Neger"; "gab vor er wollte ein paar Tabackspfeifen haben"; "er solche bei den Krämern suchen müsse"; "ob er Hinterhalt oder was er im Sinne hatte"; "bis hierher . . . noch nichts Übles"; "der allermächtigsten und gnädigsten Protection des Weltheilands"; "wenn ich nur dankbar genug sein könnte." Journals of Henry Melchior Muhlenberg, PM95A (1778); *Journals of Henry Melchior Muhlenberg*, March 8, 1778, 3:135. Tappert and Doberstein transcribe and translate "starker Neger" as "huge Negro," which changes the meaning. Wolfgang Splitter relies on Tappert and Doberstein's transcription and translation and argues that Mühlenberg was intimidated by the physical stature of the black man knocking on his door late at night. Splitter, "'Neger,' Miterlöste,' 'Nebenmenschen,'" 313.

81. "Dass man auch ohne schwarze Sklaven leben und Nahrung und Kleider finden könne, wenn man gottselig seie und sich begnüge und nicht mehr aus der Welt herausnehem will as man herein gebracht hat." Journals of Henry Melchior Muhlenberg, PM95A (1774); *Journals of Henry Melchior Muhlenberg*, October 13, 1774, 2:586.

82. "Liess sich von feindseligen Leuten anstiften und begehrte frei zu sein oder einen anderen Meister zu haben"; "missgünstigen Nachbarn"; "weil das Camisol nicht similar Coleur vom Rocke hätte." Journals of Henry Melchior Muhlenberg, PM95A (1751); *Journals of Henry Melchior Muhlenberg*, January 1751, 1:265–66.

83. "Nunmehr kommt so viel verdorbenes Volk herein und treibt es so arg, dass der Name [deutsch] stinkend wird." Journals of Henry Melchior Muhlenberg, PM95A (1751); *Journals of Henry Melchior Muhlenberg*, August 11, 1751, 1:304.

CHAPTER 8

How the Quakers Worked with Moravians, Germans, the French, the British, and Enslaved and Free Africans

All in the Antislavery Cause

MAURICE JACKSON

The Quaker onslaught against slavery was led by Anthony Benezet, who was born to Huguenot (Protestant) parents Jean Étienne Benezet and Judith de la Méjenelle in Saint-Quentin, Picardy, France, on January 31, 1713, and baptized the next day. After the revocation of the Edict of Nantes in 1685, the Huguenots faced intensifying religious persecution, and many were forced to join the Roman Catholic Church. Anthony's father, Jean, had belonged to a nonviolent Huguenot resistance group called "Inspirés de la Vaunage," but in 1715 he fled with his young family to Holland and then to England. Anthony would later tell a friend, François, marquis de Barbé-Marbois, of his family's oppression by French persecutors: "one of my uncles was hung by those intolerants, my aunt was put in a convent, two of my cousins died in the galleys, and my fugitive father was hung in effigy for explaining the gospel differently from the priests, and the family was ruined by the confiscation of his property."[1] Perhaps for these reasons, Anthony Benezet came to have a deep sympathy for other oppressed and exiled people, particularly enslaved Africans.

While moderately successful during sixteen years in England, Jean Benezet wanted more for his family, and he moved them to Philadelphia in 1731. Although Quakers associated with them during their first years in Philadelphia, the Benezet family was not Quaker; Anthony's father and several of his sisters soon joined the Moravian Brethren. Jean also admired the great English evangelist George Whitefield, and revealed his own sympathy for blacks by contributing to Whitefield's unsuccessful attempt to start the Nazareth training school for blacks on five thousand acres of land near the Delaware River. Perhaps more than any other individual's work in the eighteenth century, that of Anthony Benezet served as a catalyst throughout the Atlantic world for the beginnings of the organized fight against the slave trade and the eventual ending of slavery. His written work, which combined Quaker principles and Enlightenment thinking with knowledge gained through a study of Africa and her history, and his own contacts with black people as a teacher and philanthropist, influenced men such as Benjamin Franklin, John Jay, and Patrick Henry in North America; Thomas Clarkson, Granville Sharpe, and William Wilberforce in England; and Condorcet and Abbé Raynal in France. His words helped inspire African-born Olaudah Equiano and Ottabah Cugoano to write and students at his Quaker school, such as the American-born black Richard Allen and Absalom Jones, to organize. In this work he inspired others of many nationalities and faiths to join him.

CONTACT WITH MORAVIANS

Jean-Étienne, now John Stephen, Benezet purchased two five-hundred-acre tracts of land from James and William Bingham. From 1735 to 1741 he resided in a large two-story house on Second Street below Race Street, in an area called Moravian Alley, which suggests he had close ties with the Moravians before he officially joined them in 1743. George Brookes cites the minutes of the Philadelphia Monthly Meeting of March 27, 1743: "Cadwaller Foulke acquainted this meeting that Stephen Benezet had been lovingly spoke to respecting his declining to attend our Religious Meetings . . . he had joined himself in the Society of Moravians."[2] Early Philadelphia Moravians often had ties to the French Prophets, and members of each group joined the other.[3] Before father Benezet took the official step of announcing to the Quaker Annual Meeting of 1743 that he had joined the Moravians, two of his daughters, Susanna and Marianne, had already done so. Susanna had married John Pyraleus, one of the first Moravian missionaries sent to America, in 1742. John Stephen Benezet had sufficient standing and ties to the Moravians that Count Zinzendorf himself stayed with the Benezet family during part of his trip to Pennsylvania (1741–43).

The count had allowed Moravians to live on his estate in Saxony, where, under his tutelage, the doctrine of "Brotherly Agreement" that outlined their tenets was developed. His associates and followers established over one hundred overseas missions and communities from the late 1720s until the mid-1740s. Pyraleus became a part of a group who began, on November 14, 1740, to construct the "Charity School for the Instruction of Poor Children Gratis in Useful Literature and the knowledge of the Christian Religion." John Stephen Benezet became a trustee of the center, named simply the New Building. Among other trustees of the school were the Reverend George Whitefield, then living in Georgia; Samuel Seward of London; and Benjamin Franklin. The New Building was later deeded to the Academy, which became the College of Pennsylvania and later the University of Pennsylvania. The *Pennsylvania Gazette* of September 12, 1751, recorded that on September 16 a Free School would be opened "by Order of the Trustees of the ACADEMY . . . at the New Building for the Instruction of poor children gratis in reading, writing and arithmetic."[4]

Around 1739 Benezet worked as a proofreader for the printer Christopher Saur the Elder.[5] Born in Germany and originally a tailor, Saur was known in English as Sower, and his son, also named Christopher, used the English variant still more frequently (as Wiggin and Erben also outline in their chapters in the present volume). After the elder Saur's arrival in Pennsylvania, he became a tool manufacturer and eventually imported printing equipment and German movable type in 1731, going on to publish, in German, religious books, including the Bible, a newspaper, and an almanac. Two other things stand out about the Saur/Sower press and its connection to the Benezet family. First, on May 20, 1751, the Saur father and son were witnesses to the signing of the will of Benezet's father, who signed his name as J. Stephen Benezet.[6] Second, when Anthony Benezet published his first work, *Observations on the Inslaving of Negros* (1760), which had not been approved by the Quakers and for which he had to find funds to print, the printer was "Christopher Sower: Germantown," the son.

During these and later years Benjamin Franklin read Benezet's pamphlets to gain knowledge of Africa and the slave trade.[7] Benezet gained early connections to Philadelphia Germans via Franklin. In Benezet's job as a proofreader for Saur, he learned invaluable lessons "in the way of accuracy of thought, expression, punctuation, and writing."[8] The younger Saur enjoyed a long-standing friendship with Franklin and surely provided one of the early contacts between Franklin and Benezet, who later worked together on education and health issues. By the early 1770s, Franklin and Benezet had cemented their bond. Benezet's brother Daniel had married Deborah Franklin's cousin in 1771, forging a family connection. The two men began to share ideas and information in earnest on a wide range of topics. Benezet used Franklin's letters as a way to search for more ammunition with which to fight slavery.

THE PEOPLE OF THE CITY OF PHILADELPHIA

During the height of Benezet's fight against slavery, Philadelphia emerged as a key industrial and maritime center. Compared with the southern colonies, Pennsylvania's slave population was relatively small. While exact numbers cannot be given prior to the 1790 federal census, the closest estimates reveal that in 1721 the white population in Pennsylvania totaled 60,000 and the black 5,000.[9] By 1750, the colony's estimated population was about 150,000, with from 7,500 to 12,000 being black.[10] Between 1750 and 1770 the city of Philadelphia's population more than doubled. By 1775, the city had a population of 19,650, and the greater Philadelphia area had 33,290 inhabitants, the largest city and urban area in colonial British America.

Benezet's Philadelphia was a complicated religious, racial, national, and ethnic mix: Anglicans, Catholics, Lutherans, Presbyterians, Mennonites, Moravians, and Quakers; English, Irish, German, Scotch-Irish, and French Huguenots; whites and blacks. Slaves came from nations and kingdoms in West Africa, including Benin, Senegal, Gorée, Guinea, and Gambia. They had been kidnapped from the Kingdom of Fida and from Dutch forts at Delmina. They were Mandingos and Fuli, Akan, and other African ethnicities. There were enslaved Africans and some who later became free people of color. They worked next to indentured servants—bond laborers—and next to the masters of both black and white.[11]

THE DEVELOPMENT OF BENEZET: QUAKER, SCHOOLMASTER, AND ANTISLAVERY LEADER

Anthony had been apprenticed to a Quaker merchant in London. As a merchant in training he was not a success, but he was attracted to his master's religion. He had a multilayered background combining knowledge of the persecution of his family with his family's close associations with the French Prophets, the Quakers, and the Moravians. Unlike his father and sister, he decided to join the Society of Friends. With them his life's central mission became the defense of another persecuted minority, the enslaved Africans. Benezet combined his mission to end slavery with his family's traditional commitment to education, leaving little wonder why he founded both a school for girls and a school for free blacks.

In Philadelphia on May 13, 1736, he married Joyce Marriot, granddaughter of prominent Quaker physician and "ministering Friend" Griffith Owen. Both children born to Joyce and Anthony died in infancy. Joyce, like her grandfather, became a "ministering Friend," a public spiritual figure in a religious community that allowed women to address religious meetings and did not believe in a "hireling ministry."

Although the eldest son of a versatile father who had now become a successful Philadelphia dry-goods importer, Anthony Benezet had no desire to join his brother in business. He wrote a friend that "I find being amongst the buyers and sellers rather a snare to me."[12] He had a small frame and a "frail constitution," and because of this he sought what he thought would be a less strenuous vocation. Equally importantly, his love of books, his mastery of several languages, his love of children, and his passion for the truth led him to become a teacher. In 1742, he took charge of the Friend's English School in Philadelphia (later renamed the William Penn Charter School). He also founded a school for Quaker girls in 1755. Nonetheless, what most distinguished Benezet from his Quaker contemporaries was his association with blacks.

Benezet began teaching blacks in his home in the evenings in 1750; after two decades of that private tutoring, he established the Friends School for Black People, later called the African Free School, which opened its doors in the summer of 1770. Benezet later wrote, "having observed the many disadvantages these afflicted people labour under in point of education and otherwise, a tender care has taken place to promote their instruction in school learning, and also their religious and temporal welfare."[13] He reverted uncharacteristically to the third person in the epilogue to his *Short Observations on Slavery*:

> A. Benezet, teacher of a school established by private subscription, in Philadelphia, for the instruction of the Black Children and others of that people, has, for many years, had opportunity of knowing the temper and genius of the Africans; particularly of those under his tuition, who have been many, of different ages... and he is bold to assert, that the notion entertained by some, that the Blacks are inferior to the Whites in their capacities, is a vulgar prejudice, founded on the Pride or Ignorance of their lordly Masters, who have kept their Slaves at such a distance, as to be unable to form a right judgment of them.[14]

Students at the school included Absalom Jones, the first priest of African descent in the Protestant Episcopal Church, and Richard Allen, the founder of the African Methodist Episcopal Church, who also greatly appreciated Benezet's work as teacher and abolitionist. Together they founded the Free African Society in 1797. Another student at what became known as Benezet's School was James Forten, the sailmaker and entrepreneur. These three free blacks had petitioned Congress to repeal the Fugitive Slave Act of 1793, and Allen and Jones assisted Dr. Benjamin Rush during the yellow fever epidemic in 1793. Forten would also lead the opposition to the American Colonization Society and its efforts to send free blacks back to uncertain lives in unfamiliar Africa.

Linking his Quaker beliefs with his growing hatred of slavery, Benezet began his career as a teacher, writer, and activist with the purpose of freeing enslaved Africans as well as educating them. There were several intellectual, religious, and social links between Benezet's Quakerism and abolitionism. The first was "that all people were equal in the sight of God" and carried an "inner light" within them. A second important influence was the Quaker doctrine of nonviolence, and a third Quaker rule was "that Friends should avoid excesses in their daily lives, as that made them and their children lazy. Benezet believed that greed, luxury, and vanity corrupted human beings and that the quest for wealth was the root of the evils of his time, including the burgeoning Atlantic slave trade. One of his early antislavery tracts argued, "Thus an insatiable desire of gain hath become the principal and moving cause of the most abominable and dreadful scene, that was perhaps ever acted upon the face of the earth."[15] Tying the slave trade to a worldwide drive for profits, Benezet wrote his friend Samuel Fothergill that "it is frequent to see even Friends, toiling year after year, enriching themselves, and thus gathering fuel for our children's vanity and corruption." He believed that anyone "who is not blinded by the Desire of Gain"[16] should recognize that "the right by which these Men hold the Negroes in Bondage, is no other than what is derived from those who stole them."[17] In 1758, the Philadelphia Yearly Meeting seemed poised to defeat a motion requiring Quakers to disavow slavery and free their slaves. Benezet, who had been silent throughout the meeting, solemnly rose. Weeping profusely, he walked to the front of the meeting and recited a well-known passage from the Book of Psalms 68:31: "Ethiopia shall soon stretch out her hands unto God." His message was that the children of Africa were God-fearing, God-loving, and worthy of God's grace. Benezet's message, backed by his life of service, carried the day.[18]

Although the Quakers had finally taken their initial stand on religious grounds, slavery continued to flourish among a much larger group of people who could not be converted by religious arguments alone. In his unending campaign against the slave trade and slavery, Benezet incorporated secular arguments from an impressive array of reading. He was a founding contributor to the Library Company of Philadelphia, and his library was full of current scientific studies; he also read from the libraries of prominent Philadelphia gentlemen including James Logan, Benjamin Rush, and Benjamin Franklin. Benezet used every available source to add rational support for his religious, moral, and ethical arguments against slavery.

Like many writers of the time—particularly Dissenters in the English-speaking world—Benezet relied heavily on biblical citations to buttress his arguments, but he found rational endorsement for his crusade in the writings of enlightened philosophers and jurists. Charles Louis Secondat, Baron de Montesquieu, clearly denounced slavery in his *The Spirit of the Laws* (1748). Montesquieu wrote, "the state of slavery is in its own nature bad. It is neither useful to the master or to the slave; not to the slave because he can do nothing through a motive of virtue; nor to the master, because by having an unlimited authority over his slaves he insensibly accustoms himself to the want of all moral values." This caused man to become "fierce, hasty, severe, choleric, voluptuous, and cruel."[19] Benezet endorsed Montesquieu's argument that slavery had a destructive effect on both the state and free men therein; he noted that slavery destroyed both the white soul and the black body.

The gentle Quaker was deeply influenced by the Scottish moral philosophers. The first of these men whom he quoted from was Francis Hutcheson, who in his *System of Moral Philosophy* (1755) declared, "no endowments natural or acquired, can give a perfect right to assume power over others, without their consent."[20] Hutcheson reasoned that "all men have strong desires of liberty and property, have notions of right, and strong natural impulses to marriage, families, and offspring, and earnest desires of their safety."[21] Hutcheson insisted that slaves who were sold into faraway countries had never legally forfeited their freedom, and he argued for universal liberty, happiness, and benevolence. Benezet generally agreed with Hutcheson, except on the right of the enslaved to use violence in resistance. As a pacifist Quaker, Benezet hoped to avoid violence through black education and white renunciation of slavery.

Benezet was also fond of Scottish jurist George Wallace's *A System of the Principles of the Law of Scotland* (1760), especially his idea that there could never be any legal title for the possession of one human being by another, and thus all transactions for human flesh were legally void. Wallace wrote, "Men and their liberty are not '*in commercio*'; they are not either saleable or purchasable.... For everyone of those unfortunate men who are pretended to be slaves, has a right to be declared free, for he never lost his liberty; he could not lose it; his Prince had no power to dispose of him."[22] At another point Wallace went a step further in his beliefs. He wrote that "property, that bane of human felicity, is too deeply rooted in Society, and is thought to be too essential to the sustenance of it, easily to be abolished. But it must necessarily be banished out of the world, before an Utopia can be established."[23] Benezet embraced natural law theory to insist that every human was born free by a right based in the law of nature. Yet the political remained religious. Government was an "ordinance of

God," and "No Legislature on Earth ... can alter the Nature of Things, or make that to be lawful which is contrary to the law of God."[24]

AFRICA AND AFRICANS

Like Adam Smith, Benezet argued that slavery diminished the productive capacity and corrupted the morals of both blacks and whites. History can be a powerful aid to revolution, and he studied African history with a clear purpose and remarkable care. In seeking to understand African folkways and customs, he read all the available English, French, and Dutch sources, consulting an impressive number of the narratives of adventurers, factors, and accountants of the Royal African Company, and the surgeons and crewmen of the slave ships. His most important works on Africa are *Observations on the Inslaving, Importing and Purchasing of Negroes* (1759), *A Short Account of That Part of Africa, Inhabited by the Negroes* (1762), and *Some Historical Observations of Guinea* (1771). This third, ambitious study was divided into twenty-one chapters discussing "the different parts of Africa, from which the Negro is brought to America." Benezet laid out several premises that directly contradicted prevailing European notions of Africa. He insisted that "scarce a country in the whole world ... is better calculated for affording the necessary comforts of life to its inhabitants," that the Africans "still retain a great deal of innocent simplicity; and, when not stirred up to revenge from the frequent abuses they have received from the Europeans in general, manifest themselves to be a humane, sociable people, whose faculties are as capable of improvement as those of other Men." Finally, he asserted that their economy and government was in many ways commendable, and "it appears that they might have lived happy, if not disturbed by the Europeans." His wide-ranging study included a description of southernmost Africa, a country "settled by Caffres and Hottentots, who have never been concerned in the making or selling slaves."[25] He explored in detail what was known of the Kongo and Old Benin, in present-day Nigeria. Later in the work he described the lives of the Jalofs, Fulani, and Mandingos of West Africa. He directly confronted the myth of the natural inferiority of Africans and the superiority of the Europeans who came to save the supposedly "feeble race." He described an abundant Africa, inhabited by people who produced only what they needed. Rare for his era, Benezet distinguished between those Africans who collaborated with slave traders and those who were victims. His understanding of the societies, tribal structures, and social geography of eighteenth-century Africa was remarkably accurate for a writer of his time. *Some Historical Accounts* became the first school textbook on Africa (and was later assigned in Reconstruction schools).

The gentle Quaker kept track, as best he could, of the number of humans forcibly taken from Africa, the number perishing during the "middle passage," and the number reaching the "new world." He extracted from the printed *Liverpool Memorandum-Book* a list of that port's slave trade, which he estimated carried thirty thousand Africans a year into American slavery. Adding an estimate for the London and Bristol trades, he concluded that "at least One Hundred Thousand Negroes [are] purchased and brought on board our ships yearly from the coast of Africa."[26] He knew that millions of enslaved Africans did not reach western shores due to disease, maltreatment, and resistance, mainly by leaping overboard during the Atlantic crossing.

Benezet was primarily addressing English-speaking audiences, and he paid special attention to the English colonies of Jamaica and Barbados. He described the white indentured servants of Barbados and argued that Europeans were as suitable as Africans for labor in the tropics. He quoted the rector of St. Lucy parish in Barbados, who believed that if there were any inadequacies among blacks in the arts or in the "common affairs" of life, it was due to lack of education and the "depression of their spirits by slavery" rather than any lack of natural ability. Benezet's evaluation of the situation for the blacks in the West Indies was confirmed by the unnamed author of *An Account of the European Settlements in America*, who wrote that "the Negroes in our colonies endure a slavery more complete, and attended with far worse circumstances, than what any people in their condition suffer in any other place in the world, or have suffered in any other period of time."[27] In *A Short Account*, Benezet had already documented the treatment of the slaves in Barbados. Using the account of Sir Hans Sloane, the well-known English author of the *History of Jamaica*, Benezet detailed the atrocities against the blacks. Making note of the disproportionate ratio of blacks to whites in South Carolina, Benezet used Sloane to describe Jamaica as having three times as many blacks as whites; because the slaves made frequent attempts to revolt, blacks were never trusted or left idle. Benezet believed that once the enslaved Africans realized their own strength, they would try to get "their Liberty, or to deliver themselves out of the miserable Slavery they are in."[28] Benezet simply used every available source and every contact to aid his cause.

Benezet closely collaborated with the Quaker leader John Woolman. He also had a tremendous influence on Franklin, who credited his pamphlets and antislavery petition efforts with the decision of the Virginia House of Burgesses to petition the king for an end to the slave trade in 1772. Benezet brought the Philadelphia physician Benjamin Rush, who later wrote anonymous tracts condemning slavery, into the struggle for black freedom. Benezet wrote many hundreds of letters, corresponding with religious leaders such as George Whitefield, John Wesley, and Moses Brown and secular leaders such as Franklin and Rush about his views on slavery and the slave trade. Wesley's *Thoughts upon Slavery* (1774) is based almost entirely on Benezet's *Some Historical Observations of Guinea*, and the Quaker thanked the founder of Methodism for using his work. Upon receiving one of Benezet's pamphlets, sent to him by the Virginia Quaker Robert Pleasants, the future patriot firebrand Patrick Henry wrote on January 18, 1773, "I take this Opportunity to acknowledge ye receipt of Anthony Benezet's book against the slave trade. I thank ye for it." Henry added ruefully, "would anyone believe that I am a Master of Slaves of my own purchase? I am drawn along by ye general Inconvenience of living without them; I will not, I cannot justify it."[29]

As the American Revolution approached, Benezet readily exploited the obvious irony of the rhetoric of revolutionaries railing against tyranny and the threat of their own "enslavement" while holding slaves themselves. In the wake of the Stamp Act crisis, he had already asked "how many of those who distinguish themselves as the Advocates of Liberty, remain insensible and inattentive to the treatment of thousands and tens of thousands of our fellow-men,"[30] the enslaved Africans. Benezet refused to accept the hypocrisy of many of his peers like Benjamin Franklin and Patrick Henry who said they opposed slavery yet owned slaves.

When kidnapped blacks were transported through Philadelphia on their way south, Benezet intervened to obtain their freedom; his actions helped lead to the formation of the Society for the Relief of Free Negroes Unlawfully Held in Bondage on April 14, 1775. Throughout the

Revolutionary War he sought to extend to the blacks the rights that the American revolutionaries had won for themselves. He wrote in *Notes on the Slave Trade,* "It cannot be, that either war, or contract, can give any man such a property in another as he has in his sheep or oxen. Much less is it possible, that any child of man, should ever be born a Slave. Liberty is the right of every human creature, as soon as he breathes the vital air. And no human law can deprive him of that right, which he derives from the law of nature."[31]

As a pacifist, Benezet had not believed in the American revolutionaries' right to use violence in resisting George III's government; surprisingly, Benezet was able to publish antiwar pamphlets in Philadelphia repeatedly during the American Revolution. He was also concerned throughout his writings with the danger that slavery would provoke violent uprisings. In a letter to his friend Joseph Phipps, Benezet wrote,

> With respect to the Danger the Southern Colonies are exposed to from the vast disproportion there is between the number of Negroes, the whites, but it was too tender a point to expose to ye view of such of the blacks, as can read. In the treatise, the proportion in South Carolina is said to be fifteen Blacks to a white, but by their own account, the difference is rather twenty to one. In Georgia and South Carolina the Negroes are not hemmed in by the some hundreds of miles, as they are in the Islands, but have a back Country uninhibited for some hundreds of miles, where the Negroes might not only retire, but who expect to be supported & assisted by the Indians.[32]

He realized that in places such as South Carolina, where blacks outnumbered whites significantly, the potential for violent revolution existed. Benezet saw the potential of African and Native American unity in the face of white rule. He was much more tolerant of the propensity of the Africans, in the words of the old Negro spiritual, to "Steal Away." Running away seemed legitimate resistance. In numerous publications he denounced laws that encouraged the murder of runaways. In his letter to Phipps he had referred approvingly to the Maroons, escaped slaves who established their own runaway communities. In South Carolina this occurred near the Sea Islands of the Atlantic Coast, but maroonage was much more common in the mountainous areas of the West Indies, in

Latin America, and especially in Brazil. Benezet alluded to the necessity to make plans for the "freedom of those amongst us, after a reasonable period of time." He called for the "use all reasonable endeavors, to enable them to procure a comfortable living, not only as an act of justice to individuals, but as a debt due to them, on account of the oppression and injustice perpetuated on them or their ancestors."[33] He later called for some reparations to the freed blacks in the form of communally shared land. This land-sharing plan was amazingly similar to African forms of communalism, or primitive communism, which existed before the European conquest and which Benezet knew from his reading.

INFLUENCE ON BRITISH, FRENCH, AND AFRICAN-BORN ABOLITIONISTS

In preparing *An Essay on the Slavery and Commerce of the Human Species, Particularly the African* (1786), the British abolitionist Thomas Clarkson wrote of Benezet's *Some Historical Account of Guinea* that "in this precious book, I found almost all I wanted."[34] Benezet's descriptions of Africa proved to be so central that William Wilberforce quoted Benezet at length in the great 1792 Parliamentary debates on ending the slave trade. At that time a motion was forwarded in favor of abolishing that trade—the first such action taken in any parliamentary body in the world. Although it did not win passage, it is credited with having brought about the beginning of the end of the international slave trade. Benezet corresponded with the founders of the Société des Amis des Noirs (Society of the Friends of the Blacks) in Paris, who initially authorized the translation of his works on Africa. Among these men were Jean-Pierre Brissot; Nicolas Caritat, marquis de Condorcet, a politician and defender of human rights, especially for women and blacks; Étienne Clavière, a peer of Brissot's in the Girondist movement; Honoré Gabriel Victor Riqueti, comte de Mirabeau, who was imprisoned because of his revolutionary activities; Abbé Guillaume-Thomas Raynal, a Jesuit priest who left the order to devote his life to politics; and Bishop Henri Grégoire, the leading antislavery figure during the French revolution.

Charles Ignatius Sancho wrote in 1778 about "the Christian—the friendly and learned Author of that most valuable book [*Some Historical Account of Guinea*]," Anthony Benezet.[35] The Quaker's work also greatly influenced the famed African-born abolitionists Quobna Ottobah

Cugoano and Olaudah Equiano. Both of these men were kidnapped as children from Africa and relied on Benezet's writings to enhance their knowledge of their homelands. The formerly enslaved Cugoano, whose *Thoughts and Sentiments on the Evil and Wicked Traffic of Slavery and Commerce of the Human Species*, first published in London in 1787, referred his readers to "the worthy and judicious" Benezet as giving "some very striking estimates of the exceeding evil occasioned by that wicked diabolical traffic of the African slave-trade."[36]

Some Historical Account of Guinea was praised two years later by Olaudah Equiano, who relied upon Benezet when telling of his native Nigeria. Equiano's dramatic kidnapping scene in *The Interesting Narrative of the Life of Olaudah Equiano or Gustavus Vassa, the African* (1789) is remarkably similar to a description printed by Benezet eighteen years earlier. He advised his readers to "see Anthony Benezet's 'Account of Guinea' throughout" to bolster his own description of the Africa of his youth, before the "arrival of the Europeans."[37] In depicting his Igbo culture and homeland in what later became Nigeria, Equiano closely followed Benezet's geographical and physical accounts.

SUMMARY

Like other opponents of slavery in the 1780s, Benezet came to focus on the abolition of the slave trade as the practical first target in the abolition of slavery. In 1783, he wrote to Britain's Queen Charlotte, urging her to help end the British slave trade. His *Notes on the Slave Trade* proclaimed the "inconsistence of slavery with every right of mankind, with every feeling of humanity, and every precept of Christianity" and "its inconsistency with the welfare, peace and prosperity of every country, in proportion as it prevails." He described the sufferings the trade brought upon the blacks, and then confronted the whites directly. First he addressed the "Captains employed in this trade." He described the kindness of the African people whom the slavers separated from their loved ones, then he admonished the slavers directly: "[You] forced them into your ships, like an herd of swine.... You have stowed them together as close as ever they could lie, without any regard to decency.... Such slavery ... is not found among the Turks at Algiers, no, nor among the heathens in America."

Benezet begged the slave-trading captains to quit their horrid trade immediately. He then turned his attention to the slave merchant, telling him that "it is your money, that is the spring of all." He challenged the morality of the slave sellers and urged them to promise that "I will never buy a slave more while I live." Moving in on the conscience of the reformed merchant and his readers, Benezet asserted, "O let his resolution be yours! Have no more any part in this detestable business."

Benezet also appealed to the plantation owner who might claim "I pay honestly for my goods, and am not concerned to know how they are come by." The goods referred to were, of course, his chattel slaves, whom the plantation owner viewed merely as part of his property. Benezet accused the planter of not being as honest as a pickpocket, housebreaker, or highwayman. He indicted him for fraud, robbery, and murder, and told him that it was his "money that pays the merchant, and thro' him the captain and African butchers," before concluding that he was "the spring that puts all the rest in motion." Thus, no one who had any part in slavery—from the "men-stealers" to the ship captain to the merchant to the plantation owner to the men or women who proclaimed innocence because they inherited the homeless slave—was truly innocent.[38]

Benezet repeatedly confronted those who claimed "that, if the English were to drop this Trade entirely, it would be immediately thereupon carried on by other Nations, to a much greater Degree than it is now." He also challenged those who asserted that an end to slavery "would lessen, if not utterly ruin, some other considerable Branches of our Commerce, especially the Sugar and the Tobacco Trades, because of the Difficulty in getting Hands enough, in the Room of the Blacks, to work and labour in those Plantations."[39] Characteristically, he answered in moral terms, reinforced with facts about the ability of white labor to perform adequately in tropical weather. Blacks were no more suited to work at hard labor in the sun than were whites. He ended by alerting whites to the "impending catastrophe" of slave revolt if the trade continued.

In early 1787, a few years after Benezet's death, a number of free blacks, including Richard Allen and Absalom Jones, met in Philadelphia to discuss forming a religious society. Feeling that their numbers were too small and their religious sensibilities too many, they instead, in April 1787, formed the Free African Society at the home of Richard Allen. Its articles of incorporation were written under the aura of Benezet and indeed specified that "it is always understood, that one of the people called Quakers . . . is to be chosen to act as Clerk and Treasurer of this useful institution."[40] Beginning in early 1789, the society held its meetings at the Quaker building known as Benezet's African School House. The society began circulating petitions modeled in part on Benezet's earlier ones, and James Forten's opposition to colonization schemes recalled that of Benezet, who was an early advocate of giving land to free blacks.

The educator wrote to his friend Benjamin Franklin on March 5, 1783, about his life teaching blacks, "I know no station in life I should prefer before it."[41] Friend Anthony Benezet died on May 3, 1784. His *Last Will and Testament* began, "Be it remembered that I, Anthony Benezet, a teacher of the Free School for the Black People of Philadelphia." In death, as in life, Benezet served as a symbol to those who fought against slavery. He usually led by quiet example and devout work. He had lived modestly and plainly, preferring to use his meager salary as a teacher to defray the cost of his writings and to run the Quaker schools. The *Pennsylvania Gazette* as well as *Watson's Annual Journal* wrote of Benezet's death on May 13, 1784, and noted that hundreds of blacks followed his coffin in the streets. The *Gazette*'s obituary provided more details of his bequests to educate blacks: "in his last will and testimony [he] bequeathed the annual; income of his whole estate, forever (after the decease of his wife), for the instruction and education of Negroe and Mulattoe children." Although Benezet said upon his deathbed, "I am dying, and feel ashamed to meet the face of my maker, I have done so little in his cause,"[42] the blacks who followed and wept at his funeral procession felt otherwise. He need not have uttered his deathbed fear that he had not done enough. The enslaved African men, women, and children whom he fought to free viewed him as a saint among sinners, a healer amidst the wounded, and a godsend amongst infidels. That is why the largest gathering of blacks in Philadelphia, up until that time, and a comparable number of whites, followed his casket along the city streets to the burial grounds of the Society of Friends. Benezet's first biographer wrote, "At the interment of his remains, . . . the greatest concourse of people that had ever been witnessed on such an occasion in Philadelphia, was present, being a collection of all ranks and professions among the inhabitants, thus manifesting the universal esteem in which he was held. Among others who paid that last tribute of respect, were many hundred black people, testifying by their attendance, and by their tears, the grateful sense they entertained of his pious efforts in their behalf."[43]

What set Benezet apart was his great imagination in using every available resource to develop new methods in the arena of antislavery politics. At the very root of his thinking was the belief that black men, women, and children were human beings equal to all others. Summing up the general feeling about the passing of Benezet, Jacques-Pierre Brissot, the famed French writer and revolutionary, wrote for humanists everywhere:

> Where is the man in all Europe, of whatever rank or birth, who is equal to Benezet? Who is not obliged to respect him? How long will authors suffer themselves to be shackled by the prejudices of society? Will they never perceive that nature has created all men equal, that wisdom and virtue are the only real criterion of superiority? Now who was more virtuous than Benezet? who more useful to society, to mankind? What author, what great man, will ever be followed to his grave by four hundred Negroes, snatched by his own assiduity, his own generosity, from ignorance, wretchedness, and slavery? Who then has a right to speak haughtily of this benefactor of men?[44]

Long after Benezet's death, antislavery advocates continued to invoke his name, and antislavery newspapers and periodicals of the early nineteenth century, time and again, resurrected his legacy. Black leaders continued to pay homage to the gentle Quaker decades after his death. In April 1836, a half century after Benezet died, James Forten Jr., the eldest son of the famed black abolitionist and student at the Benezet School, spoke before the Philadelphia Female Anti-Slavery Society: "You are called fanatics. Well, what if you are? ... There is an eloquence in such fanaticism, for it whispers hope to the slave; there is sanctity in it, for it contains the consecrated spirit of religion; it is the fanaticism of a Benezet, a Rush, a Franklin, a Jay."[45] That the descendant of a slave invoked the name of Benezet first among those in the antislavery crusade shows the depth of black admiration for the man who dedicated his life to their cause and internationalized the struggle for their freedom.

Notes

1. François, marquis de Barbé-Marbois, *Our Revolutionary Forefathers: The Letters of François, marquis de Barbé-Marbois During His Residency in the United States as Secretary of the French Legation,* trans. and ed. Eugene Parker Chase (1969; repr., Freeport, N.Y.: Books for Libraries Press, 1990), 139.

2. George S. Brookes, *Friend Anthony Benezet* (Philadelphia: University of Pennsylvania Press, 1937), 19.

3. Hillel Schwartz, *The French Prophets: The History of a Millenarian Group in Eighteenth-Century England* (Berkeley: University of California Press, 1980), 203.

4. *Pennsylvania Gazette,* September 12, 1751.

5. "Anthony Benezet," in *Quaker Biographies: A Series of Sketches,* vol. 3 (Philadelphia: For sale at Friends' Book Store, 1912), 88.

6. Samuel Small Jr., *Genealogical Records of George Small, Philip Albright, Johann Daniel Dünckel, William Geddes Latimer, Thomas Bartow, John Reid, Daniel Benezet, Jean Crommelin, Joel Richardson* (Philadelphia: J. B. Lippincott, 1905), 197.

7. Namely, Benezet's *Observations on the Inslaving, Importing and Purchasing of Negroes* (Germantown, Pa.: Christopher Sower, 1758) and *A Short Account of That Part of Africa, Inhabited by the Negroes* (Philadelphia, 1762). Early copies of Benezet's works were donated to the Library Company of Philadelphia. Franklin wrote, "I find in Capt. Seagrave's Account of his Voyage to Guinea" that "a Dutch Ship came into the Road and some of the blacks going on Board her were treacherously seized and carried off as Slaves." Benjamin Franklin, *A Narrative of the Late Massacres, in Lancaster County* (Philadelphia, 1764), 306. It seems that Franklin simply misspelled the captain's name and was referring to Captain William Snelgrave, who in 1734 published *A New Account of Some Parts of Guinea, and the Slave Trade.* Benezet had made use of Snelgrave's *New Account* many times, and Franklin seems to have discovered him by way of Benezet.

8. Brookes, *Friend Anthony Benezet,* 27, 28–29. The name of the paper was *Der hochdeutsch pennsylvanische Geschicht-Schreiber, oder, Sammlung wichtiger Nachrichten aus dem Natur- und Kirchen-Reich* (The High German Pennsylvania Recorder of Events, or Collection of Important news from the Realm of Nature and the Church). Ibid., 27n21.

9. Evarts B. Greene and Virginia D. Harrington, *American Population Before the Federal Census of 1790* (New York: Columbia University Press, 1932), 114–15; Ira Brown, "Pennsylvania's Antislavery Pioneers, 1688–1776," *Pennsylvania History* 55, no. 2 (1988): 59–60.

10. Merle Gerald Brouwer, "The Negro as Slave and as a Free Black in Colonial Pennsylvania" (Ph.D. diss., Wayne State University, 1972), 17.

11. *Pennsylvania Journal,* May 27, 1762; *Pennsylvania Gazette,* May 6, 1762.

12. *Friends' Miscellany* 3, no. 3 (1832).

13. Anthony Benezet, *A Short Account of the People Called Quakers: Their Rise, Religious Principles and Settlement in America* (Philadelphia: Enoch Story, 1783), 34–35.

14. Anthony Benezet, *Short Observations on Slavery* (Philadelphia, 1781), 11–12.

15. Anthony Benezet, *A Caution and a Warning to Great Britain and Her Colonies* (Philadelphia: Henry Miller, 1766), 16.

16. Anthony Benezet to Samuel Fothergill, November 27, 1758, Haverford College Quaker Collection.

17. Anthony Benezet, *A Short Account of That Part of Africa, Inhabited by the Negroes* (Philadelphia, 1762), 64.

18. Maurice Jackson, *Let This Voice Be Heard: Anthony Benezet, Father of Atlantic Abolitionism* (Philadelphia: University of Pennsylvania Press, 2009), 56.

19. Charles de Secondat, Baron de Montesquieu, *The Spirit of the Laws,* trans. and ed. Anne M. Cohler, Basia C. Miller, and Harold S. Stone (Cambridge: Cambridge University Press, 1989), bk 15, chap. 1, 246; 1st ed., Paris, 1748.

20. Francis Hutcheson, *A System of Moral Philosophy* (Edinburgh, 1755), bk II, chap. 5, sec. ii, 301.

21. Ibid., bk. 1, chap. 1, sec. i.

22. George Wallace, *A System of the Principles of the Laws of Scotland* (Edinburgh, 1760), 95–96. Benezet first used this quote in *A Short Account of That Part of Africa.*

23. Wallace, *System*, 90.
24. Benezet, *Short Account of That Part of Africa*, 52.
25. Anthony Benezet, *Some Historical Account of Guinea* (Philadelphia: 1771), ii, 1, 4.
26. Anthony Benezet, *A Caution and Warning to Great Britain and Her Colonies, in a Short Representation of the Calamitous State of the Enslaved Negroes in the British Dominions* (Philadelphia: Henry Miller, 1766), 30.
27. Anon., *An Account of the European Settlements in America*, vol. 2 (London, 1757), 120.
28. Benezet, *Short Account of That Part of Africa*, 57.
29. Patrick Henry to Robert Pleasants, January 18, 1773, Haverford College Quaker Collection.
30. Benezet, *Caution and Warning*, 3.
31. Benezet, *Notes on the Slave Trade*, 8. Benezet did not accept the Aristotelian notion that some men were born to be slaves or Hobbes's view that the powerful had the right to enslave the weak.
32. Anthony Benezet to Joseph Phipps, May 28, 1763, Haverford College Quaker Collection.
33. Benezet, *Short Account of That Part of Africa*, 27–28.
34. Thomas Clarkson, *The History of the Rise, Progress, and Accomplishments of the Abolition of the African Slave-Trade by the British Parliament*, 2 vols. (London, 1808), 1:208–9.
35. Ignatius Sancho, "Letter LVII to Mr. F[isher] Charles Street, January 27, 1788," in *Letters of the Late Ignatius Sancho, an African*, ed. Vincent Carretta (New York: Penguin Books, 1989), 111–12.
36. Quobna Ottobah Cugoano, *Thoughts and Sentiments on the Evil and Wicked Traffic of Slavery and Commerce of the Human Species*, ed. Vincent Carretta (New York: Penguin Classics, 1999), 75.
37. Olaudah Equiano, *The Interesting Narrative of the Life of Olaudah Equiano, Written by Himself*, ed. Robert J. Allison (New York: Bedford, 1995), 39n1.
38. Benezet, *Notes on the Slave Trade*, 1, 3, 6–7, 7.
39. Benezet, *Short Account of That Part of Africa*, 59–60.
40. William Douglass, *Annals of the First African Church in the United States of America, Now Styled the African Episcopal Church of St. Thomas* (Philadelphia, 1862), 17.
41. Anthony Benezet to Benjamin Franklin, March 5, 1783, Haverford College Quaker Collection.
42. Roberts Vaux, *Memoirs of the Life of Anthony Benezet* (Philadelphia, 1817), 132.
43. Ibid., 134.
44. Jacques-Pierre Brissot, *A Critical Examination of the Marquis de Cha[s]tellux's Travels, in North America, in a Letter Addressed to the Marquis* (Philadelphia, 1788), 85. The original letter, dated July 1, 1786, is held at Trinity College, Atkinson Library, Hartford, Conn.
45. Philip S. Foner and George E. Walker, eds., *Proceedings of the Black State Conventions, 1840–1865*, vol. 1, *New York, Pennsylvania, Indiana, Michigan, Ohio* (Philadelphia: Temple University Press, 1979), 125.

PART 4

The Languages of Wood and Stone

CHAPTER 9

Communicating Through Wood and Stone
Building a New World Identity in Pennsylvania

CYNTHIA G. FALK

In 1777, when the British invaded Germantown, only a few miles from their strategic and symbolic target of Philadelphia, British general William Howe made his headquarters in a two-story house built just a few years earlier as a country residence for David Deshler, an immigrant from Heidelberg, and his wife, Mary Deshler, the daughter of French Huguenot parents who had fled to the Rhine River Valley and then the New World.[1] Five years later, when yellow fever drove American president George Washington from the new United States capital in Philadelphia, he too made his temporary home in David Deshler's former residence. The physical form of the Deshler house made it desirable to Deshler, Howe, and Washington alike. It was "situate[d] on the west side of the main street ... commanding an agreeable prospect of the adjacent country." The façade was symmetrical, the stone walls finished with stucco scored to resemble masonry blocks, and the cornice adorned with classical detailing (fig. 9.1). A central front door provided visitors with access to a passage leading to more formal rooms at the front of the house, "all finished in the most elegant manner." A kitchen, located within "suitable back buildings," offered space for cooking and other work well away from the refined core of the building.[2]

FIGURE 9.1 David Deshler house, Germantown, Pa., 1772–74. A smaller attached building behind the main core of the house predates the formal front structure and likely served as David and Mary Deshler's house before 1772. After the main portion was built, it became the kitchen.

FIGURE 9.2 John Wister house, now known as Grumblethorpe, Germantown, Pa., 1744.

The history of the Deshler house's early occupants—German-speaking immigrant, British general, American president—suggests that a well-understood and commonly shared understanding of the characteristics of a well-appointed house emerged in the years leading up to the American Revolution. However, the form of the Deshler house was the result of decades of experimentation in Pennsylvania and elsewhere. A generation earlier, the country house of David's uncle John Wister, built in 1744, would have stood out in Germantown because of its large size, durable stone construction, and well-crafted finish (fig. 9.2). Yet, with its two first-floor doors, one leading directly into a principal room, as well as a second-floor door and balcony, it lacked the restricted access and classical symmetry of the later Deshler residence. By 1806, it had become so outdated in appearance that a new generation of the Wister family gave it a facelift, closing off one of the two front doors, removing the second-story door and balcony, and stuccoing the stone façade to create a more uniform appearance.[3]

The decisions made by the Wister and Deshler families in regard to their houses illustrate the importance of nonverbal communication in early America. Particularly in areas where multiple languages were spoken and scripted, the babel of verbal and written communication might be overcome through messages coded in a medium other than words. Visual and tactile statements had the potential to supplement other types of communication, potentially even overcoming confusion among people who did not speak the same tongue. Furthermore, aesthetic missives could engage people who were either unable to read or whose reading ability was restricted to a language other than that of a given text.[4]

Material culture communicates differently than language, particularly standard prose. Henry Glassie likens artifacts to poetry or music in their ambiguity, allusiveness, repetition, and transformations, and he notes that those who study physical things have "the strange responsibility of putting into words that which is not verbal." In his seminal study of clothing, Grant McCracken argues that material culture is "extremely limited in its expressive range" and "is a relatively impoverished means of communication," yet he concludes it "has certain virtues not shared by language" that make it worthy of study.[5] Despite the challenges of interpretation, the potential of material culture as an expressive medium is real. Kasey Grier and Jules Prown, who both use the literary concept of metaphor as a way to understand material culture, demonstrate that material manifestations could develop broadly understood meanings within their cultural context(s) and that their messages can still be uncovered today.[6] In the case of the Deshler house, the physical building served as a symbol for the abstract qualities of authority and affluence. This metaphor was strong enough to persuade its original owners, a British general, and an American president all of the building's worth.

Material expressions are especially valuable because they can transcend those messages conveyed through written and spoken word. They can impart information not readily conveyed in other ways because it is either taken for granted or is unlikely to be spoken publicly or recorded.[7] For the Wisters, renovations of the family's house in the early nineteenth century demonstrated a feeling that the previous generation was out of touch and unfashionable, something unlikely to be uttered in a medium accessible two centuries later.

Material messages, by their very nature, have the potential to be long lasting.[8] The Germantown houses of the Wister and Deshler families continue to communicate today much about their owners and users and the time periods in which they were built. These two buildings articulate that a fundamental change—one that embodied, among other things, the very conception of what a house should look like and the behaviors it should support—occurred between the mid-eighteenth century and the start of the American Revolution.[9] They also reveal the changing nature of ethnic distinctiveness in the same time period. As the use of the Deshler house by both Howe and Washington indicates, elite Europeans and European Americans in the last quarter of the eighteenth century shared a common desire to live in a large masonry house where entrance was mitigated by an interior passage and work, especially kitchen work done by nonfamily members, including, in some cases, enslaved people, was separated from other household activities.[10]

In the early 1750s, however, when David Deshler and his wife, Mary, purchased the property on which the house would be built, he could not have anticipated the increasingly standardized form his house would take just two decades later. Through the mid-eighteenth century, houses like his were only slowly becoming common. The designs of such buildings represented original rather than regularized responses to new needs and desires. For Pennsylvanians of German descent who participated in this transitional episode, erecting such a house was one way to forge a new identity, one shaped by their ethnic background and heritage but also fundamentally forward thinking in its execution. The houses that resulted undertook expressive tasks that went beyond those usually articulated through more traditional forms of language.[11] To understand their messages requires attention to how meaning is registered nonverbally through visual, tactile, and other sensory means.[12]

It is perhaps easiest to understand the communicative power of architecture by focusing on a building type intentionally designed to be symbolic. Religious buildings not only serve the practical function of sheltering a gathered body but also provide space for sacred rituals and, through their iconography, or lack thereof, express beliefs about spirituality, the divine, and the afterlife. Augustus Lutheran Church in Providence, Pennsylvania, where Henry Melchior Muhlenberg preached, was constructed beginning in 1743, shortly after the European clergyman's arrival (fig. 9.3). The designers of the stone building included an apse-like polygonal end, gambrel roof, side entrance, stacked windows, and a stone inscribed in Latin dedicating the building and recognizing adherence to the Augsburg Confession.[13]

FIGURE 9.3 Augustus Lutheran Church, Trappe, Upper Providence Township, Montgomery County, Pa., 1743.

These features become more noteworthy when comparing Augustus Lutheran with other religious buildings found in Pennsylvania at the same time. In the 1740s, many congregations met in the houses of parishioners, or sometimes even barns, not yet able to expend resources to construct purpose-built meeting places.[14] When they did build, religious groups in Pennsylvania constructed meetinghouses, which tended to be house-like in scale, especially in rural areas. While sometimes constructed of stone, many were of more humble materials, often log.[15]

Augustus Lutheran stood out, especially among religious building outside of the city of Philadelphia, because it physically looked different. It was nonresidential in character, the polygonal end suggested the form of European church buildings, as did the gambrel roof.[16] The stone walls indicated permanence, and the second-story windows denoted a balcony. Those who designed Augustus Lutheran avoided features such as arched windows, a two-story entry, or brick construction, all of which were found at St. Michael's Lutheran in Philadelphia, which was begun at roughly the same time (see fig. 10.7). Yet they did create a building that looked like and functioned as a church.

Inside, the floor plan and finishes shaped the way people behaved by directing their vision toward the pulpit and altar area (fig. 9.4). The interior of Augustus Lutheran contrasted notably with the interior of meetinghouses, which tended to have seating oriented toward a long wall. In Quaker meetinghouses in Pennsylvania, a removable partition separated areas used by men and women during business sessions.[17] The physicality of the space both signified religious practices and encouraged practitioners to conform to them. On the most basic level, its features communicated how the building was used, but when further dissected, they also conveyed an understanding of God and the appropriate ways to show reverence and devotion.

A 1759 map of the Province of Pennsylvania demonstrates through visual representations and textual descriptors that buildings like Augustus Lutheran served functions that were not exclusively religious. On the map, the church becomes a landmark (fig. 9.5). Its labeling is especially telling and demonstrates the importance of using both material and textual sources to gain the fullest sense of meaning. In Providence, the structure used by the Reformed was identified as a "Dutch Meet"; farther southeast stood a "Quak^r Mt^g." The Lutherans, on the other hand, had a

COMMUNICATING THROUGH WOOD AND STONE 255

FIGURE 9.4 Interior, August Lutheran Church, Trappe, Upper Providence Township, Montgomery County, Pa., 1743.

FIGURE 9.5 Detail from "To the Honourable Thomas Penn and Richard Penn, Esqrs., true & absolute proprietaries & Governours of the Province of Pennsylvania & counties of New-Castle, Kent & Sussex on Delaware this map of the improved part of the Province of Pennsylvania. / Is humbly dedicated by Nicholas Scull. Engraved by Ja. Turner. Printed by John Davis" (Philadelphia: Nicholas Scull, 1759). Augustus Lutheran Church is located just under the large letter L in Philadelphia County, the county of which Trappe, or Providence, was part before the creation of Montgomery County; below the Lutheran Church is the Dutch (Reformed) Meet[ing] and still further below a Quaker Mt^g.

church. This nomenclature undoubtedly recognized common parlance, but it also confirmed the physicality of the buildings.[18] In 1759, Augustus Lutheran was a monumental structure with distinct church-like features that would have been recognizable to those traveling on the road from Reading to Philadelphia.

In studying religious buildings like Augustus Lutheran, relationships between architectural form, liturgy, and ritual are an obvious focus. Yet the 1759 map, a form of material culture in and of itself, confirms that religious structures served secular functions as well, and in this they were not unlike other types of buildings, including houses. Throughout the eighteenth century the majority of buildings in Pennsylvania were not grand masonry structures, such as the Wister and Deshler houses or Augustus Lutheran, which all survive today. Most houses were built of log, they were one story, and they were small—often only one room. Over half of the houses in Germantown at the close of the eighteenth century were less than five hundred square feet in footprint; by comparison, the main block of the Deshler house measured forty-five by forty feet, or 1800 square feet.[19] When visiting Philadelphia in 1744, Maryland doctor Alexander Hamilton wrote, "the majority of the houses [were] mean and low."[20]

The Germantown house of the Wisters, built in the same year as Hamilton's visit, must then have been noteworthy. With more than forty feet of street frontage and a full two stories high, the building was hardly low or mean. As a 1748 Germantown real estate advertisement in the *Pennsylvania Gazette* noted, a two-story stone house was special, "conveniently situated for a gentleman, storekeeper, or tradesmen."[21] At the Wister house the level of refinement went one step further. While the side and back walls were made of randomly shaped pieces of Wissahickon schist, those that formed the façade had been carefully fashioned into rectangular blocks that fit together well and created an orderly appearance. This further differentiated the Wister house from other area stone residences, including the neighboring one, also owned by Wister, which had less refined, uncoursed façades.

If a stone house was good, a brick house was even better. Daniel Hiester's Montgomery County brick house was advertised in the *Pennsylvania Gazette* later in the century as "one of the best houses in that part of the country."[22] The meaning of materials was so well understood that in

Schaefferstown a wood-frame house was actually fitted with painted plaster to look as if it was brick. This example, through its faux finish, ironically confirms that recognizing what a building was made from helped the people who saw it understand where it, and by extension its owners, fell within an established hierarchy. As a communicative medium, the Schaefferstown house conveyed knowledge of design, grounded in a desire for durability and orderliness, in this case coupled with a contrived artificiality.

There was more to a house than just whether it was wood, stone, or brick, however. While less visible from the exterior, a building's floor plan controlled how interior spaces were experienced.[23] Among German immigrants and their descendants, multiple-room houses followed a distinct three-room floor plan, especially before the mid-eighteenth century (fig. 9.6).[24] Entry was directly into the kitchen, which was dominated by a large cooking fireplace. To the rear of the fireplace were two more rooms, one of which likely served for sleeping and the other for eating and daily living. The careful observer might pick up on the arrangement from the exterior due to the asymmetrical façade, with the door to one side, and the off-center chimney (fig. 9.7).[25]

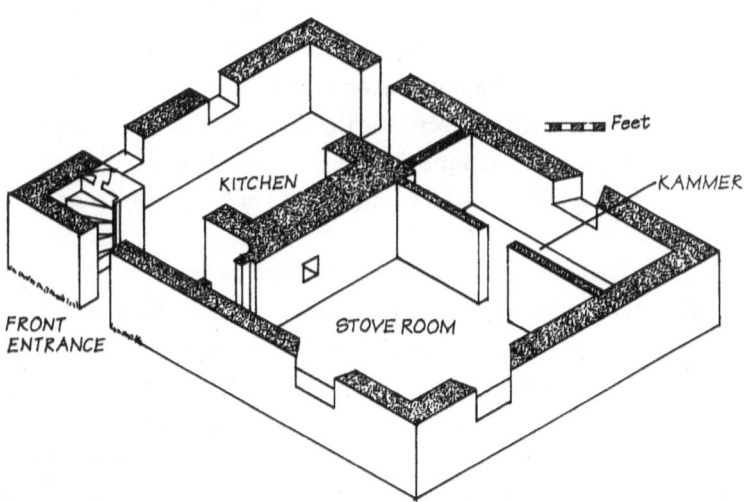

FIGURE 9.6 Isometric projection of first-floor plan, Hans Mirtel Gerick house, Exeter Township, Berks County, Pa., 1741.

FIGURE 9.7 Heinrich and Anna Maria Zeller house (Fort Zeller), Newmanstown, Millcreek Township, Lebanon County, Pa., ca. 1745. The interior plan of the house was made manifest by the slightly off-center placement of the chimney along the roof ridge.

This three-room plan in Pennsylvania did not duplicate a traditional form in Continental Europe.[26] Rather, it built upon a smaller two-room plan that Benjamin Franklin graphically depicted in his book *Observations on Smoky Chimneys* and that he associated with "the lower people among the northern nations of Europe, and . . . the poorer sort of Germans in Pennsylvania." In describing the two-room plan, Franklin noted its key feature: a stove "compos'd of Five Iron Plates scru'd together," which he found used in the Germanic areas of both Europe and Pennsylvania.[27]

The box-like stove's cast-iron plates formed its top, bottom, and three sides (fig. 9.8). On its fourth side, the stove abutted the rear wall of an adjacent fireplace. As Franklin described it, it was like "a kind of Oven revers'd, its Mouth being without, and Body within the Room that is to be warmed by it."[28] In addition to cast-iron examples, contemporary observers also reported "earthen" and "pottery-ware" stoves of this type.[29] By the 1760s, a related type of stove, formed of six iron plates, began to replace the five-plate stove, which had to be installed abutting a fireplace.

FIGURE 9.8 Jamb, or five-plate, iron stove, Isaac Zane, Marlboro Furnace, Frederick, Virginia, ca. 1768; stove support, Philip Erpf, Schaefferstown, Pa., 1765.

The newer stove type was freestanding, and a stovepipe provided venting to a chimney or the exterior.[30]

The feature that united three-room entry-kitchen houses in Pennsylvania with smaller two-room variations was the stove-heated room, or *Stube*. While many of the messages communicated by houses were visual in nature, the use of a stove for heat was also tactile. Comparing stoves with fireplaces, more often used for heating in British American houses, Henry Melchior Muhlenburg wrote, "open fireplaces ... freeze a person on one side and broil him on the other. Like the sun, which warms only one side of our dark planet, these fireplaces heat only one side of our bodies unless we turn continuously on our own axis like a roast on a spit."[31]

In the eighteenth century, houses with entry-kitchen and stove-heated rooms varied from one-story log buildings to larger multiple-story stone residences. However, by the second half of the century, some individuals experimented with different designs for their dwellings. One option was to partition the kitchen to create a distinct entry, thus dividing the work space from the main entrance.[32] The message was about separation, both of work and of people. The kitchen, where sights, sounds, and smells focused on labor and production, now was further divided from spaces used for activities such as dining. One could enter a house with a separate entry and kitchen and be escorted to a more formal stove-heated room, where food was served and consumed, without having to experience the space where meals were produced or, in cases where servants or slaves did the preparations, the people who made them possible.

While the creation of an entry was one way to segregate spaces for work and other more refined activities was only one option, and not the one that would have the most lasting impact in the New World. In the mid-eighteenth century, from the 1740s through at least the Revolutionary War, Pennsylvanians of German descent began to experiment with a whole new type of house, one that had a through passage.[33] The Moravians in Pennsylvania used this arrangement with some regularity as they built communal buildings in Bethlehem, Nazareth, and Lititz. The first Single Brothers' house in Bethlehem, built in 1744, had a central passage with two fireplaces, which existed to provide access to stoves in the main first-floor rooms (figs. 9.9 and 9.10).[34] In this setting, cooking facilities could be located in other places, so the new floor plan was largely about regulating access, and perhaps maintaining heat.

In single-family residences, adding a central passage often went hand-in-hand with creating work spaces toward the rear of the house. At Oley forge, the Johannes Lesher house maintained the integral back-to-back relationship between the stove room and kitchen, but the kitchen was located in a rear corner rather than at the front door. Instead of a cooking fireplace, what one saw upon entering the house was a prominent staircase, suggesting the presence of a suite of rooms on the full second story and the ability of the owner to make a grand entrance from them (figs. 9.11 and 9.12).[35] The Isaac and Catherine Meier house may have been very similar to the Lesher house when originally built, but an addition on one end of the building eventually allowed the kitchen to be removed from the main core entirely (fig. 9.13).

COMMUNICATING THROUGH WOOD AND STONE 261

FIGURE 9.9 First Single Brothers' house, later converted to Single Sisters' house, Bethlehem, Northampton County, Pa., 1744.

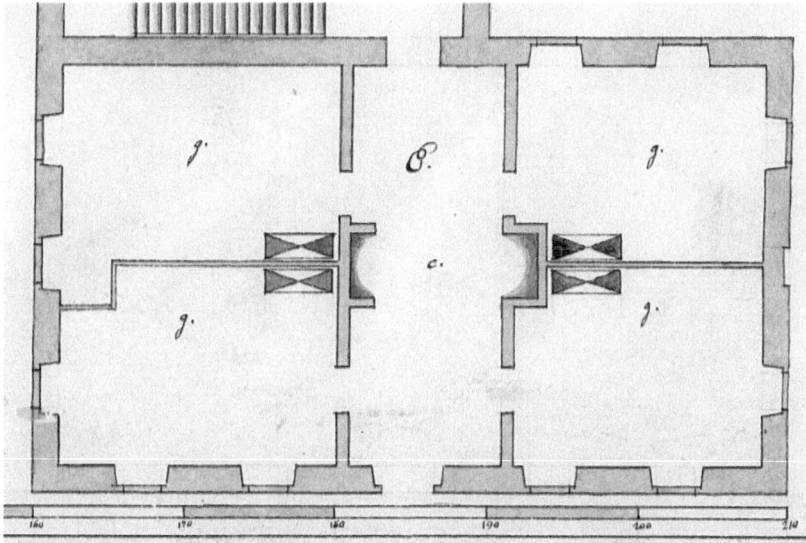

FIGURE 9.10 First-floor plan, first Single Brothers' house. The location of stoves, fed from fireplaces within the center passage, is shown by rectangular boxes marked with an X pattern.

FIGURE 9.11 Johannes Lesher house (Oley Forge mansion), Oley Township, Berks County, Pa., ca. 1750–55.

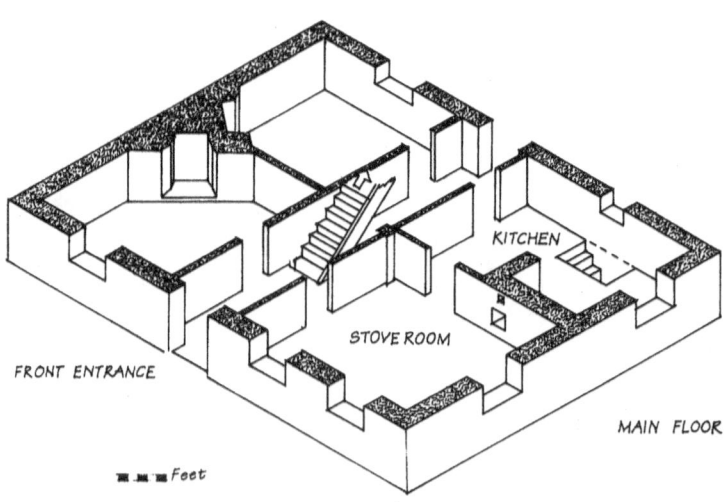

FIGURE 9.12 Isometric projection of first-floor plan, Johannes Lesher house, Oley Township, Berks County, Pa.

FIGURE 9.13 Isaac and Catherine Meier house, Myerstown, Lebanon County, Pa., ca. 1757.

In the mid-eighteenth century, Pennsylvanians, especially Pennsylvanians of German descent, were just beginning to experiment with these new plans. The liminal nature of their new houses was expressed on their exteriors. Eventually the five-bay arrangement utilized at the Deshler house would become typical, but in the 1740s and '50s there was not yet standardization. The Lesher house maintained some of the asymmetry of the entry-kitchen house, with two windows to one side of the front door—in the room heated by the closed stove—and only one on the other side, where a fireplace would have provided more light. The Meier house had three bays across its more symmetrical façade, while the earlier Single Brothers' house in Bethlehem had five. These buildings represented a new form, and those who built them were still working out what components were important and how they could be best combined.

By building a house with a central passage and an orderly façade, some Germans in Pennsylvania bought into new trends that existed throughout Europe and the European colonies. When William Penn's colonial secretary, James Logan, had his country house built in Germantown in the 1720s, he opted for a two-story brick abode with six rooms on the first floor of the main structure—one of which served as a formal

FIGURE 9.14 James Logan house, Stenton, Germantown, Pa., 1723–30.

entry and another as the stair hall—and a detached kitchen building. The façade of the house featured a central front door flanked on either side by three first-floor windows carefully sized to create a sense of balance with the six windows located across the second-floor level (fig. 9.14).[36] To the west, in Chester County, Joseph and Mary Pennock, both of whom had personal or family connections within the colonial government, also chose brick for their 1738 house, which included a broad through passage and separate kitchen ell but, like the Lesher house, only had four bays across its front (fig. 9.15).[37]

The new style of building, whether built for people of British extraction like James Logan and Joseph Pennock or for those whose families hailed from Continental Europe, emphasized order and control. The dwellings shared a common design that separated work and formal spaces. But individuals like the Meiers and Leshers incorporated features like closed heating stoves as a way to make the model work for them. Through its decorative features, the Peter and Rosina Margaretha Wentz house provides another way of understanding the variations. The house has a central passage with a stairway tucked away behind a door rather

FIGURE 9.15 Joseph and Mary Pennock house, now known as Primitive Hall, West Marlboro Township, Chester County, Pa., 1738.

than being prominently located within the central passage (fig. 9.16). It incorporates references to classical architectural elements such as pilasters, cornices, and a decorative entablature as well as corner cupboards with glass doors for showing off consumer goods. Yet paint analysis shows that it was decorated with patterned dados that may have been inspired by wallpaper, but created a somewhat different aesthetic.[38]

The use of paint is especially distinctive in the kitchen of the Wentz house, where black polka dots adorned the walls floor to ceiling. The use of painted dots and other shapes may reflect a traditional European practice, like the use of the closed stove. A Bavarian doctor who toured Pennsylvania associated the decoration specifically with German settlers. He noted that inside Pennsylvania German houses "everything [was] daubed with red."[39] Other surviving examples suggest the kitchen was a common place to continue this practice, perhaps because of the impracticality of wallpaper in this space.[40] The visual message could then only be retrieved by those with interior access to a typically private area. At the Wentz house, however, everyone who entered the front door could see the

FIGURE 9.16 Center passage as viewed from the front door, Peter and Rosina Margaretha Wentz house, Worcester Township, Montgomery County, Pa., 1758.

distinctive decoration, which—even though it was executed in paint—communicated a familiarity with a trend toward patterned walls among those who could afford imported wallpaper. It also communicated another aesthetic motivation, one grounded in Continental European identity. When families like the Wentzes explored new house models at midcentury, they did so in ways that conveyed otherwise unstated messages about the multiple influences that informed their domestic environments.

In 1759, Benedict and Anna Eschleman erected their new house in Lancaster County. It had a center passage, rear kitchen, stove-heated front room, and five-bay façade—although the bays were not quite evenly spaced because the stove-heated room was larger than any other on the main floors of the house. The Eschleman house included corner cupboards with solid doors for storing goods. The kitchen may have been lavishly decorated with spots, although today only a few are still visible around the fireplace.

The Eschleman house, like Augustus Lutheran Church, was also physically labeled by its occupants. Materials, floor plan, stove heat, and painted dots all provided forms of nonverbal communication. However, not all houses built by Pennsylvania Germans were without textual references. In the Eschlemans' case, a carved stone prominently indicated in German that Benedict Eschleman and his wife, Anna, built their house in 1759 (fig. 9.17). Another stone conveyed a variation of Psalm 127:1, "WO GOTT _____ UM HAUSZ _____ CHT GIBT SEIN _____ ST SO ARBEIT _____ DERMAN UMSONST 1759."

The Eschlemans were not alone in the practice of embellishing their residence with words in the German language. Often stones displaying names, dates, and phrases were decorative in nature. They required skill to produce and provided an aesthetic detail. Using two was a way to continue an emphasis on symmetry. While scriptural passages were not especially common, the labeling of a house with the names of both husband and wife was not unusual. The inclusion of both names should not be read as an assertion of gender equality in the eighteenth century, but it does communicate the fundamental roles of both men and women in creating and maintaining a sizable house of this type.[41] Further, the use of the German language on the stones provided an external message about the linguistic preferences of those inside.

But what of eighteenth-century houses that were not designed with date stones inscribed with textual messages? As mute objects devoid of text, what did these houses communicate in the eighteenth century? Specifically, what did large masonry houses with passages, segregated work spaces, stove-heated rooms, and distinctive decorative embellishments mean to the people who occupied them? What did they impart to those

FIGURE 9.17 Date stone, Benedict and Anna Eshleman house, Conestoga Township, Lancaster County, Pa. The Eshlemans prominently labeled their house "BENEDICT / ESCHLEMAN UND / SEINE HAUSFRAU / ANNA HABEN DE / SES HAUS GEBAU / ANNO 1759" (Benedict Eshleman and his wife Anna have built this house 1759). The companion date stone included a variation of Psalm 127:1a, "Except the Lord build the house, they labor in vain that build it."

who observed them when they were new? And what is left for them to reveal today?

On the most basic level, houses, like other buildings, conveyed messages about wealth. Larger buildings typically cost more, and the use of stone or brick required the skills of a mason as well as a carpenter for construction. Masonry also made a building more durable and suggested a degree of permanence that wood did not.

In the years leading up to the American Revolution, however, houses like the one built by David Deshler in Germantown communicated not only that their owners had money to build but also a style of life that required different types of spaces. Unlike entry-kitchen houses, where access was directly into a work space, these new houses had passages that mediated entry by forming an intermediate space separating the interior from the exterior world. At the same time, kitchens, as work spaces, were removed from the front of the house, and more formal spaces were added for entertaining.

While commonly understood by the 1770s, the form epitomized by the Deshler house did not spring up all in one piece. As house owners and builders experimented with new forms at midcentury, there was not a single solution, and surviving buildings represent various attempts to work out new ideas to suit local and individual needs. While the desire for new floor plans was shared by people of various ethnic backgrounds in Pennsylvania, people of German descent made their own modifications to suit cultural preferences. Some of their tactics were highly visual: the use of paint to embellish wall surfaces, for example. Other elements engaged the other senses. In some cases, the use of stoves provided a different type of radiant heat. When these building were in use, distinct foodways may have further enhanced their ethnic character through smell and taste.

The house built by Johan Peter and Maria Magdalena Troxell not far from the Lehigh River in what is now Lehigh County on the eve of the Seven Years' War shows just how variable and exploratory the new form was (fig. 9.18). The floor plan includes an almost symmetrical

FIGURE 9.18 Johann Peter and Maria Magdalena Troxell house, Egypt, Lehigh County, Pa., 1756.

arrangement, with two kitchens at the back of the house and two stove-heated rooms at the front. The arrangement is mirrored upstairs, with matching chambers at the front and two smaller rooms to the rear. Why? What can this arrangement tell us about the way the space was used? Was it the result of an effort to maintain the spatial arrangement between the kitchen and stove room while still incorporating a partial center passage? Or was this building shared in some way? Its second owner bequeathed the property to two of his sons, but it is unknown whether Troxell family members practiced similar joint occupancy.[42] The date stone on the building, listing the names of only a husband and wife, tells of a traditional single-family arrangement. Other types of written sources to help answer such questions are not immediately forthcoming, so we are left to interrogate the building.

What the Troxell house conveys is that much about the New World was still new in 1756. On the eve of the Seven Years' War in North America, the Troxells went about building a house on the frontier. They used some traditional features, such as closed stoves, and made use of stone, a material that long had been associated with strength and financial means. But the overall result was quite novel. As part of the design, the Troxells labeled their building with their names and included a blessing in German asking God to keep their house from danger.[43] Like many colonial Pennsylvanians, despite the sense of risk, they forged ahead, using their house to create spaces that suited the cultural needs resulting from who they were, where they were, and when they were.

Two decades later, David Deshler experienced firsthand the effects of war when his fashionable house fell into the hands of British general William Howe as the Battle of Germantown raged around it. But something fundamental had changed in Pennsylvania between 1756 and 1777, between the Seven Years' War and the American Revolution. The architecture of these two families' dwellings helps us understand it. Both the Troxells and the Deshlers built sizable masonry houses that embraced new desires for separation, order, and display. But the Troxells did so in a way that was inventive, novel, and, as a result, still hard to completely understand. Deshler, on the other hand, participated in a shared culture, one that was so well understood that both a British general and an American president could appreciate and even participate in it. The multiple languages of Babel—literal, visual, and sensory—were becoming more easily understood, at least by European Americans, as Pennsylvanians left behind the liminality of the mid-eighteenth century. While the best houses had once been original innovations, they increasingly embraced a standardization of form and finish that transcended cultural groups and rose above local taste.

Notes

1. Mary (Le Fevres) Deshler died of scarlet fever on February 25, 1774, around the time of the completion of the building, and for that reason I refer to it as widower David Deshler's house. Anna Coxe Toogood, *Historic Structure/Furnishing/Grounds Report, Deshler Morris House, Bringhurst House, Historical Data Section, Independence National Historical Park, Pennsylvania* (Denver: Denver Service Center Branch of Historic Preservation, Mid-Atlantic/North Atlantic Team, National Park Service, United States Department of the Interior, [1980?]), 20.

2. John L. Cotter, Daniel G. Roberts, and Michael Parrington, *Buried Past: An Archaeological History of Philadelphia* (Philadelphia: University of Pennsylvania Press, 1992), 343–46; Toogood, "Historic Structure/Furnishing/Grounds Report," 11–12, 21–22. Quotations from real estate advertisements, *Pennsylvania Gazette*, April 14, 1782, and May 12, 1784 (accessed through Accessible Archives).

3. Cotter, Roberts, and Parrington, *Buried Past*, 337–39; "Grumblethorpe," Historic American Buildings Survey, call no. HABS PA,51-GERM,23- (accessed through the Library of Congress, American Memory).

4. Henry Glassie, *Folk Housing in Middle Virginia* (Knoxville: University of Tennessee Press, 1975), 11–12; Glassie, *Material Culture* (Bloomington: Indiana University Press, 1999), 44–45.

5. Glassie, *Material Culture*, 47; Grant McCracken, *Culture and Consumption: New Approaches to the Symbolic Character of Consumer Goods and Activities* (Bloomington: Indiana University Press, 1988), 69.

6. Katherine C. Grier, "Material Culture as Rhetoric: 'Animal Artifacts' as a Case Study," in *American Material Culture: The Shape of the Field*, ed. Ann Smart Martin and J. Ritchie Garrison (Knoxville: University of Tennessee Press for the Henry Francis DuPont Winterthur Museum, 1997), 75–94. Also on metaphors, see the work of Jules Prown, who builds from anthropologist James Fernandez: Jules Prown and Kenneth Haltman, *American Artifacts: Essays in Material Culture* (East Lansing: Michigan State University Press, 2000), 18–21.

7. McCracken, *Culture and Consumption*, 68–69; Glassie, *Folk Housing in Middle Virginia*, 20; Grier, "Material Culture as Rhetoric," 76. Grier draws the comparison to metaphor, noting, "'A is B' creates meaning as the maker and listener employ a mental screening process that is almost always beneath the level of self-consciousness."

8. Glassie, *Material Culture*, 45–46; Prown and Haltman, *American Artifacts*, 12.

9. For a similar argument about colonial Delaware, see Richard L. Bushman, *The Refinement of America: Persons, Houses, Cities* (New York: Vintage Books, 1992), 3–29.

10. At the Deshler house, enslaved people were certainly part of the labor force during George Washington's tenancy. See Burt Froom, "Washington's Germantown Servants and Slaves," http://www.wman.net/wp-content/uploads/2015/08/Yesterday-Mt.-Airy-24.pdf.

11. McCracken, *Culture and Consumption*, 68–69; Daniel Miller, ed., *Material Cultures: Why Some Things Matter* (Chicago: University of Chicago Press, 1998), 5–6.

12. W. J. T. Mitchell, "There Are No Visual Media," *Journal of Visual Culture* 4, no. 2 (2005): 257–66; Fiona Candlin, "The Dubious Inheritance of Touch: Art History and Museum Access," *Journal of Visual Culture* 5, no. 2 (2006): 137–54.

13. Charles H. Glatfelter, *Pastors and People: German Lutheran and Reformed Churches in the Pennsylvania Field, 1717–1793* (Breinigsville, Pa.: Pennsylvania German Society, 1980–81), 1:379–80, 2:102, 104, 158. For additional illustrations of Augustus Lutheran, see Margaret Bye Richie, John D. Milner, and Gregory D. Huber, *Stone Houses: Traditional Homes of Pennsylvania's Bucks County and Brandywine Valley* (New York: Rizzoli, 2005), 145–47.

14. Glatfelter, *Pastors and People*, 2:152–55.

15. Catherine C. Lavoie, "Quaker Beliefs and Practices and the Eighteenth-Century Development of the Friends Meeting House in the Delaware Valley," in *Quaker Aesthetics: Reflections on a Quaker Ethic in American Design and Consumption*, ed. Emma Jones Lapsansky and Anne A. Verplanck (Philadelphia: University of Pennsylvania Press, 2003), 156–87, especially 169–71; Vernon H. Nelson and Lothar Madeheim, "The Moravian Settlements in Pennsylvania in 1757: The Nicholas Garrison Views," *Pennsylvania Folklife* 19, no. 1 (1969): 7, 9, 13; Glatfelter, *Pastors and People*, 2:154–55, 157, table 7.

16. Lorsch Abbey, for example, had a similar-shaped end and roof form. Although it was closed during the Reformation and burned in 1621 during the Thirty Years' War, the building was documented and publicized in a copperplate engraving entitled *Kloster Lorsch* by Matthäus Merian the Elder in 1645. To see the engraving and learn more about the structure based on archaeology, visit: www.iwr.uni-heidelberg.de/groups/ngg/Lorsch/.

17. Lavoie, "Quaker Beliefs," 183.

18. The Upper Providence Friends Meetinghouse, which currently stands in Oaks, Pennsylvania, dates to the early nineteenth century. The stone building is a single story with a central front door on its long side, which is flanked on either side by two windows, creating a five-bay façade. It replaced an older, perhaps smaller, building, which would have been depicted on the map. It is difficult to know just what the building used by the Reformed congregation in Providence looked like in the mid-eighteenth century. Michael Schlatter wrote in 1746 that services took place "in a barn, since the poor congregation there has hitherto not been able to build a church." A structure of unknown design was erected the following year and represented on the Scull map of 1759. See Glatfelter, *Pastors and People*, 1:380, 2:155.

19. On the preponderance of one-story log houses in late eighteenth-century Pennsylvania, see Cynthia G. Falk, "Symbols of Assimilation or Status? The Meanings of Eighteenth-Century Houses in Coventry Township, Chester County, Pennsylvania," *Winterthur Portfolio* 33, nos. 2–3 (1998): 128; Scott T. Swank, "The Architectural Landscape," in *Arts of the Pennsylvania Germans*, ed. Catherine E. Hutchins (New York: W. W. Norton for the Henry Francis du Pont Winterthur Museum, 1983), 24–27, tables 1–9. Of the eight townships and two borough wards covered by these sources, only in Lower Salford Township, Montgomery County, were the greatest number of houses not one-story log structures. For statistics on Cumberland County farther west, see Nancy Van Dolsen, *Cumberland County: An Architectural Survey* (Carlisle, Pa.: Cumberland County Historical Society, 1990), 3, fig. 1. In all eleven townships Van Dolsen surveyed, the majority of houses were built of logs. In all but three (Carlisle, Newton, and West Pennsboro), the average house was one or one-and-a-half stories. On Germantown, see Stephanie Grauman Wolf, *Urban Village: Population, Community, and Family Structure in Germantown, Pennsylvania, 1683–1800* (Princeton, N.J.: Princeton University Press, 1976), 35. In 1798, while the majority of houses in Germantown were stone (83.5 percent)—perhaps due to the more urban setting—51.1 percent were less than 500 square feet. The largest one-hundred-square-foot range was 300–399 square feet, into which 22.9 percent of houses fell. According to a real estate advertisements placed by Deshler, his house was 45 feet by 40 feet exclusive of the work spaces to the rear. Real estate advertisements, *Pennsylvania Gazette*, April 14, 1782, and May 12, 1784 (accessed through Accessible Archives).

20. Alexander Hamilton, *Hamilton's Itinerarium, Being a Narrative of a Journey from Annapolis, Maryland Through Delaware, Pennsylvania, New York, New Jersey, Connecticut, Rhode*

Island, Massachusetts and New Hampshire from May to September, 1744 (Saint Louis: William K. Bixby, 1907), 20.

21. Real estate advertisement, *Pennsylvania Gazette*, March 29, 1748 (accessed through Accessible Archives).

22. Real estate advertisement, *Pennsylvania Gazette*, January 29, 1783 (accessed through Accessible Archives); Valeria Elizabeth Clymer Hill, *A Genealogy of the Hiester Family* (Lebanon, Pa.: Report, 1903), 25; Daniel Hiester's house is also discussed or illustrated in H. Winslow Fegley, *Farming, Always Farming: A Photographic Essay of the Rural Pennsylvania German Land and Life Made by H. Winslow Fegley* (Birdsboro, Pa.: Pennsylvania German Society), 92, fig. 79; G. Edwin Brumbaugh, "Colonial Architecture of the Pennsylvania Germans," *Pennsylvania German Society Proceedings* 41 (1933): pl. 92.

23. In studying house types, field workers such as Henry Glassie have chosen to focus on floor plan, rather than building materials or decorative elements, as the best way to understand use and meaning at the time of construction. See Glassie, *Folk Housing in Middle Virginia*, 33–34; Henry Glassie, "A Central Chimney Continental Log House," *Pennsylvania Folklife* 18, no. 2 (1968–69): 33–34.

24. Robert C. Bucher, "The Continental Log House," *Pennsylvania Folklife* 12, no. 4 (1962): 14–19; Glassie, "Central Chimney Continental Log House," 32–39; Edward Chappell, "German and Swiss," in *America's Architectural Roots: Ethnic Groups That Built America*, ed. Dell Upton (Washington, D.C.: Preservation Press, 1986), 68.

25. Bavarian doctor Johann David Schöpf observed of Pennsylvania houses, "if of one chimney only, placed in the middle, the house should be a German's and furnished with stoves, the smoke from each led into one flue and so taken off; if of two chimneys, one at each gable end there should be fire places, after the English plan." See Johann David Schöpf, *Travels in the Confederation, 1783–1784*, trans. and ed. Alfred J. Morrison, 2 vols. (Philadelphia: William J. Campbell, 1911), 1:125.

26. William Woys Weaver, "The Pennsylvania German House: European Antecedents and New World Forms," *Winterthur Portfolio* 21, no. 4 (1986): 244, 253, 257–58, 264.

27. Benjamin Franklin, "An Account of the Newly Invented Pennsylvanian Fire-Places," in *The Papers of Benjamin Franklin*, ed. Leonard W. Labaree et al., 41 vols. to date (New Haven, Conn.: Yale University Press, 1961–), 2:429. See also Franklin, *Observations on Smoky Chimneys, Their Causes and Cure: With Considerations on Fuel and Stoves* (London: I. and J. Taylor, 1793), 28.

28. Franklin, "Account," 2:429.

29. David Seibt to his brother, December 20, 1734, in *The Journals of David Schultze*, trans. and ed. Andrew S. Berky (Pennsburg, Pa.: Schwenkfelder Library, 1952), 1:55; Sir Benjamin Thompson, Count Rumford, *Essay IV: Of Chimney Fire-places, with Proposals for Improving Them, to Save Fuel, to Render Dwelling-houses More Comfortable and Salubrious, and, Effectually to Prevent Chimnies from Smoking* (London, 1796), 304.

30. Philip E. Pendleton, *Oley Valley Heritage: The Colonial Years, 1700–1775* (Birdsboro, Pa.: Pennsylvania German Society; Oley, Pa.: Oley Valley Heritage Association, 1994), 79–81.

31. Henry Melchior Muhlenberg, *The Journals of Henry Melchior Muhlenberg*, trans. and ed. Theodore G. Tappert and John W. Doberstein, 3 vols. (Philadelphia: Evangelical Lutheran Ministerium of Pennsylvania and Adjacent States and Muhlenberg Press, 1942), 2:379.

32. For more on this type of house, which Charles Bergengren calls *Kreuzehausen*, see Bergengren, "The Cycle of Transformations in the Houses of Schaefferstown, Pennsylvania" (Ph.D. diss., University of Pennsylvania, 1988), 74–80, 155, 170–73; Sally McMurray and Nancy Van Dolsen, eds., *Architecture and Landscape of the Pennsylvania Germans, 1720–1920* (Philadelphia: University of Pennsylvania Press, 2011), 40, 48.

33. Bergengren, "Cycle of Transformations," 80–91, 155, 175–81; McMurray and Van Dolsen, *Architecture and Landscape*, 49–55.

34. William J. Murtagh, *Moravian Architecture and Town Planning: Bethlehem, Pennsylvania, and Other Eighteenth-Century American Settlements* (Chapel Hill: University of North

Carolina Press, 1967), 36–39, 65. The most accurate information on the original floor plan of the structure comes from a 1766 map of Bethlehem reproduced in Ralph Grayson Schwarz, *Bethlehem on the Lehigh* (Bethlehem: Bethlehem Area Foundation, n.d.), 18, and floor plans of the Gemeinhaus and related buildings in Bethlehem from the collection of the Moravian Archives Herrnhut, Germany, dating to 1751 (TS Mp.216.15).

35. Pendleton, *Oley Valley Heritage*, 77–79.

36. Cotter, Roberts, and Parrington, *Buried Past*, 332–34.

37. Margaret Berwind Schiffer, *Survey of Chester County, Pennsylvania, Architecture, 17th, 18th and 19th Centuries* (Exton, Pa.: Schiffer, 1984), 68–71, 385–87; Richie, Milner, and Huber, *Stone Houses*, 218–21.

38. Albert T. Gamon, "Peter Wentz Farmstead," *Antiques* 72, no. 4 (1982): 788–95; Richie, Milner, and Huber, *Stone Houses*, 132–39; Wendell Garrett, *American Colonial: Puritan Simplicity to Georgian Grace* (New York: Monacelli Press, 1995), 163, 165; National Heritage Corporation, "Master Plan: Peter Wentz Farmstead, Volume 1: The Plan and Program" (January 1975), 37, 43.

39. Schöpf, *Travels in the Confederation*, 1:104.

40. Cynthia G. Falk, "Personal History for the Visiting Public," in the published roundtable "The Gemberling-Rex House: From Eighteenth-Century Tavern to Nineteenth-Century Home to Twenty-First Century Museum, A Public History Roundtable," *Pennsylvania History* 75, no. 1 (2008): 59, fig. 6.

41. Cynthia G. Falk, *Architecture and Artifacts of the Pennsylvania Germans: Constructing Identity in Early America* (University Park: Penn State University Press, 2008), 97.

42. Northampton County, Pennsylvania, Will Book 1, 352–54. The manuscript will of Peter Steckel, dated February 11, 1784, and written in the German language, is also on file with Northampton County, file #1086.

43. John K. Heyl, "The Building of the Troxell-Steckel House," *Proceedings of the Lehigh County Historical Society* 14 (1944): 112; Charles R. Roberts, "The Steckel House," *Proceedings: Lehigh County Historical Society* 13 (December 1942): 22–23; National Register of Historic Places Inventory—Nomination Form, Troxell-Steckel House, State Historic Preservation Office, Harrisburg, Pa.

CHAPTER 10

Germans in Colonial Philadelphia
Ethnicity, Hybridity, and the Material World

LISA MINARDI

At first glance, the small walnut cabinet on turned feet looks like any other so-called spice box made in southeastern Pennsylvania during the early to mid-eighteenth century (fig. 10.1). It is fitted on the interior with drawers to provide secure, compartmentalized storage for costly imported spices, as well as coins and other small valuables. Although Pennsylvania spice boxes are generally thought of as English and typically Quaker objects, this example has several features that indicate it was made by a German émigré craftsman. Set into the center of the door is an inlaid bird; its feathers and the stump on which it perches are embellished with incised lines, sand shading (in which pieces of wood are darkened by scorching them in hot sand), and dyes or stains to achieve a polychrome effect—all traditional Germanic marquetry techniques. On the interior, the use of tulip-shaped hinges and drawer construction with thin wedges driven into the pins of the dovetails is also indicative of Germanic craftsmanship. In 1763, a different German émigré woodworker made a set of chairs for his pastor, Lutheran minister Henry Melchior Muhlenberg (1711–1787). Built of mahogany, the chairs have through-tenoned side rails, two-part vertical glue blocks, and compressed ball-and-claw feet typical of Philadelphia seating furniture (fig. 10.2). Each is ornamented with a pierced splat, fluted rear stiles, and carved shells in

FIGURE 10.1 Spice box, Philadelphia area, ca. 1740. Walnut and mixed-wood inlay. H 16 in., W 14¼ in., D 10⅛ in.

FIGURE 10.2 Pair of side chairs made for Henry Muhlenberg, attributed to Leonard Kessler, Philadelphia, 1763. Mahogany. H 40½ in., W 21½ in., D 17 in.

the rococo style. Thanks to a detailed family provenance and an entry in Muhlenberg's journal in which he noted paying Leonard Kessler £10.2.6 for making a set of "new chairs," we know that these chairs were made by a German craftsman for a fellow German patron. Otherwise, the chairs would be identifiable only as fairly elaborate yet typical examples from mid-eighteenth-century Philadelphia.[1]

These objects challenge us to rethink not only what is English and what is German about colonial Pennsylvania, but also whether these are even the most relevant questions—particularly in the cosmopolitan milieu of early Philadelphia. Although some recent studies have argued for the importance of Germans as culture brokers and active participants in transatlantic networks, there continues to be an emphasis on defining people as English or German.[2] This "monolingual fallacy," as noted in Bethany Wiggin's introduction to this volume, has led to questionable "monocultural" or "monoethnic" assumptions about Pennsylvania German people and their material worlds. In fact, as the objects discussed in this chapter will demonstrate, being German in colonial Pennsylvania had multiple meanings. This was particularly true in Philadelphia, the social and political capital of the most ethnically diverse colony in British North America. Although most German-speaking immigrants arrived via Philadelphia and then moved outside the city, a sizable number remained. Spurred by large waves of immigration and natural increase, Philadelphia's German population reached a height of 45 percent in 1760. The presence of so many German-speaking people—who largely did not settle in ethnic enclaves but wherever space permitted—had a profound impact on the city's ethnic, cultural, linguistic, religious, and material life.[3] Yet heretofore the vast majority of studies have focused almost exclusively on Philadelphia's English-speaking inhabitants or on rural Pennsylvania Germans and their material culture (such as painted chests and Fraktur, or decorated manuscripts).[4]

In order to move beyond the predominant stereotypes of Philadelphia as an English-dominated "Quaker City" and Pennsylvania Germans as country bumpkins who adorned their homes with quaint folk art, we must set aside such monoethnic, either-or assumptions. Material culture evidence can shed light on how factors such as religion, socioeconomic status, and locale (particularly urban vs. nonurban) influenced the choices made by Pennsylvania German consumers.[5] In the following chapter, two groups of furniture made in or near Philadelphia will be explored, as well as colonial Philadelphia's two German Lutheran churches. The first group of furniture, distinguished by the use of inlaid parrot motifs, is readily identified as Germanic in origin by its construction and decoration. With the second group, I explore ethnically anonymous objects through the work of Leonard Kessler and the rococo chairs he made for Henry

Muhlenberg. Both groups include furniture made by and for German immigrants, challenging us to move beyond monoethnic models and to reconsider what it meant to be German in colonial Pennsylvania. I then examine the architecture and furnishings of St. Michael's and Zion Lutheran Churches, both of which were built before the Revolutionary War and demolished soon after the Civil War.[6] Using these three groups as case studies, I argue that material objects were critical to German speakers' formation of a hybrid identity in which ethnicity, language, religion, and locale each played a prominent role—particularly in the cosmopolitan setting of early Philadelphia.

PARROT-INLAID FURNITURE

Following the "discovery" of the Americas in 1492, Europeans became fascinated with its exotic flora and fauna. Images of armadillos, monkeys, alligators, jaguars, and dazzlingly colorful parrots became popular symbols of the New World and imperial conquest, while animal bodies were commoditized along with goods such as silver, chocolate, and tobacco. Parrots were one of the most prized New World commodities from the very beginning. On his return voyage of 1493, Columbus brought a pair of Cuban Amazon parrots back to Europe as a present for Queen Isabella. By the 1600s, hundreds of parrots were being imported each year, leading to the establishment of specialized shops and even bird-sellers' guilds in major cities.[7] Parrots began to figure prominently in allegorical depictions of America, which was often personified as a scantily clad woman wearing a feathered skirt, cape, and headdress with a parrot at her side. Parrots were also commonly illustrated on maps of the New World, such the 1747 *Plan Von Neu Ebenezer* depicting the Salzburger settlement near Savannah, Georgia.[8] German artisans and consumers were particularly fond of the bird; in the 1700s, there was a veritable craze for parrot iconography, especially on furniture. Maximilian II Emanuel, elector of Bavaria, owned a cabinet made of exotic imported woods with images of two large parrots inlaid on the inside of the doors, while Frederick the Great and Maria Amalie Auguste (wife of Frederick August III, elector of Saxony) owned commodes that were prominently inlaid with parrot motifs. From about 1720 to 1760, furniture decorated with parrot images was so popular in Baden-Württemberg and especially Hohenlohe that the term *Papageienschrank* or "parrot cupboard" came into use. Less expensive painted furniture embellished with parrots was also widely popular.⁹

Objects embellished with images of exotic parrots enabled Europeans to experience the Americas without ever leaving home. The birds' colorful plumage was aesthetically pleasing, and their unique ability to mimic human speech was a source of wonderment. This latter trait also made it possible to draw parallels between parrots and indigenous people, affirming a dark sense of European superiority in the process. Kept in cages or chained to perches, articulate parrots were sometimes viewed as a subservient form of humanity and likened to subordinate or enslaved peoples.¹⁰ Most German artists worked from drawings or print sources, especially as ornithology books became increasingly available. By 1750, three major studies with illustrations of North American birds were published: Mark Catesby's *Natural History of Carolina, Florida and the Bahama Islands* (1729–47), Eleazar Albin's *A Natural History of Birds* (1731–38), and George Edwards's *A Natural History of Uncommon Birds* (1743–51). Many engravings from these books were copied by Johann Michael Seligmann of Nuremberg and published in his nine-volume *Sammlung verschiedener ausländischer und seltener Vögel* (Collection of various foreign and rare birds, 1749–76). Although some artists studied live parrots, many used taxidermy specimens as the basis of their illustrations—resulting in rather stiff, lifeless depictions of birds carefully posed on branches, their wings tucked firmly at their sides.¹¹

Given the enormous interest in parrots by German artisans and their patrons, it is little surprise that German-speaking immigrants carried this fascination with them to Pennsylvania. There many also encountered live parrots for the first time: the Carolina parrot (*Conuropsis carolinensis*). Now extinct, this colorful green bird with a red and yellow head was the only parrot species indigenous to North America and was once common in the mid-Atlantic region (fig. 10.3). In the 1750s, the schoolmaster Gottlieb Mittelberger extolled the "very wonderful" birds in Pennsylvania, writing, "it is impossible to overpraise their beautiful colors and their lovely songs." He described the Carolina parrot as "grass-green ones, with red heads."¹² Two large parrots are prominently inlaid on the doors of one of the earliest known examples of Pennsylvania German furniture, a *Kleiderschrank* or clothes cupboard dated 1741

FIGURE 10.3 *The Parrot of Carolina*, in Mark Catesby, *Natural History of Carolina, Florida and the Bahama Islands* (London, 1729–47).

(fig. 10.4). This architectonic piece of furniture has flat pilasters inlaid with flowering vines and shells along with ornately carved capitals and bases modeled after the Corinthian order. Made by the same unknown émigré craftsman as the parrot-inlaid spice box (see fig. 10.1), the inlay is embellished with engraving, scorching, and dyes or stains. Inlaid on two of its four drawers are the initials "MI AM," enabling a tentative identification of the original owner as Michael Amenzetter (1696–1784), a German immigrant who settled in Philadelphia and was a member of St. Michael's and Zion Lutheran Church. He likely immigrated before 1727, as his name does not appear in the lists of arrivals that Philadelphia began requiring in that year; or he arrived in a different city. In 1741, Michael would have been forty-five years old, which is in keeping with the fact that such costly furniture was typically acquired by established households rather than newlyweds. Unfortunately, although Michael's death is recorded in the church records, no estate papers have been located that might verify his ownership of this piece. The same anonymous craftsman who made the parrot-inlaid spice box and wardrobe can be linked to at least two other pieces of furniture: a tall clock case dated

FIGURE 10.4 Schrank, Philadelphia area, 1741. Walnut and mixed-wood inlay. H 76 in., W 75¼ in., D 27½ in.

FIGURE 10.5 Detail of the lid of a slant-front desk, Philadelphia area, ca. 1750. Walnut and mixed-wood inlay.

1740 and a slant-front desk. The clock is inlaid with flowering vines, while the lid of the desk is adorned with flowers, two parrots, and a human figure in feathered cape and headdress (fig. 10.5).[13]

Also working in or near Philadelphia, a second German émigré craftsman built and inlaid two clock cases with parrots on the pendulum doors. One has a movement by Augustin Neisser (1717–1780) of Germantown and the other a movement by Joseph Wills (1700–1759) of Philadelphia. The door of the Wills clock case is inlaid with a parrot perched on a flowering branch, hovering above a pastoral vignette complete with buildings, agricultural fields, and a fence (fig. 10.6). Although distinct from the previous group of inlaid furniture, the decoration, robust moldings, and construction of these clock cases indicate that they were also built by a cabinetmaker trained in Continental Europe. Both Neisser and Wills had close ties to the German-speaking community. Neisser was

FIGURE 10.6 Detail of the inlaid parrot on a tall clock case, Philadelphia area, ca. 1745. Walnut and mixed-wood inlay.

born in Schlen, Moravia, and moved as a young boy to the estate of Count Nicholas Ludwig von Zinzendorf in Herrnhut, where he joined the Moravian faith. He immigrated to America in 1736 and three years later settled in Germantown, where he worked as a clock- and watchmaker until his death. Wills was a native of Devonshire, England; he immigrated to Philadelphia in the 1730s and married a German woman, Maria Dorothea, who died in 1757 and was buried in the graveyard of St. Michael's and Zion Lutheran Church.[14] Even without our knowing the individual cabinetmakers who made this furniture, the use of Germanic decoration and construction practices forces us to rethink traditional questions of whether an object (or person, in the case of Joseph Wills) is English or German. Whether the subject is a parrot-inlaid spice box or an English clockmaker who married a German Lutheran, a bifurcated English-versus-German approach obscures the historical reality of cultural hybridity and exposes the limitations of a monoethnic focus.

The presence of stiff, taxidermy-like imagery on these American-made objects also reveals that although Pennsylvania German craftsmen had readier access to live parrots than their European counterparts, they continued to use Old World methods of depiction rather than make direct observations from nature. In part, this may be due to their awareness of the customary manner in which parrots had long been depicted in European art and a desire to not deviate from the norm. This consistency, while lacking in verisimilitude, helped to make the continued use of parrot imagery an important form of memory art that recalled the German craze for parrot iconography as a potent symbol of New World exotica and transatlantic exchange. Objects such as a spice box provided a container designed to store yet more exotic commodities. Large wardrobes were used to store bed linens, clothing, and other textiles, much of which was imported, while desks helped people to write, organize, and store the letters, receipts, invoices, and other documents pertaining to life in a transatlantic world. Images of parrots, whether printed on a map or inlaid on the door of a cupboard, provided German-speaking consumers in both Europe and America with a powerful vehicle for communicating knowledge about the New World and ownership of its resources via international trade networks.

The sophisticated carving and inlay on this group of furniture also reveal the high level of craftsmanship executed by German émigré woodworkers in colonial Philadelphia, dispelling misconceptions that few if any Pennsylvania Germans made or owned fashionable, urban objects. At the same time, the parrot-inlaid furniture is overtly Germanic due to its decorative motifs and techniques of inlay and construction. In many cases, however, a cabinetmaker's ethnic identity can be virtually invisible in the absence of a signature, label, or other documentation—particularly in urban areas, where there was a strong tendency toward conformity to particular furniture forms, decoration, and construction methods. The chance discovery of Leonard Kessler, a German cabinetmaker and woodcarver who made furniture for the Muhlenberg family, provides an opportunity to explore this issue in more detail. The sophisticated rococo carving executed by Kessler and other Pennsylvania German woodworkers, including multiple craftsmen working in or near the towns of Lancaster, Manheim, and Reading from about 1765 to 1800, reveals the fallacy of claims such as that "in the Germanic communities of Pennsylvania, rococo ornament was seldom employed, and then usually only on special commission." Hundreds of chairs, clock cases, desks, high chests, dressing tables, looking glasses, long rifles, stove plates, and other forms—all embellished with rococo ornament—indicate otherwise and reveal the shortcomings of focusing strictly on painted furniture and other stereotypical examples of Pennsylvania German material culture.[15]

LEONARD KESSLER

One of the leading cabinetmakers of any ethnic background in colonial Philadelphia was Leonard Kessler, a member of St. Michael's and Zion Lutheran Church. Born on September 4, 1737, Kessler emigrated from Germany about 1750. His marriage to Anna Maria Ritschauer on October 3, 1758, was witnessed by Jacob Shoemaker, Reinhardt Uhl and his wife, and the brothers Scheubele/Scheuffele. Both Reinhardt Uhl and Jacob Scheubele (later Schieffelin) were Kessler's brothers-in-law, married to his wife's sisters, Christina Catharina and Regina Margaretta Ritschauer. The Schieffelin family Bible notes Regina's birthplace as Mühlhausen an der Enz, a town in Württemberg; presumably all three sisters were born there and immigrated to Philadelphia. The name of the third party who attended the wedding, Jacob Shoemaker, provides an important clue as to Kessler's training as a cabinetmaker. No Jacob Shoemaker appears in the records of St. Michael's and Zion Lutheran Church or the German Reformed Church in Philadelphia as a baptismal sponsor, communicant, or witness to a wedding except for this one instance, implying a relationship with Kessler other than that of a family member or coreligionist. Given that Kessler emigrated from Germany as a young man and would have apprenticed in Philadelphia, Shoemaker is very likely the man who trained him and can thus reasonably be identified as the turner Jacob Shoemaker Jr. (1692–1772) of Philadelphia.[16]

Three generations of Schumachers/Shoemakers were woodworkers, beginning with Jacob Sr., a Quaker who emigrated from Mainz, Germany, in 1683 and was one of the original settlers of Germantown. He moved to Philadelphia about 1715 and worked there approximately five years. In 1722, he bequeathed his "turning tools and all the other timber materials utensils and Tools belonging to the Trades of Turning and

Wheel Making" to his son Jacob Jr., whose shop was located on Market Street next to that of Caspar Wistar, another German émigré. Jacob Jr. probably trained his own son, Jonathan Shoemaker (1726–1793), who worked as a joiner by 1750 and in 1752 acquired a shop on the west side of Second Street. In 1767, Jonathan relocated to Third Street near Arch. Although only one piece of furniture signed by Jonathan Shoemaker is known (a walnut chest-on-chest), drawings made by one of his apprentices reveal that his shop produced a variety of sophisticated forms, including large case pieces and cabriole leg chairs typical of Philadelphia furniture.[17]

No signed or labeled furniture by Leonard Kessler is known, but significant details of his life and work are noted in the journals of Lutheran minister Henry Melchior Muhlenberg. A member of St. Michael's and Zion Church, Kessler was the only cabinetmaker that Muhlenberg is known to have patronized when he lived in Philadelphia from 1761 to 1776. In October of 1762, Kessler was hired to build a chimney door for the parsonage; for this and other cabinetwork he was paid more than £12, some of which he returned to Muhlenberg as a contribution to the pastor's salary. When Muhlenberg's five-year-old son died in 1764, Kessler built the coffin. On October 22, 1765, the St. Michael's church council passed a resolution that charged "Mr. Ehwald and Mr. Kessler, two master carpenters ... with supervising the alterations in the pews in the front section of St. Michael's Church." On January 21, 1763, Muhlenberg paid Kessler £10.2.6 for "new chairs." At least six chairs from this set are known, one of which is marked "XII," indicating that there were originally twelve or more (see fig. 10.2). Although £10.2.6 is low for a set of twelve mahogany chairs with fluted stiles and carved ornament (which by the 1772 Philadelphia price book would have cost more than £25), Philadelphia was in a postwar economic depression in the early 1760s. Kessler may have charged Muhlenberg a lower price for the chairs simply because he needed the work, or he may have given his pastor a discount. Muhlenberg also paid for the chairs in January, the time of year when parishioners often contributed toward his salary. Although much more elaborate chairs were available in Philadelphia, these chairs do have a number of embellishments and would have been well suited to Muhlenberg's relatively modest means. A large set of chairs was an occupational necessity for the minister, who frequently hosted sizable groups of visitors at his home. Nor would just any chairs suffice. Muhlenberg was keenly aware of the need for keeping up appearances, remarking that when in the city he "would not dare" wear the clothing his wife made for him "unless I wanted the children on the streets to laugh at me behind my back."[18] Such statements reveal that distinctions between city and country were often just as important, sometimes more so, than English versus German. Muhlenberg was more concerned about presenting a reasonably fashionable appearance when in the city, which required tailored rather than homemade garments, than he was about appearing more or less German. Thus, it is unsurprising that Muhlenberg felt the need to upgrade his household furniture by acquiring a fashionable set of new chairs soon after he moved from Trappe, then a small rural village, to Philadelphia.

Careful examination of the Muhlenberg chairs reveals a number of distinctive features that identify seating furniture from Kessler's shop, including flared, scrolled ears decorated with four pairs of crescent-shaped chip cuts, the topmost pair being located on the apex of the ear and not visible from the front; pierced splats with large scroll volutes and high, straight plinths; scallop shells with unusually small flanges on the front seat rail; and ball-and-claw feet with pronounced knuckles. The ruffled shell cartouches on the crest rails were derived from those on other Philadelphia chairs with carving attributed to French émigré Nicholas Bernard, but subtle differences help distinguish his and Kessler's work. On the Muhlenberg chairs, the volutes flanking the leaf at the bottom are slightly overscale, like those on the splat, and the concave sides of the cabochons in the cartouche are gently curved, rather than sharply peaked, at the waist. Based on the Muhlenberg chairs, it is evident that Kessler also made less ornate examples, including ones with plain rear stiles, solid splats, and/or no carving. Although these chairs can be firmly attributed to Kessler through the subtle but distinctive details in their construction and carving, nothing about them even hints at the ethnic identity of either the maker or owner. Instead, the chairs are a standard Philadelphia model of the mid-1700s.

Documentary evidence sheds light on Kessler's interactions with other woodworkers, both German and English, again reminding us of the need to move beyond monoethnic models in the study of colonial Pennsylvania. In 1769, he witnessed the will of joiner John Gaul. Eleven years later, Kessler and Anthony Leckler inventoried the stock of Johann Michael Barendt, a joiner and musical instrument maker. Barendt's will stipulated that "all my Tools of my Trade shall be particularly mentioned in the Inventory or Appraisement of my Estate and be put up and carefully kept . . . for the use of my beloved son John," so Kessler was likely selected for this task due to his knowledge of woodworking tools. The following year, carpenter George Adam Pfister appointed as executors of his estate "my worthy and Esteemed Friends Leonerd Kessler of the said City Cabinetmaker and Michael Bowes of the same Place Victualler," together with his wife. Kessler also did carving work for cabinetmaker Benjamin Randolph, who belonged to St. Paul's Anglican Church in Philadelphia, and sold walnut boards, chair legs, coffins, and other items to Quaker cabinetmaker David Evans (1748–1819), who lived and worked at 115 Arch Street.[19]

In addition to chairs, Kessler also built significant case pieces, including a desk for which Friederich Schenckel, a leather breeches maker in Philadelphia, paid him £22. It was described as a mahogany desk-and-bookcase and valued at $25 when Schenckel died in 1810. A final indication of Kessler's range of work is suggested by the inventory taken when he died in 1804. In addition to "One lot Joiner's Tools (very old)," valued at fifty cents, there was an extensive list of furniture, including an eight-day clock and case, a desk-and-bookcase, six chairs, a chest of drawers, two bureaus, two tea tables, a stand, fire screen, and chest—all of mahogany—together with twelve chairs, a bureau, table, and tea table in walnut. Likely most, if not all, of this furniture was made by Kessler, as it made good business sense for a cabinetmaker to make pieces for his own household rather than pay someone else to do it.[20]

Kessler was evidently quite successful as a cabinetmaker. The 1783 Philadelphia occupational tax assessment, based on yearly income, shows that he was one of eleven woodworkers who paid a tax of £100; only three cabinetmakers paid a higher amount, while most were taxed at £30 to £50. In 1765, Kessler took out an insurance policy for his "Dwelling house, Kitchen and Work Shop," located on the north side of Arch (or Mulberry) Street between Third and Fourth. The house was three stories tall and measured fifteen feet wide by twenty-five-and-a-half feet deep. The front room on the first floor was partitioned off for a shop where Kessler could meet with customers and tend to his accounts. Behind the house was a kitchen that measured eleven by sixteen feet, two-and-a-half stories high; there was also a two-story workshop of nineteen feet, six inches by fifteen feet. The three buildings were together insured for £200, the house at £150, kitchen at £35, and shop at £15. By the time the property was resurveyed in 1772, wainscoting had been added in the house and the kitchen expanded to twenty-seven feet, six inches by eleven feet. The house and kitchen now totaled 1,752 square feet of living space (not counting the attic), with an additional 588 square feet for the workshop. This puts Kessler squarely in the category of middling-to-wealthy Philadelphians, who on average occupied three-story houses with approximately 2,000 square feet. By way of comparison, the average Philadelphia laborer lived in a two-story house of about 500 square feet.[21]

Church records indicate that Leonard and Mary Kessler raised six children: Leonard Jr., John, Michael, Elizabeth, Rachel, and Anna Maria / Hannah; a seventh child, Jacob, died in infancy. Details about Kessler's personal life found in the journals of his pastor, Henry Muhlenberg, reveal that he was an active participant in congregational life. On November 7, 1761, Muhlenberg recorded his first visit from "Mr. Kessler, the joiner." The Muhlenbergs had just moved to the city on October 29, relocating from Trappe in what is now Montgomery County. This was the first of many visits the pastor would receive from Kessler, as the congregation was in the midst of a bitter controversy over church leadership and the cost of building a new schoolhouse. Kessler was one of the chief complainants against the current trustees and elders, who were accused of mismanaging church funds and trying to avoid annual elections. Muhlenberg paid a visit to Kessler's home on December 30 to discuss the situation. The controversy soon worsened, and after church on January 10, 1762, Muhlenberg recorded that "two dissatisfied members, Messrs. Leonhard Kessler and Enderle, delivered written complaints to my house." Two weeks later, Muhlenberg was invited to dine at the home of Kessler's brother-in-law, Reinhard Uhl. When he arrived, he found "Messrs. Fuchs and Kuhn, former elders, together with Leonhard Kessler and their wives." The church dispute gave Kessler cause for concern about his spiritual state. On a Tuesday in early February of 1762, Muhlenberg noted in his journal, "Toward evening had a visit from the joiner, Mr. Kessler, who conferred with me concerning his spiritual condition and requested me to pray with him." Later that week Muhlenberg was visited by "Messrs. Kessler and Enderle, with whom I conferred and prayed, for they were awakened—Mr. Enderle by Pastor Völcker and Pastor Starck in Frankfurt, Mr. Kessler here." The three men also discussed a religious tract that Kessler had brought along—*The Gospel of Nicodemus*, reprinted at Ephrata—which Muhlenberg denounced as "papistic abominations."[22]

When these fragments of information are combined with extant furniture, tax records, insurance policies, and other sources, a more complete picture of Leonard Kessler emerges. In addition to being German, he was a father, husband, neighbor, cabinetmaker, Lutheran, and Philadelphian preoccupied not just with making furniture but also with his family, friends, and spiritual matters. By the 1790s, Kessler had profited enough from his trade that he acquired several rental properties and began to make potash (used in soapmaking, textile bleaching, and glassmaking). He also acquired a hearse, which he advertised as a "commodious Carriage for the conveyance of the Dead either out or into town." Since Kessler also made coffins, this was probably a logical expansion of his existing business. As he grew older, these diverse investments enabled Kessler to escape the repetitiveness of working at a single trade and provided income that was not as physically demanding as cabinetmaking. Beginning in 1798, Kessler is listed in the Philadelphia city directories as a "gentleman," indicating that he had retired. By the time of his death on January 27, 1804, at the age of sixty-six, he had achieved a substantial degree of material comfort. In addition to the extensive assortment of mahogany and walnut furniture noted above, he owned twelve silver spoons and sugar tongs, a silver pocket watch, silver shoe buckles, three looking glasses, thirty-three books, two German Bibles, and a ten-plate stove. The latter object suggests that Kessler preferred to heat his house in cold weather with a typically Germanic stove rather than an open fireplace, as was common in English households.[23]

ST. MICHAEL'S AND ZION LUTHERAN CHURCH

When Henry Melchior Muhlenberg arrived in Philadelphia in 1742, he was appalled by the "leaky slaughterhouse" (a rented facility) in which he had to preach his first sermon. He soon led the Lutheran congregation to acquire a lot on Fifth Street at Appletree Alley and embark on the construction of a church. Dedicated in 1748, St. Michael's was an impressive brick edifice that cost a substantial £1,607 to build and measured 45 by 70 feet (fig. 10.7). It was also the first church in Philadelphia to have a steeple tower, although the weight of the tower caused the exterior walls to bow and it had to be removed in 1750.[24] Among the church's original furnishings was a small, domed-lid chest inlaid with flowers and, on the lid, an image of the Agnus Dei, or Lamb of God (fig. 10.8). It was probably built to transport and store communion wafers; two crude slots were later cut into the lid to convert it into a ballot or alms box. Like the parrot-inlaid furniture discussed above, the chest has features that indicate it was likely made by a German émigré craftsman. St. Michael's had a seating capacity of eight hundred but was soon overcrowded. A brick schoolhouse was built in 1761 to provide additional space, and in 1765 the church's pews were altered to accommodate more people. The congregation soon became so large that these measures proved insufficient, even with the use of a third building (Whitefield Hall or New Building at the

FIGURE 10.7 Old Lutheran Church on Fifth Street, Philadelphia, 1800. Drawn and engraved by William Russell Birch and Thomas Birch, Philadelphia, 1800, and published in *Birch's Views of Philadelphia* (Philadelphia: W. Birch, 1800).

FIGURE 10.8 Chest, Philadelphia, ca. 1750. Walnut with mahogany and maple inlay. H 8¼ in., W 12¼ in., D 8 in.

FIGURE 10.9 New Lutheran Church on Fourth Street, Philadelphia, 1799. Drawn and engraved by William Russell Birch and Thomas Birch, Philadelphia, 1799, and published in *Birch's Views of Philadelphia* (Philadelphia: W. Birch, 1800).

College of Philadelphia), so a lot was acquired at Fourth and Cherry on which to build a new church (fig. 10.9). Robert Smith was hired as the architect, and construction began in 1766. Its brick exterior featured Venetian windows, brick pilasters, and ornately carved pediments and cornices together with a balustrade of urns on the roof. The interior was equally grand, with eight large fluted columns supporting the arched ceiling and galleries ornamented with a Doric entablature. When completed, Zion measured 108 by 70 feet and had seating capacity for 2,500; it was one of the largest public buildings in the country and cost more than £9,500 to construct. The church was dedicated on two successive days in June of 1769, with services held in German the first day and English on the second.[25]

In 1786, the congregation hired David Tannenberg, a Moravian, to make what would be the largest and finest organ built in eighteenth-century America. With three manuals (or keyboards) and thirty-four stops, it was Tannenberg's masterpiece and cost a staggering £1,500— he was not a member of the congregation. Measuring 24 feet wide, 27 feet high, and 8 feet deep, the case had five towers and more than one hundred pipes. On the central tower was an image of the sun rising above the clouds and flanked by gilded eagles, while the side towers had figures of trumpeting angels. The dedication of the organ in 1790 was held over three days due to the large crowds that attended, and Michael Billmeyer of Germantown printed a special pamphlet in German for the occasion.[26] Tragically, this magnificent organ did not last long. A devastating fire in December 1794 caused the church roof to collapse, gutting the interior and destroying the organ. The congregation decided to rebuild and hired William Colladay to oversee the project. Tannenberg offered to rebuild the organ for £3,000, but it was postponed for financial reasons and not completed until 1811. On November 27, 1796, the rebuilt church was consecrated. Two years later, on December 26, 1799, some four thousand people crowded into Zion to attend the state memorial service for George Washington, following a funeral procession that began at the Pennsylvania State House (now Independence Hall). Bishop William White, rector of Christ Church, led the service, and General Richard Henry Lee of Virginia delivered his famous eulogy from the pulpit. Eight years earlier, on March 22, 1791, Zion was used for Benjamin Franklin's memorial service due to its enormous capacity. A photograph of Zion taken in 1866 during the church's centennial celebration shows the post-1794 interior, with its elegant wineglass pulpit and sounding board topped with a blaze finial and neoclassical ornament on the galleries (fig. 10.10). Little else is known about the interior, as Zion was torn down in 1869; three years later, St. Michael's suffered the same fate.[27]

FIGURE 10.10 Photograph of Zion Lutheran Church interior, Philadelphia, Pennsylvania, 1866. On the wall behind the pulpit is a banner with an image of Henry Muhlenberg.

With the loss of these two buildings, the most tangible vestiges of Philadelphia's German community disappeared and its heritage was increasingly forgotten. Monocultural stereotypes of Philadelphia as the "Quaker City" have long obscured the German presence and reinforced a pervasive myth of English-speaking dominance that emphasizes the city's Quakers and Anglicans to the near-total exclusion of its sizable German-speaking population. When Henry Muhlenberg's son, Frederick, was elected the first speaker of the U.S. House of Representatives on April 4, 1789, by a landslide vote of 23–7, the *Philadelphische Correspondenz* proclaimed that "the blood of the grandchildren of our grandchildren will proudly well up in their hearts when they will read in the histories of America that the first Speaker. . . . was a German, born of German parents in Pennsylvania."[28] Yet Frederick Muhlenberg has rarely made the history books. His unpopular tie-breaking vote to fund the Jay Treaty in 1796 led to a fall from political power, followed by his early demise in 1801 at the age of fifty-one, likely have something to do with this. But the larger reason returns to the issue of how Pennsylvania German culture has come to be defined. Generations of scholars, antiquarians, and museum curators alike have interpreted objects such as a parrot-inlaid *Kleiderschrank* as Pennsylvania German, but not a rococo chair such as those made by Leonard Kessler. Thus, a redware teapot is easily recognized as Pennsylvania German, but not a silver sugar bowl—even when

FIGURE 10.11 Teapot, southeastern Pennsylvania, 1779. Lead-glazed red earthenware. H. 5⅝ in.

FIGURE 10.12 Sugar bowl by Christian Wiltberger, Philadelphia, ca. 1800. Silver. H 10¼ in.

both were made by German-speaking artisans living in Pennsylvania (figs. 10.11 and 10.12). As a result, our understanding of Pennsylvania German culture has been homogenized and compressed into a heavily skewed perception of what in reality was an extraordinarily diverse, dynamic, cosmopolitan, and often hybrid society. People such as the Muhlenbergs—along with other influential, affluent, and frequently urban

German speakers—do not conform to the rural peasant stereotype to which we are accustomed. Nor do the Muhlenbergs fit within the usual exalted ranks of the Founding Fathers or the English-speaking, Quaker mythology that characterizes most studies of the mid-Atlantic and colonial Philadelphia. Thus, when it is discovered that many elite Pennsylvania Germans such as the Muhlenbergs furnished their houses with stylish mahogany furniture, silver, china, and other expensive "English" goods, it becomes all too easy to interpret their actions as assimilation.[29] Why the distinction?

Being German in colonial Pennsylvania has come to be defined as ethnically distinctive, a boundary that during this period was much less rigid or clear than we think of it today. Ethnic identity was a much more fluid concept—especially in Philadelphia's cosmopolitan, multicultural society. Some objects, such as the group of parrot-inlaid furniture, evince strong connotations of their Germanic origins. Yet, as the rococo-style chairs made by Leonard Kessler demonstrate, material goods were not always ethnically distinctive. Ethnicity can also be expressed through language, religion, heating preferences, foodways, and other less tangible means. Nor was ethnicity always an either-or (English/German) choice, or even the foremost issue of one's identity. Many status-conscious, affluent Germans living in Philadelphia or elsewhere in southeastern Pennsylvania were first and foremost concerned with presenting a fashionable appearance. It simply may not have mattered to them whether the dovetails in a chest were wedged or the moldings were applied with wooden pegs versus nails, so long as the piece was well built and the overall appearance suited. Such objects helped people to become active participants in the lingua franca of sociability and refinement. Like people, material goods can have multiple identities; they cannot simply be consulted as a litmus test for evidence (or lack thereof) of a particular ethnicity. By furnishing their houses with fashionable goods, German-speaking consumers in colonial Pennsylvania were not necessarily seeking to become less German or more English. At the same time, Philadelphia craftsmen drew on both Continental and British sources to forge a diverse material world within a locally specific urban context. In the Babel that was colonial Pennsylvania, ethnicity, language, religion, and locale were all factors in shaping the formation of hybrid identities that were increasingly multicultural—and American—rather than German or English.

Notes

This essay includes text and images first published in Lisa Minardi, "Philadelphia, Furniture, and the Pennsylvania Germans: A Reevaluation," in *American Furniture*, ed. Luke Beckerdite (Hanover: University Press of New England for the Chipstone Foundation, 2013), 196–292; reproduced here with permission. These themes are explored more fully in my dissertation, "Germans in the Quaker City: Ethnicity, Religion, and Material Life in Early Philadelphia" (working title).

1. Henry Melchior Muhlenberg, *The Journals of Henry Melchior Muhlenberg*, trans. and ed. Theodore G. Tappert and John W. Doberstein, 3 vols. (1942; repr., Camden, Maine: Picton Press, 1980), 2:590.

2. On Germans as culture brokers and transatlantic participants, see, for example, Rosalind Beiler, *Immigrant and Entrepreneur: The Atlantic World of Caspar Wistar, 1650–1750* (University Park: Penn State University Press, 2008); Katherine Carté Engel, *Religion and Profit: Moravians in Early America* (Philadelphia: University of Pennsylvania Press, 2009); Diane E. Wenger, *A Country Storekeeper in Pennsylvania: Creating Economic Networks in Early America, 1790–1807* (University Park: Penn State University Press, 2008).

3. On German immigration, see Marianne Wokeck, *Trade in Strangers: The Beginnings of Mass Migration to North America* (University Park: Penn State University Press, 1999), esp. 37–46, 53. On Philadelphia's German population, see Marie Basile McDaniel, "Divergent Paths: Processes of Identity Formation Among German Speakers, 1730–1760," in *A Peculiar Mixture: German-Language Cultures and Identities in Eighteenth-Century North America*, ed. Jan Stievermann and Oliver Scheiding (University Park: Penn State University Press, 2013), 189. On ethnic settlement patterns, see Billy G. Smith and Paul Sivitz, "Notes and Documents: Identifying and Mapping Ethnicity in Philadelphia in the Early Republic," *Pennsylvania Magazine of History and Biography* 140, no. 3 (2016), 393–411.

4. See, for example, Russell F. Weigley, ed., *Philadelphia: A 300-Year History* (New York: W. W. Norton, 1982). Scott T. Swank et al., *Arts of the Pennsylvania Germans*, ed. Catherine E. Hutchins, exh. cat. (New York: W. W. Norton for the Henry Francis du Pont Winterthur Museum, 1983).

5. On material culture and ethnic identity, see Cynthia G. Falk and Lisa Minardi, "Pennsylvania, German, and Beyond," in *A Shared Legacy: Folk Art in America*, exh. cat. (New York: Skirra Rizzoli and Art Services International, 2014), 61–77; Cynthia G. Falk, *Architecture and Artifacts of the Pennsylvania Germans: Constructing Identity in Early America*, Publications of the Pennsylvania German Society 42 (University Park: Penn State University Press, 2008), esp. 1–11.

6. St. Michael's and Zion Churches were two distinct buildings owned and used by a single congregation known as St. Michael's and Zion.

7. See, for example, Alfred Crosby, *The Columbian Exchange: The Biological and Cultural Consequences of 1492* (Westport, Conn.: Greenwood, 1972); also Marcy Norton, *Sacred Gifts, Profane Pleasures: A History of Tobacco and Chocolate in the Atlantic World* (Ithaca, N.Y.: Cornell University Press, 2008). On parrots, see Louise E. Robbins, *Elephant Slaves and Pampered Parrots: Exotic Animals in Eighteenth-Century Paris* (Baltimore: Johns Hopkins University Press, 2002), esp. 109.

8. On European views of America, see Hermann Wellenreuther, "Amerika in Europa: Europäische Bilder and Vorstellung von Amerika vom 16. Bis ins 19. Jahrhundert," in *Freiheit, Fortschritt, und Verheißung: Blickwechsel zwischen Europa und Nordamerika seit der frühen Neuzeit* (Halle: Franckeschen Stiftungen, 2011), 13–27. For examples of maps depicting parrots, see Margaret Beck Pritchard and Henry G. Taliaferro, *Degrees of Latitude: Mapping Colonial America* (Williamsburg, Va.: Colonial Williamsburg Foundation, 2002), 83, 103, 112, 135. A copy of the New Ebenezer map is in the collection of the Museum of Early Southern Decorative Arts, acc. no. 2867.

9. On parrots and material culture, see Lisa Minardi, "Parrots and Empire in Early Modern Germany and America" (unpublished manuscript., University of Delaware, 2013). On Max Emanuel's cabinet, see Renate Eikelmann et al., *Prunkmöbel am Müncher Hof: Barocker*

Dekor unter der Lupe, exh. cat. (Munich: Bavarian National Museum, 2011), 50–51. On Maria Amalie Auguste's commode, see Wolfram Koeppe et al., *Extravagant Inventions: The Princely Furniture of the Roentgens*, exh. cat. (New York: Metropolitan Museum of Art, 2012), 88–91. On the *Papageienschrank*, see *Barockmöbel aus Württemberg und Hohenlohe 1700–1750*, exh. cat. (Ulm: Wüttembergisches Landesmuseum Stuttgart, 1985), 28–29.

10. Bruce Boehrer, "Men, Monkeys, Lap-Dogs, Parrots, Perish All! Psittacine Articulacy in Early Modern Writing," *Modern Language Quarterly* 59, no. 2 (1998): 171–93; Boehrer, *Parrot Culture: Our 2500-Year Long Fascination with the World's Most Talkative Bird* (Philadelphia: University of Pennsylvania Press, 2010), 1–5.

11. Amy R. W. Meyers and Margaret Beck Pritchard, *Empire's Nature: Mark Catesby's New World Vision* (Chapel Hill: University of North Carolina Press, 1998), passim.

12. On the Carolina parrot, see Joseph M. Forshaw, *Parrots of the World* (Princeton, N.J.: Princeton University Press, 2010), 312–13; Carole Boston Weatherford, *The Carolina Parakeet: America's Lost Parrot in Art and Memory* (Minneapolis: Avian Publications, 2005); Gottlieb Mittelberger, *Journey to Pennsylvania*, ed. Oscar Handlin and John Clive (Cambridge, Mass.: Harvard University Press, 1960), 57.

13. Michael Amenzetter's death is recorded in the church's records; see *18th Century Records of the German Lutheran Church at Philadelphia, Pennsylvania (St. Michael's and Zion)* (hereafter *SM&Z*), ed. F. Edward Wright, trans. Robert L. Hess, 5 vols., on *Pennsylvania German Church Records* CD-ROM, 5:1262. For more information on Amenzetter and this group of related furniture, see Minardi, "Philadelphia, Furniture," 213–29; also Wendy A. Cooper and Lisa Minardi, *Paint, Pattern, and People: Furniture of Southeastern Pennsylvania, 1725–1850* (Winterthur, Del.: Henry Francis du Pont Winterthur Museum, 2011), 29–31.

14. On Neisser, see William J. Murtaugh, *Moravian Architecture and Town Planning: Bethlehem, Pennsylvania, and Other Eighteenth-Century American Settlements* (Philadelphia: University of Pennsylvania Press, 1967), 5. On Wills, see Brian Loomes, *Watchmakers and Clockmakers of the World*, vol. 2 (London: N. A. G. Press, 1976), 255. The translated church records describe Maria Dorothea as the "English wife of Joseph Wills," but this is likely a mistake in the translation; the original intention was to identify Joseph, rather than his wife, as English. See *SM&Z*, 5:1096.

15. See Morrison H. Heckscher and Leslie Greene Bowman, *American Rococo, 1750–1775: Elegance in Ornament*, exh. cat. (New York: Harry N. Abrams, 1992), 59. For alternative views, see Minardi, "Philadelphia, Furniture," 200–203; also Falk, *Architecture and Artifacts*, 178–94.

16. Three men by the name of Johann Leonard Kessler emigrated from Germany to Philadelphia between 1749 and 1754; see Ralph Beaver Strassburger and William John Hinke, *Pennsylvania German Pioneers: A Publication of the Original Lists of Arrivals in the Port of Philadelphia from 1727 to 1808*, 3 vols. (Norristown, Pa.: Pennsylvania German Society, 1934), 1:397, 449, 661. Witnesses at Leonard Kessler's marriage are named in *Pennsylvania German Church Records of Births, Baptisms, Marriages, Burials, etc., from the Pennsylvania German Society Proceedings and Addresses*, 3 vols. (Baltimore: Genealogical Publishing, 1983), 1:658.

17. See Minardi, "Philadelphia, Furniture," 231–32.

18. Muhlenberg, *Journals*, 1:280, 564, 581–82, 590, 727; 2:35, 276–77, 766; 3:13. For a detailed discussion of the Muhlenberg chairs and other examples attributable to Kessler, see Minardi, "Philadelphia, Furniture," 233–37. On Henry Muhlenberg, see Hermann Wellenreuther, Thomas Müller-Bahlke, and A. Gregg Roeber, eds., *The Transatlantic World of Heinrich Melchior Mühlenberg in the Eighteenth Century* (Halle: Franckeschen Stiftungen, 2013); Lisa Minardi, *Pastors and Patriots: The Muhlenberg Family of Pennsylvania* (Collegeville, Pa.: Berman Museum of Art, 2011).

19. Will of John Gaul, dated January 16, 1769, proved February 1, 1769, Winterthur Library, Downs Collection, Philadelphia will books microfilm 1769, no. 239; Will of John Michael Barendt, dated August 31, 1780, proved October 15, 1780, Winterthur Library, Downs Collection, Philadelphia will books

microfilm 1780, no. 331; Will of George Adam Pfister, dated July 16, 1781, proved September 24, 1793, Winterthur Library, Downs Collection, Philadelphia will books microfilm 1793, no. 268. When Randolph's tools, lumber, hardware, and other shop equipment were dispersed in 1778, Kessler was paid "for a lot of carved work to be sold at auction" by the vendue master, John Ross; see Nancy Ann Goyne, "Furniture Craftsmen in Philadelphia, 1760–1780: Their Role in a Mercantile Society" (M.A. thesis, University of Delaware, 1963), 65. On Evans, see Eleanore P. Gadsden, "When Good Cabinetmakers Made Bad Furniture: The Career and Work of David Evans," in *American Furniture*, ed. Luke Beckerdite (Hanover: University Press of New England for the Chipstone Foundation, 2001), 65–87; also Gadsden, "From Traditional Cabinetmaking to Entrepreneurial Production: David Evans (1748–1819)" (M.A. thesis, University of Delaware, 2000). Daybooks of David Evans, Winterthur Library, Downs Collection, microfilm, passim.

20. The desk purchase is noted in Friederich Schenckel's account book of 1770 to 1775 (translation): "Bought a desk from carpenter Leonhart Köseler on February 24, 1773, for 22 pounds." The account book is in the Pennsylvania German Archives, Myrin Library, Ursinus College; thanks to Alan Keyser for this information and translation. Inventory of Leonard Kessler, taken April 27, 1804, Winterthur Library, Downs Collection, Philadelphia will books microfilm 1804, no. 16.

21. The initial survey is dated July 1, 1765, and the resurvey is dated August 4, 1772. The Philadelphia Contributionship Digital Archives, policy no. 1018. Information about workers' housing is from Bernard L. Herman, cited in Amy Hudson Henderson, "Furnishing the Republican Court: Building and Decorating Philadelphia Homes, 1790–1800" (Ph.D. diss., University of Delaware, 2008), 88.

22. *SM&Z*, 1:115, 143, 188, 252, 291; 5:1190; Muhlenberg, *Journals*, 1:467, 471, 475, 481, 486, 488, 490.

23. *Pennsylvania Packet, and Daily Advertiser*, Philadelphia, October 4, 1790, Early American Newspapers Database; *Pennsylvania Packet, and Daily Advertiser*, Philadelphia, October 22, 1790, Early American Newspapers Database; inventory of Leonard Kessler, taken April 27, 1804, Winterthur Library, Downs Collection, Philadelphia will books microfilm 1804, no. 16. On stoves, see Cynthia G. Falk, "Of Dwelling Houses, Painted Chests, and Stove Plates: What Material Culture Tells Us About the Palatines in Early New York," in Stievermann and Scheiding, *Peculiar Mixture*, 90–91, 101–3.

24. Muhlenberg, *Journals*, 3:36; see also 1:68–69.

25. Charles E. Peterson, *Robert Smith: Architect, Builder, Patriot, 1722–1777* (Philadelphia: Athenaeum of Philadelphia, 2000), 76; Muhlenberg, *Journals*, 2:277. Zion's dimensions are taken from the 1788 fire insurance survey; Philadelphia Contributionship Digital Archives, policy no. 2423.

26. Minardi, "Philadelphia, Furniture," 199–200; Raymond J. Brunner, *That Ingenious Business: Pennsylvania German Organ Builders* (Birdsboro, Pa.: Pennsylvania German Society, 1990), 85–87.

27. Minardi, "Philadelphia, Furniture," 197, 276; Peterson, *Robert Smith*, 89–93.

28. Minardi, *Pastors and Patriots*, 57–60; also Margaret C. S. Christman, *The First Federal Congress, 1789–1791* (Washington, D.C.: Smithsonian Institution Press for the National Portrait Gallery and the U.S. Congress, 1989), 31, 219–21. The *Philadelphische Correspondenz* is quoted in ibid., 219.

29. On ethnicity and status, see Falk, *Architecture and Artifacts*, 14–21, 194–97.

CONTRIBUTORS

CRAIG ATWOOD is the Charles D. Couch Professor of Moravian Theology and Director of the Center for Moravian Studies at Moravian College in Bethlehem, Pa. He is the author of *Community of the Cross: Moravian Piety in Colonial Bethlehem* (2004) and *The Theology of the Czech Brethren from Hus to Comenius* (2013), both published by Penn State University Press.

PATRICK M. ERBEN is Professor of English at the University of West Georgia, where he teaches early American literature. He is the author of "To Direct / My Loving Countrymans Defect': Translingual Education in German-Speaking Pennsylvania, 1683–1760," in *New Perspectives on German-American Educational History*, edited by Jürgen Overhoff and Anne Overbeck (Klinkhardt, 2017).

CYNTHIA G. FALK is Professor at the Cooperstown Graduate Program, a master's degree program in museum studies sponsored by the State University of New York College at Oneonta. She is the author of *Barns of New York: Rural Architecture of the Empire State* and *Architecture and Artifacts of the Pennsylvania Germans; Constructing Identity in Early America* (Cornell University Press, 2012). She served as the coeditor of *Buildings and Landscapes*, the journal of the Vernacular Architecture Forum, from 2012 to 2017, and is Deputy Mayor of the Village of Cooperstown.

KATHERINE FAULL is Presidential Professor of German and Humanities at Bucknell University. She is most recently the author of *Speaking to Body and Soul: Instructions for the Moravian Choir Helpers, 1785–1786* (Penn State University Press, 2017).

WOLFGANG FLÜGEL is currently engaged as a researcher at the Institut für Sächsische Geschichte und Volkskunde Dresden. He received the degree of D.Phil. in Early Modern History from the Technische Universität Dresden. After completing his dissertation, "Konfession und Jubiläum: Zur Institutionalisierung der lutherischen Gedenkkultur in Sachsen 1617–1830," in 2005, he worked within the framework of the "Lutherdekade" in connection with the Reformation Anniversary in 2017. In this context, his publications also focused on German Lutherans in North America in the eighteenth and early nineteenth centuries. His most recent essay is "1817 in Amerika: Das Reformationsjubiläum als Minderheitenphänomen," in *Jubiläum: Literatur- und kulturwissenschaftliche Annäherungen*, edited by Franz M. Eybl, Stephan Müller, and Annegret Pelz (V&R Unipress, 2017), 139–77.

KATHARINE GERBNER is Assistant Professor of History at the University of Minnesota. Her research explores the religious dimensions of race, authority, and freedom in early America, the Caribbean, and the Atlantic world. Her first book, *Christian Slavery: Conversion and Race in the Protestant Atlantic World* (University of Pennsylvania Press, 2018), shows how debates among slave owners, black Christians, and missionaries transformed the practice of Protestantism and the language of race.

MAURICE JACKSON teaches in the History, African American Studies, and Music departments at Georgetown University. He is author of *Let This Voice Be Heard: Anthony Benezet, Father of Atlantic Abolitionism* (University of Pennsylvania Press, 2010), and coeditor of *African Americans and the Haitian Revolution* (Routledge, 2009), *Quakers and Their Allies in the Abolitionist Cause, 1754–1808*, and *DC Jazz: Stories of Jazz Music in Washington* (Routledge, 2015). He issued "An Analysis: African American Employment, Population, and Housing Trends in Washington, D.C.," 2017. He is at work on a manuscript entitled "Halfway to Freedom: The Struggles and Strivings of African Americans in Washington, DC."

LISA MINARDI is Executive Director of the Speaker's House, home of Frederick Muhlenberg, in Trappe, Pa. Her most recent publication are the chapters "Fraktur and Visual Culture" and "Pennsylvania German Decorative Arts" in *Pennsylvania German Studies: A Research Guide*, edited by Simon J. Bronner and Joshua R. Brown (Johns Hopkins University Press, 2017).

JÜRGEN OVERHOFF is Professor of the History of Education at the Westfälische Wilhelms-Universität Münster, where he is also the Director of the Center for German-American Educational History. He has published numerous monographs and articles on early modern political thought, constitutional history, and the theory and practice of education in the Age of Enlightenment. He earned wide acclaim for his books on Frederick the Great, George Washington, and Charles-Louis de Montesquieu, all of which went into several editions: *Friedrich der Große und George Washington* (Klett-Cotta, 2011); *Montesquieu: Meine Reisen in Deutschland, 1728–1729* (Cotta, 2014).

BIRTE PFLEGER is Professor of History at the California State University, Los Angeles. She is the author of *Ethnicity Matters: A History of the German Society of Pennsylvania* (German Historical Institute, 2006). Most recently her article "Language, Ethnicity, and Citizenship in the Early Republic" appeared in *Pennsylvania Legacies*, published by the Historical Society of Pennsylvania (September 2016). She is currently researching the life and legacy of Kurt Molzahn, a German-born Lutheran clergyman in Philadelphia convicted of espionage for Nazi Germany in 1942, tentatively titled "Vergangenheitsbewältigung: The Pastor Who Was a Nazi Spy."

BETHANY WIGGIN is Associate Professor of German at the University of Pennsylvania, where she is the Founding Director of the Penn Program in Environmental Humanities. She is the author of *Novel Translations: The European Novel and the German Book, 1680–1730* (Cornell University Press, 2011) co-editor of *Un/Translatables: New Maps for Germanic Literatures* (Northwestern University Press, 2016), and co-editor of the special issue of the *German Studies Review, The Fall, or the Rise, of Monolingualism?* (2018). She is currently at work on *Germanopolis: Utopia Found and Lost in Penn's Woods*.

INDEX

Note: page numbers in italics refer to figures; those followed by n refer to notes, with note number.

An Account of the European Settlements in America (1757), 237
Account of the Province of Pennsylvania in America (Penn), 175
acculturation
  importance of language in, 147
  increase in, after American independence, 149
  language as marker of, 148
  rejection by some groups, 149
acculturation of German Lutherans
  and balance between change and cultural conservation, 149
  and development of hybrid American culture, 295
  ethnic mobility trap and, 150–51
  and generational conflicts over use of English, 151
  higher levels among elite and socially ambitious, 151
  higher levels in areas of frequent mixing, 151
  pastors leading, 148–49
  political events and, 151
  resistance to, 151–52
  willingness to accept, 148–49
  See also Charity Schools movement
Achenwall, Gottfried, 134, 135–36, 145n22
African Free School, 232–33
Albin, Eleazar, 279
Allen, Richard, 233, 242
Allen, William, 59

Almanac (Saur), 23, 35n53
Amenzetter, Michael, 280
American Babel (Shell), 5, 9
American Plan of Zinzendorf, 85–88
  and creation of Philadelphian Church of God, 88
  missions to European colonists, 86–87
  missions to Native Americans, 85–86
American Revolution, German service in, and claims to full citizenship, 203
Ames, William, 196–97n20
Anglophone culture
  efforts to convent German immigrants to, 21, 25, 43
  efforts to influence politics of German residents, 46
Anglophone scholarship, and monolingual fallacy, 11, 32n28
Antes, Henry, 88
Apter, Emily, 32n32
architecture of German immigrants in colonial Pennsylvania
  adoption of English design elements, 263–64, 264, 265
  characteristic stove design, 258–59, 259
  characteristic three-room plan, 257, 257–58, 258
  development of shared understanding of house design, 249–51, 252, 263–65, 269, 270–71
  eighteenth century experimentation in, 251, 252–53, 259–60, 263, 266–67, 269–70

interior decoration, 265–66, 266, 267, 269
introduction of central hallway, 252, 260, 261, 263
as landmarks, 254–56, 255
modest size and materials of most houses, 256
separation of kitchen from living areas, 252, 260, 264, 268–69, 269–70
as statement of identity, 252–53
use of stove-heated rooms, 259, 260, 261, 264, 269, 273n25, 289
verbal labels on, 267, 268, 270
architecture of German immigrants, and nonverbal communication, 251–52, 267–70
about wealth, 268
house size as, 256
materials used as, 256–57, 268
in religious buildings, 253, 253–56, 255
Armbrüster, Anthon, 45, 61
Armbrüster, Gotthard, 14, 33n39, 45
Arnold, Edmund C., 66
Atlantic history, and English American nationalism, 9, 31–32nn17–18
Augustine (saint), 42
Augustus Lutheran Church (Providence, Pennsylvania, 1743), 253, 253–56, 255

Babel
colonial language and culture diversity compared to, 2
Pennsylvania colony as, 18, 21
recasting of parable as celebration of diversity, 5, 30, 68
Babel, Tower of
Nimrod as builder of, 41–42
symbolic meaning of, 42, 67–68
Baer, Friederike, 163
Bannet, Eve Tavor, 32n28
Barbados
economic ties to Pennsylvania colony, 178
Fox's visit to, 177–78
as primary destination for Quakers in 1660s–70s, 177
Barbados, Quaker slaveowners in
conversion ethic justifying, 177–78, 186–88
emigration to Pennsylvania colony, 178, 187
gradual decline of, 193
number of, 196n6
Pennsylvania Quakers' request to cut off slave imports to Pennsylvania, 191

"To the General Meeting off ffriends In Barbados" letter to (1698), 191
Barendt, Johann Michael, 287
Baron Munchhausen's Narrative of His Marvellous Travels and Campaigns in Russia (Raspe), 134, 145n16
Bauman, Richard, 8, 9–10
Bechtel, Anna Margarethe. *See* Jungmann, Anna Margarethe Bechtel
Bechtel, Johannes, 101, 118
Beck, Ulrich, 30
Behr, Burchard Christian von, 134
Beissel, Conrad, 49–50, 71n31, 71n34, 88
Benedict and Anna Eschleman house (Conestoga Township,1759), 267, 268
Benezet, Anthony
on African collaborators with slave trade, 237
African history and culture, study of, 236
on African people, characteristics of, 236
on Africans' natural abilities, 237
antiwar pamphlets against American Revolution, 239
arguments constructed against slavery, 234–36
background of, 228–30, 232
calls for emancipation and reparations, 240
as catalyst of antislavery movement, 229
death of, 243
on destructiveness of slavery to both slave and owner, 234–35, 236
and development of new methods of antislavery activism, 244
early career as merchant's apprentice, 232
emancipation of slaves as life's mission, 232, 233
extensive reading by, 234–36
founding of Quaker girls' school, 232
and Free African Society, 233
freeing of kidnapped blacks by, 238
and Friends School for Black People, founding of, 232–33
funeral, large black attendance at, 243, 244
on illegitimacy of slavery, 234, 239, 246n31
influence of, 229, 231, 240–41, 244
on irony of rhetoric in American Revolution, 238–39
joining of Quakers, 232
Last Will and Testament of, 243
letter-writing campaign against slavery, 238

Benezet, Anthony (*continued*)
and Library Company of Philadelphia, 234
and natural law theory, 235–36
notable black students of, 233
Observations on the Inslaving of Negros, 230–31
and Philadelphia Germans, connections to, 231
predictions of slave revolt, 238, 239
Quaker faith of, and abolitionism, 233–34
and Quaker policy on slavery, influence on, 234
rejection of violent opposition to slavery, 235
research on slave trade, 237
Saur family and, 29, 194, 202, 230–31
on slave colonies of Jamaica and Barbados, 237–38
and slave trade, efforts to end, 241–42
on slave trade, evil origins and results, 234, 241–42
support for Native American grievances, 35n58
support for runaway slaves, 239–40
teaching career of, 232
teaching of blacks, 232–33
translation of works into French, 240
wife and children of, 232
Woolman and, 238
works on Africa, 236
Benezet, Jean Étienne [John Stephen], 228–30, 232
Benezet's African School House, 243
Bernard, Nicholas, 286
Bethlehem, Moravian commune at, 89–91
establishment of, 85
first residents of, 116
first Single Brother's House (1744), 260, 261, 263
as fullest expression of Moravian principles, 77, 89
as Moravian headquarters in North America, 89
as multilingual community, 89
music at, 89
polyglot singing at, 77
sexual practices, opposition to, 90
as threat to American economic values, 90
as threat to patriarchal order, 90
as threat to social order, 89–91

women on governing board of, 89
and Zinzendorf's American Plan, 85–88
Beyhülfe Vor die Teutschen Um Englisch zu Lernen (1751), 155
bilingualism among German immigrants
Charity Schools and, 60, 66
and debate on language of Lutheran services, 160–63
Franklin College and, 159–60
political overtones of debate on, 163–64
support for, 158–59
See also English language, German immigrants' use of
bilingual society, Franklin and Smith's inability to envision, 66–67
Billmeyer, Michael, 292
Block, Kristen, 176–77, 178
Boehme, Jacob, 42
Boltzius, Johann Martin, 54–55, 84, 85
Book of Discipline (1704), 192–93
Bowes, Michael, 287
Brickhouse, Anna, 45
Briggs, Charles, 8, 9–10
Brissot, Jean-Pierre, 240, 244
British Parliament, debate on ending slave trade, 240
Brookes, George, 229
Brown, Moses, 238
Brunnholtz, Peter, 152, 153, 154, 158
Buck-Morss, Susan, 31n12
Büninger, Martha, 107
Büttner, Anna Margarethe. *See* Jungmann, Anna Margarethe Bechtel
Büttner, Gottlob, 119, 120

Calvinists, German, concerns about free environment of colonies, 20–21
Carey, Brycchan, 177
Carondowana, 110
Catesby, Mark, 279, 280
Charity School for the Instruction of Poor Children Gratis in Useful Literature and the knowledge of the Christian Religion, 230
Charity Schools movement, 56–67
assimilation of German immigrants as goal of, 58, 59–60
bilingualism in, as tool of power and coercion, 60, 66
British withdrawal of funding in French and Indian War, 156

education of German immigrant children in English language and culture as goal of, 19, 56, 154
  as effort to impose Anglophone Protestantism, 21, 43
  financial problems of, 166n47
  fundraising for, 58
  German opposition to, 29, 155–56
  as imperialist project, 43, 57, 60, 66
  Mühlenberg's reasons for supporting, 59, 154–55, 156
  need for local supporters, 58–59
  and oppressive type of bilingualism, 56
  See also *Eine Kurtze Nachricht Von der Liebreichen Anstalt / A Brief History of the Charitable Scheme* (Smith)
Charlotte (Queen of Britain), 241
Charter of Privileges of Pennsylvania
  freedom of conscience in, 52
  guarantee of right not to bear arms, 14, 45
Cheyfitz, Eric, 44
Cheyney, Edward Potts, 133
Children's School, Germantown, 101
Christison, Wenlock, 179
Cincinnatus, as model for creation of cultural unity, 2
Clarkson, Thomas, 229, 240
classical education, as tool for creation of cultural unity, 2
Clavière, Étienne, 240
clockmakers, German, 281–82
Coates, Ta-Nehisi, 31n12
Colladay, William, 292
Collinson, Peter, 13, 14–15, 45, 57, 58, 60
Condorcet, Nicolas Caritat, marquis de, 240
Crell, John, 14, 17
Crell, Joseph, 71n27
Crèvecoeur, Hector St. John de, 19, 215
Cugoano, Quobna Ottobah, 229, 240–41
cultural identity
  language as marker of, 147, 148
  religion as marker of, 147
Curieuse Nachricht von Pennsylvania (Falckner), 104

Delaware Indians, conflict with settlers (1755)
  Quaker and pacifist efforts to mediate, 23–24
  Saur's sympathetic reporting on, 24, 25–28, 29
Deshler, David and Mary, 249, 270, 271n1

Deshler house (Germantown, 1772–74), 250
  architecture of, 249
  and development of shared understanding of house design, 251, 263, 270–71
  and eighteenth century architectural experimentation, 252–53
  nonverbal communication by, 252, 268
  notable occupants of, 249, 270
  size of, 256
Dimock, Wai-Chee, 32n32
Dippel, Johann Konrad, 37n64
disciplines, academic
  and obscuring of racism at heart of European idealism, 31n12
  as product of imperial project, 23
diversity of language and culture in colonial America
  effort to homogenize, as imperialist project, 43
  as exercise of freedom, 24
  and other "possible pasts," 29
  parallels to modern U.S., 10
  suppression of, in scholarship, 12–13
  See also Babel
diversity, fear of disorder resulting from
  among German clergy, 20–22
  and assumed normativity of English, 9
  Smith on, 2, 13
Dunn, Richard S., 177, 196n6

education of German immigrants
  Franklin College and, 159–60
  immigrant resistance to, 160
  lack of higher education institutions, and deacademization of clergy, 156–57
  Lutheran seminary, establishment of, 156, 157
  orientation toward English use, 157
  plans for German university, 157
  See also Charity Schools movement
Edwards, George, 279
Ehlich, Konrad, 10
Eine Kurtze Nachricht Von der Liebreichen Anstalt / A Brief History of the Charitable Scheme (Smith), 61–66, 62
  on advantages of learning English, 61–63
  attacks on Saur in, 63, 64, 65
  bilingualism in, as tool of power and coercion, 66
  conception of Germans as slaves and dupes, 65

Eine Kurtze Nachricht Von der Liebreichen Anstalt / A Brief History of the Charitable Scheme (Smith) (*continued*)
   on dire consequences of rejecting Charity School education, 63–64
   Franklin and, 66
   on full citizenship's dependence on adoption of English language and culture, 64–65
   implied hierarchy of languages in, 63
   side-by-side bilingual columns in, 66, 67
   stress on bilingual mutuality and balance in, 61
Einige Anmerkungen über Nord-Amerika und über dasige Grosbrittanische Colonien (Achenwall), 135–36, 145n22
Ellis, Elizabeth, 9
emancipation
   black inferiority arguments against, 214
   and concerns about black ownership of white indentured servants, 213
   German-speakers' opposition to, 213–14, 215–16
   Pennsylvania passage of, 214, 222n9
   private property arguments against, 213–14, 216
   types of arguments against, 216
Endress, Christian, 161, 163, 165
English language, German immigrants' use of
   and concerns about loss of German identity, 162
   for everyday dealings, 147, 148
   and generational conflicts, 151
   and increased Anglicization of names, 164–65
   increase in, 152
   Lutheran clergy's resistance to translation of devotional literature, 161
   and need to open Lutheran services to English, 165
   and pastor's need for fluency, 152–53
   and recasting of German identity as cultural and ethnic, 164
   and upward mobility, 164
English-only view of American nation
   need to move beyond, 3–4, 9–11, 32n28
   as product of imperial tradition, 3, 9, 43
Ephrata Cloister
   Beissel as leader of, 88
   Saur's wife and, 41, 49–50
   sexual abstinence at, 92
Equiano, Olaudah, 229, 240–41
Eschleman, Benedict and Anna, 267

Eschleman house (Conestoga Township,1759), 267, 268
An Essay on the Slavery and Commerce of the Human Species, Particularly the African (Clarkson), 240
ethnic identity, essential, dominance of concept in scholarship, 11, 32–33n29
ethnic mobility trap, German immigrants and, 150–51
Evangelical Magazine, 160
Evans, Eavid, 287
Evans, Lewis, 135
An Exhortation and Caution to Friends Concerning Buying or Keeping of Negroes (1693), 184

Falckner, Daniel, 104
Firmian, Leopold Anton von, 140
Fogleman, Aaron, 21, 75–76, 90
Forbes, John
   background of, 24
   questioning of Saur about French and Indian War reporting, 22–23, 25–28
   Saur on, 29
   Smith on, 24–25
Forten, James, 233, 243
Forten, James, Jr., 244
Fothergill, Samuel, 234
Foulke, Cadwaller, 229
Fox, George
   Gospel Family-Order, 178, 187, 188, 193
   on slavery, 177–78, 187, 193
Francke, August Hermann
   and Halle Foundations, 83
   influence on Whitefield, 137
   influence on Ziegenhagen, 139
   on modern Nimrods, 42
   and Moravians in Pennsylvania, opposition to, 84–85, 87
   Mühlenberg's feud with Saur and, 53–54
   and Mühlenberg's hope for seminary in Pennsylvania, 156
   and Paedagogium Regium, 136, 140, 141
   and Pietist research on Pennsylvania settlement possibilities, 104
   sending of Mühlenberg to Pennsylvania, 140
   Zinzendorf as student of, 83, 104
   See also *Kurtzer Bericht von der gegenwärtigen Verfassung des Paedagogii Regii zu Glaucha vor Halle* (Franke)
Francke, Gotthilf, 83
Francke Foundations in Halle, 21, 83, 148

Franklin, Benjamin
　Benezet and, 229, 231, 234, 238, 243, 245n7
　and bilingual society, inability to envision, 66–67
　and Charity Schools, assimilation of German immigrants as goal of, 58, 59–60, 154
　and Charity Schools, founding of, 56, 57
　effort to homogenize Pennsylvania groups, as imperialist project, 43
　funeral service of, 292
　German printing partners, and efforts to undermine Saur family's influence, 45
　historians' reevaluation of, 69
　honorary doctorate awarded to, 133
　and New Building, 230
　as Nimrod, 44, 57, 66
　Observations on Smokey Chimneys, 258
　Poor Richard's Almanac, 14, 23
　pseudonymous publications by, 70–71n27
　and Saur family printers, efforts to undermine influence of, 45, 46–51, 67
　and Saur Jr., friendship with, 231
　as slaveowner, 238
　and Smith's *Marania* plan, interest in, 13
　support for imperial political order, 68
　as suspected runaway servant, 207
　Woolman and, 238
　See also *Die Hoch-Teutsche und Englische Zeitung / High Dutch and English Gazette*; "Observations Concerning the Increase of Mankind" (Franklin); *Pennsylvania Gazette*; *Philadelphische Zeitung*; *Plain Truth* (Franklin)
Franklin, and Pennsylvania militia
　efforts to convince German immigrants of need for, 14–15, 44–45
　efforts to fund, 33n35
　German immigrants' opposition to, 14–15, 18, 45, 155
　See also *Plain Truth* (Franklin)
Franklin, and Philadelphia Academy
　description of, for German professors, 135–36
　investigation of English and Scottish models for, 133
　investigation of German models for, 133–36, 143–44, 145n21
　Observations relative to the Intentions of the Original Founders of the Academy in Philadelphia, 143
　and Paedagogium Regium as potential model, 136–37, 139–41
　as president of board of trustees, 131
　Proposals Relating to the Education of Youth in Pennsylvania on, 137, 138
　role in founding of, 131–32
　views on curriculum, 138–39, 143
Franklin, on German immigrants
　characteristic house design of, 258
　as danger to dominance of English language, 16–18, 57, 150
　as danger to English culture of colony, 20
　as danger to political unity of colony, 18, 43–44, 60
　efforts to undermine political power of, 45–46, 46–51, 67
　growing political influence of, 13–14, 45–46
　influence on opinions in England, 58
　methods for assimilating, 58
　racialized description of, 19–20, 207
　separatism of, 14–18, 57–58
　swarthiness of, 207
　unregulated presses run by, 57
Franklin College, 159–60
Free African Society, 233, 242–43
freedom, debate across languages on meaning of, 30
French and Indian War
　drafting of indentured servants in, 211
　fear caused by, 12
　Moravian loyalty in, as issue, 86
　and Native Americans, colonists' fear of, 86
　Pennsylvania Quakers' refusal to support, 211
　Saur's opposition to, 23–24
　Saur's reporting on, General Forbes' questioning of Saur about, 22–23, 25–28
Friendly Association
　founding of, 23–24
　multilingual history, need for, 35n58
　Saur and, 28, 29, 30
　support for Delaware grievances, 23–24, 35n58
Friend's English School, 232
Friends School for Black People, 232–33
Frost, J. William, 187–88
Fur, Gunlög, 102
Furly, Benjamin, 175
furniture by German immigrants
　chairs made for Henry Melchior Mühlenberg, 275–76, 276, 285–86, 295
　characteristics of, 275
　clock cases, 280–81, 281–82, 282

furniture by German immigrants (*continued*)
   and cultural hybridity of cosmopolitan Philadelphia, 277, 282, 286–87
   false stereotypes about, 283–84
   high level of craftsmanship in, 283
   hybrid cultural identity of, 278
   inlaid chest (ca. 1750), 290, 291
   Kleiderschrank [clothes cupboard] (1741), 279–80
   parrot/bird inlay motifs on, 275, 276, 278–83, *281*, 295
   Shoemaker family and, 284–85
   slant-front desk (1750), 280–81, *281*
   spice box (ca. 1740), 275, 276, 280
   See also Kessler, Leonard

Gaul, John, 286
General Idea of the College of Mirania (Smith), 13
George II (king of England), 56–57
"The German American Tradition Reconsidered" (Sollors), 5
German clergy, on Saur as Nimrod, 42–43, 53
German immigrant children, plan to educate. *See* Charity Schools movement
German immigrants
   achievement of white status, and adoption of Anglo racism, 203, 220
   characterization as "tawny" or "swarthy" by Anglos, 19, 21, 202, 206–7
   Charity School's efforts to assimilate, 21, 43, 58, 59–60
   decline in, in last third of eighteenth century, 151
   development of English-speaking German American identity, 163, 171n92
   encouragement to assimilate, as imperialist project, 44
   English-speakers' anxiety at influx of, 150
   and ethnic mobility trap, 150–51
   German Lutheran and Calvinist concerns about, 20
   high rate of marriage outside group, 46
   hopes for maintaining German subculture, 151–52
   increase after 1820s, 151
   large number in eighteenth century, 104, 149–50, 277
   move outside Philadelphia, 277
   number of slave owners, 206
   in Pennsylvania, limited involvement with slave labor, 205–6
   and Pennsylvania militia, opposition to, 14–15, 18, 45, 155
   scholars' tendency to focus on rural contingent of, 277, 293–95
   and slave labor, competition with, 212–13
   support for bilingualism in, 158–59
   tendency to concentrate in Pennsylvania, 166n10
   uneducated, concerns about effects of freedom on, 20–22
   See also acculturation of German Lutherans; architecture of German immigrants in colonial Pennsylvania; education of German immigrants; Franklin, on German immigrants; furniture by German immigrants; slavery, German immigrants' views on; *other specific topics*
German language
   decline of, as concern to German immigrants, 151–52
   decline of, in last third of nineteenth century, 158
   Helmuth on importance of retaining for worship, 159
   instruction in, at University of Pennsylvania, 157–58
   Kunze on importance of retaining for worship, 158–59
   Lutheran pastors' support for German educational system, 159
   Mühlenberg on importance of retaining for worship, 147, 152–53
   Mühlenberg on necessity of dropping to save Lutheran Church in America, 153, 155
   as second-most-spoken language in colonial mid-Atlantic, 11
German Society of Pennsylvania (GSP), 208–10, 224nn38–39
Germantown, Pennsylvania
   founding of, 175
   as quasi-independent chartered borough, 181
Germantown Quaker meeting
   founding of, 175
   leverage with other Quakers, 182
   place in Quaker meeting hierarchy, 195n2
Germantown Quaker meeting resolution condemning slavery (1688), 175–76, 182–83

arguments for equality of blacks and whites, 182
comparisons of black slaves and Turkish-enslaved Quakers, 182
as first in American colonies, 175
influence of arguments in, 183–84, 188–89, 194, 197n31
on inherent violence of slavery, 183
move through Quaker bureaucracy, 183
rejection of Yearly Meeting, 183
Germantown Quakers
European origins of, 181, 196–97n20
familiarity with persecution, 181, 182
as mostly former Mennonites, 181, 196–97n20
and rights-based antislavery arguments, development of, 176, 183–84, 194
settlement together as group, 181
Gersdorf, Henrietta Sophia von, 85
Gilberts, John, 180–81
Giles, Paul, 10
Glassie, Henry, 251
globalism
early modern, and colonial diversity of language and culture, 3
and monoglot nations as obsolete, 30
Gnadenhütten mission, 107, 112, 114, 118, 120
Gospel Family-Order (Fox), 178, 187, 188, 193
Gray, George, 186–88
Great Awakening, Moravians and, 87
Greenblatt, Stephen, 44
Grégoire, Henri, 240
Grier, Kasey, 251–52
GSP. *See* German Society of Pennsylvania
Gutenberg diagram, 66

Hadley, John, 133
Haidt, Valentin, 89
Halle (Prussia)
and New Ebenezer settlement, 140
as Pietist center, 83, 84–85, 88, 104
See also Francke Foundations in Halle; Paedagogium Regium (Halle)
Hamilton, Alexander, 256
Handschuh, Johann Friedrich, 153, 156
Hans Mirtel Gerick house (Exeter Township, 1941), 257
Hassencamp, Johann Matthäus, 135
HDEG. *See Die Hoch-Teutsche und Englische Zeitung / High Dutch and English Gazette*
Helmuth, Justus Heinrich Christian

and acculturation of German Lutherans, 148–49, 158
assignment to North America, 148
and debate on language of Lutheran services, 160, 161–62
and founding of Marshall College, 159
and German language education, 160
hopes for maintaining German subculture, 152
on importance of retaining German for worship, 159
and Lutheran seminary, 157
and Mosheim Society, 160
as opinion leaders, 148
politics of, 163
support for bilingualism in German immigrants, 159
support for German educational system, 159
Henry, Patrick, 229, 238
Hepburn, John, 194
Hiester, Daniel, 256
Hiester House, 256
High German American Calendar (1754), 151
Hirsch, Alison Duncan, 102, 108, 114
Hirschberg, synod of, 125n19
Die Hoch-Teutsche und Englische Zeitung / High Dutch and English Gazette (HDEG)
Anglicization of Germans as goal of, 61
bilingualism in, as tool of power and coercion, 43, 44, 60
on English as models for Germans, 49
on Germans as unreliable citizens, 49
Saur's response to attacks from, 53
side-by-side bilingual columns in, 47, 51, 60–61
and visual representation of superiority of English language, 51, 60–61
Die Hoch-Teutsche und Englische Zeitung, editorial attacking Saur in, 46, 50–52
criticism of Saur's poor writing, 51
Mühlenberg as probable author of, 50–51, 55
on Saur as heretic and seducer, 50–51
on Saur as unfit to discuss theology, 51–52
writer of, as Nimrod, 53
Die Hoch-Teutsche und Englische Zeitung, letter attacking Saur in, 46, 48, 49
comparison of Saur to Nimrod in, 41, 42, 49, 50, 55
on Saur trying to shoot his wife, 41, 49
writer of, as Nimrod, 53

Howe, William, 249, 270
Huguenots, persecution of, 228
Hutcheson, Francis, 235

idealism, European, racism as central to, 31n12
imperial tradition
    academic disciplines and, 23
    Charity Schools and, 43, 57, 60, 66
    cultural homogenization as project of, 43
    English-only view of American nation as product of, 3, 9, 43
    Franklin and, 68
    Mühlenberg and, 68
    resistance to, and creation of spaces of coexistence, 4
    use of translation as tool of conquest, 44–45
indentured servants and redemptioners
    auctioning and resale of, 207, 213
    cost of, in eighteenth century, 206
    drafting of, in French and Indian War, 211, 225n50
    runaway, as subject to capture and sale, 207
    runaway, Philadelphia newspaper ads for, 205–6, 211
    shortages of, in French and Indian War, and increased use of slave labor, 211–12, 225n49
    taxes on, vs. taxes on slaves, 208, 224n38
indentured servants and redemptioners, German immigrants as
    and employers' view of slaves and indentured servants as interchangeable, 210–12
    fear of being lumped in with slave labor, 206–10, 213, 220
    GSP as advocate for rights of, 208–10, 224n38
    laws declaring rights of, vs. black slaves, 203, 208–9
    laws prohibiting separation of families, 210
    robbing of, during Atlantic passage, 209
Indian Song for Peace (Smith), 19
The Interesting Narrative of the Life of Olaudah Equiano or Gustavus Vassa, the African (Equiano), 241
Ireland, Owen, 216
Isaac and Catherine Meier house (Myerstown, ca. 1757), 260, 263, 263, 264
Isaacson, Walter, 132

Jablonski, Daniel Ernst, 80
James and Mary Pennock house (West Marlboro Township, 1738), 264, 265
James Logan house (Germantown, 1723–30), 263–64, 264
Jay, John, 162, 229
Johannes Lesher house (Oley Forge, ca. 1750–55), 260, 262, 263, 264
Johan Peter and Maria Magdalena Troxell house (Egypt, 1756), 269, 269–70
Jones, Absalom, 233, 242
Jordan, Winthrop, 223n14
Joseph and Mary Pennock house (West Marlboro Township, 1738), 264, 265
Jostes, Birgit, 10
Judah, David, 143
Jungmann, Anna Margarethe Bechtel, 118–21
    activities in missionary work, 107–8
    background of, 118
    in Bethlehem, 119, 120, 121
    colleagues in missionary work, 102, 114, 116, 119, 122
    death of husband and son, 120
    first marriage of, 119
    fluency in Indian languages, 107–8, 120
    funeral of, 121
    on life as missionary, 119
    missionary colleagues of, 107
    missions served in, 102, 107, 114, 119, 120, 121
    recruitment to missionary work, 101, 118–19
    second marriage of, 120
    success as missionary, 101–2, 107
Jungmann, Johannes, 102, 120

Kalm, Peter, 204
Keith, George, 184, 185–86
Keppele, Henry, 224n39
Kessler, Leonard
    characteristics of furniture made by, 286
    children of, 288
    and cultural hybridity of cosmopolitan Philadelphia, 286–87
    economic success of, 287–88, 289
    furniture and carpentry work for Friedrich August Mühlenberg, 275–76, 276, 285–86, 295
    marriage of, 284
    as member of St. Michael's and Zion Lutheran Church, 284, 285, 288–89
    migration to America, 284
    Mühlenberg as minister to, 288–89

range of furniture types produced by, 287
side-businesses of, 289
training as cabinetmaker, 284
Kunze, Johann Christoph
and acculturation of German Lutherans, 148–49, 150–51, 158
on America as promised land, 171n92
assignment to North America, 148
and debate on language of Lutheran services, 160, 162, 163
on German language, decline in use of, 158
on importance of retaining German for worship, 158–59
and Lutheran seminary, 157
as opinion leaders, 148
support for bilingualism of German immigrants, 158–59
Kurtzer Bericht von der gegenwärtigen Verfassung des Paedagogii Regii zu Glaucha vor Halle (Franke), 139–41
as account of Paedagogium Regium rules and regulations, 141
discussion about, among Philadelphia Academy trustees, 140–41, 142
English translation for Philadelphia Academy, 140, 142
as gift to Franklin from Ziegenhagen, 139–40
influence on Philadelphia Academy's rules and regulations, 141–43

Labaree, Leonard W., 140
language
Enlightenment neo-Platonist view of, 44
as inherently plural, 8–9
as mark of cultural identity, 147–48
and modernity's separation of subjectivity and science, 8, 31n16
See also English language; German language
language of larger society
as citizenship requirement, 162
ethnic mobility trap and, 150–51
failure to learn, as handicap for social advancement, 148, 150
immigrants' use for everyday dealings, 147, 148
Latin: Study of a World Language (Leonhardt), 10–11

Latour, Bruno, 8
Die Lautere Wahrheit (Franklin, Crell trans.), 14, 17, 45
Leckler, Anthony, 287
Lemay, A. Leo, 70–71n27
Leonharet, Jürgen, 10–11
Lesher house (Oley Forge, ca. 1750–55), 260, 262, 263, 264
Letters from an American Farmer (Crèvecoeur), 19, 215
Levi, Moses and Nathan, 143
Levy, Barry, 184
Library Company of Philadelphia, 234
linguistic borders, individuals moving between, 4
linguistic diversity of colonial America, imperial projectors' efforts to silence, 9
Liu, Lydia, 3
Logan, James, 234, 263
Logan house (Germantown, 1723–30), 263–64, 264
Lorsch Abbey, 272n15
Luther, Martin, 42, 158
Lutheran Church in America
admission of blacks to congregations, 217, 226n65
concerns about parishioners in free environment of colonies, 20–21
deacademization of clergy in, 156–57
debate on language of services in, 160–64
development of English-speaking congregations, 163
growth of political and class divisions in, 163–64
increasing use of English, and need for English services, 165
lack of higher education institutions, and deacademization of clergy, 156–57
as largest Pennsylvania denomination by 1775, 201
Mühlenberg on necessity of dropping German language to save, 153, 155
Mühlenberg on schools' role in preserving, 154
Mühlenberg's efforts to preserve, 156
pastors shaping, 148
political overtones of language debate in, 163–64
as stronghold of German ethnicity, 148
See also acculturation of German Lutherans

Lutheran parochial schools, teacher shortages in, 154
Lutheran seminary in Pennsylvania
  establishment of, 156, 157
  integration into University of Pennsylvania, 157

Mack, Johanna "Jannetje" Rau
  background of, 112
  colleagues in missionary work, 102, 107, 114, 119, 120, 122
  missions served in, 107, 112–14, 120
  and Montour, 110
  recruitment to missionary work, 112
Mack, Martin, 102, 112, 113, 114, 120
Manning, Susan, 32n28
"...map of the improved part of the Province of Pennsylvania . . . ." (Turner), 254–56, 255
Marcus, Greil, 23
Marriot, Joyce, 232
Maryland, Quaker slaveowners in, 179, 196n12
material culture
  fashionable, German participation in, 295
  fashionable, tendency to identify as English, 295
  German, and cultural hybridity of cosmopolitan Philadelphia, 277, 282, 286–87, 293–95, 294–95
  nonverbal communication by, 251–52
  See also architecture of German immigrants in colonial Pennsylvania; furniture by German immigrants
McCracken, Grant, 251
McDaniel, Marie Basile, 46
Meier house (Myerstown, ca. 1757), 260, 263, 263, 264
Meniolagomekah mission, 107
Merrell, James, 35n58, 102, 108–9, 123n6
Merritt, Jane, 3, 102, 107
"Methodus der Wilden bekehrung" (Zinzendorf), 106, 113
Michaelis, Johann David, 134, 135, 136
Middle States, Quaker slaveowners in, 178–80
militia ("Voluntary Association" for the defense of Pennsylvania), 45
  efforts to fund, 33n35
  Franklin's efforts to convince German immigrants of need for, 14–15, 44–45
  German immigrants' opposition to, 14–15, 18, 45, 155

Saur's opposition to, 23, 45
  See also *Plain Truth* (Franklin)
Mirabeau, Gabriel Victor Riqueti, comte de, 240
Mittelberger, Gottlieb, 20, 21–22, 34n48, 204, 279
modernity
  instrumental conception of language in, 8
  separation of subjectivity and science in, 8, 31n16
monoglot nations, as obsolete in globalized world, 30
monolingual fallacy, 8–9, 9–11, 29, 277
Montesquieu, Charles Louis Secondat, Baron de, 234–35
Montour, Andrew, 108, 110, 112–13
Montour, Isabelle, 110, 112–13
Moravians
  accusations of doctrinal chamelionism against, 83
  adoption of Augsburg Confession, 80
  adoption of early church rituals, 79–80
  beliefs of, 76, 78, 91–93
  beliefs, critiques of, 98–99n70
  beliefs, difficulty of determining, 91
  black community members, reluctance to accept, 205
  claimed descent from Hussite Unity of the Brethren, 78, 81
  controversy stirred by missions of, 81–82, 83, 85, 86
  cultural identity of, 147–48
  development of name for, 80–81
  embrace of all people and races as equals, 76, 77
  exile from Moravia and Bohemia, 79
  forced withdrawal from aggressive missions, 88, 94
  and gender norms, challenges to, 77, 89, 90–91, 92, 93
  gradual adoption of traditional practices, 76, 91, 94
  increased opposition to, with increased success, 83, 94
  legal status of, as issue, 80, 81, 82–83
  migration to U.S., increased radicalism following, 77
  missions to Native Americans, 76, 84, 85–86
  missions to slaves, 76, 81, 84
  as multiethnic, international church, 82

and Native American languages, production of religious texts in, 85
and Native Americans, views on, 86
New York's expulsion of missionaries, 112
and nonhierarchical multilingualism, commitment to, 77, 82, 85–86, 89
opponents' pursuit to North America, 75
as organized and energetic, 75
polyglot singing by, 77, 82, 89
rapid growth of, 75, 230
recognition as church by British Parliament, 76, 82
religious conflicts of eighteenth-century Europe and, 77–83
riot against, 83, 87, 93
on sanctity of human body, 91–92
scapegoating of, 94
sexual practices, controversy stirred by, 92–93
and slavery, views on, 204–5
success in attracting followers, 93–94
as threat to patriarchal order, 90–91
as threat to social order, 75–76, 77, 82–83, 89–90
Tropus plan of, 82
Wachovia Tract, purchase of, 76
Zinzendorf's influence on, 89
See also Bethlehem, Moravian commune at; women as Moravian missionaries to Indians; Zinzendorf, Nicholas Ludwig von, Count
Moravians, ecumenism of
and association with fringe elements, 88
controversy surrounding, 81
as threat to confessional identities, 76, 77, 88
and welcoming of worshipers without requiring change of denomination, 79, 82
Moravians at Herrnhut village (Saxony), 75
aggressive missions of, 81–82
and Brotherly Agreement, 80, 230
controversy surrounding, 81
establishment of, 78–79
power rivalry with Pietists at Halle, 83, 84–85
practices adopted by, 79–80
separate common houses for single men and women, 80
as threat to religious and political order, 78, 81

Zinzendorf's Philadelphian project and, 79
Moravians in British North America, 84–88
architecture of, 260, 261
arrival as organized missionary force, 84
colonists' need for teachers and, 154
colonists' need for trained clergy and, 86–87
educated clergy of, 84
first colony in Georgia, 84
and loyalty in Seven Years War, as issue, 86
Lutheran opposition to Moravians in Pennsylvania, 84–85
massacre at Gnaddenhütten, 86
missions to European colonists, 86–87
Morgan, Cadwallader, 185, 186, 193, 197n31
Morris, Lewis, 178
Mosheim Society, 160, 161, 162, 171n78
mother tongue, native speakers of, assumed primacy of, 9–11
Mühlenberg, Friedrich/Frederick August, 160–61, 162, 293
Mühlenberg, Gotthilf Heinrich, 159, 161
Mühlenberg, Heinrich "Henry" Melchior
and acculturation of German Lutherans, 148–49, 158
on America as "western desert," 171n92
arrival in America, and encounter with slaves, 199
assignment to North America, 140, 148
and Augustus Lutheran Church, 253
and building of St. Michael's Church, 289–90
and Charity Schools, 56, 59, 154–55, 156
death of son, 285
and debate on language of Lutheran services, 147, 152–53, 155, 161, 162
desire for seminary in Pennsylvania, 156
efforts to preserve Lutheran Church in America, 156
effort to homogenize Pennsylvania groups, as imperialist project, 43
Francke as mentor of, 42, 46, 54
on free blacks, 216, 217, 218, 219
furniture and carpentry work by Kessler for, 275–76, 276, 285–86, 295
on German language, importance of retaining for worship, 147, 152–53
on German language, necessity of dropping, to save Lutheran Church in America, 153, 155

Mühlenberg, Heinrich "Henry" Melchior (*continued*)
    German servants, troubles with, 219–20
    and immigrant Pietists, efforts to return to fold, 20–21
    on importance of fashionable appearance, 11, 286
    journal, inaccuracies in English translation of, 33n32
    as minister to Kessler, 288–89
    ministry in New York, 55–56
    on Moravian beliefs, 83, 87, 99n70
    and Moravians in Pennsylvania, opposition to, 84–85, 86, 87, 88, 93, 154
    multilingual ministry of, 55–56
    as Nimrod, 44, 55, 59
    as opinion leaders, 148
    and Paxton Boys murders, 86
    and Philadelphia Academy, son's education at, 144
    and polyglot hymn singing, 56
    on poor morals of later German immigrants, 219–20
    and proliferation of religious opinions, concerns about, 56
    on schools, shortage of teachers in, 154
    on schools' role in preservation of Lutheranism, 154
    on stove heat, benefits of, 259
    support for German educational system, 159
    support for imperial political order, 68
    travels in South, 199–200, 219
Mühlenberg, and Saur
    criticism of, as Nimrod-like, 42–43
    criticism of Bible printed by, 54
    desire for printing press to challenge, 53, 54, 59
    efforts to undermine, 59, 67
    Mühlenberg as probable author of *HDEG* editorial attacking Saur, 50, 55
    on Saur's attacks on clergy, 54–55
    Saur's verbal attacks on, 53–54
Mühlenberg, on English language
    need for, in ministering to acculturated Lutherans, 152–53
    need for, in representing church in public, 153
    use for everyday dealings, 147, 148, 151, 152
Mühlenberg, on slavery, 216–20
    benefits of not keeping slaves, 219
    benign nature of, in Pennsylvania, 204, 216, 217–18
    condemnation of slave owners unwilling to teach Christianity to slaves, 199
    condemnation of white fornicators with slaves, 199
    early distaste for, 199
    feared retribution for wrongs of, 218
    later acceptance as American norm, 199–200, 216–20, 222n8
    as non-German institution, 200–201, 200–201
    representativeness of views on, 204, 223n16
    views on slaves, 200, 216, 217
Mühlenberg, John Peter Gabriel, 144, 163, 216–17, 220
Mühlenberg family, sophistication of, 294–95
Mulsow, Martin, 30
multilingualism, as normative state, 8–9, 9–11
multilingualism in colonial mid-Atlantic, 4
    and cultural and linguistic transactions, 30
    mix of languages, 3
    need to recover lost voices of, 23
    Saur and, 24
multilingualism in Pennsylvania, Crèvecoeur on, 19
Münchhausen, Gerlach Adolph, Baron von, 134
Münchhausen, Hieronymus Carl Friedrich von, 134

nationalist phase in American culture, and English monolingualism, 10
Native Americans
    Christian conversions of, as discounted, 86, 125n28
    colonists' fear of, in Seven Years War, 86
    grievances against settlers, Quaker and pacifist support for, 23–24
    Moravian missions to, 76, 84, 85–86
    Moravians' views on, 86
    native identity after conversion to Christianity, 109
    and Paxton Boys murders, 86
    Pietist views on, 104
    Quakers' Friendly Association to support, 23–24, 28, 29, 30, 35n58
    Saur's sympathetic reporting on, 24, 25–28, 29
    and translation as tool of imperial conquest, 44

See also French and Indian War; women as Moravian missionaries to Indians
A Natural History of Birds (Albin), 279
Natural History of Carolina, Florida and the Bahama Islands (Catesby), 279, 280
A Natural History of Uncommon Birds (Edwards), 279
Neisser, Augustin, 281–82
Newbie, Nathan, 179–81
New Building, 230, 290–91
New Ebenezer settlement, 140
Nimrod
    attackers on Saur as, 41, 42–43, 53, 55, 65
    as biblical tyrant and deceiver, 41–42, 67
    as builder of Tower of Babel, 41–42
    Franklin as, 44, 57, 66
    as master propagandist, 67–68
    Smith as, 44, 57, 66
Nitschmann, Anna, 101, 114, 118
Nitschmann, David, 80
Notes on the Slave Trade (Benezet), 239, 241–42

"Observations Concerning the Increase of Mankind" (Franklin)
    Franklin's latter efforts to remove criticisms of German immigrants from, 34n41
    on French threat, 18
    on German immigrants as danger to dominance of English language, 16–18
    on German immigrants as danger to political unity, 18
    publication history of, 33–34n41
    racialized description of German immigrants in, 19–20, 207
"Observations for the Explication of the Foregoing Accounts." See *Kurtzer Bericht von der gegenwärtigen Verfassung des Paedagogii Regii zu Glaucha vor Halle* (Franke)
Observations on Smokey Chimneys (Franklin), 258
Observations on the Inslaving, Importing and Purchasing of Negroes (Benezet), 236
Observations on the Inslaving of Negros (Benezet), 230–31
Observations relative to the Intentions of the Original Founders of the Academy in Philadelphia (Franklin), 143
Oceanic Atlantic history, and move beyond idea of English-speaking American nation, 3

Oley Forge mansion. See Johannes Lesher house (Oley Forge, ca. 1750–55)

Paedagogium Regium (Halle)
    curriculum at, 137, 141, 143
    founding of, 136
    Francke and, 136, 140, 141
    Philadelphia Academy and, 136–37, 139–41, 141–43
    strong discipline at, 141–42
    Zinzendorf as student at, 104
parrots
    Carolina parrot, 279, 280
    European fascination with, 278, 279
    Europeans' comparison to indigenous people, 279
    as symbol of New World, 278, 283
parrots as furniture inlay motif
    conventions of representations, 283
    in furniture made by German immigrants, 275, 279–83, 295
    image sources used for, 279, 283
    popularity in Germany, 278–79
Pastorius, Francis Daniel, 153, 175, 181
Paxton Boys, 86
Peace of Westphalia, 78, 80, 81
Pedagogium. See Paedagogium Regium (Halle)
Pemberton, Israel, 24, 35n58
Penn, John, 209
Penn, William
    advertisement of Pennsylvania colony to German- and Dutch-speaking Protestants, 175
    and Germantown Quakers, 181
    missions to German Mennonites, 196–97n20
    on slavery, 210
Pennock, James and Mary, 264
Pennock house (West Marlboro Township, 1738), 264, 265
Pennsylvania colony
    economic ties to Barbados, 178
    laws distinguishing indentured servants from black slaves, 208–10
    mass immigration in mid-eighteenth century, 149
    as transnational space, 11
Pennsylvania Gazette
    on Benezet's funeral, 243
    on opening of New Building, 230
    real estate ads in, 256

Pennsylvania Gazette (continued)
  runaway slave and servant ads in, 205–6, 223–24n27
The Pennsylvania Gazette, 61, 70n27, 137
Pensylvanische Berichte
  attacks on pastor Bartholemäus in, 49, 52–53, 54
  circulation of, 46
  on Forbes' questioning of Saur, 22–23, 25–28
  runaway slave and servant ads in, 205–6, 211, 223nn24–25
  Saur's response to attacks from *HDEG* in, 53
Pestana, Carla, 21
Peter and Rosina Margaretha Wentz house (Worcester Township, 1758), 264–66, 266
Peters, Richard, 46
Pfister, George Adam, 287
Philadelphia, in eighteenth century
  as diverse, cosmopolitan city, 277, 282, 286–87, 293, 295
  false stereotype as Quaker city, 293, 295
  first White House in, 225n46
  German immigrants in, as often ignored in historical accounts, 277, 293
  large number of German immigrants in, 104, 149–50, 277
  mix of religions, races and ethnicities in, 46, 231
  slave population of, 231
  white population of, 231
Philadelphia Academy/College
  addition of medical school, 133
  founding of, 131–32
  Lutheran community leaders' support of, 144
  and New Building, 230
  Paedagogium Regium as potential model for, 136–37, 139–41
  Paedagogium Regium influence on, 141–43
  religious observances at, 144
  renaming as University of Pennsylvania (1791), 131
  Smith as head of, 2, 19
  strict discipline at, 142–43
  students, broad range of religious affiliations in, 143
  students, Jewish, 143
  See also University of Pennsylvania

Philadelphia Academy/College, Franklin and
  description of, for German professors, 135–36
  investigation of English and Scottish models for, 133
  investigation of German models for, 133–36, 143–44, 145n21
  Observations relative to the Intentions of the Original Founders of the Academy in Philadelphia, 143
  and Paedagogium Regium as potential model, 136–37, 139–41
  as president of board of trustees, 131
  Proposals Relating to the Education of Youth in Pennsylvania on, 137, 138
  role in founding of, 131–32
  views on curriculum, 138–39, 143
Philadelphia Academy/College curriculum
  emphasis on modern rather than classical languages, 132, 138–39, 143
  emphasis on moral philosophy, 132
  vs. other colonial colleges, 132, 138
  range of subjects in, 132, 143
  religion in, 136, 138, 143–44
  Whitefield on, 137–40
Philadelphian movement, 79, 84, 88
Philadelphische Correspondenz, 162
Philadelphische Zeitung, 61
Pietists
  Halle as center of, 83, 84–85, 88, 104
  and Moravians, 79
  preference for emotional sermons, 156
  research on Pennsylvania settlement possibilities, 104
  rivalry with Moravians, 83, 85, 88
Piles, Robert, 188–90
Plain Truth (Franklin), 14, 15, 16
  German translation of, 14, 17, 45
  Saur's responses to, 45, 69n19
  support for militia resulting from, 14
  and translation as tool of imperial conquest, 44–45
Plan Von Neu Ebenezer (1747), 278
Pleasants, Robert, 238
Pliny the Elder, 1, 2
Powell, Joseph, 116, 117, 118
Powell, Martha Pritchett, 115–18
  background of, 115–16, 126n43
  at Bethlehem, 116, 118
  challenges to faith of, 109
  colleagues in missionary work, 116, 117, 120, 122

migration to America, 116
missions served at, 116–17, 118
recruitment by Zinzendorf, 116
power and oppression, masking of, by blaming dissidents, 67–68
Pratt, Mary Louise, 3
Priest, William, 213
Primitive Hall (West Marlboro). *See* Joseph and Mary Pennock house (West Marlboro Township, 1738)
Proposal for Erecting Indian Schools (Smith), 19
Proposals Relating to the Education of Youth in Pennsylvania (Franklin), 137, 138
Proprietary Party, 46
Protestant groups in Pennsylvania, use of translation to overcome factionalism, 44
Protestants of eighteenth century, persecution in Holy Roman Empire, 78
Prown, Jules, 251–52
purification, epistemology of, 8
Pütter, Johann Stephan, 134, 135, 145n21
Pyraleus, John, 230

Quaker meetinghouses, design of, 254
Quakers
 in founding of Germantown, Pennsylvania, 175
 and prophetic dream tradition, 190
Quakers, from England and Wales
 acceptance of limited form of slavery, 176
 concerns about family order, 193
 focus on slavery's impact on Quaker owners, 176
 See also Quakers, from Wales and Cheshire
Quakers, from Germany. See *entries under* Germantown
Quakers, from Wales and Cheshire
 antislavery activism by, 193
 family practices of, 184–85
 settlement apart from English Quakers, 184
 as slaveowners, 185
Quakers and slavery
 caution about manumission, 190
 concerns about effects on slaveowners, 189–90, 191
 concerns about impact of slaves in Quaker household, 176, 180–81, 184, 185, 186, 188–90, 193

concerns about lack of discipline in Quaker families, 191–93
concerns about slaves' sexual misconduct, 185, 193
conversion ethic justifying slaveowners, 176, 177–78, 186–88, 191
debates on, in Monthly, Quarterly, and Yearly meetings, 185, 191–92, 193–94, 197n31
development of international debate on, 194
differences in German/Dutch vs. English/Welsh views, 176, 177
disciplining of slaves as issue, 179–80
efforts to establish "godly" slaveholding, 178
efforts to integrate slaves into household, 178–79
exclusion of slaveowners from Pennsylvania congregation (1773), 202
An Exhortation and Caution to Friends Concerning Buying or Keeping of Negroes (1693), 184
and fear of slave rebellion, 183, 189
Fox's views on, 177–78
Golden Rule arguments against slavery, 182, 188
gradual move toward antislavery position, 194–95, 202
majority of Quakers as not anti-slavery, 176
Piles's letter rejecting slave ownership, 188–90
rights-based arguments against slavery, 176, 183–84, 194
and risk of drawing "bad" slaves, 185
sexual misconduct with slaves, 180–81
slave auctions, condemnation of, 191
treatment of slaves as issue, 180
and tribalist antislavery arguments, 186, 193, 197n35
Yearly Meeting statement on slavery (1696), 186
See also Germantown Quaker meeting resolution condemning slavery (1688); Germantown Quakers; Quaker slaveowners
Quakers and slave trade
 appeal to London Yearly Meeting to restrict, 193–94
 London Yearly Meeting statement on, 194
 Philadelphia Yearly Meeting policy on, 186, 190, 193, 202, 234

Quakers in Pennsylvania
    Book of Discipline (1704), 192
    campaign against superfluous furniture
        and dress (early 1700s), 192
    campaign to increase discipline in Quaker
        households (late 1690s), 191–93
    campaign to purge worldliness (1694),
        185–86
    and household Gospel Order, 192
Quaker slaveowners in Barbados
    as common, 177
    conversion ethic justifying, 177–78, 186–88
    emigration to Pennsylvania colony, 178, 187
    gradual decline of, 193
    number of, 196n6
    Pennsylvania Quakers' request to cut off
        slave imports to Pennsylvania, 191
    "To the General Meeting off ffriends In
        Barbados" (1698) letter to, 191
Quaker slaveowners in Maryland, 179, 196n12
Quaker slaveowners in Middle States, 178–80
Quaker slaveowners in Pennsylvania, 178,
    180–81
Quaker slaveowners in Virginia, 179–80
Quakers slaveowners in Pennsylvania, 178,
    180–81

race, as little-used term before early nineteenth
    century, 204
racism, as central to European idealism, 31n12
Randolph, Benjamin, 287
Raspe, Rudolph Erich, 134, 145n16
Raynal, Guillaume-Thomas, 229, 240
Reiche, Karl Christoph, 213–14, 226n65
Reise nach Pennsylvanien (Mittelberger), 20,
    21–22, 34n48
religion, as mark of cultural identity, 147
religious buildings of eighteenth century,
    nonverbal communication in, 253,
    253–54, 255
religious conflicts in eighteenth-century
    Europe, 77–83
    complexity of, 78
    and exile of Moravians from Moravia and
        Bohemia, 79
    and religious dissent as social and politi-
        cal dissent, 78
Richter, Daniel, 3, 30
Roeber, Anthony Gregg, 28, 160
Roman Empire, as model for creation of cul-
    tural unity, 2, 12, 13
Rush, Benjamin, 233, 234, 238

St. Michael's and Zion Lutheran Church
    Kessler as member of, 284, 288–89
    Kessler's carpentry work for, 285
    members of, 280, 282
    See also Zion Lutheran Church (Fourth
        and Cherry Streets, Philadelphia)
St. Michael's Church (5th Street, Philadel-
    phia), 254, 290
    construction of, 289–90
    demolition of, 292–93
    financial dispute at, 288–89
    inlaid chest owned by, 290, 291
    schoolhouse built at, 288, 290
    use of New Building, 290–91
*Sammlung verschiedener ausländischer und
    seltener Vögel* (Seligmann), 279
Sancho, Charles Ignatius, 240
Saur, Christoph
    Almanac, 23, 35n53
    attack on Ephrata to recover wife, 49
    background of, 23, 37n64
    Beissel and, 49–50
    Benezet and, 29, 194, 202, 230–31
    career of, 230
    and Charity Schools, opposition to, 29,
        155–56
    comparison to Nimrod by Franklin and
        others, 41, 42–43, 53, 55, 65
    criticisms of Moravians, 88
    as culture broker, 30
    diverse, polyglot American experienced
        by, 12–13
    engagement with public sphere, 28–29
    exclusion from American canon, 12–13, 23
    on Forbes, 29
    and freedom to express opinion, 24
    and French and Indian War, opposition
        to, 23–24
    Friendly Association and, 28, 29, 30
    German Bible printed by, 23, 52
    German Bible, clergy's criticism of, 51–52,
        54
    and German right to linguistic and cul-
        tural distinctiveness, 43–44, 67, 68
    and human rights advocacy, 29, 30
    and immigrants' learning of English,
        views on, 155
    influence of, 29, 46
    Mühlenberg's efforts to undermine, 59
    and multilingualism in Pennsylvania col-
        ony, 24, 29–30
    as nonconformist pacifist, 23

and Pennsylvania militia, opposition to, 23, 155
questioning by British official about French and Indian War reporting, 22–23, 25–28
and race as little-used term before early nineteenth century, 204
rebuttals of Franklin's *Plain Truth*, 45, 69n19
and slavery, 205
and Smith's education plan, opposition to, 23, 29
Smith's efforts to undermine, 58
support for aggrieved Indians, 23–24
verbal attacks on dissenters seeking personal gain, 71–72n34
verbal attacks on traditional clergy, 25, 27, 28, 42–43, 50, 52–53, 53–54, 54–55, 72n42
writing style of, 28
See also *Pensylvanische Berichte*
Saur, Mühlenberg and
Mühlenberg as probable author of *HDEG* editorial attacking Saur, 50, 55
Mühlenberg criticism of, as Nimrod-like, 42–43
Mühlenberg on Saur's attacks on clergy, 54–55
Mühlenberg's criticism of Bible printed by, 54
Mühlenberg's desire for printing press to challenge, 53, 54, 59
Mühlenberg's efforts to undermine, 59, 67
Saur's verbal attacks on Mühlenberg, 53–54
Saur, Christoph, Jr., 50
Benezet and, 29, 230, 231
Franklin and, 231
Saur, Marie Christine
joining of Beissel's Seventh-day Baptists, 41, 50, 71n31
Saur's attack on Ephrata community to recover, 49
Saur's attempt to shoot, 41
Saur family printing business, Franklin's efforts to undermine influence of, 45, 46–51
Schaum, Johann Helfrich, 154, 156
Schenckel, Friedrich, 287, 298n20
Schlatter, Michael, 56–57, 58
Schmick, Johann, 102, 107
Schmick, Johanna, 102, 107, 122

Schmidt, Anna Catharine Riedt, 114–15
background of, 114
colleagues in missionary work, 112, 120, 122
fluency in Indian languages, 114
missions served in, 114–15, 117
and Montour, 110
Schmidt, Anton, 114–15
Schmidt, Georg, 83
Schneider, Hans, 83
scholarship
Anglophone, and monolingual fallacy, 11, 32n28
on Colonial America, decolonization of, 9
dominance of essential ethnic identity in, 11, 32–33n29
suppression of diversity of language and culture in colonial America, 12–13
tendency to focus on rural contingent of German immigrants, 277, 293–95
Schutt, Amy, 102, 121
Seligmann, Johann Michael, 279
Sensbach, Jon, 204–5, 222n8
Seven Years War. See French and Indian War
Seward, Samuel, 230
Shamokin
as crossroads town of multiple tribes, 109–11, *111*, 117
as lawless frontier town, 113, 117
Shamokin mission, 107
arrival of Macks at, 112–13
and cultural gulf with traders, 117
diaries of, 102, 117
establishment of, 110–11
need for women missionaries at, 126n40
Powells at, 116–17
Schmidts at, 114–15
Sharpe, Granville, 229
Shekomeko
Moravian mission at, 114, 119, 120
Zinzendorf in, 114
Shell, Marc, 5, 9
Sheshequin mission, 121
Shikellamy, 109, 113, 114, 117, 118, 126n40
Shoemaker, Jacob, Jr., 284–85
Shoemaker, Jacob, Sr., 284–85
Shoemaker, Jonathan, 285
A Short Account of That Part of Africa, Inhabited by the Negroes (Benezet), 236, 237
single-language communities, difficulty of identifying in multilingual colonial environment, 4

slavery
    antislavery arguments, rights-based, development by Germantown Quakers, 176, 183–84, 194
    and hardening of racial distinction, 203
    importance of slave labor in colonies, 11, 33n31
    number of slaves in Pennsylvania, 215
    Pennsylvanians' framing as southern problem, 215
    and white's claimed inability to work in tropical weather, 237, 242
    See also Quakers and slavery
slavery, German immigrants' views on
    on benign nature of Pennsylvania slavery, 204
    and employers' tendency to regard slaves and indentured servants as interchangeable, 210–12
    and fear of black ownership of white indentured servants, 213
    German efforts to attain full free white status and, 202, 203, 207
    and hopes for conversion of slaves to Christianity, 201
    indentured servants' fear of being lumped in with slave labor and, 206–10, 213, 220
    initial ambivalence about, 204–5
    initial focus on heathenness rather than skin color in, 201, 204
    limited antislavery activism outside Quakers, 202
    minimal engagement with slave labor, 205–6
    and race as little-used term before early nineteenth century, 204
    and slave labor as competition for free laborers, 212–13
    societal pressure to accept, 205
    turn to support for black slavery, 201–2, 203, 207
slaves
    cost of, in eighteenth century, 206
    inability to legally marry, 210, 224–25n44
    Moravian missions to, 76, 81–82
    number owned per capita in Pennsylvania, 198n38
    in Philadelphia, African origins of, 231
    runaway, Philadelphia newspaper ads for, 205–6, 223nn24–25

slave trade
    arguments for continuing, 242
    Benezet on evil origins and results of, 234, 241–42
    Benezet's efforts to end, 241–42
    Benezet's research on, 237
    British Parliamentary debate on, 240
    increased imports to Philadelphia, 1750–60, 211–12
    See also Quakers and slave trade
Sloane, Hans, 237
Smith, Robert, 291
Smith, William
    on Anglophone Protestantism, obligation to spread, 25
    bilingualism publications by, as tool of power and coercion, 44
    and bilingual society, inability to envision, 66–67
    bombast of, 28
    on diversity of language and culture, danger of, 2
    effort to homogenize Pennsylvania groups, as imperialist project, 43
    on Forbes, 24–25
    General Idea of the College of Mirania, 13
    Indian Song for Peace, 19
    as Nimrod, 57, 66
    and Philadelphia Academy, 2, 19
    and primacy of English, commitment to, 12, 19, 20
    Proposal for Erecting Indian Schools, 19
    and Roman Empire as model for creation of cultural unity, 13, 19
    and Saur, efforts to undermine, 58, 67
    support for imperial political order, 68
    See also *Eine Kurtze Nachricht Von der Liebreichen Anstalt / A Brief History of the Charitable Scheme* (Smith)
Smith, and Charity Schools
    assimilation of German immigrants as goal of, 58, 59–60
    founding of, 19, 20, 56, 58
    fundraising for, 58
    need for local supporters for, 58–59
    Saur's opposition to, 29
Société des Amis des Noirs, 240
Society for Promoting Religious Knowledge and the English Language Among the German Emigrants in Pennsylvania. *See* Society for the Promotion of the

Knowledge of God Among the Germans
Society for the Promotion of the Knowledge of God Among the Germans, 57, 154
Society for the Relief and Instruction of Poor Germans, 59
Society for the Relief of Free Negroes Unlawfully Held in Bondage, 238
Soderlund, Jean, 176, 197n35
Sollors, Werner, 5, 23
Some Historical Account of Guinea (Benezet), 237, 240, 241
Some Historical Observations of Guinea (Benezet), 236, 238
Southeby, William, 197n31
Spangenberg, August Gottlieb, 85
The Spirit of the Laws (Montesquieu), 234–35
Splitter, Wolfgang, 222n8
Stievermann, Jan, 32n19
stoves
  typical design used by German immigrants, 258–59, 259
  use for room heat, as characteristic of German immigrant house designs, 259, 260, 261, 264, 269, 273n25, 289
sugar bowl (Wiltberger), 293, 294
Susquehanna country, 109–11, *111*
  as liminal space, 109–11, *111*, 117
  Moravian missions in, 102, 107
  women in, and reduced violence, 108
  Zinzendorf in, 85, 106
  See also women as Moravian missionaries to Indians (1740s–50s)
System of Moral Philosophy (Hutcheson), 235
A System of the Principles of the Law of Scotland (Wallace), 235

Tannenberg, David, 292
Teage, Penticott, 191, 193
teapot (southeastern Pennsylvania, 1779), 293, 294
Teedyuskung, 26, 27, 28, 29, 35n58
Tennant, Gilbert, 98–99n70
Thirty Years War, end of, 78
Thomson, David, 56
Thoughts and Sentiments on the Evil and Wicked Traffic of Slavery and Commerce of the Human Species (Cugoano), 241
Thoughts upon Slavery (Wesley), 238
Timothée, Louis, 61
To Live Upon Hope (Wheeler), 109

"To the General Meeting off ffriends In Barbados" (1698), 191
translation
  use by imperial boosters as tool of conquest, 44–45
  use by radical Protestant groups in Pennsylvania to overcome factionalism, 44, 69n12
translation zones
  and power relations, 3
  as site of continuous negotiation, 4
Tropus plan, 82
Troxell, Johan Peter and Maria, 269
Troxell house (Egypt, 1756), 269, 269–70
True History of the Real Condition of the Destitute Congregations in Pennsylvania (Schlatter), 56–57

University of Göttingen, Franklin's visit to, 134–36, 143–44, 145n21
University of Pennsylvania
  founding of, 131
  German language instruction in, 157–58
  integration of Lutheran seminary into, 157
  renaming of Philadelphia Academy as (1791), 131
Upper Providence Friends meetinghouse (Oaks, Pennsylvania), 255–57, 272n18

Vigera, Johann Friedrich, 142
Vincens, Simone, 110
Virginia, Quaker slaveowners in, 179–80
"Voluntary Association" for the defense of Pennsylvania. See militia

Waldstreicher, David, 223n27
Wallace, George, 235
Ward, W. R., 81
Washington, George
  employment of workers of various backgrounds, 210–11
  funeral service of, 292
  stay in Deshler House, 249
Watson's Annual Journal, 243
Weiser, Conrad, 90, 114
Weiss, Lewis, 209
Wellenreuther, Hermann, 33n29
Wentz house (Worcester Township, 1758), 264–66, 266
Wesley, Charles, 137
Wesley, John, 98n70, 137, 238

Wheeler, Rachel, 102, 109, 119
White, Richard, 4
White, William, 292
Whitefield, George, 89, 98n58, 137–40, 229, 230, 238
Wilberforce, William, 229, 240
Wilkison, Thomas, 217, 218
Wills, Joseph, 281–82
Wiltberger, Christian, 294
Wister house [Grumblethorpe] (Germantown, 1744), 250, 251, 252, 256
women as Moravian missionaries to Indians (1740s–50s)
  activities in missionary work, 107–8, 117–18, 119, 121
  and circulation among missions, 107
  and extralinguistic communication among women, 108
  greater agency than women missionaries of 1770s, 102–3
  and identity-changing interactions, 109
  importance within Zinzendorf's strategy for converting Indians, 106
  as mediators and agents of translation, 108–9
  and militia gangs, 103–4
  mission records on, 103–4
  missions and missionaries, 107–8
  and Moravian influence on individual nurturing of converts, 105–6
  motives for missionary work, 121
  network of, 102, 111, 121–22, 122
  past experiences, value of, 110
  and Pennsylvania mission map for 1740–70s, 107, 108
  perceptions of Susquehanna country, 103
  reliance of Indian women on, 121
  sources on, 122–23
  spheres of influence of, 107
  success of, 106, 107, 114–15, 119
  as under-researched, 102
  Zinzendorf's recruitment of, 101–2, 114
  See also Jungmann, Anna Margarethe Bechtel; Mack, Johanna "Jannetje" Rau; Powell, Martha; Schmidt, Anna Catharine Riedt
Woolman, John, Benezet and, 238
Wyalusing mission, 121

Zeisberger, David, 102, 121, 126n40
Ziegenhagen, Friedrich Michael, 53, 139–40
Zinzendorf, Benigna von, 101, 118–19
Zinzendorf, Nicholas Ludwig von, Count
  American Plan of, 85–88
  Brotherly Agreement, 80
  and complex negotiations on Moravian status, 80
  exile from Saxony, 81
  hope to establish ecumenical church in British North America, 84, 85
  individual nurturing of converts, 105–6
  John Stephen Benezet and, 230
  on method for converting heathens, 106, 113
  on missionaries' demeanor toward non-Christians, 104–5
  mission theology, development of, 104, 119
  on Montour, 110
  as Moravian leader, 76, 79
  and Moravian missions to Native Americans, 85–86, 106
  Mühlenberg on, 87
  multiple ordinations of, 80
  and nonhierarchical multilingualism, 77
  and Philadelphian movement, 79, 84, 88
  and Pietism, 96n16
  Saur's criticisms of, 71–72n34
  sheltering of Moravians on estate, 78, 79, 230, 282
  stay with Six Nations, 85, 106
  as student of Francke, 83, 104
  theology of, 91–93
  on transformation of converted heathens, 105
  and Tropus plan, 82
  visit to Moravian missions in West Indies, 105, 124n15
  and women missionaries, recruitment of, 101–2, 112, 114, 116, 118–19
Zion Lutheran Church (Fourth and Cherry Streets, Philadelphia), *291*, 293
  construction of, 291
  demolition of, 292–93
  described, 291–92
  destruction by fire, and rebuilding, 292
  funeral services for Washington and Franklin held at, 292
  ornate organ at, 292

www.ingramcontent.com/pod-product-compliance
Lightning Source LLC
Chambersburg PA
CBHW030300010526
44108CB00038B/833